The Society for Old Testament Study

BOOK LIST
1995

Printed for the Society

ISSN 0309 0892

ISBN 0 905495 18 7

PRINTED BY W. S. MANEY AND SON LTD, HUDSON ROAD LEEDS LS9 7DL

Contents

One copy of the *Book List* is supplied free to all members of the Society.

Copies of this *Book List* may be obtained from The Society for Old Testament Study, P.O. Box YR7, Leeds LS9 7UU, England. Back Numbers of the *Book List* are also available from the address. Orders should not be accompanied by payment; an invoice will be sent. The price of a single copy is £15.00 including postage. Payment should be made by cheque in sterling payable to the Society for Old Testament Study, or direct to Post Office Giro Account No. 50 450 4002.

Customers in the U.S.A. should order from Scholars Press.

Review copies of books for the *Book List* should be sent to the Editor:

Professor Lester L. Grabbe
Department of Theology
University of Hull
Hull HU6 7RX
England

PREFACE

Well over 500 books are reviewed or noticed in this issue. This number attests not only to the burgeoning work in 'core' Old Testament study but also to the increasing number of publications in related disciplines which have implications for the Hebrew Bible and ancient Israel. This number of reviews would not be possible without the help of a dedicated band of reviewers who often agree to review at some inconvenience to themselves. I am grateful to everyone of them. In addition, a number of reviewers have kindly gone on to make book suggestions to me or provided extra reviews or otherwise helped in the editorial process:

Dr A. Abela, Professor G. W. Anderson, Mrs M. Barker, Professor P. R. Davies, Mr J. Eaton, Dr J. F. Elwolde, Canon C. J. A. Hickling, Professor G. H. Jones, Dr P. M. Joyce, Professor W. G. Lambert, Professor A. R. Millard, Dr S. C. Reif, Mr M. E. J. Richardson, Dr W. G. E. Watson, Professor R. N. Whybray, Dr N. Wyatt. The following continued to provide help with books and reviews from their own countries: Professor K. Jeppesen and Professor G. L. Prato. Messrs W. S. Maney and Son have provided their valuable support, with special thanks to Mr D. Brown and Miss Liz Rosindale.

The following abbreviations and symbols are employed as in earlier issues:

B.L.	= *Book List*
Eleven Years	= *Eleven Years of Bible Bibliography* 1957
Decade	= *A Decade of Bible Bibliography*
Bible Bibliog.	= *Bible Bibliography 1967–1973:*
	Old Testament (1974)

UNIVERSITY OF HULL   LESTER L. GRABBE

1. GENERAL

AHITUV, S. and LEVINE, B. A. (eds): *Avraham Malamat Volume* (Eretz Israel 24). 1993. Pp. 241*, 197 (Hebrew). (Israel Exploration Society, Jerusalem. Price: $90.00. ISBN 965 221 023 4)

This volume has something for almost everyone concerned with Old Testament studies, ranging from archaeological through historical and literary to theological, reflecting Abraham Malamat's wide interests. There are thirty essays in European languages and twenty-nine in Hebrew, with English summaries of all not in English. Notable are W. G. Dever on 'Cultural Continuity, Ethnicity in the Archaeological Record, and the Question of Israelite Origins'; B. Halpern, 'The Exodus and the Israelite Historians,' finding genuine recollections of Late Bronze Age conditions; K. A. Kitchen, 'The Tabernacle — A Bronze Age Artefact'; A. Lemaire, 'La Syrie-Palestine vers 800 av J.-C.,' reconstructing an historical situation from biblical and extra-biblical texts; C. Meyers, 'Toponyms in the Eschatology of Zechariah 9'; R. Rendtorff, 'Some Observations on the Use of El in the Hebrew Bible,' noting it does not occur alone in Genesis to denote the High God but elsewhere is often an appellative. In Hebrew I. Eph'al studies Jeremiah 37:13; A. Demsky, 'The Genealogy of Asher (1 Chron. 7:30–40)'; M. Weinfeld, 'The Davidic Empire — Realization of the Promise to the Patriarchs'; B. Oded offers an Assyrian perspective on Leviticus 26:6, 'peace in the land'; and A. Rofé discusses 'The Family-Saga as a Source for the History of the Settlement'. I. Beit-Arieh publishes two ostraca from Horvat 'Uza, both listing names; S. Talmon edits two texts of Leviticus from Masada, both identical with the Massoretic Text; and B. Porten lists and discusses Aramaic ostraca, mainly from Elephantine. Other essays look at methods of study (N. K. Gottwald, C. Schäfer-Lichtenberger, J. A. Soggin), details from Mari texts (M. Anbar, A. Finet, M. Greenberg on *ḥerem*, V. Hurowitz, S. Paul), excavations at Beth-Shean (A. Mazar), Kadesh-Barnea (D. Ussishkin), the Jericho region in the last days of Judah (E. Stern). A worthy tribute to an esteemed scholar.

A. R. MILLARD

BALENTINE, SAMUEL E. and BARTON, JOHN (ed.): *Language, Theology and the Bible. Essays in Honour of James Barr*. 1994. Pp. xiv, 418. (Clarendon Press, Oxford. Price: £45.00. ISBN 0 19 826191 8)

The title of this weighty Festschrift provides the guide to its organization. Following a biographical sketch and articles on Barr's 'quest for sound and adequate biblical interpretation' (S. Balentine) and on Barr as 'critic and theologian' (J. Barton), there follow articles on language, theology and exegesis, and the Bible through the centuries. Language articles include: translation and emendation (B. Albrektson); scribal additions in the Hebrew Bible (E. Tov); post-biblical Hebrew vocalization (J. Hughes); the translation of the Septuagint (R. Hanhart); philology in Psalm 74:13a (J. Greenfield); and Isaiah and Israeli Hebrew (E. Ullendorff). Articles on biblical theology include: story and history in the Old Testament (E. Nicholson); the sociology of morality in Israel (D. Knight); Terah's age at death (J. Emerton); the concept of the state in Deuteronomy (L. Perlitt); the Nehemiah memoir (J. Blenkinsopp); the theological significance of biblical poetry (P. Miller); the centre of the Psalms (J. Mays); Isaiah 35 (W. Harrelson); and the future of the 'Servant Songs' (H. Barstad). The Hebrew Bible is viewed in a variety of contexts in articles on: biblical myth and rabbinic midrash (M. Fishbane); contours of ancient Judaism (W. Green); a 16th-century commentary on the Song of Songs (Jane Barr); 17th-century biblical scholarship (B. Childs); Newton and the Bible (M. Wiles); Karl Budde (R. Smend); historical method and value systems (J. McIntyre); and the search for structures 'behind'

biblical texts (D. Ritschl). The volume concludes with a bibliography of
Barr's publications and an author index. The wide range of these articles, the
stimulus they provide, and the warmth with which they are offered provide a
fitting tribute and testify to the stature and significance of Professor Barr's
own work.
                                                                D. J. REIMER

BAR-ASHER, MOSHE; GARSIEL, MOSHE; DIMANT, DEVORAH; and MAORI,
YESHAYAHU (eds): *'ywny mqr' wpršnwt, krk g: spr zykrwn lmšh gwšn-
gwtštyyn (Studies in Bible and Exegesis. Vol. III: Moshe Goshen-Gottstein–in
Memoriam* (Bar-Ilan Departmental Researches: Department of Bible). 1993.
Pp. xi (Eng.), 437 (Heb.). (Bar-Ilan University Press, Ramat-Gan. N.P.
ISBN 965 226 079 7)

   As with earlier volumes in this impressive series, the range is so wide that
one can do no more than indicate the general parameters and authorship of
these essays, which stand as a worthy memorial to a master of Semitic
languages and literatures. Matters relating to the grammar, syntax and
literary devices of the Hebrew Bible are dealt with by I. Gottlieb, S. Kogut,
M. Garsiel and B. Kedar-Kopfstein, while E. Tov, I. Yeivin, D. Lyons,
Y. Maori and J. S. Penkower touch on its Masoretic and pre-Masoretic
textual history. The Syro-Hexapla, Septuagint and Targum occupy the
attention of Š. Assif, D. Dimant, D. Weissert and S. A. Kaufman, with
contributions from D. Boyarin, A. Goshen-Gottstein, S. Sharvit and M. A.
Zipor on various aspects of rabbinic literature, and from S. Japhet on
medieval compilatory commentaries (such as that of Joseph Qara on Job) and
M. Perez on Ibn Janaḥ's exegetical methodology. The remainder of the
volume contains a comparative study of pre-Islamic Palestinian Syriac and
Samaritan Aramaic by M. Bar-Asher, and Aramaic poetic parody for Purim
edited by J. Yahalom and M. Sokoloff, and a study of changing Jewish
attitudes to miracles by R. Kasher. There are also a brief English appreciation
of Goshen-Gottstein and a bibliography of his works but no indexes or
English summaries.
                                                                S. C. REIF

BEGG, CHRISTOPHER T. (ed.): *Old Testament Abstracts.* Vol. 17. 1994.
Pp. 755. (Catholic Biblical Association of America, Washington, DC. Subs.
price: $26.00. ISSN 0364 8591)

   OTA continues to provide a valuable and up-to-date service to scholars.
There are some fourteen-hundred periodical abstracts and over two hundred
book notices, while the arrangement in twenty-five sections makes possible a
rapid overview of relevant material.
                                                                M. A. KNIBB

BIDERMAN, SHLOMO and SCHARFSTEIN, BEN-AMI (eds): *Myths and Fictions* (Philosophy and Religion 3). 1993. Pp. vii, 397. (Brill, Leiden–New
York–Köln. Price: fl. 185.00/$105.75. ISBN 90 04 09838 0; ISSN 0924 7904)

   This volume, third in a series to emerge from Tel Aviv (not noted thus far
in *B.L.*), has thirteen contributions which fall into two parts, on theory and
historical practice. In the latter section, the essays by J. Agassi on halakhah
and haggadah and by J. A. Dally on mythological motifs in John's Gospel will
be of most direct interest. In the former section, the editors write on kinds of
truth ('Is it all our fancy?'); S. Rosen, 'the whole story'; E. Deutsch, truth and
mythology; L. E. Goodman, mythic discourse; B.-A. Scharfstein, how to
justify the reductive explanation of myths; L. J. Hatab, evolution and creation — a Heideggerian response; C. Crittenden, myths, stories and existence;

and P. J. McCormick, fictions of modernity. This is not the place to pinpoint large numbers of problems, but there remains at times a sense of *déjà lu* in much of this, and not from the authorities cited in the notes. Perhaps we have reached the stage where little new and useful can be written on myth, which is a pity, because it ought to be a topic of primary importance to Old Testament scholarship.

N. WYATT

BORMANN, LUKAS; DEL TREDICI, KELLY; and STANDHARTINGER, ANGELA (eds): *Religious Propaganda and Missionary Competition in the New Testament World. Essays Honoring Dieter Georgi* (Supplements to Novum Testamentum 74). 1994. Pp. xiii, 570. (Brill, Leiden–New York–Köln. Price: fl. 225.00/$128.75. ISBN 90 04 10049 0; ISSN 0167 9732)

Each of the twenty-five contributors was asked to respond to Tertullian's motto — 'What has Athens to do with Jerusalem, the Academy with the Church, Christians with heretics?' The result is a disparate collection of essays under various headings which are introduced by a confusing article by I. Gruenwald entitled 'The Study of Religion and the Religion of Study'. I will limit my remarks to the section entitled Jewish Sources. K. Baltzer implausibly argues that the servant of Isaiah 52:13 is Moses who is taken up to a high place to come to his Lord. The text is said to stand somewhere between Deut. 34 and *Testament of Moses* 10:8–10; 11:5–6, 8. J. J. Collins offers a study of the political propaganda in Egypt. He compares the 2nd century BCE sections of *3 Sibylline Oracle* with the *Potter's Oracle* and shows that, in contrast to later *Sibylline Oracles*, the first Sibyl evinces positive relations between Jews, Greeks and Egyptians (pp. 68–69). A. T. Kraabal investigates relations between the well-established Jewish community in Sardis and their Gentile neighbours at the turn of the era. Finding little support for Georgi's view that 'Jews had a widespread missionary awareness' (p. 77). K. concludes that most Graeco-Jewish literature was not written for Gentiles, but for Jews (p. 82). Angela Standhartinger identifies two diverging approaches in the way that the rape of Dinah was read in Hellenistic Jewish literature. The first suppresses Dinah's perspective, whereas the second makes her plight central and thus provides evidence that in some communities violence to women was a theological problem about which Hellenistic Jewish women were far from silent (pp. 115–16). Finally, G. Barth's paper surveys various primary sources from the late Second Temple and early rabbinic periods which demonstrate that belief in life beyond death was not universally accepted.

D. J. BRYAN

BUNNENS, G. (ed.): *Abr-Naharain. An Annual Published by the Department of Classical and Near Eastern Studies, University of Melbourne.* Vol. 31. 1993. Pp. vii, 143. (Peeters, Louvain. Price: BEF 1200. ISSN 0065 0382)

This annual continues seamlessly under its new editor. B. gives generous thanks to his predecessor, T. Muraoka. Brian E. Colless (pp. 1–35) returns to the subject of the Byblos syllabary (see also his article in volume 30). He adopts the term 'Gublaic' for the Bronze Age texts from Byblos (Gubla). Text D, a royal proclamation, is explained line by line. A. S. Jamieson (pp. 36–92) writes on 'The Euphrates Valley and Early Bronze Age Ceramic Traditions'. The discussion is mainly concerned with pottery and there are illustrations showing the author's typology, but there is also a section on the EB historical background. A. Korotayev (pp. 93–105), using 'Sabaic' inscriptions, applies social anthropological models to the study of the structure of ancient South Arabian society. T. Muraoka and Z. Shavitsky (pp. 106–09) provide a further instalment in 'A Biblical Hebrew Lexicon of Abraham Ibn-Ezra: Daniel'. Finally R. Snir (pp. 110–25) studies poetic aspects of an inscription, partly in Nabataean Aramaic, partly in Arabic, recently discovered at 'Avdat. This inscription has generated much interest since its publication in 1986 because of its claim to be the earliest Arabic. Reviews complete the volume.

J. F. HEALEY

CANCIK, HUBERT; GLADIGOW, BURKHARD; and KOHL, KARL-HEINZ (eds): *Handbuch religionswissenschaftlicher Grundbegriffe*. Band 3: *Gesetz-Kult*. 1993. Pp. 488. (Kohlhammer, Stuttgart–Berlin–Köln. Price: DM 148.00; sub. price DM 128.00/SwF 129.00/AS 999. ISBN (set) 3 17 010531 0; (vol. 3) 3 17 009555 2)

Volume 2 was welcomed in *B.L.* 1991, p. 10. Although the Old Testament is often not specifically addressed in entries, a number of articles still have potential interest for the Old Testament scholar, including *Gesetz*, *Gottesvorstellungen*, *Heil*, *das Heilige*, *Herrscherkult*, *Hexe/Hexenmuster*, *Historismus/Historizismus*, *Identität*, *Ideologie*, *Initiation*, *Inspiration*, *Integration*, *Interpretationsmodelle*, *Intoxikation (rituelle)*, *Irrationalismus/das Irrationale*, *Jenseits*, *Kanon*, *Klassengesellschaft*, *Klassifikationssysteme*, *Königtum (sakrales)*, *Kommunikation*, *Konflikt*, *Konversion/Apostasie*, *Krieg*, *Krise*, *Kult*.

L. L. GRABBE

CHIA, PHILIP (ed.): *Jian Dao. A Journal of the Bible and Theology*. Vol. 1/1. 1994. Pp. 1–135. (Alliance Bible Seminary, Hong Kong. Price: (US) $25 p.a.)

The Chinese name of Alliance Bible Seminary in Hong Kong is also the title of this new journal that seeks to establish a scholarly forum for Asian (or perhaps more accurately Chinese) biblical and theological perspectives. Written in Chinese and English (appended with bilingual abstracts for the most part), the articles are not exclusively by Asians. In fact, one of the aims is to establish a meaningful dialogue between 'Asian' and 'Western' (though, it would seem, not Afro-Caribbean, South American and other) perspectives. Published under the aegis of a conservative Christian seminary, this publication reflects a growing maturity and confidence in Asian biblical scholarship and theological thinking. It is to be wondered whether the publication of articles in Chinese would not hinder the very dialogue which it is attempting to foster.

T. H. LIM

COUNTRYMAN, L. WILLIAM: *Biblical Authority or Biblical Tyranny? Scripture and the Christian Pilgrimage*. 1994 (rev. ed.). Pp. xi, 125. (Trinity Press International, Valley Forge PA. Price: $12.00. ISBN 1 56338 085 4)

This is a slightly revised edition of a book first published in 1982 (not noted in *B.L.*). C. attempts to rescue the Bible's authority for Christians by looking at all the problematic elements in the book and seeking to steer a middle course (Anglicanism's famous *via media*, no doubt) between the Scylla of fundamentalism and the Charybdis of critical thought. It is, by and large, a very sensible book, fully recognizing the errors (historical, moral, scientific) of and in the Bible while affirming that it is the Word of God. The Bible is for C. 'wonderfully deep, convoluted, and perplexing' and the task for Christians is to understand that 'it is the Word of God *as we have it*'. By this qualification he means that it must be read *as it is* and 'not as corrected and systematized by the theological labours of any number of well-meaning, pious, scholarly people' (p. 21). That seems to me to be a fine policy for Christians: the Bible is to be taken 'warts and all, so to speak'. It is of course *a*

Christian reading and will therefore have only a very limited appeal to the millions of non-Christians who read the Bible and probably no appeal at all to those many biblical scholars who eschew traditional forms of belief commitment. But of its kind this is a very sensible little book which may be recommended to all earnest seekers after truth in the religious communities of the West.

R. P. CARROLL

DAVIS, MALCOLM C.: *A Catalogue of the Pre-1850 Books in the Cecil Roth Collection.* 1994. Pp. 119. (The Brotherton Library, University of Leeds. Price: £15.00. ISBN 0 9024 54 08 0)

Those interested in information about significant collections of printed Hebraica and Judaica in the United Kingdom will be grateful to the efficient compiler, and to the University Librarian in the University of Leeds. Brief introductory material is followed by 918 entries describing books and pamphlets in the fields of Bible, liturgy, Marrano literature, rabbinics and Anglo-Judaica. The works are written in a variety of European languages, as well as Hebrew, and there is a small percentage of other, unrelated material. Each entry lists the author, title, format, place of publication and publisher, and any relevant bibliographical reference, with the earliest editions dating from the first half of the 16th century. The Hebrew titles, though sometimes sharply abbreviated, are printed in the original language and information is supplied about which works are bound together. Altogether a well-produced and useful reference tool, though unfortunately not provided with indexes.

S. C. REIF

DAWES, STEPHEN V.: *Adam Clarke. Methodism's First Old Testament Scholar* (Cornish Methodist Historical Association Occasional Publication 26). 1994. Pp. 36. (Cornish Methodist Historical Association; available from the Treasurer, Pelmear Villa, Carharrack, Redruth, Cornwall TR16 5RB. Price: £1.70. ISBN 0 9509323 7 X)

Adam Clarke's Bible Commentary was begun in 1798 and first published in eight volumes between 1810 and 1826. An edited six-volume edition later appeared in 1881. Clarke, like that other early pioneer of historical criticism of the Bible Samuel Davidson, was of Irish origin. He was born close to Londonderry in 1762 and died of cholera in 1832. This short sketch examines Clarke's critical comments relating to the Davidic authorship of the Psalms and the question of the dual authorship of the Book of Isaiah. The criticism is very moderate, but reveals a genuine awareness of the issues although, in the main, Clarke strives for a devotional style drawn from the tradition of Matthew Henry. The study is much to be welcomed, if only to whet one's appetite to learn more about the influential tradition of commentary-writing and biblical interpretation in Great Britain from the Napoleonic period, especially among the Methodists and Dissenters which has been much neglected.

R. E. CLEMENTS

DONNER, HERBERT: *Aufsätze zum Alten Testament aus vier Jahrzehnten* (Beihefte zur Zeitschrift für die alttestamentliche Wissenschaft 224). 1994. Pp. vi, 311. (de Gruyter, Berlin–New York. Price: DM 168.00. ISBN 3 11 014097 7; ISSN 0934 2575)

The fifteen essays reproduced here were first published between 1959 and 1992. The preface disclaims a single common theme; yet a number of recurring and linked interests are manifest from the titles: (1) nature and origin of the office of the queen mother in the Old Testament; (2) the 'king's friend'; (3) adoption or legitimation? remarks on adoption in the Old Testament against the background of ancient oriental laws; (4) 'Here are your gods, Israel'; (5) the literary shape of the Old Testament Joseph story; (6) Balaam pseudopropheta; (7) the rejection of King Saul; (8) Isaiah LVI 1–7: an instance of repeal within the canon — implications and consequences; (9) the saying about Issachar (Gen. 49:14–15) as source for the early history of Israel; (10) Psalm 122; (11) 'Seek ye out of the book of the Lord, and read!' a contribution to the understanding of Israelite prophecy; (12) the reliable prophet: considerations of 1 Macc. 14:41ff and Ps. 110; (13) 'As it is written', origin and meaning of a formula; (14) prophecy and prophets in Spinoza's *Theologico-Political Tractate*; and (15) the redactor: reflections on precritical acquaintance with Holy Scripture. Essays 9 and 10 were first published in English, and the two contributions at the end have been extracted from the otherwise chronological order to form a small group on scripture introduced by the latest.

A. G. AULD

EXUM, J. CHERYL and BRETT, MARK G. (eds): *Biblical Interpretation. A Journal of Contemporary Approaches*. Vol. 2/1–3. 1994. Pp. vi, 376. (Brill, Leiden. Price: fl. 112.00/$64.00 p.a. ISSN 0927 2569)

Volume 2/1 is devoted to The Bible and Popular Culture, with Alice Bach as the guest editor. A smart introduction, full of insight, by Bach is followed by Amy-Jull Levine on Jesus and women; Jennifer A. Glancy on the construction of gender in Mark 6:17–29; John H. Elliott on the evil eye and the Sermon on the Mount; Robin M. Jensen on the offering of Isaac in Jewish and Christian traditions; and Rudy V. Busto on Motolinia's account of the *Caída de nuestros primeros padres* (a colonial Mexican religious play performed in 1539 and based on the Christian reading of Genesis 2–3). Volume 2/2 is the more standard collection of discrete articles: Mark Coleridge on 'Why bother with Biblical Studies?'; Gerald West on reading the Joseph story with the poor and marginalized communities in South Africa; Timothy K. Beal on divine abjection in the Hebrew Bible; Ingrid Rosa Kitzberger on an intertextual reading of John 13:1–20 and Luke 7.36–50; and Anthony C. Thiselton on the Cretan liar paradox in Titus 1.12,13. Some twenty-seven pages of book reviews also appear in this issue. Volume 2/3 is devoted to Commitment, Context and Text: Examples of Asian Hermeneutics, with R. S. Sugirtharajah as guest editor. He provides a very thoughtful piece on Asian biblical hermeneutics. George M. Soares-Prabhu offers an interpretation of Matt. 28.16–20 in the light of a Buddhist text; Hisako Kinukawa looks at Mark 5.25–34 from a Japanese feminist context; Khiok-Khng Yeo discusses 1 Cor. 8 and Chinese ancestor worship; Archie C. C. Lee examines the Chinese creation myth of Nu Kua and Gen. 1–11; D. N. Premnath analyses the concepts of *Rta* and *Maat*; S. J. Samartha looks at the relational hermeneutics involved in religion, language and reality. There are also responses to these articles. These contributions constitute an impressive year's output by this very fine new journal and amply fulfil its claim to be 'A Journal of Contemporary Approaches'.

R. P. CARROLL

FABRY, HEINZ–JOSEF and RINGGREN, HELMER (eds): *Theologisches Wörterbuch zum Alten Testament*. Band 7, Lfg. 9–11 (cols. 1025–1348). 1994. Pp. 192. (Kohlhammer, Stuttgart. Price: DM 191.80/AS 1496/SwF 191.00. ISBN 3 17011553 7)

This triple fascicle comprises thirty-seven articles and the final part of E. Otto's article on *šeba'* with *šābū'ōt* (*B.L.* 1993, p. 11). By far the most

GENERAL

GENERAL   13

substantial article here is that on *šūb* (A. Graupner and Fabry) with fifty-nine columns including two and a half columns of bibliography. Next comes *šīr* (Fabry, G. Brunert, M. Kleer, G. Steins, U. Dahmen) — surprisingly long, but treating of music and musical terms in the ancient Near Eastern world, as well as the psalms and the liturgical use of song in Israel generally. Another substantial article is that on Shaddai (H. Niehr, Steins). There are separate articles on *šābat* and *šabbāt* both by E. Haag, the latter surprisingly brief. *šāgāh* and *šāgag* are taken together in a single article as augmentations of the basic morpheme *šg* (T. Seidl). L. Ruppert in three articles, *šḥr* ('black, blackness'), *šaḥar* I and *šāḥar* II, distinguishes between *šaḥar* 'dawn' and the divine name *Šaḥar*. *šāḥat*, 'ruin' (J. Conrad) and *šaḥat*, 'pit' are also treated separately. Other articles include *šōpār* (H. Ringgren), *šūšan*, 'lily' (H. Schmoldt), *šḥt*, slaughter (R. E. Clements), *šākab* (W. Beuken), *šākaḥ* (H. D. Preuss), *šᵉkem* (J. Milgrom) and *šākan* (M. Görg).

R. N. WHYBRAY

FABRY, HEINZ–JOSEF and RINGGREN, HELMER (eds): *Theologisches Wörterbuch zum Alten Testament*. Band 8, Lfg. 1–3 (cols. 1–384). 1994. Pp. 192. (Kohlhammer, Stuttgart. Price: DM 179.00/AS 1396/SwF 179.00. ISBN 3 17011553 7)

This triple Lieferung comprises thirty-one complete articles and one uncompleted one. The longest is that on *šēm* (F. V. Reiterer and Fabry, fifty-three columns), followed by *šālōm* (F.-J. Stendebach), *šāmayim* (R. Bartelmus), *šālah* (F.-L. Hossfeld, M. van der Velden and U. Dahmen), *šāmar* (F. García López) and *šāma'* (U. Rüterswörden). The article on *ša'ar*, 'gate' (E. Otto) runs so far to twenty-seven columns and appears to be far from complete. It is unfortunate that that on *šemeš* (E. Lipiński) is disproportionate to its religious significance, extending only to nine columns. Otherwise the editors continue to take a broad view of what is theologically important: there are, for example, articles on *šeleg*, 'snow' and *šulhān* (both by A. Ernst), *šālap*, 'draw (a sword), takes off (a shoe)' (P. Mommer), and *šēn* ('tooth') (A. S. Kapelrud).

The article on *šālōm* includes a lengthy discussion of the etymology of the word and its relationship to, *inter alia*, the verb *šlm* and the adjective *šālēm*. There is further discussion of this question in the separate articles on *šālēm* (K.-J. Illman) and *šᵉlāmīn* (Th. Seidl).

R. N. WHYBRAY

GRAHAM, WILLIAM A: *Beyond the Written Word: Oral Aspects of Scripture in the History of Religion*. 1993 (1987). Pp. xiv, 306. (Cambridge University Press. Price: £14.95/$19.95. ISBN paper 0 521 44820 4)

The book reviewed in *B.L.* 1989, pp. 16–17, is now available in paperback.

ED.

GREENSTEIN, EDWARD and MARCUS, DAVID (eds): *Semitic Studies in Memory of Moshe Held = The Journal of the Ancient Near Eastern Society*. Vol. 19. 1989. Pp. viii, 181. (Jewish Theological Seminary, NY. Price: $20.00. ISSN 0010 2016)

The sixteen essays here reflect Held's interests in the Old Testament and the ancient Near East, including Proverbs 23:7 (K. Barker), the 'Held method' for comparative Semitic philology (C. Cohen), Hebrew *'rb* (L. Freedman), Ezekiel's abnormalities (S. Garfinkel), the syntax of 'yes' in

Hebrew (E. Greenstein), breast-feeding (M. Gruber), Genesis 41:16 (M. Lichtenstein), Judges 11:4–11 (D. Marcus), the accession year and Davidic chronology (E. Merrill), biblical *rḥm* I and II (S. Sperling), the imagery of clothing, covering and overpowering in Semitic (N. Waldman), and divine names in the Psalms (R. Youngblood). Other articles are on Spinoza as the father of biblical scholarship, the institution of *sugāgūtum* at Mari, a bibliography of cuneiform mathematical texts, and inscriptions from Ashurnasirpal II's palace. An appreciation of Held and a list of his publications complete the volume.   L. L. GRABBE

HAUSER, ALAN J. and SELLEW, PHILIP (eds): *Currents in Research: Biblical Studies*. Volume 1. 1993. Pp. 215 (Sheffield Academic Press. Price: £14.50/$20.00. ISSN 0966 7377)

HAUSER, ALAN J. and SELLEW, PHILIP (eds): *Currents in Research: Biblical Studies*. Volume 2. 1994. Pp. 280. (Sheffield Academic Press. Price: £14.50/$20.00. ISSN 0966 7377)

This new journal will be welcomed by all students of biblical studies. Keeping up with developments in scholarship, especially outside one's area of specialism, is always a serious task, and it becomes more so as journals and monographs multiply. Volume 1 has articles on the archaeology of Galilee in the Roman period, Ezra-Nehemiah and the Persian period, Job, Proverbs and Qohelet, Isaiah, the social world of premonarchic Israel, the Q gospel source, and feminist biblical criticism. Volume 2 gives surveys on Ezekiel, archaeology of the Persian and Hellenistic periods, the Psalms, Targumic studies, apocalypses and apocalypticism and also on the epistle of Hebrews, the book of Revelation, the *Gospel of Thomas*, and the quest of the historical Jesus.   L. L. GRABBE

HELTZER, MICHAEL; SEGAL, ARTHUR; and KAUFMAN, DANIEL: *Studies in the Archaeology and History of Ancient Israel in Honour of Moshe Dothan*. 1993. Pp. 278 (Heb.), 249*. (Haifa University Press. N.P. ISBN 965 311 013 6)

The Hebrew section of this monumental volume honouring the archaeologist Moshe Dothan, noted particularly for his work at Ashdod and Akko, begins with a list of his publications. The English section begins with a brief appreciation of Dothan and abstracts in English of the contributions published in Hebrew (and French, German and Italian!). The time-span covered by the contributions is wide and they are ordered chronologically. About half deal with aspects of the Roman period and later, down to the Crusades. A few are prehistoric. Of particular interest from the Old Testament point of view will be B. Oded, 'Ahaz's Appeal to Tiglath-Pileser III in the Context of the Assyrian Policy of Expansion' (pp. 63*–71* — English), Y. Avishur, 'The Narratives of the Binding of Isaac and Abraham's Exodus from Haran — Structure, Style and Language' (91–106 — Hebrew) and A. Malamat, 'Two Parallels between New Mari Prophecies and Biblical Prophecy' (107–10 — Hebrew). Of more general religious interest will be M. G. Amadasi Guzzo, 'Astarte in Trono' (163*–80* – Italian) and R. Hachlili, 'Characteristic Features of Synagogue Architecture in the Land of Israel' (157–94 — Hebrew). The selection of these few contributions for mention does not do justice to this fine collection.   J. F. HEALEY

HOPFE, LEWIS M. (ed.): *Uncovering Ancient Stones. Essays in Memory of H. Neil Richardson.* 1994. Pp. xviii, 270. (Eisenbrauns, Winona Lake IN. Price: $32.50. ISBN 0 931464 73 0)

What began as a Festschrift has become a memorial volume which the editor himself did not live to see in print. All but one of the nineteen essays relate in some way to the Old Testament and fall into three sections. Under the Hebrew Bible in its Time are slaying the serpent of Isaiah 27:1 (B. Anderson), two unifying female images in Isaiah (K. Darr), a reading of Isaiah 40–55 (A. Johnston), the 'fortresses of Rehoboam' (T. Hobbs), the Lachish letters and official reactions to prophecy (S. Parker), perception of shame in the divine-human relationship (L. Bechtel), and *ḥyl* as God-language (J. Foster). Archaeology and the Bible discusses an epistemology of archaeology, texts, and history-writing (W. Dever), demographic aspects of the Israelite settlement (I. Sharon), Palestinian stamp-glyphic art in the Assyrian and Persian periods (E. Stern), and the origins of Roman Mithraism (Hopfe). The Hebrew Bible and its Later Uses examines laws concerning idolatry in the *Temple Scroll* (L. Schiffman), method in Septuagint lexicography (G. Chamberlain), the semantic field of 'idolatry' (C. Kennedy), the use of the Old Testament in Stephen's speech (R. Anderson), Isaiah in the development of the Christian canon (W. Farmer), the tabernacle in Samaritanism (J. Purvis), the Bible in recent English translation (E. Frerichs), and biblical hermeneutics and contemporary African theology.   L. L. GRABBE

HUPPER, WILLIAM G. (ed.) *An Index to English Periodical Literature on the Old Testament and Ancient Near Eastern Studies*, Volume v (American Theological Library Association Bibliographical Series 21). 1992. Pp. xliv, 708. (Scarecrow Press, Metuchen NJ and London. Price: $72.50. ISBN 0 8108 2618 6)

HUPPER, WILLIAM G. (ed.) *An Index to English Periodical Literature on the Old Testament and Ancient Near Eastern Studies*, Volume vi (American Theological Library Association Bibliographical Series 21). 1994. Pp. lii, 728. (Scarecrow Press, Metuchen NJ and London. Price: $72.50. ISBN 0 8108 2822 7)

Each volume in this series covers a different section of the Old Testament. Only volume II has been reviewed in the *B.L.* (1990, p. 17). Volume v covers history of religions (worship, cult, temples, festivals, Jewish sects, mythology, religions of the surrounding peoples), epigraphical and philological studies (Hamito-Semitic languages, relevant Indo-European languages, Elamite), and the Bible as literature. Volume VI indexes critical and exegetical studies on the Old Testament, textual criticism and exegesis of the Apocrypha and Pseudepigrapha, and studies on Philo, Josephus, Hillel (what 'works of Hillel' do we have?), and rabbinic writings.   L. L. GRABBE

KIDA, K. et al. (eds): *Annual of the Japanese Biblical Institute.* Vol. 19. 1993. (The Japanese Biblical Institute, Tokyo. Price: ¥3090. ISBN 4 947668 10 5)

This volume comprises two Old Testament and two New Testament articles. S. Nagano, 'The Elders of Israel in Exodus 24:9–11', discusses the passage against the background of the phrase 'the elders of Israel' in Ezekiel and the Deuteronomistic History and in the light of recent treatments of the elders in the Old Testament generally. This pericope, the work of the late Yahwist, reflects neither a priestly nor a Deuteronomistic point of view; it is not nationalistic but, like the reference to Jethro in Exod. 18:12, universalistic in intention. A. Tsukimoto, in 'The Background of Qoh 11:1–6 and Qohelet's Agnosticism', interprets this passage as expressing Qohelet's characteristic view that it is impossible to predict the future. Vv. 3–5 refer to the worthlessness of divination, which was practised not only in ancient Mesopotamia but also in the Hellenistic period and in later times. They refer in turn to meteorological, rhabdomantic (*'ēṣ* here means 'rod') and birth divination. Qohelet's 'agnosticism' is a recognition of human inability to predict the future, which leads to absurdity and negates the fundamental values of human life. He advises the acceptance of life as it is, but finds faith in 'fearing God' in his mysterious being.

R. N. Whybray

KIEFFER, RENÉ (ed.): *Svensk exegetisk årsbok*, 59. 1994. Pp. 216. (Uppsala. Graphic Systems, Stockholm. ISSN 1100 2298)

This issue contains three articles on Old Testament subjects. A. Runesson argues that when the active participle is used to express creation, a continuing but not cyclic process is indicated. T. D. Mettinger contributes a discerning account of the *Religionsgeschichte Israels* by R. Albertz, emphasizing its religio-sociological approach. F. Lambert writes with an ample bibliography on tribal influences in Old Testament tradition. There are also articles on miracle culture and parable culture in Mark 4–11 (V. K. Robbins), the narrative structure of Mark (D. Hellholm), quotations from Isaiah 6 amd 53 in John 12 (A. Ekenberg), baptism in the Didache and the Shepherd of Hermas (L. Hartman), and the tasks facing New Testament scholarship (M. Hengel). In addition, twenty books are reviewed.

G. W. Anderson

LANG, BERNHARD: *Eugen Drewermann, interprète de la Bible* (Théologies). 1994. Pp. 172. (Cerf, Paris. Price: Fr 118.00. ISBN 2 204 04884 4; ISSN 0761 4330)

Eugen Drewermann's large volumes of psychological interpretation of the Bible have been best sellers in Germany in recent years, and interest in the author has been heightened by opposition to his work by his Roman Catholic superiors. Drewermann's Paderborn colleague, Bernhard Lang, has not only added French to the various languages in which he writes; he has provided a helpful introduction to Drewermann's work which is also a powerful plea for a multi-faceted approach to biblical interpretation. The influences upon Drewermann which L. traces include the German Romantic tradition and Kierkegaard as well as the great modern psychologists. Lang also notes similarities with the work of Eliade, and devotes a section to a precursor, the Swiss Protestant pastor Oskar Pfister. The latter part of the book is devoted to an examination of Genesis 2–3 and the New Testament Infancy narrative of Luke. In the case of Genesis, three readings provided by L. on the basis of his own and others' interpretations (structural, historical and mythological) precede Drewermann's exposition.

J. W. Rogerson

LANG, BERNHARD, et al. (eds): *Internationale Zeitschriftenshau für Bibelwissenschaft und Grenzgebiete*. Vol. 39. 1992–93. Pp. xiv, 469. (Patmos, Düsseldorf. Price: DM 158.00. ISBN 3 491 66039 4; ISSN 0074 9745)

The higher ratio of entries per page noted for the previous number (*B.L.* 1994, p. 16) has been held, though some few book reviews occupy more than a side. However, this welcome volume is some one-sixth larger than Band 38.

A. G. Auld

LEHMANN, REINHARD G.: *Friedrich Delitzsch und der Babel-Bibel-Streit* (Orbis Biblicus et Orientalis 133). 1994. Pp. xvi, 444. (Universitätsverlag, Freiburg (Schweiz); Vandenhoeck & Ruprecht, Göttingen. Price: SwFr 130.00. ISBN (Universitätsverlag) 3 7278 0932 9; (Vandenhoeck & Ruprecht) 3 525 53768 9)

Friedrich Delitzsch, the Assyriologist, son of Franz Delitzsch the Old Testament scholar, shocked much of the western reading world in 1902 with a lecture in which he claimed that much of Hebrew religion, including monotheism, was derived from Babylonian sources, a theme he followed up in other lectures and publications. A very public controversy ensued, and in *Die grosse Täuschung* (1920) he pushed matters still further so that he laid himself open to the charge of anti-Semitism. L.'s work is a detailed study of the whole matter, publishing for the first time many letters to and from Delitzsch bearing on the issues, reprinting cartoons from then current periodicals, and re-creating the events and Delitzsch's intellectual and spiritual development with a mass of documentation. The scholarly issues raised are not studied: the work is history of exegesis, not a consideration of Babylonian influence on the Hebrews. The author concludes that Delitzsch was not in the full sense anti-Semitic, but was pushed by the heat of the controversy into an extreme stance.

W. G. LAMBERT

LEMAIRE, ANDRÉ and OTZEN, BENEDIKT (eds): *History and Traditions of Early Israel — Studies Presented to Eduard Nielsen, May 8th 1993* (Supplements to Vetus Testamentum 50). 1994. Pp. vii, 165. (Brill, Leiden–New York–Köln. Price: fl. 135.00/$77.25. ISBN 90 04 09851 8; ISSN 0083 5889)

The studies in this volume, presented to Eduard Nielsen on the occasion of his seventieth birthday, are a fitting tribute to his distinguished scholarly work. A reconstruction of the route and objectives of Pharaoh Sheshonq's campaign in Palestine by the late G. W. Ahlström has been edited by Diana Edelman. R. A. Carlson investigates the interplay of tradition and innovation, fact and fiction, in 2 Samuel 6. J. A. Emerton discusses various renderings of Psalm 68:16f. and concludes that v. 16a is a question. S. Holm-Nielsen argues that Jerusalem fell to David because the water supply was cut off and not because Joab climbed Warren's Shaft. A. S. Kapelrud examines Genesis 3 in the light of Sumerian and Babylonian myths. A. Lemaire reconsiders the composition and date of the Abraham traditions in the light of recent discussion. N. P. Lemche offers a detailed criticism of the views of F. Stolz and K. Engelken on the Canaanites. M. Ottosson gives an account of the Scandinavian archaeological expedition to Tell el-Fukhar and its results. B. Otzen examines the literary motif of 'the promoting mother' in the Ugaritic texts and the Old Testament. M. Saebø reconsiders the divine names and epithets in Genesis 49:24b–25a, taking full account of the text-critical and form-historical problems. J. A. Soggin contributes a study of Genesis 34 which he regards as of late date and unrelated to Israel's occupation of the land. J. Strange argues that Joshua is 'a Hasmonean manifesto'. M. Weinfeld gives a comparative presentation and analysis of the laws in the Covenant, Priestly, and Deuteronomic codes concerning the relations of Israel to the Canaanites.

G. W. ANDERSON

METZGER, BRUCE M. and COOGAN, MICHAEL D. (eds): *The Oxford Companion to the Bible*. 1993. Pp. xxi, 874 + 14 maps. (Oxford University Press. Price: £35.00. ISBN 0 19 504645 5)

A Companion is evidently not quite a biblical encyclopaedia, though it contains articles on all the books of the Bible, on its principal characters, realia and theological topics. This Companion at any rate also contains short articles on the Bible in modern culture (e.g. Dance and the Bible, African American Traditions and the Bible), and on the transmission and diffusion of the Bible (e.g. Illustrated Bibles, Chapter and Verse Divisions). Articles in M.'s field of textual history are first-class, articles on biblical books tend toward the conventional, while some of the other articles are frankly unworthy of the volume. The article on Women, for example, begins with the palpable falsehood that before the exile 'women in Israel enjoyed a status and freedom comparable to that of men'. The article on Marx and the Bible ignores Marxist biblical criticism altogether. The article on 'Israel, History of' ends at 722; as far as I can see, there is no article on history of post-exilic Judaea at all. In general, it is hard to see how a volume in which contributors were urged to present their own views and in which the editors disclaim any responsibility for 'dogmatic unanimity' can also be an 'authoritative reference' (pp. vi, viii). Authoritativeness and postmodernism are odd bed fellows.

D. J. A. CLINES

MILLS, WATSON E.: *Lutterworth Dictionary of the Bible*. 1994. Pp. xxx, 993 + 62 plates. (Lutterworth, Cambridge. Price: £30.00. ISBN 0 7188 2918 2)

The contributors to this volume are members of the National Association of Baptist Professors of Religion; however, in many ways they represent a cross section of (mostly) American biblical scholars, and a number of their names will be recognized by most readers. About 1450 succinct entries (signed and with a pronunciation guide) on the main expected topics will make this a useful quick reference, especially for students. As one would expect, the quality of the entries varies considerably. There is some bibliography at the end of the longer entries, but it tends to be fairly basic and not always particularly helpful, with no dates or place of publication. Of more use are the cross references at the end of many articles and also an index of entries listed by contributor.

L. L. GRABBE

MÜLLER, HANS-PETER: *Mensch-Umwelt-Eigenwelt. Gesammelte Aufsätze zur Weisheit Israels*. 1992. Pp. 243. (Kohlhammer, Stuttgart. Price: DM 128.00/AS 999/SwFr 129.00. ISBN 3 17 012200 2)

This volume contains a collection of essays on Old Testament wisdom literature written on various occasions since 1970. Job and Kohelet have two pieces each: one essay on Job debates the conflict between old and new modes of thought contained in the book, the second discusses the real nature of God's 'answer' to Job. Of the essays on Kohelet, one discusses the commonly held decline in wisdom expertise at the time of the book's composition, the second viewing Kohelet as a 'strange guest' fitting awkwardly into the 'feast' of wisdom books; the book's position in the Christian canon also is discussed against the background of the death of God controversy. Other articles cover the educational aspects of wisdom (with many references to Tobit), and wisdom's interpretation of mortality — particularly in Gen. 3:19 and Eccl. 3:21 — in the light of ancient parallels, including Greek tragedy and comedy and grave inscriptions. The use of the term, 'riddle' (*ḥidot*) is also examined. Links between wisdom and apocalyptic and between wisdom and anthropology are traced in the last two articles (previously unpublished). M. claims to cover all wisdom books of the Old Testament: it is unfortunate that that *doyen* of wisdom, Ben Sira, falls in the Apocrypha and is therefore omitted almost entirely!

J. G. SNAITH

NELLEN, HENK J. M. and RABBIE, EDWIN (eds): *Hugo Grotius–Theologian. Essays in Honour of G. H. M. Posthumus Meyjes* (Studies in the History of Christian Thought 55). 1994. Pp. xi, 275. (Brill, Leiden–New York-Köln. Price: fl. 135.00/$77.25. ISBN 90 04 10000 8; ISSN 0081 8607)

All who admire the Dutch Dioscuri Erasmus and Grotius will obtain and read this magnificent Festschrift. The bibliography alone, complete for the period 1840–1993 in six out of the thirteen subsections, would justify the expense. Only two of its thirteen essays deal with Old Testament and Jewish themes. François Laplanche writes on 'Grotius et les religions du paganisme dans les *Annotationes in Vetus Testamentum*' (pp. 53–63), emphasizing both his indebtedness to Maimonides and G. J. Vossius and also his ability to supplement them from his own classical reading (he was in fact an early practitioner of what later was to be called comparative religion). Grotius stressed the inapplicability of the prohibition of idolatry to current debates within 17th-century Christianity. Edwin Rabbie surveys 'Hugo Grotius and Judaism' (pp. 99–120) and concludes, just possibly with more hindsight than precision: Grotius 'has never had any real interest in Jews as individuals nor in Judaism as a religious practice. For that he has met too few Jews, and Judaism was too remote from him . . . His point of view was and remained that of a philologist' (p. 119). Ten of the essays are in English, the rest in French. On pp. 206; 274, correct the reference to 1 Peter 1:10–11.

                                                                                J. L. NORTH

NOLL, MARK A.: *The Scandal of the Evangelical Mind*. 1994. Pp. ix, 274. (Eerdmans, Grand Rapids MI; Inter-Varsity Press, Leicester. Price: $19.99/£11.99. ISBN (Eerdmans) 0 8028 3715 8; (Inter-Varsity) 0 85111 1483)

This is a critique from the inside. N. writes as a committed evangelical, but gives a 'cri du cœur on behalf of the intellectual life' (p. ix). For him the scandal of the evangelical mind is that there is no evangelical mind; that is, there is no intellectual endeavour toward the whole spectrum of modern learning from an evangelical perspective. N. argues his case eloquently, and one hopes that it will strike a chord in many evangelicals. He himself is optimistic that progress is possible, though his view is that evangelicalism has a large amount of baggage inessential to Christianity. The question remains, however, whether the freedom of thought necessary for such an intellectual critique can be sufficiently compatible with evangelicalism.

                                                                                L. L. GRABBE

NORTH, ROBERT (ed.): *Elenchus of Biblica 1991* (Elenchus of Biblical Bibliography 7). 1994. Pp. 1062. (Pontifical Biblical Institute, Rome. Price: Lire 170.000. ISBN 88 7653 602 7)

The superb *Elenchus* returns for 1991 to average length, despite coverage of a few more publications. Our own editorial change of mid-1992 is 'anticipated' on p. 103. The opening page answers the question 'Why does our Elenchus come so late? (mid–1994 for 1991)' with some excerpts from Father North's editorial diary.

                                                                                A. G. AULD

NUMBERS, RONALD L.: *The Creationists*. 1992. Pp. xvii, 458. (University of California Press. Price: £13.95/$15.00. ISBN paper 0 520 08393 8)

In recent years, 'creation science' has been become a major controversy and even a political issue in the United States. As an ex-creationist, N. is a knowledgable critic on the subject. However, his criticism is mainly indirect as he gives a fascinating and sympathetic history of creationism's development since the time of Darwin, through such figures as George McCready Price to Whitcomb and Morris and finally to the current situation in America. One point made abundantly clear is that creationism is an outgrowth of religion, whatever scientific data are assembled in support of it.

L. L. GRABBE

ORD, DAVID ROBERT and COOTE, ROBERT B.: *Is the Bible True? Understanding the Bible Today.* 1994. Pp. xii, 132. (SCM, London. Price: £7.95. ISBN 0 334 00745 3)

Addressing the questions of whether truth is co-terminous with fact and, if not, whether both may be equally trustworthy as a basis for life, this book confronts the difficulties the Bible presents to believing and non-believing readers alike. The important influence wielded by readers' home cultures on their interpretation of any text is discussed with a view to raising the awareness of modern readers that, in reading the Bible, they confront an ancient text from an alien culture. O./C. claim that the 'real' differences between gospel stories are vital to understanding the nuances intended by the individual writers and should not be glossed over to give a unified version of events, then lead the reader through many Bible stories, from Old Testament and New, showing how their liberal approach opens up the Bible to the modern mind in a way that integrates the events in biblical narrative with modern life experience and with modern modes of thought. Meaning is valued as highly as fact or truth, and although many of the illustrations and examples from modern life are American in origin, they are well enough known in European culture to make their meanings clear.   H. A. McKAY

PORTER, STANLEY E.; JOYCE, PAUL; and ORTON, DAVID E. (eds): *Crossing the Boundaries. Essays in Biblical Interpretation in Honour of Michael D. Goulder* (Biblical Interpretation Series 8). 1994. Pp. xviii, 381. (Brill, Leiden–New York–Köln. Price: fl. 145.00/$83.00. ISBN 90 04 10131 4; ISSN 0928 0731)

Of the twenty-four contributions to this Festschrift five are directly devoted to The Hebrew Bible in Context: Historical and Literary Perspectives: 'When Did Jehu Pay Tribute?' (W. G. Lambert); 'The Minor Prophets — One Book or Twelve?' (R. Coggins); '"A Bloodless Compromise"'? the Question of an Eschatological Ritual in Ancient Israel' (J. H. Eaton); 'The Structure and Composition of Proverbs 22:17–24:22) (R. N. Whybray); 'The Song of Songs: Mystification, Ambiguity and Humour' (G. I. Emmerson). Another three open up 'Views beyond the Biblical Boundaries', two of which deal with aspects of Judaism: 'Do God-fearers Make Good Christians?' (J. M. Lieu); 'Sadducees and Essenes after 70 CE' (M. Goodman). A final trio debate Method in Biblical Interpretation: 'Historical Criticism and Literary Interpretation: Is There Any Common Ground?' (J. Barton); 'First among Equals? The Historical-Critical Approach in the Marketplace of Methods' (P. Joyce); 'Typology' (F. Young). The remaining contributions discuss New Testament themes, several with Old Testament ramifications, e.g. 'The Origin of Armageddon: Revelation 16:16 as an Interpretation of Zechariah 12:11' (J. Day). An appreciation of Michael Goulder (by D. Nineham) and a bibliography of his published work (by S. E. Porter) complete the volume.

J. L. NORTH

SÁRKÖZI, A. (ed.): *Acta Orientalia Academiae Scientiarum Hungaricae*. Tom. 46. 1992–93. Pp. 412. (Akadémiai Kiadó, Budapest. HU ISSN 0001 6446)
This volume contains nothing relevant to Old Testament studies.

J. A. EMERTON

SMITH, WILFRED CANTWELL: *What Is Scripture? A Comparative Approach*. 1993. Pp. x, 381. (Fortress, Minneapolis. Price: $19.00. ISBN 0 8006 2608 7)
This is the American edition of the book reviewed in *B.L.* 1994, p. 19.

ED.

SPOTTORNO DÍAZ-CARO, MARÍA VICTORIA (ed.): *Sefarad. Revista de estudios hebraicos, sefardíes y de Oriente Próximo*. Vol. 53. 1993. Pp. 453. (Consejo Supérior de Investigaciones Científicas, Madrid. Price: 6,000 ptas. ISSN 0037 0894)
J.-L. Cunchillos publishes a 7th-century BC Phoenician inscription (*l'šmnh* or *l'šmny*) from T. Doña Blanca (Cádiz), with various suggestions as to how the final letter might be interpreted. With J.-P. Vita, Cunchillos also presents a new study of an Ugaritic letter advising of the destruction of a city. M. T. Rubiato details recent excavations at Hazor, which have uncovered a 9th- or 8th-century crematorium, an unexpected large building from the Late Bronze Age, destruction linked to Amos's earthquake, a 19th–18th-century tablet containing Amorite and Hurrian names, and a letter on the transfer of women perhaps addressed to Ibni-Adad, King of Hazor. García Martínez defends his 'non-messianic' interpretation of 4Q521:10, 4Q285:4, and 4Q246. N. Fernández Marcos reflects on intertestamental misogynist rewriting of biblical history, linking this to dualism and a concentration on impurity. In another article, Fernández concludes that house-churches show no clear dependence on synagogues, especially from the perspective of art and archaeology. A. Alba and C. Sainz de la Maza present a letter of the apostate Abner of Burgos in which the Jews are argued to be descendants of Edom (with Obadiah's Sefarad and Sarphat as places in Edom, not Spain and France). G. Nador shows how 'paradox' is used as a technical logical term in two Midrash Rabbah texts, both concerning Laban. Articles on medieval and later Judaism include studies on Jonah ibn Janaḥ's *Sefer ha-Shorashim*, the Kabbalah, and Columbus's *Book of Prophecies*.

J. F. ELWOLDE

SPOTTORNO DÍAZ-CARO, MARÍA VICTORIA (ed.): *Sefarad. Revista de estudios hebraicos, sefardíes y de Oriente Próximo*. Vol. 54. 1994. Pp. 224. (Consejo Supérior de Investigaciones Científicas, Madrid. Price: 6,000 ptas. ISSN 0037 0894)
L. Alonso lists thirteen similarities of expression (not calques) between Biblical Hebrew and Spanish, English, German, etc. C. Herranz and G. Seijas present a short study of *ashishah* ('raisin cake'?), although they overlook the evidence from Qumran of particular relevance to Isa. 16:7. M.-J. de Azcárraga analyses oversized letters in biblical manuscripts (e.g., Dt 6.4) and other Masoretic works. Jesús-Luis Cunchillos and J. P. Vita present various corrections and additions to the Ugaritic material held in their Database of Northwest Semitic philology (BDFSN). M. T. Rubiato describes how the Hazor of Ahab's time is gradually being excavated. A number of

22 GENERAL

articles relate to medieval and later Judaism. As usual, the fascicle contains valuable detailed book reviews and summaries of non-Spanish biblical journals.

J. F. ELWOLDE

TÅNGBERG, ARVID (ed.): *Text and Theology. Studies in Honour of Professor dr. theol. Magne Sæbø Presented on the Occasion of His 65th Birthday.* 1994. Pp. 381. (Verbum, Oslo. Price: NKr 298.00. ISBN 82 543 0647 8)

The range of subjects discussed in the contributions to this impressive volume reflects the extent and variety of the honorand's scholarly work. I. Asheim writes on apocalyptic and belief in creation with reference to Luther's teaching. T. Austad discusses the election of Israel and its place in Christian belief. H. M. Barstad argues that alleged Akkadian loanwords in Isaiah 40–55 are not evidence for its Babylonian origin. K. Berge examines the place of deliverance and blessing in Westermann's thought. E. Baasland contributes a study of the concept *noema* in 2 Corinthians. R. E. Clements evaluates the contributions of J. Kitto and W. Smith to the understanding of the Bible. J. Jeremias examines the influence of Hosea on Jeremiah. A. S. Kapelrud demonstrates the similarity between Sumerian and Israelite accounts of temple building. M. Kartveit discusses the identity of the prophets referred to in Zechariah 13:2–6. E. E. Knudsen surveys pronominal forms of final weak nouns in biblical Hebrew. O. C. M. Kvarme considers recent translations of the New Testament in a Jewish setting. E. Larsson describes the impact of Jewish-Christian dialogue on Christian theology. H. Graf Reventlow evaluates the Job commentary of Didymus the Blind. D. Rian comments on autobiographical passages in Mowinckel's writings. O. Skarsaune examines the differences between the early Christian canon of the Old Testament and the Jewish Bible and the reasons for them. O. Skjevesland contributes an essay on homiletics. J. A. Soggin discusses the historicity of Ezra. S. Storøy comments on the theme of poverty in Proverbs 14:20. Tångberg inquires whether the classical prophets preached repentance. K. W. Weyde argues that the references to Jacob in Hosea 12:4f. are a typological interpretation of the Genesis traditions.

G. W. ANDERSON

TIFFIN, LEE: *Creationism's Upside-Down Pyramid. How Science Refutes Fundamentalism.* 1994. Pp. 229. (Prometheus Books, Amherst, NY. Price: $29.95. ISBN 0 87975 898 8)

Unlike some writers on the subject, T. is not anti-religion; on the contrary, he himself has a theology degree and has been a church pastor. His work gives a good summary of the basis of 'scientific creationism'. The last section of the book (part 3) discusses the politics in the USA of the attempt to introduce creationism into the school curriculum as an 'alternative' to evolution. The weakness of the book is its organization. It is not clear how the contents of part 1 differ from part 2, since they overlap considerably, nor is the order of topics in each clear. T. also fails to understand that the most effective way to argue against creationism is not with sarcastic overkill. The best argument is frequently a simple statement of the arguments on each side; also, he often fails to give due attention to the scientific arguments used to oppose the creationists'. (A book such as N. Eldredge's *The Monkey Business* does a better job of this.) Nevertheless, the book is a useful contribution to the debate. (See also R. L. Numbers above.)

L. L. GRABBE

WALLIS, GERHARD: *Mein Freund hatte einen Weinberg. Aufsätze und Vorträge zum Alten Testament* (Beitrage zur Erforschung des Alten Testaments und des Antiken Judentums 23). Mit einem Geleitwort von Walter Dietrich. 1994. Pp. 301. (Lang, Frankfurt–Bern–New York. Price: SwF. 33.00. ISBN 3 8204 1174 7; ISSN 0722 0790)

W. succeeded to the Old Testament chair in Halle held by Otto Eissfeldt and occupied it from 1959 until his retirement in 1990. During this time he was one of the leading scholars in his field in the German Democratic Republic. This volume of collected essays covers the areas of the history of Israel, the history of tradition, and prophecy (including theology and ethics). There are three previously unpublished articles: 'Aufnahme und Überwindung kanaanäischer Vorstellungen und Eigenarten durch Alt-Israel', 'Gottesvorstellung und Gotteserfahrung der alttestamentlichen Weisheitsliteratur', and 'Hermann Gunkel. Zum 100. Geburtstag am 23. Mai 1962'. Particularly interesting is Wallis's memorial address for his distinguished predecessor on the first anniversary of his death on 23 April 1974. Now that travel to Eastern Germany presents no problems, it will be much easier for foreigners to appreciate W.'s account of Eissfeldt's family background, linked as it was to the Eisfelder (*sic*) Talmühle, which can be visited on the Harzer Schmalspurbahn with its powerful steam locomotives.

J. W. ROGERSON

ZOBEL, HANS-JÜGEN: *Altes Testament — Literatursammlung und Heilige Schrift. Gesammelte Aufsätze zur Entstehung, Geschichte und Auslegung des Alten Testaments* (Beihefte zur Zeitschrift für die alttestamentliche Wissenschaft 212). 1993. Pp. vii, 306. (de Gruyter, Berlin–New York. Price: DM 138.00. ISBN 3 11 013982 0; ISSN 0934 2575)

This is a selection of essays, some previously unpublished, by Z. collected and edited by former pupils to mark his sixty-fifth birthday. As the subtitle suggests, they cover a wide range of issues on the origin, history, and interpretation of the Old Testament. After an opening essay which discusses the relationship between the Old Testament as a literary collection or holy scripture, the first section deals with the Sitz im Leben of Deut. 33:6–25, the meaning of Cis- and Trans-Jordan for the history of early Israel, the use of 'Greater Judah' in the pre-Davidic period, the prophet in Israel and Judah, and Hosea and Deuteronomy. The second section covers the relationship of Yahweh to El and Baal, the divine triad in the ancient Near East and the Old Testament, history and tradition in the theology of Israel and Judah, 'Old and New' in deutero-Isaiah and in the psalms and prophets. The collection is completed by essays on Hebraists at the University of Wittenberg (1502–1817), the history of the Deutschen Evangelischen Instituts für Altertumswissenschaft des Heiligen Landes, the life and work of Wilhelm Gesenius, and Otto Eissfeldt as theologian. The essays display typical careful scholarship but are rather dated given the shifts which have taken place in the discipline in the last few years.

K. W. WHITELAM

2. ARCHAEOLOGY AND EPIGRAPHY

ARNAUD, DANIEL: *Texte aus Larsa. Die epigraphischen Funde der 1. Kampagne in Senkereh-Larsa 1933* (Berliner Beiträge zum Vorderen Orient: Texte 3). 1994. Pp. 25 + 42 plates. (Dietrich Reimer Verlag, Berlin. Price: DM 48.00. ISBN 3 496 02510 7)

This is a volume of cuneiform copies with brief notes identifying the texts, and also lists of personal names. For cuneiformists, not Old Testament scholars.

W. G. LAMBERT

BEIT-ARIÉ, MALACHI: *Hebrew Manuscripts of East and West. Towards a Comparative Codicology* (Panizzi Lectures 1992). 1993. Pp. xiv, 124. (The British Library, London. Price: £16.00. ISBN 0 7123 0306 5)

Here, in edited form, are the Panizzi Lectures by one of the foremost Israeli experts in codicology and palaeography. The chapters are entitled 'Medieval Hebrew Manuscripts as Cross-Cultural Agents', 'The Art of Writing and the Craft of Bookmaking' and 'Scribal Re-making: Transmitting and Shaping Texts'. There are copious illustations of the highest quality: four in colour and fifty-two in black and white. The author surveys the socio-cultural situations, influences and relationships of the Jewish scribes all round the Mediterranean and over much of Europe, giving a succinct descriptive typology of all the main script-types with their several backgrounds. A small book, but beautiful and fascinating.

R. P. R. MURRAY

BEN-TOR, AMNON (ed.): *The Archeology of Ancient Israel*. Translated by R. Greenburg. 1992. Pp. xxi, 398. (Yale, New Haven CT — London, Price: $50.00; paper $27.50/£19.95. ISBN 0 300 04768 1; paper 0 300 05919 1)

This book aims to provide an up-to-date overview of the archaeology of the biblical periods. The Neolithic, Chalcolithic and early Bronze Ages are included on grounds that they provide the background (settlement patterns, economic and socio-political setting) for the central events of biblical history. However, this is not a book of 'biblical archaeology' in the misguided sense of the term. Indeed, a section in the Introduction deals very clearly with the interrelation (its relevance and limitation) between archaeology and the Bible (pp. 7–9). Now that the accumulated wealth of material is so great, each period is presented by a respective specialist. The material is up to date and clearly presented. The various aspects dealt with include public and private architecture, everyday objects, industry and crafts, art, cult, trade relations, and also discussion on the important characteristics of each period. Numerous photographs and drawings supplement the text. Originally based on an introductory course for the Open University, Israel, a wider readership will now benefit by this publication.

J. R. DUCKWORTH

BIRAN, AVRAHAM: *Biblical Dan*. English version by Joseph Shadur. 1994. Pp. 280 + 272 illustrations. (Israel Exploration Society, Jerusalem. Price: $32.00. ISBN 965 221 020 X)

This book, first published in Hebrew in 1992, is most welcome because it furnishes the only substantial account of the excavations which B. has been directing at the site of Laish/Dan since 1966. But it is also frustrating, as there are still no technical reports, even preliminary ones, to which one can go for further clarification and information. Nevertheless the book provides a useful and readable account of the history of the city, with lavish illustrations which include pottery drawings, sections and plans as well as photographs. The first seven chapters deal with the Neolithic and Bronze Age remains. The remaining chapters, which are longer, describe the early Iron Age levels, which can to some extent be correlated with Judges 17–18; evidence of metal-working (bronze apparently); the sacred precinct where the shrine (re)built by Jeroboam I for the 'golden calf' is argued to have continued in use until the 4th century AD; the Israelite gates and other fortifications; and the evidence from the 8th century BC and later. Finally, one of several additions made for the English edition gives details and a photograph of the 9th-century Aramaic stele fragment from the site: two further pieces have subsequently been discovered.

G. I. DAVIES

CHARLESWORTH, JAMES H. (ed.): *The Dead Sea Scrolls: Hebrew, Aramaic, and Greek Texts with English Translations. Volume 1: Rule of the Community and Related Documents* (The Princeton Theological Seminary Dead Sea Scrolls Project 1). With F. M. Cross, J. Milgrom, E. Qimron, L. H. Schiffman, L. T. Stuckenbruck, and R. E. Whitaker. 1994. Pp. xxiii, 185. (Mohr, Tübingen; Westminster John Knox, Louisville KY. Price: DM 168.00. ISBN (Mohr) 3 16 146199 1; (Westminster) 0 664 21994 2)

This is the first of the Princeton Project's ten volumes of texts (preceded by a Graphic Concordance [*B.L.* 1992, p. 134] and to be crowned by a Lexical Concordance) — thanks to C.'s talent for bringing money, people and institutions together. This volume includes 1QS, 1QSa, 1QSb, 5Q13; then 4Q159, 4Q513 and 4Q514(=4QOrd^{a-c}). The series obviously addresses a dual audience. Scholars get a critical text (for 1QS this includes 4Q readings), and the inclusion of only 'obvious' restorations is a better policy than some other editions, though still subjective (and transgressed here!). No restorations at all would be better.

For the non-scholar, there is much packaging: preface, foreword, and general introduction precede introductions, text, translation and notes on the individual documents. The editors' own ideas also intrude, not always helpfully: we read that 1QS is organically related to 1QSa and 1QSb because written by the same hand on the same scroll; portions of 1QS were memorized during the two years' probation; *the* Messiah appears in 9:11; the community dates from the mid-2nd century BCE; the sect prayed at sunrise and sunset so as to bring light back to the earth. All wrong, or dubious. Two oddities: a table of 'technical terms uniformly rendered' — where *yḥd* can be any of 'the Community, common, each other, together, one, unity', whereas *'rṣ* is 'earth, land' and *ḥkmh* 'wisdom' (*technical?*); and the obligatory reference to 'original language' — irrelevant to the texts in this volume. But scholars can ignore the fripperies and be grateful for, at last, a standard critical edition of virtually all the Qumran non-biblical texts.   P. R. DAVIES

DEUTSCH, R. and HELTZER, M.: *Forty New Ancient West Semitic Inscriptions.* 1994. Pp. 100. (Archaeological Center Publication, 7 Magal Dagim Street, Old Jaffa 68036, Israel. N.P. ISBN 965 222 511 8)

The longest inscriptions presented are dedications, one Phoenician, six Aramaic, to the *štrm* of Sharon on six bronze vessels and a cymbal. Found during building work with other objects, they evidently come from a Phoenician shrine of the 5th century BC. Discussion of the divine and personal names and the phrase 'for his life' argues for an Arabian connection, although the grounds appear very slight. Five bronze arrowheads are the oldest texts included, assigned palaeographically to the 11th century BC. One duplicates that of Zakarbaal king of Amurru in Beirut Museum, the others bear West Semitic names, some known, some hitherto unknown. A slab, reputedly cut from a tomb at Khirbet el-Kom, carries two Hebrew graffiti, rendered 'Bless your stone-cutters' and 'In this will rest the elders'. Pecked in Hebrew on a small pottery decanter of Iron Age II type is the notice, 'Belonging to Mattanyahu, wine for (cultic) libation — (one) quarter', the unit of measurement being uncertain (the pot has a capacity of 1.27 litres), but Ex. 29:40 and Lev. 23:13 have similar phrases. The most numeous inscriptions are seals and impressions. The ten bullae include another example of 'Berekyahu son of Neryahu, the scribe', commonly identified with Jeremiah's secretary, this one with a fingerprint! Two bullae were impressed for royal servants, one for a prison gate-keeper. The seven seals include one of a king's servant, one of an 'attendant', one of a 'guide' (*nhl*) and one of a woman. Five bronze weights are engraved with their values. All of these objects, now in private collections, are accidental or illicit discoveries, so none has an archaeological provenance. Nevertheless, the authors have done a valuable service in publishing them, adding to knowledge of West Semitic onomastics, religion and language (note the bowl, no. 39, has both *zy* and *d* in the same Aramaic text).

A. R. MILLARD

FREYDANK, HELMUT: *Mittelassyrische Rechtsurkunden und Verwaltungstexte III* (Ausgrabungen der Deutschen Orient-Gesellschaft in Assur: E. Inschriften, VII. Keilschrifttexte aus mittelassyrischer Zeit). 1994. Pp. 82. (Mann Verlag, Berlin. Price: DM 29.00. ISBN 3 7861 1746 2)

These hand-copies of eighty-six cuneiform texts with catalogue entries and indices bring the finds of this type of administrative documents found at Ashur near to completion. Fifty-five of these documents have already been published elsewhere with translations and commentaries. The rest also relate to the supply of common commodities to the main temples there. As such their bearing on the Old Testament is limited to possible parallels to similar Semitic practices found in the later First Temple period at Jerusalem.

D. J. WISEMAN

GEVA, HILLEL (ed.): *Ancient Jerusalem Revealed*. 1994. Pp. xvi, 336. (Israel Exploration Society, Jerusalem. Price: $40.00. ISBN 965 221 021 8)

The revelations of twenty-five years' excavations in Jerusalem are truly impressive. Despite the overburden of medieval and modern buildings and the repeated destructions and dismantlings, much has been learnt about the city in biblical times, although major gaps remain. This volume 'continues and complements' *Jerusalem Revealed* (*B.L.* 1976, p. 26), bringing together reports collected from the journal *Qadmoniot*. After the editor's introductory survey, fifteen papers discuss remains from the 'First Temple Period,' seventeen the 'Second Temple Period' and seven 'Later Periods'. Y. Shiloh's City of David site and the supposed gateway on the Ophel yielded the principal Iron Age ruins, a little from the 10th century, some from the 9th–8th and more from the 7th–6th, as might be expected, given the processes of destruction and survival. Walling on the west edge of Mount Zion is held to prove the city extended so far in the late Monarchy. Inscriptions include the texts of the 45 bullae from the City of David. Tombs from all periods inevitably feature strongly, some well known (like Ketef Hinnom, 'Caiaphas'), others easily overlooked. With them belong studies of ossuaries and finely carved sarcophagi of the Second Temple era. There are numerous maps, plans, black and white photographs, and eight pages of coloured pictures.

A. R. MILLARD

GOPHER, AVI: *Arrowheads of the Neolithic Levant. A Seriation Analysis* (American Schools of Oriental Research Dissertation Series 10). 1994. Pp. xviii, 325. (Eisenbrauns, Winona Lake IN. Price: $47.50. ISBN 0 931464 76 5)

This comprehensive doctoral study was completed in 1985, revised in 1990, and the preface contains a summary of discoveries up to 1993. After an introduction (ch. 1), a survey of previous research (ch. 2) and a definition of terminology (ch. 3), the author presents a careful evaluation of the sites which have yielded arrowheads then sets out thirteen principal types (ch. 4). The survey of sites (ch. 5) discusses the contexts and illustrates examples from each provenance, assessing the frequency of arrowheads in each stone tool assemblage. That is the basic material which ch. 6 analyses. Four major groups appear, each seeing the rise and decline of certain types of arrow, with those in the 'Southern Levant' usually coming later in the development of each than those to the north and north-east, something which ch. 8, 'The Geographical Aspect' examines within the whole Neolithic context. 'Absolute Chronology' (ch. 7) attempts to set the groups in time with the aid of radiocarbon dating (a list of dates forms an appendix). The conclusions (ch. 9) integrate the results to argue for a 'general homogeneity characterizing the Levantine Neolithic lithic industries' which probably applies to other aspects of the culture also. Various appendices give details of sites and statistical tables. There is no attempt to discover the uses or effectiveness of the different shapes of arrowheads!

A. R. MILLARD

HEALEY, JOHN F.: *The Nabataean Tomb Inscriptions of Mad'in Salih. Edited with Introduction, Translation and Commentary* (Journal of Semitic Studies Supplement 1). 1993. Pp. xiv, 298, 55 (Arabic) + 3 maps, 38 drawings/photos, 13 plates. (Oxford University Press. Price: £40.00. ISBN 0 19 922162 6; ISBN 0022 4480)

This volume serves as an auspicious beginning of a new series in Semitic Studies, and will hopefully prove to be a model for future volumes. It is a text edition of Nabataean tomb inscriptions from the Nabataean site of Hegra in Arabia from the first century AD The volume presents a complete text edition of each inscription, with an extensive philological commentary and notes on each inscription. In addition, the book contains autograph copies as well as photographs of the inscriptions, and indices with proper names and a glossary, as well as a lengthy bibliography. The author's introductory notes include a brief summary of Nabataean history, as well as a discussion of the grammar of the inscriptions, and general affinities with other Semitic languages. The Akkadian parallels must be viewed with caution, since individual cognate words known to us from Akkadian may have been used in Nabataean through the spread of Aramaic during the Persian period. It is likely that certain standard legal formulas were widespread in Aramaic, some of which originally being derived from Akkadian; the appearance of a few such standard legal terms in Nabataean (see pp. 43–44) may be interesting linguistically, but not culturally significant.

M. J. GELLER

HENTEN, JAN WILLEM VAN and HORST, PIETER WILLEM VAN DER (eds): *Studies in Early Jewish Epigraphy* (Arbeiten zur Geschichte des Antiken Judentums and des Urchristentums 21). 1994. Pp. ix, 290. (Brill, Leiden–New York–Köln. Price: fl. 135.00/$77.25. ISBN 90 04 09916 6; ISBN 0169 734X)

This interesting volume collects nine papers from a 1992 Utrecht conference. There is no attempt to present an overview of current analysis, nor any real dialogue between the, mainly specialized, papers except through the editors' introduction. Some treat familiar issues from a new perspective: G. Lüderitz, 'What is the Politeuma?' and T. Rajak, 'Inscription and Context: Reading the Jewish Catacombs of Rome'. Others contrast the 'religiosity' of epitaphs with literary texts, posing sharply questions of Jewish-non-Jewish interaction: J. Strubbe, 'Curses against Violation of the Grave', A. Bij de Vaate, 'Alphabet Inscriptions from Jewish Graves', and P. van der Horst, 'Jewish Poetical Tomb Inscriptions'. The former question is also examined directly by W. Horbury, 'Jewish Inscriptions and Jewish Literature in Egypt, with Special Reference to Ecclesiasticus', and by J. W. van Henten in his comparison of 'A Jewish Epitaph in a Literary Text: 4 Macc 17:8–10' with contemporary Jewish and non-Jewish epitaphs. Inevitably, the strongest impression is one of variety — illustrated by David Noy's assessment of 'The

28   ARCHAEOLOGY AND EPIGRAPHY

Jewish Communities of Leontopolis and Venosa' — and a mix of the expected and unexpected: G. Mussies on 'Jewish Personal Names in Some Non-Literary Sources' (including a discussion of Ja'el of Aphrodisias). Most of the essays include examples, with fuller collections being appended to those by Strubbe and van der Horst.

J. LIEU

HERBORDT, SUZANNE: *Neuassyrische Glyptik des 8.–7. Jh. v. Chr. unter besondere Berüchsichtigung der Siegelungen auf Tafeln und Tonverschlüssen* (State Archives of Assyria Studies 1). 1992. Pp. xx, 276 + 36 plates and 1 map. (Neo-Assyrian Text Corpus Project, Helsinki. Price: $39.50. ISBN 951 45 6047 7)

This is a meticulous study of the impressions of both cylinder and stamp seals on Assyrian documents (all legal) and on bullae and related clay lumps from Assyrian sites dating to the 8th-7th centuries. The function of sealing is dealt with in detail, and the designs are studied by a gathering of relevant data, though there is no deep study of Neo-Assyrian art. The catalogue is exemplary, but the drawings lack something in quality, and the photographs are not well reproduced. The book is relevant to study of sealing under the Israelite monarchy.

W. G. LAMBERT

HERRMANN, CHRISTIAN: *Ägyptische Amulette aus Palästina/Israel. Mit einem Ausblick auf ihre Rezeption durch das Alte Testament* (Orbis Biblicus et Orientalis 138). 1994. Pp. xxiii, 828 + 80 figures and 70 plates. (Universitätsverlag, Freiburg (Schweiz); Vandenhoeck & Ruprecht, Göttingen. Price: DM 340.00/SwF 295.00/AS 2652. ISBN (Universitätsverlag) 3 7278 0933 7; (Vandenhoeck & Ruprecht) 3 525 53773 5)

This unwieldy and expensive volume attempts to present a corpus of all the Egyptian-type amulets excavated in Palestine during 1898–1992, in catalogue-form, all drawn, with a generous selection of photographs; some 1400 pieces are included. In the Introduction, the author attempts to sketch the variations in types of amulets through late Bronze IIB to Roman times. He also points out that the heaviest concentration in the finds of these amulets is in the Iron Age IIB, *c.* 930–700 BC. That excess of paganising use of such talismans in Judah and Israel of the divided monarchy impels the author to attempt to identify these amulets with the *gillulim* of the Old Testament (pp. 83–91) — which is, frankly, unconvincing in many contexts. But, more subtly, this concentration may be a reflex of the syncretism and idolatry condemned by the prophets and orthodox circles (Deuteronomic so miscalled) at this period. A corpus of these little objects is impractical, as ongoing and future excavations will yield still more, but it will be useful as a work of reference.

K. A. KITCHEN

HOPPE, LESLIE J.: *The Synagogues and Churches of Ancient Palestine*. 1994. Pp. v, 145. (Liturgical Press, Collegeville MN. Price: $11.95. ISBN 0 8146 5754 0)

Clearly written and well documented, this book provides a good introduction to the ways Jews and Christians of the Roman and Byzantine periods expressed their religious beliefs through the construction of places of worship. Both groups adapted the Greco-Roman basilica to their own liturgical needs, but architectural variations show that there was no 'typical' synagogue or church. Religious art and architecture was influenced as much by current fashions and popular beliefs as by 'orthodox' religious tenets. Extravagance of building reflects economic prosperity rather than local piety. The location of remains points to a concentration of Jews in Galilee and to Christians in the

Judaean and Samaritan hills. Problems that still remain unresolved include the origin of the synagogue as an architectural form; how to identify a building as a synagogue or church; the question of Jewish Christianity

J. R. DUCKWORTH

HUTTENHÖFER, RUTH (ed.): *Ptolemäische Urkunden aus der Heidelberger Papyrus-Sammlung (P. Heid. VI)*. 1994. Pp. xxi, 199 + 32 plates. (C. Winter, Heidelberg. Price: DM 130.00. ISBN 3 8253 0143 5)

H. publishes twenty-five Greek texts from Ptolemaic Egypt, mainly administrative documents. They include official correspondence, records relating to grain transport, receipts for grain and taxes, lists of names, petitions, and some private documents. Each text has an introduction and commentary, and a translation is provided (except for the fragmentary ones). Of particular interest are three references to *Samareios* (texts 367, 375, 382). This is not the city in Palestine but one in the Faiyum; however, it seems to have Jewish (Samaritan?) settlers, as indicated by the name Dositheos (texts 375, 382; cf. also 381).

L. L. GRABBE

ISAACS, HASKELL D. with the assistance of COLIN F. BAKER: *Medical and Para-Medical Manuscripts in the Cambridge Genizah Collections* (Cambridge University Library Genizah Series 11). 1994. Pp. xxi, 144 + 20 plates. (Cambridge University Press. Price: £70.00/$110.00. ISBN 0 521 47050 1)

This excellently-produced catalogue of 1616 documents, mostly in Arabic/Judaeo-Arabic and usually with a 'medical' connexion (often loose), has various useful indices, photographs, bibliography, and introduction. Each item is accompanied by a note describing its contents or an outstanding feature. The author states that eye disease and fevers are the commonest themes. Problems to do with sex and eating also rank highly, matched by a curious lack of texts on childhood illnesses. There are occasional comments on the transmission of Greek and Romance words into Hebrew and Arabic, and the material also gives some insights into Jewish society and Jewish-Muslim relations (e.g. items 689, 692, 1061, 1600, and 1601). Of the 155 items in Hebrew only, Moses ibn Tibbon's translation of Maimonides on Hippo-crates' *Aphorisms* accounts for twenty.

J. F. ELWOLDE

KIENAST, B., in collaboration with S. Sommerfeld: *Glossar zu den altakkadischen Königsinschriften* (Freiburger altorientalische Studien 8). 1994. Pp. ix, 406. (Franz Steiner, Stuttgart. Price: DM 116.00/SwF 116.00/AS 905. ISBN 3 515 04249 0; ISBN 0170 3307)

The bilingual cultural which prevailed in the first Semitic Empire under Sargon the Great is evident from the Old Akkadian royal inscriptions, which were edited by I. J. Gelb and B. Kienast in the same series (*FAOS* 7, 1990). The numerous errors in the Gelb/Kienast volume which were noted by reviewers have been corrected in the present glossary to the inscriptions, which also includes indices of divine names, personal names, geographical and temple names. The respective Sumerian and Akkadian glossaries are individually useful as concordances to the inscriptions, but also provide important bilingual information. The words found in bilingual texts are cited in both languages in full contexts. The glossaries also give a list of Sumerian logograms with Akkadian equivalents, which is a convenient tool for reading the texts. The glossaries themselves could have been improved with additional grammatical analysis of the verbal forms, but the glossary is not necessarily intended to replace the lexicon.

M. J. GELLER

King, Philip J.: *Jeremiah. An Archaeological Companion*. 1993.
Pp. xxvi, 204, (Westminster/John Knox, Louisville KY. Price: $27.00. ISBN
0 664 21920 9)

The author is not concerned with addressing at first hand the knotty
historical problems associated with the book of Jeremiah but with illustrating
and illuminating the text by drawing on the artefactual and inscriptional
evidence, particularly from recent years. Many aspects of everyday life in late
7th- and early 6th-century Judah are clarified and illuminated by the judicious
way the author brings together archaeological evidence (much of it unpublished or not easily available) and the biblical text. The subject matter
includes political, religious, social and economic issues. Clearly written and
well illustrated the book is as fascinating as it is illuminating. Chapters on
Jeremiah, the prophet and the book; historical background; and geographical
setting broaden the scope of the book to include the non-specialist reader.
Moreover the author's balanced approach shows how current interdisciplinary archaeology can best contribute to biblical studies.

J. R. Duckworth

Layton, R. (ed.): *Who Needs the Past? Indigenous Values and Archaeology* (One World Archaeology 5). 1994 (1989). Pp. xxiv, 215. (Routledge,
London–New York. Price: £16.99. ISBN 0 415 09558 1)

Shennan, S. J. (ed.): *Archaeological Approaches to Cultural Identity*
(One World Archaeology 10). 1994 (1989). Pp. xxvii, 317. (Routledge,
London–New York. Price £17.99. ISBN 0 415 09557 3)

Both these volumes are part of a series of publications coming out of the
World Archaeological Congress held in Southampton in 1986. Neither of
them investigates Israel specifically; rather their value is more in general
questions of methodology which may be suggestive to historians of Israel as to
how they might apply recent work from other areas of scholarship. Many of
the essays relate archaeology and social anthropology. The volume edited by
L. examines how a variety of cultures have looked at their own past, including
one on Egypt's use of the past in the 3rd and 2nd millennium BC (pp. 131–49).
A number of the essays here touch on oral tradition and its relation to written
records. The volume edited by S. considers the question of objectivity in
archaeological interpretation (generally supporting a qualified or limited
objectivism) and also shows the problematic nature of identifying material
culture with ethnicity.

L. L. Grabbe

Lemche, N. P., and Müller, M. (eds); *Fra dybet* (Forum for bibelsk
Eksegese 5). 1994. Pp. 286. (Museum Tusculanums Forlag, København.
Price DKR 195. ISBN 87 7289 295 1)

The fifth volume of 'Forum for biblesk Eksegese', an annual for the
Department of Biblical Exegesis at University of Copenhagen, is a Festschrift
presented to one of the Old Testament members, John Strange on his sixtieth
birthday. The title 'Out of the Depths' is a play on both the archaeological and
theological engagement of J.S. He is a scholar with many interests and among
the nineteen contibutions, essays are published on subjects normally not
found in an exegetical Festschift, e.g. 'Physicists and the Bomb' by the former
vice chancellor of the University of Copenhagen, O. Natan, for whom J.S.
was deputy for a time. Of most interest are the articles about J.S.'s special
field, biblical archaeology: F. G. Andersen (Hellenistic glass ceramics from
Tell el-Fukhar), S. Holm-Nielsen (a summer's day at Umm Queis),
P. McGovern (the Sea Peoples at Beth Shan), and I. Thuesen (the walls of

Jericho); on Old Testament exegeses: B. Ejrnæs (the Septuagint in Danish Bible tradition), J. Høgenhagen (prophet and prophetic writing), N. P. Lemche ('what have we done, and where are we going?), A. Munk (does Ecclesiastes reach a compromise on futility?), E. Nielsen (the book of Joshua, especially ch. 5) and T. L. Thompson (exegetical and theological implications of understanding Exodus as a collected tradition).

K. JEPPESEN

LEVINE, LEE I. (ed.): *The Galilee in Late Antiquity*, 1992. Pp. xxiii, 410. (Jewish Theological Seminary, distributed by Harvard University Press, Cambridge MA and London. Price: $35.00/£27.95; paper £14.95. ISBN 0 674 34113 9; paper 0 674 34114 7)

These papers from a 1991 conference will interest historical, literary, linguistic, cultural, and religious students of Hellenistic, Roman and Byzantine periods alike. H. C. Kee argues that in the 1st century CE the word *synagogē* refers to gatherings in homes rather than to purpose-built structures, and underlines the bilingual Greek and Aramaic culture of Galilee. D. Edwards and Sean Freyne similarly explore the cultural interaction of Hellenistic and Semitic, urban and rural in Galilee. (Problems of interpreting Josephus' *Vita* inevitably reappear.) A. J. Saldarini sees Matthew as originating from a group regarding itself but not accepted as Jewish. A. I. Baumgarten locates the Ps.-Clementine authors, who know and admire rabbinic Judaism, in 2nd-century Galilee. U. Rappaport portrays 1st-century Galilee as more peaceful and less anti-Roman than generally assumed; Z. Safrai complements this by postulating the Roman army's positive effect on the local economy. Third-century Jewish sources, however, viewed the Roman military presence more negatively (A. Oppenheimer). M. Goodman examines the 3rd-century Roman view of the Jews as a religious people and the *nasi* as their religious leader. The possibility of a distinct Galilaean *halakha* is denied by L. H. Schiffman. The rabbis (S. J. D. Cohen), Rabbi Hanina (S. S. Miller), the sages and the synagogue (L. I. Levine), Mishnaic Hebrew's Galilaean background (G. A. Rendsburg), the value of Galilaean Targumic material for understanding Jewish society (A. Shinan), and the practice of Targum (which did not drive out knowledge of Hebrew) in Galilee (S. D. Fraade), though here labelled 'late antiquity', are not without importance to students of the Hebrew scriptures. The final, archaeological section incorporates synagogues (G. Foerster), Sepphoris (E. M. Meyers, J. F. Strange), and social aspects of burial in Beth She'arim (Z. Weiss). A most valuable up-date.

J. R. BARTLETT

Masada IV. The Yigael Yadin Excavations 1963–1965. Final Reports (Masada Reports). 1994. Pp. 368 (Israel Exploration Society, Jerusalem. Price: $90.00. ISBN 965 221 026 9)

Originally planned as the fifth volume of the excavations, this final report publishes a selection of the considerable material remains found at Masada. Studies on lamps, textiles, basketry, cordage, wood remains, *ballista* balls, and human skeletal remains, together with accompanying photographs, give the reader a vivid impression of life during the short habitation of the site. All of the material remains, the skeletal finds excepted, do not contradict the Masada story as known through Josephus's writings. The discovery of a mere twenty-five skeletons of men, women and children, however, act as a corrective against the inflated figure of 960 which Josephus gives for the inhabitants who committed suicide together.

T. H. LIM

Noy, David: *Jewish Inscriptions of Western Europe. Volume 1: Italy (excluding the City of Rome), Spain and Gaul.* 1993. Pp. xxi, 385 + 32 plates. (Cambridge University Press. Price: £60.00/$95.00. ISBN 0 521 44201 X)

The first volume of the Cambridge Jewish Inscriptions Project was reviewed in *B. L.* 1993, p. 32. The new volume is the first of two on the inscriptions of Western Europe, the second of which will be devoted to Rome. All Jewish inscriptions before 700 CE are collected (192 in all). Any in Frey's *Corpus Inscriptionum Judaicarum* which do not meet the criteria used by the Project are also included in two appendixes (though not in the indexes). The detailed indexes are both welcome and problematic. Because the inscriptions are in Greek, Latin, or Hebrew (or sometimes a mixture), an attempt is made to integrate words from all languages rather than indexing them separately, though the principle used is not always clear. Also, since there are eight categories (names, personal details, religion, formulae, and the like) with a number of subdivisions in some cases, the user may have to wade through the entire set to check for certain types of information. It remains to be seen whether this is the best arrangement for the indexes, but all will be grateful for this new edition of the inscriptions. However, the bibliographical information should include publishers as well as place of publication. What good is it to know that something was published in London or New York?

L. L. Grabbe

Olmo Lete, Gregorio del: *Tell Qara Qūzāq - I. Campañas I–III (1989–1991)* (Aula Orientalis Supplementa 4). 1994. Pp. 321 + 21 plates, 7 plans, numerous ill. (Editorial Ausa, Sabadell, Barcelona. N.P. ISBN 84 605 0359 3)

Two of the reasons why Tell Qara Qūzāq was selected for excavation were its size and its advantageous location. We now know, for example, that early on it functioned as a storage and redistribution centre for cereals. It was, in fact, important right into Roman times. With commendable rapidity the results of three archaeological campaigns conducted on this site by the 'Mision Arqueologica de la Universidad de Barcelona in Siria' are presented in detail, accompanied by plans, maps, photographs, tables and drawings. The volume is in three parts and a survey of the contents is provided here. Part I, Archaeology, comprises brief accounts of the campaigns and of the topography of the site and over one hundred pages on the pottery. Part II, Analysis of Material, deals with radiocarbon dating, palaeobotany the stone industry, metallurgy, potter's marks and ornamentation. In Part III, Setting, are discussed geoarchaeology, grain silos, the ancient Near Eastern context of the site, the influence of the Romans, coins, a seal, and the area and its inhabitants as they are today. We look forward to future reports of this quality from the Spanish team on their subsequent archaeological campaigns in Syria.

W. G. E. Watson

Postgate, J. N.: *Early Mesopotamia. Society and Economy at the Dawn of History.* 1992. Pp. xxiii, 367. (Routledge, London–New York. Price: paper £18.99. ISBN 0 415 11032 7)

Although the book was designed as a textbook for students of Near Eastern history and archaeology as well as for the general reader, it must be used with caution. The book contains much valuable material, but suffers from several serious flaws. First, there is nothing to indicate whether the many ancient texts translated were originally in Sumerian or Akkadian, which is potentially misleading to the unsuspecting reader. This lack of identification of Sumerian and Akkadian sources reflects a problem in the author's methodology, which assumes a seamless divide between Sumerian and Akkadian civilizations, as if 'Mesopotamia' was a single cultural and historical entity. Such an approach needs to be explained by the author, since much can be distinguished and contrasted between Sumerian and Akkadian texts. Moreover, the 'dawn' of civilization is drawn from sources rooted in the second millennium BC, without thought as to the major changes which occurred between the Ur III and Old Babylonian periods. Finally, although much good use is made of texts to reconstruct the history, relatively little of the archaeology of Mesopotamia is expounded in the book, except for the excellent illustrations provided in the plates.

M. J. GELLER

RAST, WALTER E.: *Through the Ages in Palestinian Archaeology. An Introductory Handbook*. 1992. Pp. xiv, 221. (Trinity Press International, Valley Forge PA. Price: $15.95. ISBN 1 56338 055 2)

This is an informative, undemanding guide to its subject by an author who knows how to select his material and present it clearly and attractively. Three chapters are devoted to method and eleven to the 'ages' of prehistory and history. Both sections of this standard layout, however, have fresh and distinctive features. Method is handled in an up-to-date way which emphasises environmental and social archaeology alongside more traditional approaches. More welcome still, from a historical point of view, is the fact that the coverage extends from the Palaeolithic age through to the Hellenistic, Roman, Byzantine and Islamic periods. Most general books on the subject ignore these later periods, despite the impressive remains which survive. Inevitably the treatment of the Old Testament period is then rather brief, but it is well done, and the wider perspectives offered by the rest of the book are ample compensation. It is a pity that the two maps were not more professionally produced: the type and layout are unclear in several respects. Nevertheless, R. has produced an excellent introduction to the archaeology of Palestine for the newcomer, one which can be warmly recommended.

G. I. DAVIES

REED, STEPHEN A. (compiler): *The Dead Sea Scrolls Catalogue. Documents, Photographs and Museum Inventory Numbers* (Society of Biblical Literature Resources for Biblical Study 32). Revised and edited by Marilyn J. Lundberg with the collaboration of Michael B. Phelps. 1994. Pp. xlvi, 558. (Scholars Press, Atlanta. Price: $89.95; paper $64.95. ISBN 0 7885 0017 1; paper 0 7885 0018 X)

This catalogue contains in one volume a complete revision of all fourteen catalogue fascicles which were published in 1991 and 1992. As it now stands it has three correlated sections. The first is a listing of all the manuscripts and other materials from Qumran, Mird, Murabba'at, ed-Daliyeh, Naḥal Ḥever and elsewhere; for each item the list contains document number, current siglum, previous sigla (including where applicable thos used in the *Preliminary Concordance*), location, photographs, current editor, and publication details. The second section is a list of all the photographs referred to in the first part and the third is a list of all the materials in the Rockefeller Museum by inventory numbers; very usefully there is also an appendix containing an alphabetical listing of the sigla used in the *Preliminary Concordance* for the Cave 4 manuscripts. As the compilers of this work acknowledge, the catalogue in its new form still represents work in progress; not only will it need to be continually updated as editors publish the principal editions of the texts for which they have responsibility and as museum holdings are checked and rechecked, but also in addition to corrections to the bibliographical information there will be new materials (such as the 1800 photographs taken by John Allegro) to be incorporated. Nevertheless this indispensable volume represents very many hours of painstaking work and provides the most comprehensive listing of Dead Sea Scrolls materials yet.   G. J. BROOKE

RICE, MICHAEL: *The Archaeology of the Arabian Gulf c. 5000–323 BC* (The Experience of Archaeology). 1994. Pp. xvii, 369. (Routledge, London–New York. Price: £50.00. ISBN 0 415 032687)

The author of this survey has had a long association with the Gulf area, having been involved in the setting up of museums in several of the states on the Arabian side of the Gulf, and is well versed in the relevant archaeological survey and excavation reports. He gives a useful and fairly full summary of early work and discussion on Bahrain (ch. 2). The main substance of the volume is in chs 7–8 where the results of archaeological work on the Arabian side of the Gulf, from the Danish expeditions of 1953 onwards, are summarized with a good selection of illustrations. There is also a section on the distinctive Gulf seals (pp. 280–99), but much of the remainder of the volume is given less usefully to Mesopotamian background derived from secondary sources. Considerable attention is given to Dilmun. The few references to the Old Testament appear mainly in this latter connection, bearing on the Eden and Flood accounts in Genesis. Otherwise reference is made to Ezek. 29:13 (misquoted as 27:3–4) improbably as relevant to the ancient suggestion that the Phoenicians came from the Gulf. There is a useful bibliography but citations in the end notes give no page references.   T. C. MITCHELL

RIMON, OFRA (ed.): *Michmanim*. Vol. 7. January 1994. Pp. 42* (Eng.), 54 (Heb.). (The Reuben and Edith Hecht Museum, University of Haifa. N.P.)

This has apparently not been noticed in the *B. L.* before. This issue has English language articles on bronze figurines depicting Reshef and Baal (I. Cornelius), basalt tripod and three-legged bowls (Z. Gal), and a statue of Hermes from Gadara (R. Gersht). The Hebrew articles cover two limestone stelae depicting Canaanites deities (R. Merhav), gems in the Hecht Museum (M. Hershkovitz), four segments of inscribed parchment from the Judaean Desert (H. Misgav), and 'Yehuda' coins from the early Hellenistic period (A. Kindler). There are Hebrew abstracts of the English-language articles, and English abstracts of those in Hebrew.   L. L. GRABBE

RIMON, OFRA (ed.): *'Purity Broke Out in Israel' (Tractate Shabbat, 13b). Stone Vessels in the Late Second Temple Period.* Catalogue 9. Spring 1994. Pp. 36* (Eng.), 36 (Heb.). (The Reuben and Edith Hecht Museum, University of Haifa. N.P.)

This is the printed catalogue to accompany a museum exhibition. It has articles on the stone vessel industry during the Second Temple period (Y. Magen) and Jewish ossuaries (L. Rahmani). The contents appear in both Hebrew and English (though the Hebrew articles have some additional Hebrew bibliography). The many photographs occur throughout the Hebrew and English sections, without duplication but with dual-language captions.

L. L. GRABBE

SCHÄFER, PETER and SHAKED, SHAUL (eds): *Magische Texte aus der Kairoer Geniza*. Band I (Texte und Studien zum Antiken Judentum 42). 1994. Pp. ix, 329. (Mohr, Tübingen. Price: DM 168.00. ISBN 3 16 146272 6; ISSN 0721 8753)

This is the first of a projected three-volume edition of the Hebrew and Aramaic magical texts from the Cairo Genizah. 'Magic' is used in a broad sense to include amulets, theoretical treatises, incantations, curses, medical and pharmaceutical texts. The texts for this particular volume seem to be selected to illustrate the range of literary genres found among the papyri. Each text has a description of the manuscript, scribal characteristics, content (including genre and themes), and parallels in other texts (where these exist). It is then transcribed in Hebrew characters and provided with a German translation and commentary. Scholarship will be grateful to the editorial team for its dedicated work on difficult and often-fragmentary texts.

L. L. GRABBE

SEGAL, ARTHUR: *Theatres in Roman Palestine and Provincia Arabia* (Mnemosyne Supplement 140). 1995. Pp. ix, 117 + 155 figures. (Brill, Leiden–New York–Köln. Price: fl. 125.00/$71.50. ISBN 90 04 10145 4; ISSN 0169 8958)

Approximately thirty theatres have been excavated from the Hellenistic period. Eight of these are pre-70, two built by Herod the Great (Caesarea and Jericho) and five Nabataean ones. The theatres of the Hellenized cities only begin in the late 1st century CE. The popularity of theatre entertainment is indicated by the criticisms and prohibitions in rabbinic and early Christian literature. S.'s architectural analysis is an important contribution to the archaeology of Roman Palestine. He discusses each known site individually, with photographs and drawings, and gives a useful summary table of the results (pp. 98–101). Some of the interpretations are less than certain. Given the later popularity of theatre performances, why must the Nabataean theatres have had primarily a ritual function (pp. 14–15)? And is it really useful to speculate that Herod's theatre in Jerusalem — which has not yet even been found — had little interest for the population (pp. 4–5)?

L. L. GRABBE

STERN, EPHRAIM: *Dor — Ruler of the Seas. Twelve Years of Excavations at the Israelite–Phoenician Harbor Town on the Carmel Coast*. English version by Joseph Shadur. 1994. Pp. 348. (Israel Exploration Society, Jerusalem. Price: $36.00. ISBN 965 221 127 7)

This is popular account of excavations carried out by S. at the important coastal site of Dor, modern Tanturah, from 1980 to 1991 (and continuing), and at the smaller neighbouring site of Tel Mevorakh from 1973 to 1976. The book gives a sensible and readable account of the results, with good maps, plans and sections and over 200 photographs, some in colour, though the illustrations are not linked in any way to the text. The earliest level reached so far (12th–11th century BC) is associated by the author with the Sikils (more familiar as Tjek[k]er), as indicated in Egyptian texts; he then finds a probable brief phase of Phoenician domination followed by levels of the United and Divided Monarchies, Assyrian and Babylonian rule, and substantial remains of the Persian, Hellenistic, and Roman periods. Individual interpretations include a coastal settlement pattern in the 12th–11th centuries of Sherden (Akko Valley), 'Sikil' (northern Sharon), Philistia (southern Palestine); attribution of a substantial city wall and gate to building under Ahab; and a

population and culture basically Phoenican from about the 11th century BC until Hellenistic times. There are no individual citations of sources but a good bibliography.
                                                                    T. C. MITCHELL

STONE, MICHAEL E. (ed.): *Rock Inscriptions and Graffiti Project. Volume 3: Inscriptions 6001–8500* (Society of Biblical Literature Resources for Biblical Study 31). 1994. Pp. 248. (Scholars Press, Atlanta. Price: $29.95; member price $19.95; paper $19.95 ($14.95). ISBN 1 55540 945 8; paper 1 55540 946 6)

The format of this volume is the same as that of the first two volumes in the set (*B.L.* 1994, p. 32). The inscriptions catalogued here, many of which have not yet been published, include about 1500 from the Sinai peninsula and about 1000 from Jerusalem (mainly the Church of the Holy Sepulchre and the Monastery of the Cross). A variety of languages is represented, with Nabataean inscriptions again the largest single group. Although nearly all the inscriptions are from late antiquity or subsequent periods, twenty-eight are in Egyptian hieroglyphs and so presumably earlier. Several indexes are included in this volume, covering all three volumes published so far.
                                                                    G. I. DAVIES

VLEEMING, SVEN P.: *Ostraka Varia. Tax Receipts and Legal Documents on Demotic, Greek, and Greek-Demotic Ostraka, Chiefly of the Early Ptolemaic Period, from Various Collections (P. L. Bat. 26)* (Papyrologica Lugduno-Batava 26). 1994. Pp. xiii, 172 + 62 plates. (Brill, Leiden–New York–Köln. Price: fl. 185.00/$105.75. ISBN 90 04 10132 2; ISSN 0169 9652)

Sixty-two ostraca are published here, many of them previously unpublished. The majority are tax receipts, illustrating and confirming the multiplicity of taxes alleged by some literary texts. Also included are some documents with regard to the sale of property and a decisory temple oath in which two brothers swear in a temple that they have not harmed another person.
                                                                    L. L. GRABBE

URMAN, DAN and FLESHER, PAUL V. M. (eds): *Ancient Synagogues. Historical Analysis and Archaeological Discovery*. Volume 1 (Studia Post-Biblica 47/1). 1995. Pp. xxxvii, 297. (Brill, Leiden–New York–Köln. Price: fl. 135.00/$77.25. ISBN 90 04 10242 6; ISSN 0169 9717)

This is the first of a two-volume collection of twenty-three essays (now all in English) on the mystery-shrouded development of the ancient synagogue between 70 CE and the 7th century CE and combines new articles with republications. Following the Preface and Reader's Guide which set the essays in context and indicate the interpretational stance of the volume — that the term *synagogue* is unproblematic and means primarily a *building* — there are contributions on The Origins of Ancient Synagogues from J. G. Griffiths (1985), L. L. Grabbe (1989), P. V. M. Flesher (1989) and A. Oppenheimer (1987); on The Development of Ancient Synagogues from D. E. Groh (1995), Y. Tsafrir (1981), G. Foerster (1987) and A. T. Kraabel (1979); on Synagogues and Settlements: Report and Analysis from D. Amit (1990), S. Dar & Y. Mintzker (1995), Z. Gal (1984) and D. Urman (1995); and on The Synagogue's Nature and the Jewish Community from Z. Safrai (1981), A. Kasher (1987), I. Gafni (1987), D. Urman (1994), A. Ilan (1987) and R. Reich (1987).
                                                                    H. A. MCKAY

ZWICKEL, WOLFGANG: *Der Tempelkult in Kanaan und Israel. Studien zur Kultgeschichte Palästinas von der Mittelbronzezeit bis zum Untergang Judas* (Forschungen zum Alten Testament 10). 1994. Pp. xvi, 424. (Mohr, Tübingen. Price: DM 228.00. ISBN 3 16 146218 1; ISSN 0940 4155)

Z. has produced an extremely detailed study of the archaeological information pertaining to the cultic organization from the Middle Bronze period to the Iron II. Each section contains a discussion of all relevant sites for a particular archaeological period with useful diagrams of strata or finds along with an excellent bibliography. Each chapter then concludes with a discussion of the cultic organization for the period. The final chapter is a discussion of sacrifice in Old Testament texts which he dates on fairly traditional grounds in which he traces a development in Israelite and Judaean sacrificial practice with the introduction of new elements such as burnt offerings. Interestingly, he concludes that there is no continuity between the late Bronze and Iron I periods in the Palestinian hill country in terms of the cult, arguing that this is related to the settlement of early Israel: Canaanite city temples are replaced by rural clan sancturaries and village cultic places. Many will disagree with his interpretations of the evidence for particular periods, especially the lack of concern with the economic features of the cult, or his use of the biblical traditions. However, Z. has produced a very fine reference work.

K. W. WHITELAM

3. HISTORY, GEOGRAPHY, AND SOCIOLOGY

ABERLE, DAVID F.: *The Peyote Religion among the Navaho*. With field assistance by Harvey C. Moore and an appendix by Denis F. Johnston. 1994 (1982, 1966). Pp. lii, 451. (University of Oklahoma Press, Norman OK–London. Price: $19.95/£17.95. ISBN 0 8061 2382 6)

In anthropological discussions relating to the Old Testament, the peyote religion of the American Southwest is often cited. The 1966 edition has become an anthropological classic and the standard work on the peyote religion. The text was not altered in the 1982 reprint, but a lengthy introduction interacted with reviewers and gave an updated bibliography. The 1994 edition, in a welcome paperback, has a further introduction which mainly focuses on a 1991 US court case.

L. L. GRABBE

BALL, WARWICK: *Syria. A Historical and Architectural Guide*. 1994. Pp. 216 + 96 plates. (Scorpion Publishing Ltd, Buckhurst Hill. Price £14.95. ISBN 0 905906 96 9)

Syria is ill-served by tourist guidebooks, especially in English. While even neighbouring Turkey has more volumes available than can fit within economy class baggage allowances, the traveller to Syria has had nothing for years beyond the *Lonely Planet Guide*, shared with neighbouring Jordan. B. has thus filled an important market niche, and in a manner that will endear him to any wandering *B.L.* reader, for he writes with intimate knowledge and elegant style on precisely those features of the land, its ancient archaeological sites, with which general guides deal only cursorily, in addition to temples, churches, castles, and mosques. The book is well-supplied with useful maps and architectural plans, together with superb photographs. The book opens with the statement, 'Syria is the Middle East's best kept secret'. This leak is authoritative.

N. WYATT

COGGINS, RICHARD: *What Future for the 'History of Israel'?* (The Ethel M. Wood Lecture, 5 May 1994). 1994. Pp. 23. (University of London. N. P. ISBN 07187 12 072)

C. notes that there has been a perceptible shift from the premise that a reconstruction of key historical 'events' is basic to an understanding of Israelite religion, and equally to a modern appreciation of the Old Testament/ Hebrew Bible. He points to the slenderness of links between the biblical story and non-biblical historical data, and refers to three recent books (by Ahlström, Garbini and P. R. Davies) as indicators of recent trends, identifying a concern with how properly to understand biblical 'histories' that (a) seem not to be historical, and (b) in any case, only deal with 'top people'. Characteristically lucid, witty and shrewd, C. comes down, gently, on the side of — dare one say — the 'angels': much Bible history writing of our age has been midrashic, and the Bible text does not by and large support a genuine historical reconstruction of 'ancient Israel'. On the future of the genre he is unwilling to prognosticate, but he looks forward to a more 'readerly engagement with the text itself'.

P. R. DAVIES

ÉLAYI, JOSETTE and SAPIN, JEAN: *Nouveaux regards sur la Transeuphratène* (Mémoires premières). 1991. Pp. 223. (Brepols, Turnhout. Price BEF 731. ISBN 2 503 50065 X)

The history of the ancient Near East has for too long been written within the context of particular histories, or even particular sub-disciplines of history, with the effect that scholars are presenting only partial views of the data, and frequently ignoring each other's work: 'we may well ask what is the place of history within such a fragmentation and compartmentalisation of disciplines: it is at the same time everywhere and nowhere' (p. 28). Bibliocentrism, which sees the entire history of the ancient world through biblical eyes, is merely one egregious example. The present work sets out to combat this tendency, presenting instead an altogether more comprehensive approach. Taking its cue from the Achaemenid History Workshops (*B.L.* 1994, p. 40) its concern is the broad philosophical one, its working example the Persian period, studied very refreshingly from a global and interdisciplinary perspective. 'Transeuphrates' (Akkadian *eber nāri*, Hebrew *'ēber hannahar*) designates Syria and Palestine *west* of the Euphrates, from a Persian viewpoint, lending a different gloss to 2 Sam. 10:16, 1 Kgs 14:15. Computer-technology, archaeology, historical geography, texts and epigraphy, ceramics and trade, numismatics and economics, and palaeosociology, and the internal politics of the Persian empire are each examined in turn for new insights into the overall picture, and methodology mixes fruitfully with examination of particular issues.

N. WYATT

ESKENAZI, TAMARA C. and RICHARDS, KENT H. (eds): *Second Temple Studies. Volume 2: Temple and Community in the Persian Period* (Journal for the Study of the Old Testament Supplement 175). 1994. Pp. 313. (Sheffield Academic Press. Price: £27.50/$42.50. ISBN 1 85075 472 1; ISSN 0264 6498)

The remarks which greeted the first collection of *Second Temple Studies* (*B.L.* 1992, p. 11) apply also to this second collection. The essays are of different types, ranging from 'thoughts for the conference' to densely argued mini-theses, with Richards providing a brief introduction to the whole. R. P. Carroll provides some discerning analysis and speculative answers in response to the question: 'so what do we *know* about the temple?' D. J. A. Clines' stimulating reading of Haggai's temple seems to deconstruct in the same way that Haggai's temple does (coincidence?)! K. R. Baltzer and P. Marinkovic

examine the temple in 2 Isaiah and Zechariah 1–8 respectively. P. R. Davies'
programmatic call for an autonomous sociological approach to the period is
answered by a bevy of studies in the book's second part, especially those by
H. C. Washington, D. Smith-Christopher, and Eskenazi/E. P. Judd which
read nicely as a sub-group on the problems of marriage in the Judaean
community. C. E. Carter's hefty (40 pp.) study of Yehud in the post-exilic
period is a goldmine of socio-archaeological data and analysis. T. Willi
elucidates the literary and theological shaping of Judaean identity in
Chronicles. S. Japhet examines the interrelatedness of historical framework
and narrative content of the 'book of Ezra-Nehemiah', while L. Grabbe's
discussion of Ezra's mission asserts the intractability of the problem. With
essays of such high standard, only two (H. V. van Rooy and G. Garbini) stand
out as disappointments.
                                                                    D. J. REIMER

GEERTZ, ARMIN W.: *The Invention of Prophecy. Continuity and Meaning
in Hopi Indian Religion.* 1994. Pp. xxi, 490. (University of California Press,
Berkeley–Los Angeles–London. Price: £33.50. ISBN 0 520 08181 1)

Hopi prophecy can only be catalogued for the past century or so, though
it may have a longer history. It seems to consist of sententious statements,
often appearing in tracts and newspaper reports, and with no claims of ecstatic
behaviour or divine appearances. Rather, it is based on traditional mythology
and is supported by (claimed or actual) carved stone tablets and petroglyphs.
Much of G.'s book necessarily discusses the inter-Hopi debate between
so-called 'Traditionalists' and other Hopis, which may not be of so much
interest. The main comparison with Israelite prophecy is in the hermeneutical
process, the development of the tradition from a mythical (theological) base
and the use and mutation of the tradition for individual propagandistic
purposes.
                                                                    L. L. GRABBE

HENNESSY, ANNE, CSJ: *The Galilee of Jesus.* 1994. Pp. ix, 77. (Editrice
Pontificia Università Gregoriana, Rome. Price: Lire 15,000. ISBN
88 7652 666 8)

This short, beautifully written study reveals H.'s first-hand knowledge of
the region of Galilee (though can one really see the hills of Moab [p. 15] to the
east?), her familiarity with the scholarly literature, and her sensible spirituality. Her interest in Galilee is 'an effort to understand the subtleties of the
ambience of Jesus' life and mission so as to appreciate his total message more
profoundly and to foster its extension into one's own life and mission' (p. 3);
in short, 'what does Galilee tell us about Jesus?' (p. 36). A description of
lower Galilee, a study of the influence of Galilaean life in the teaching of
Jesus, and an analysis of the different portrayals of Galilee by the four
evangelists lead to a final chapter on the contemplative pilgrim in Galilee. Not
exactly a typical academic monograph, but scholarly, profitable, and attractive.
                                                                    J. R. BARTLETT

HUSS, WERNER: *Der makedonische König und die ägyptischen Priester.
Studien zur Geschichte des ptolemaiischen Ägypten* (Historia-
Einzelschriften 85). 1994. Pp. 238. (Franz Steiner, Stuttgart. Price:
DM 80.00. ISBN 3 515 06502 4)

H. has written an important study with implications for history, society,
and religion in Ptolemaic Egypt. The relationship of the native Egyptian
priesthood to the Greek court was a complex one: the priests were seen as

40   HISTORY, GEOGRAPHY AND SOCIOLOGY

substitutes for 'the priest' who was the king, yet the Greeks were also seen as invaders. The priests were also dependent on the crown for their income and position and yet were part of the conquered masses, not the ruling classes. Thus, at different times and different places the priests would respond to an order of the king sometimes with agreement, sometimes with reservation, and sometimes with rejection or even enmity. This last is evident in such 'resistance literature' as the *Demotic Chronicle* and the *Potter's Oracle*. Not the least valuable aspects of this study are the comprehensive tables and lists (cataloguing original sources with regard to temple building, priestly prosopography, and the like) and the detailed footnotes.   L. L. GRABBE

HUTTON, RODNEY R.: *Charisma and Authority in Israelite Society*. 1994. Pp. x, 229. (Fortress, Minneapolis; SCM, London. Price: $15.00/£11.50. ISBN 0 8006 2832 2)

The author's primary concern is with Weber's famous dichotomy between charismatic and institutional forms of authority which has had great influence in Old Testament studies. H. states his general conclusion clearly: 'the purpose of this book has been to challenge at every step the notion that one can easily divorce institution from charisma' and perhaps today few students of Israelite society would wholly dissent from this. But the particular value of his work lies in the detailed discussion of those areas where Weber's distinction has often been thought to apply. Thus, after a preliminary chapter surveying the broader issues, he deals in turn with the nature of Mosaic authority, the judges, kingship, the prophets, the priesthood and finally the wisdom tradition. Undoubtedly, H. makes out a most convincing case for his main thesis, but his study often ranges far beyond it, particularly in the area of recent sociological approaches to the Old Testament. His opinions are always stimulating and well argued, even if one cannot always agree with them — for example, in his rejection of the influence of ancient Near Eastern concepts of kingship on the ideology of even the earliest Israelite monarchy. The author's English style does not make for easy reading, but this is a significant contribution.   J. R. PORTER

JACOBY, F.: *Die Fragmente der griechischen Historiker, Dritter Teil: Geschichte von Städten und Völkern (Horographie und Ethnographie). C. Faścicle 1: Commentary on Nos. 608a–608*. Edited by Charles W. Fornara. 1994. Pp. ii, 113. (Brill, Leiden–New York–Köln. Price: fl.80.00/$45.75. ISBN 90 04 09975 1)

The monumental work of J. was left incomplete at his death. Now Fornara has taken up the torch with plans to complete the commentary on IIIC, making use of J.'s notes where available. The writers covered in this fascicle are Hellanicus of Lesbos and Aristagoras.   L. L. GRABBE

JAGERSMA, H.: *A History of Israel to Bar Kochba. Part I: The Old Testament Period; Part II: From Alexander the Great to Bar Kochba*. 1994 (1-vol. edn). Pp. xv, 224. (SCM, London. Price: £20.00. ISBN 0 334 02577 X)

Parts I and II were originally published separately (*B.L.* 1983, p. 35; 1986. p. 38). These are now issued together in one volume but in unrevised form.   ED.

JOHNSON, DOUGLAS H.: *Nuer Prophets. A History of Prophecy from the Upper Nile in the Nineteenth and Twentieth Centuries* (Oxford Studies in Social and Cultural Anthropology). 1994. Pp. xx, 407. (Clarendon Press, Oxford. Price: £40.00. ISBN 0 19 827907 8)

Although acknowledging his debt to earlier researchers, such as E. Evans-Pritchard, J. has produced a work which goes well beyond any previous studies of Nuer prophecy, from the 19th century to as recently as 1992. He catalogues the prophets and their activities in their actual social setting (as opposed to some hypothetical *Sitz im Leben*) but also charts the use and reuse made of earlier prophecies by later figures and the frequent claim of how the earlier prophecies were 'fulfilled'. The media by which those earlier prophecies are handed down (stories about the prophets and songs) are also clarified. There is much here of interest to any student of the Old Testament prophetic tradition.

L. L. GRABBE

KALBERG, STEPHEN: *Max Weber's Comparative-Historical Sociology.* 1994. Pp. xi, 221. (University of Chicago. Price: $18.95. ISBN 0 226 42303 4)

When it comes to comparative-historical studies, Weber has been rather neglected in recent years in favour of Marx and Braudel. K. argues that the problems encountered by the main schools of recent sociological thought (world systems theory, interpretive historical approach, and causal analytical approach) could benefit greatly from the use of Weber. Contrary to the assertions of many of his critics, Weber had a comprehensive system of causal analysis which underlies his studies. Admitting that only parts of this are explicit, K. attempts to reconstruct the whole underlying method and show how it can benefit contemporary sociological studies.

L. L. GRABBE

KNOPPERS, GARY N.: *Two Nations Under God. The Deuteronomistic History of Solomon and the Dual Monarchies. Volume 1: The Reign of Solomon and the Rise of Jeroboam.* (Harvard Semitic Monographs 52). 1994. Pp. xv, 302. (Scholars Press, Atlanta. Price: $31.96. ISBN 1 55540 913 X)

KNOPPERS, GARY N.: *Two Nations Under God. The Deuteronomistic History of Solomon and the Dual Monarchies. Volume 2: The Reign of Jeroboam, the Fall of Israel, and the Reign of Josiah.* (Harvard Semitic Monographs 53). 1994. Pp. xvii, 349. (Scholars Press, Atlanta. Price: $31.96. ISBN 1 55540 914 8)

This work stands firmly within the approach to the deuteronomistic history (Dtr H) of the 'Cross school'. Of the two editions of Dtr H the first is pre-exilic and has as its focus the reform of Josiah. This was effectively the definitive stage, at least as far as the Dtr presentation of the monarchy is concerned, for the exilic or post-exilic additions to the pre-exilic work qualify but do not repudiate the very positive presentation of the united monarchy, especially in 1 Kings 1–10. The author develops Cross's approach especially through refining the description of the Dtr attitude to the northern kingdom. The negative presentation in 1 Kings 11, according to which Solomon committed apostasy in setting up high places, allows the rise of Jeroboam and the foundation of the northern kingdom to be presented as legitimate. The sin of Jeroboam lay in his establishment of a counter cultus to the temple in Jerusalem, not in his political moves. Because Josiah abolished the cult established by Jeroboam, he reversed the cultic degeneration of both kingdoms and could be presented as the inheritor of the Davidic-Solomonic kingdom.

Dtr H sees the monarchy as playing a central role in conserving traditional beliefs and endorses a royal role in promoting the Jerusalem temple. In this, Dtr royal ideology goes far beyond the much more restructive view of Deut. 17:14–20, so that Josiah's actions in centralizing the cult represent a triumph of Dtr ideology rather than of deuteronomic law. This is an interesting study, with extended textual and exegetical treatment of selected sections of the deuteronomistic history. One might have wished, however, for more conciseness, so that the distinctiveness of the author's own approach could be clearer.

A. D. H. MAYES

LEWIS, D. M., et al. (ed.): *The Cambridge Ancient History*. Vol. V: *The Fifth Century B.C.* 1992. Pp. xvi, 603. (Cambridge University Press. Price: £70.00/$105.00. ISBN 0 521 23347 X)

LEWIS, D. M., et al. (ed.): *The Cambridge Ancient History*. Vol. VI: *The Fourth Century B.C.* 1994 (2nd ed.). Pp. xix, 1077. (Cambridge University Press. Price: £85.00/$150.00. ISBN 0 521 23348 8)

BOARDMAN, JOHN (ed.): *The Cambridge Ancient History. Plates to Volumes V and VI. The Fifth and Fourth Centuries B.C.* 1994 (new ed.). Pp. xii, 208. (Cambridge University Press. Price: £45.00/$70.00. ISBN 0 521 23349 6)

CROOK, J. A.; LINTOTT, ANDREW; RAWSON, ELIZABETH (ed.): *The Cambridge Ancient History*. Vol. IX: *The Last Age of the Roman Republic, 146–43 B.C.* 1994. Pp. xviii, 929. (Cambridge University Press. Price: £85.00/$145.00. ISBN 0 521 25603 8)

Two of the three main volumes here have contributions relating directly to the history of the Jewish people. There is also much that provides important background information on the Mediterranean world and the historical context of the Jews in the Hellenistic and Roman periods. Volume V relates entirely to mainland Greece wars and the Greek colonies in Sicily after the Persian wars, including chapters on Greek cults and religion. Volume VI devotes a chapter to Persia and a large section to lands under Persian rule, including Mesopotamia (M. W. Stolper), Cyprus and Phoenicia (F. G. Maier), and Egypt (A. B. Lloyd). The chapter on Persian Judah (H. Tadmor) gives an interesting interpretation, though many will think it fails to give sufficient weight to the literary nature of the book of Ezra. In addition there is a regional survey of western and northern parts of the Greek world and chapters on Greek history and the beginning of Macedonian dominance, society and economy, the *polis*, and Greek culture and science. As expected, Volume IX covers the period of Roman history indicated by its title. The Jews were important in this history and figure in the chapter on Pompey in the East (A. N. Sherwin-White) and the excellent study on the Jews under Hasmonean rule (T. Rajak).

L. L. GRABBE

LONG, V. PHILIPS: *The Art of Biblical History* (Foundations of Contemporary Interpretation 5). 1994. Pp. 247. (Zondervan, Grand Rapids MI. Price: $17.95. ISBN 0 310 43180 8)

Writing a book on biblical history for this conservative series was never going to be an easy task. Its natural readership could be expected to meet much recent discussion with disfavour or outright hostility. The title of this work locates it within the tradition of Robert Alter's *Art of Biblical Narrative* and *Art of Biblical Poetry*, part of a deliberate move on L.'s part to describe biblical histories as artistic productions rather than simply factual reports. The book is both informative and readable, and makes use of a wide range of dialogue partners. One senses that L. wants to convince his readers both that modern historical study of the Bible is not necessarily a threat, and that the soundness of his own faith is not in jeopardy. There is a bit of having one's cake and eating it too in this. L. chides T. L. Thompson, for instance, for not recognizing that revelation comes both in event and word, but this 'criticism' fails to convey Thompson's point that such claims for divine activity are not properly addressed by historical discourse. There is much of value in these pages; L. should expect attacks on all sides which is, perhaps, a good sign.

D. J. REIMER

MACCHI, JEAN-DANIEL: *Les Samaritans: histoire d'une légende. Israël et la province de Samarie* (Le Monde de la Bible 30). 1994. Pp. 191. (Labor et Fides, Geneva. Price: SwF 142.00. ISBN 2 8309 0712 4)

The title of this study could be misleading. Only the first chapter is directly concerned with the Samaritans, summarizing the way in which recent scholarship has shown their distinctive characteristics to have emerged in the last centuries BCE. Then the main body of the book looks at the traditions embodied in 2 Kings 17; explores what is known of Assyrian practice in regard to conquered territories, with some interesting and by implication rather horrifying analyses of the practice of large-scale deportation; and sets this in the context of the development of Israel's religious beliefs toward something which can legitimately be described as monotheism. The role of ideology in the setting out of past history by both Jews and Samaritans is thus amply demonstrated.

R. J. COGGINS

MATHIAS, DIETMAR: *Die Geschichtstheologie der Geschichtssummarien in den Psalmen* (Beiträge zur Erforschung des Alten Testaments und des Antiken Judentums 35). 1993. Pp. 297. (Lang, Frankfurt–Bern–New York. Price: SwF 30.00. ISBN 3 631 44223 8; ISSN 0722 0790)

The *Geschichtssummarien* referred to in the title of this work are those in Psalms 78; 105–06; and 135–36; but there is here no detailed discussion of 135–36, which the author has dealt with in another publication. The point of departure is von Rad's theory of a 'little historical Credo'. It is as a contribution to that debate that the *Geschichtssummarien* (which von Rad called 'free variations of the Credo in cultic lyric') are examined with regard to form, links with tradition, and the theology of history. The somewhat elusive literary term 'Topos' is held to express their character. It is argued on lingusitic grounds that these Psalms are exilic or post-exilic, and on traditio-historical grounds that they are dependent on the completed Pentateuch and therefore are a creation of the post-exilic community. Accordingly it is maintained that there are no grounds for the view that they have developed from the 'little historical Credo'. They link the *Geschichte* of Israel with Yahweh's action and presuppose a special relationship between Yahweh and Israel. They have a particular relevance to the post-exilic community in its infidelities and afflictions.

G. W. ANDERSON

MELLERSH, H. E. L.: *Chronology of the Ancient World 10,000 B.C. to A.D. 799* (Chronology of World History). 1994 (1976). Pp. ix, 500. (Helicon, Oxford. Price: £40.00. ISBN 0 09 178259 7)

STOREY, R. L.: *Chronology of the Medieval World 800 to 1491* (Chronology of World History). 1994 (1973). Pp. xii, 705. (Helicon, Oxford. Price: £40.00. ISBN 0 09 178264 3)

WILLIAMS, NEVILLE: *Chronology of the Expanding World 1492 to 1762* (Chronology of World History). 1994 (1969). Pp. x, 700. (Helicon, Oxford. Price: £40.00. ISBN 0 09 178269 4)

WILLIAMS, NEVILLE and WALLER, PHILIP: *Chronology of the Modern World 1763–1992* (Chronology of World History). 1994 (2nd edn). Pp. xvi, 1136. (Helicon, Oxford. Price: £40.00. ISBN 0 09 178274 0)

These four volumes give a valuable reference tool for historians and others. Readers will be most interested in the volume on the ancient world. Each two-page spread covers a specific period of time (a decade once the year 600 BC is reached). The main events are listed in chronological order on the left-hand pages, while the accompanying right-hand page gives dates under five headings: A Politics, Law and Economics, B Science and Discovery, C Religion and Philosophy, D The Arts, E Literature, and F Births and Deaths. Ancient historians know that many dates depend on a good deal of interpretation and are often far from certain. However, at least the more uncertain dates (in the judgement of the editors) are given in lighter type, though readers may not always find it easy to distinguish the two sorts of type. It was not possible to give the sources for each date, but a bibliography of the main works consulted would have been desirable. Readers will be pleased to know that volumes can be purchased separately, though the entire set is expected soon to be available on CD-ROM for £150.   L. L. GRABBE

MILLARD, A. R.; HOFFMEIER, JAMES K.; and BAKER, DAVID W. (eds): *Faith, Tradition, and History. Old Testament Historiography in Its Near Eastern Context.* 1994. Pp. xiv, 354. (Eisenbrauns, Winona Lake IN. Price: $34.50. ISBN 0 931464 82 X)

These essays are all written from a conservative theological perspective reassessing recent work on the history of Israel which questions the nature of the biblical traditions. They provide a positive treatment of the biblical traditions and their use for historical construction. The volume opens with a consideration of the current state of Old Testament historiography (Yamauchi) which sets the tone for the following essays. Millard reviews various genres and their relevance for the historian. However, he does not deal with the implications of recent literary studies despite the title of the essay. The rest of the volume contains studies on scribes as transmitters of tradition (Baker), the Sumerian historiographic tradition and its implications for Genesis 1–11 (Averbeck), genealogical history as charter (Chavalas), the Weidner Chronicle and the idea of history in Israel and Mesopotamia (Arnold), history and legend in early Hittite historiography (McMahon), the historical reliability of the Hittite Annals (Wolf), the structure of Joshua 1–11 and the Annals of Thutmose III (Hoffmeier), Joshua 10:12–15 and the Mesopotamian celestial omen texts (Walton), asking historical questions of Joshua 13–19 (Hess), Judges 1 in the Near Eastern literary context (Younger), Deborah among the Judges (Block), reflections on Samuel amd the institution of the monarchy (Gordon), how did Saul become king? (Long), in search of David (Gordon), the covenant foundation of history and historiography (Niehaus), and the oscillating fortunes of history within Old Testament theology (Martens). Underlying many of the studies is the belief that the deity is revealed in history; therefore, it is of vital importance to defend the biblical traditions at all costs, although Martens provides a balanced consideration of the benefits and drawbacks of such an approach. The essays are well researched and documented, providing an interesting counterview to the minimalists and revisionists they take as their debating points.

K. W. WHITELAM

MOMIGLIANO, ARNALDO: *The Classical Foundations of Modern Historiography* (Sather Classical Lectures 54). With a Foreword by Riccardo Di Donato 1990. Pp. xiv, 162. (University of California Press, Berkeley–Los Angeles–Oxford. Price: $12.00. ISBN 0 520 07870 5)

M.'s contributions on ancient history are always instructive. Although the focus is on classical history and historians (Herodotean versus Thucydidean tradition, Tacitus, Fabius Pictor), the first article will be of particular interest to Old Testament historians: Persian, Greek, and Jewish historiography. There is also an essay on the origins of ecclesiastical historiography.

L. L. GRABBE

MOTYER, ALEC: *A Scenic Route Through the Old Testament.* 1994. Pp. 151. (Inter-Varsity Press, Leicester–Downers Grove IL. Price: £3.99. ISBN 0 85111 152 1)

This is for readers who have minimal knowledge of the Old Testament, and its aim is to inform and to enthuse. It takes six basic themes and gives an introduction to each, followed by four weeks' related readings. It does not set out to be a work of scholarship, and consequently (apart from the concise and helpful section on history, which is approached with some caution) it comes over as rather bland and uncritical. It is the transcript of a series of lectures given to a church group, and the conversational style and abundance of exclamation marks would have profited from some rigorous editing.

E. B. MELLOR

REYES, A. T.: *Archaic Cyprus. A Study of the Textual and Archaeological Evidence* (Oxford Monographs on Classical Archaeology). 1994. Pp. xxiii, 200 + 57 plates. (Clarendon Press, Oxford. Price: £50.00. ISBN 0 19 813227 1)

Based in part on an Oxford D.Phil., this excellent monograph deals with Cyprus in the period from the mid-8th to late 6th-centuries BC, addressing specifically questions of chronology, relations with foreign powers and internal contacts between the different parts of the island (at least ten separate kingdoms in the mid-7th century). R. revises the framework established by E. Gjerstad which emphasized successive disruptive incursions by the Assyrians, Egyptians and Persians. He finds instead the evidence of cooperation with outside powers and cultural continuity. In accordance with this he casts doubt on the continued separate existence of 'Eteocypriots' who were supposed to be resistant to the outsiders. The relationship with the Assyrians is seen as informal; the Egyptians did not dominate the island and Egyptian cultural influence came via Phoenicia; although Cyprus became part of the fifth Persian satrapy (with Syria and Palestine), its kings retained some autonomy. There are extremely useful bibliographies provided (including guides to archaeological and epigraphic material) as well as maps and chronological tables. There is also a glossary of technical terms (do students of ancient Cyprus have to be told what an architectural capital is and that a column is a vertical support?).

J. F. HEALEY

RÜGER, HANS PETER (ed. and trans.): *Syrien und Palästina nach dem Reisebericht des Benjamin von Tudela* (Abhandlungen des Deutschen Palästinavereins 12). 1990. Pp. xi, 80. (Harrassowitz, Wiesbaden. Price: DM 52.00. ISBN 3 447 02881 5; ISSN 0173 1904)

Benjamin of Tudela visited Palestine and Syria between 1166 and 1168 as part of a larger journey that included Europe and Asia Minor. His description of the area, its main cities, its principal buildings and its Jewish inhabitants (including the numbers of Jews in each place and their occupations) during the period of Crusader rule is an important source for social history and topography. The late Hans Peter Rüger completed his translation of the relevant part of the *Sefer ha-Massa'ot* in 1987, and his version is accompanied by an introduction, commentary and bibliography that are models for this type of work, drawing extensively upon Jewish, Christian, and Arabic sources. The book has a value far beyond its main aim of providing a translation of Benjamin's account.   J. W. ROGERSON

SOGGIN, J. ALBERTO: *An Introduction to the History of Israel and Judah*. Translated by John Bowden. 1993 (2nd edn). Pp. xxii, 474. (Trinity Press International, Valley Forge PA. Price: $30.00. ISBN 1 56338 073 0)

This is the American edition of the volume reviewed in *B.L.* 1994, p. 41.

ED.

STERLING, GREGORY E.: *Historiography and Self-Definition. Josephos, Luke-Acts and Apologetic Historiography* (Supplements to Novum Testamentum 64). 1992. Pp. xvi, 500. (Brill, Leiden–New York–Köln. Price: fl. 220.00/$ 125.75. ISBN 90 04 09501 2)

S.'s conception of 'apologetic historiography' as a distinct literary genre with its own continuous history is the dominant theme in this book. In support of the case for the existence of the genre, he offers fully documented and up-to-date accounts of relevant authors, and then goes on to draw parallels with Luke-Acts intended to validate the author's membership in the set. The result, whatever the force of S.'s argument, is a large and unusually useful volume. We have here, which scarcely exists in English, a full-length study of Greek ethnography, from Hecataeus of Miletus, through Herodotus, and on to the Hellenistic authors. This will be welcome to all interested in ancient historiography, whether classical or biblical, as will S.'s well-informed description of Josephus' *Antiquities* (including the biblical books). Apologetic historiography is, for S., the kind concerned with the defence of a nation. Luke-Acts defends the Church in equivalent terms; so the line of interpretation he follows is the one which stresses Greek historiographical elements, with considerable emphasis on prefaces, speeches and other formal Greek features. Once again, however, S. is nothing if not complete, and readers will be interested in his analysis of the way the Septuagint has influenced Luke-Acts. An excellent bibliography lacks little.   T. RAJAK

STIEGLER, STEFAN: *Die nachexilische JHWH-Gemeinde in Jerusalem. Ein Beitrag zu einer alttestamentlichen Ekklesiologie* (Beiträge zur Erforschung des Alten Testaments und des Antiken Judentums 34). 1994. Pp. 176. (Lang, Frankfurt–Bern–New York. Price: SwF 24.00. ISBN 3 631 45899 1; ISSN 0722 0790)

This 1987 dissertation was concerned to provide biblical material relevant to the conversations then taking place between 'established' and 'free' churches in the German Democratic Republic. Since then there have been many changes both in the political world and in biblical scholarship, so the work has a somewhat dated air. The post-exilic sources are scrutinized in detail, with most attention given to Ezra and Nehemiah and what they offer, in the lists and elsewhere, concerning the nature of the community. S. is more confident in his reconstruction of the history of the Persian period than many other scholars would be. The second main chapter discusses the various terms used to describe the community, and the last attempts a reconstruction of its predominant interests and concerns. It was open to converts (the obvious implications of the opposition to mixed marriages by Ezra and Nehemiah are played down); Sabbath-observance was of major importance, circumcision less so than is sometimes thought. The whole community could be described as a 'theocratic democracy'. Overall it is an interesting survey, the main limitation being the lack of reference to the considerable body of recent literature in the area.

R. J. Coggins

TROMPF, G. W. (ed.): *Cargo Cults and Millenarian Movements. Transoceanic Comparisons of New Religious Movements* (Religion and Society 29). 1990. Pp. xviii, 456. (Mouton de Gruyter, Berlin–New York. Price: DM 168.00. ISBN 3 11 012186 2)

Cargo cults, millenarian movements, and the like have sometimes been used for comparative purposes in trying to understand prophecy, apocalypticism, and related phenomena in ancient Israel. The ten essays by various specialists are organized geographically. T. gives an introduction and also a long essay on cargo and the millennium in the Pacific region, from California to Melanesia. The section on white America has essays on Mormonism and the Adventist movements. The section on Melanesia and easten Indonesia looks at various movements and religio-cultural change in the region. The section on Black America and Africa examines the Ras Tafarian movement in Jamaica, the Black Muslims in America, and the independent churches in Namibia 1920–50. In a work of this nature, there is no excuse for endnotes instead of proper footnotes.

L. L. Grabbe

WELLHAUSEN, JULIUS: *Prolegomena to the History of the Israel.* With a reprint of the article *Israel* from the *Encyclopaedia Britannica*. Preface by W. Robertson Smith. Foreword to the Scholars Press edition by Douglas A. Knight (Scholars Press Reprints and Translations Series). 1994 (1885). Pp. xvi, xvi, 552. (Scholars Press, Atlanta. Price: $44.95: member price $29.95. ISBN 1 55540 938 5)

This is a reprint of the original English edition of 1885. It retains the preface to that edition by W. Robertson Smith, who did much to popularize German critical studies to the English-speaking world, not least Wellhausen's historical-critical work on the Pentateuch. What is new to this edition is the foreword by Douglas A. Knight which is an appraisal of the man, his scholarly work in general, and the *Prolegomena* in particular. Reissued on the sesquicentennial of Wellhausen's birth the work is still relevant to ongoing research.

J. R. Duckworth

WILKEN, ROBERT L.: *The Land Called Holy. Palestine in Christian History and Thought.* 1992. Pp. xvi, 355. (Yale University Press, New Haven CT–London. Price: $40.00/£30.00; paper $16.00/£10.50. ISBN 0 300 05491 2; paper 0 300 06083 1)

The stated aim of this book is to give an account of 'how the land of the Bible, the land of Israel, the land of Canaan, if you will, became a Holy Land to Christians' (p. xiv). It gives a general account of the history of the land and of attitudes to it from Old Testament times to the Moslem conquest, with particular reference to Christian efforts to oppose Jewish interpretations of biblical promises about a return to the land, and the conviction of Christian pilgrims and of monks living in Palestine that the land was a special holy spot for Christians. The book seems to be aimed at a popular rather than a learned readership, and it never seems to answer the question what the phrase 'holy land' means. Readers will find many irritating, if not alarming, mistakes to add to the fact that the author displays little awareness of the present state of Old Testament studies. Thus we get Tiglath-pileser II as the great Assyrian empire builder of the 8th century, while Antiochus Epiphanes accedes in 175 CE (clearly a typographical error, but an unfortunate one). The Genizah in Cairo is said to have been discovered early in the present century, while the Beth Alpha synagogue is located 'in Scythopolis'. Most astonishing is the fact that, in a work that lists articles in Hebrew in the bibliography, the author seems to think that the Hebrew word for land, when anarthrous, is *aretz*!

J. W. ROGERSON

4.   TEXT AND VERSIONS

BROTZMAN, ELLIS R.: *Old Testament Criticism. A Practical Introduction.* Foreword by Bruce K. Waltke. 1994. Pp. 208. (Baker, Grand Rapids MI. Price: $10.99. ISBN 0 8010 1065 9)

Although there have been a number of books on this subject in the last few years, including Tov's encyclopaedic work of 1992 (*B.L.* 1993, p. 53), few have been written with the student so much in mind. B. does not aim at comprehensiveness, for that would clog the mind of the beginner; rather, he gives enough information which not only whets the student's appetite but supplies sufficient practical information for the work of Old Testament textual criticism.

Following a well-judged chapter on writing in the ancient Near East, B. deals with the history of the transmission of the biblical books until the present day, including a introductory chapter (4) on the Dead Sea Scrolls. The author then (chs 5–8) describes the practical steps involved in determining the most original readings. Here he discusses the errors that have crept into the text over the years, the principles for establishing the best text and, usually, the practical outworking of theory by applying it to the text of the book of Ruth (ch. 8). This latter exercise, along with the welcome Appendix 'An English Key to *BHS*', ensure that this will be a very useful tool in introducing the student to the Hebrew Bible.

R. B. SALTERS

CHOURAQUI, ANDRÉ: *Reflexionen über Problematik und Methode der Übersetzung von Bibel* (Lucas-Preis 1993). Herausgegeben von Luise Abramowski. 1994. Pp. 66. (Mohr, Tübingen. Price: DM 39.00. ISBN 3 16146202 5)

This short work contains C.'s lecture on the occasion of his award of the Lucas prize for 1993 by the Protestant Theological Faculty of the University of Tübingen. As a 'son of Israel' born in French-speaking Algeria, the author is very conscious of problems and developments in Jewish-Christian relations, and also of the relationships between them and the Koran-reading world. He touches on several issues of concern for the translators of the three relevant sacred writings — the Old Testament, the New Testament, and the Koran. Passing references are made to the history of translation within these three great traditions and to the aims, methods and problems of those engaged in translating sacred texts. The lecture is followed by an appreciation of C.'s work by Luise Abramowski and comments on the award of the Lucas prize for 1993 by Eberhard Jüngel.

G. H. JONES

CLARKE, E. G. (ed.): *Newsletter for Targumic & Cognate Studies*. Vol. 21. 1994. Pp. 12, 7. (Department of Near Eastern Studies, University of Toronto, Ontario. Price: $5.00 p.a. ISSN 0704 59005)

Fifteen publications (three volumes and twelve articles) on the Targums and considerably more on cognate subjects (principally Aramaic) are listed in this issue. A number of book reviews are also noted.

R. P. GORDON

DORIVAL, GILLES (trans. and annot.): *Les Nombres* (La Bible d'Alexandrie 4). With collaboration of Bernard Barc, Geneviève Favrell, Madeleine Petit, Joëlle Tolila. 1994. Pp.604. (Cerf, Paris. N.P. ISBN 2 204 05014 8)

The publication of the Book of Numbers in the French Septuagint series completes the Pentateuch (cf. *B.L.* 1993, p.48). This new volume follows the established pattern. The introduction investigates the following topics: 1. Is there a unity in the book? (A clue is found in the Greek title, 'Numbers'.) 2. The Greek text. 3. Comparison of Greek and Masoretic text: divisions of the text; pluses and minuses. 4. What is the Hebrew text underlying the Greek? 5. The Septuagint as a translation. 6. Intertextuality. 7. Targumisms. 8. An original exegesis (traces of a new exegesis of the Bible similar to that found later in the rabbinic tradition). 9. Distinctive aspects of the Greek vocabulary. 10. The chronological structure of the book. 11. Some notes on the language. The French translation is accompanied by detailed notes, including comparisons with the Hebrew text and discussions of the Greek exegetical traditions, Jewish and Chistian. There are three indexes, of Greek words, place names and topics. The completion of the Pentateuch is a landmark in the history of the project. Eleven volumes are already announced in the next phase.

N. R. M. DELANGE

DRAZIN, ISRAEL: *Targum Onkelos to Leviticus. An English Translation of the Text With Analysis and Commentary (Based on the A. Sperber and A. Berliner Editions)*. 1994. Pp. xvi, 278. (Ktav, Hoboken NJ. Price: $59.50 ISBN 0 88125 470 3)

In 1980 D. published *Targum Onkelos to Deuteronomy*, and in 1982 his *Targum Onkelos to Exodus* appeared (*B.L.* 1992, pp. 45–46). The present volume follows the layout of these earlier works. An Introduction (pp. 1–32), largely statistical in nature, is followed by the Aramaic text and an English translation on facing pages. All the translation is printed in the same typeface so that one does not see at a glance where the biblical text ends and the targumic deviation or addition begins.

D. notes that Targum Onkelos 'was not designed for scholars', that its 'principal aim was to present the simple meaning of the Torah's Massoretic text', and that nothing should be read into its paraphrases 'other than an attempt to capture the text's general meaning' (pp. 2–3). He regularly compares the rendering of Onkelos with other Targum versions, and he notes that his study reveals the remarkably close relationship to *Sifra* (p. 26).

M. MAHER

GROSSFELD, BERNARD: *The Targum Sheni to the Book of Esther: A Critical Edition Based on MS. Sassoon 282 with Critical Apparatus*. 1994. Pp. xvii, 195 + plates of the manuscript. (Sepher-Hermon Press, New York. Price: $49.95. ISBN 0 87203 142 X)

This edition complements G.'s translation of both the Targums of Esther which appeared in 1991. The base text is Sassoon 282, which is given both in transcription and facsimile; however, as a result of analysing further text-witnesses, G. here presents a modified account of the manuscript grouping. He now distinguishes four families, one of which represented by the majority of manuscripts, he identifies as the 'Mainstream Tradition'. It would have been helpful if he had spelled out more fully the statistical method which he has used to determine the families. The tables of 'Manuscript Comparisons' (pp. 89ff.) are rather enigmatic. Have G.'s statistics been distorted by indiscriminate counting of significant and insignificant data? His tentative proposal that Targum Sheni was composed in 'the early part of the 7th century C.E., but quite possibly earlier, perhaps even the 4th century C.E.' (p. xi) will probably carry little conviction. The author(s) of Targum Sheni knew Aramaic only as a literary language and since their models were in both eastern and western Aramaic they mixed features from both dialects. This strongly suggests the work could have been composed no earlier than c. 800 CE. Recently there has been a welcome upsurge of interest in the Targumim of the Hagiographa. G.'s work sets a new standard for editing these unjustly neglected works.

P. S. ALEXANDER

HANHART, ROBERT (ed.): *Esdrae liber II* (Septuaginta. Vetus Testamentum Graecum Auctoritate Academiae Scientiarum Gottingensis editum 8/2). 1993. Pp. 249. (Vandenhoeck & Ruprecht, Göttingen. Price: DM164.00; sub. price DM140.00. ISBN 3 525 53400 0)

This edition of 2 Esdras (the Greek versions of Ezra and Nehemiah) follows almost twenty years after the publication of the Göttingen edition of 1 Esdras (*B.L.* 1975, pp. 39–40) which, together with the editions of Esther, Judith and Tobit, was also prepared by H. It follows the standard pattern of the series but, as is now customary, the section in the introduction on the history of the text contains only sufficient to enable the user to interpret the apparatus, and a separate volume on the textual history is in preparation. In the section on the versions, H.'s fully-justified criticisms of Pereira's evaluation of the Ethiopic evidence deserve mention. This volume conforms to the high standards associated with the Göttingen edition, not least in the clarity and economy with which the evidence in the apparatus is presented, and the editor and publishers are to be congratulated on its appearance.

M. A. KNIBB

HENGEL, MARTIN and SCHWEMER, ANNA MARIA (eds): *Die Septuaginta zwischen Judentum und Christentum* (Wissenschaftliche Untersuchungen zum Neuen Testament 72). 1994. Pp. xii, 325. (Mohr, Tübingen. Price: DM 238.00. ISBN 3 16 146173 8; ISSN 0512 1604)

This is a product of a Tübinger Oberseminar 1990/1991, and is a timely reminder of the significance of the Septuagint in late antiquity, Judaism, and nascent Christianity. R. Hanhart discusses the Septuagint between the first translations and the acceptance of it as Sacred Writ by the Church at the time of Origen. J. Schaper takes up the issue of the exegesis of the Septuagint Psalter, with particular reference to eschatology and messianism. A. M. Schwemer indicates interesting links between the Septuagint and the *Vitae Prophetarum*. G. Veltri contributes two papers, one contributing to the

TEXT AND VERSIONS 51

discussion of the rabbinic background to the work of Aquila, the other discussing the significance of *Novelle 146* of Justinian. Christoph Markschies examines the concept of Hebraica Veritas in Jerome as a background to the Protestant understanding of Scripture. M. Hengel's 100-page contribution deals with a series of issues centering on the Christian reception and development of the Septuagint, although there is also a section on its development in a Jewish context. There are comprehensive indexes.

G. J. NORTON

LANE, DAVID J.: *The Peshitta of Leviticus* (Monographs of the Peshitta Institute Leiden 6). 1994. Pp. xv, 184. (Brill, Leiden–New York–Köln. Price: fl. 125.00/$71.50. ISBN 90 04 10020 2; ISSN 0169 9008)

The ongoing publication of the Leiden Peshitta has given a considerable stimulus to the scholarly investigation of this version of the Old Testament. This is the latest in a small series of monographs written by some of the contributors to the Leiden edition. Each contributor has been responsible for a particular book or books; hence the present monograph's concern with Leviticus. It makes several significant advances in the study of the Peshitta, with its evaluation of manuscript 7a1 as a median text, its evaluation of the text and apparatus of the Leiden Edition, its emphasis on the study of the translation method, its examination of the earlier printed editions and their textual affinities, and its relating the whole investigation of the text and tradition of the Peshitta to the context of Syrian Church history. It will be indispensable to future students of the Peshitta, and a salutary guide to all who make use of this version in the textual criticism of the Hebrew Bible.

A. GELSTON

LAPIDE, PINCHAS: *Ist die Bibel richtig übersetzt? Band 2* (Gütersloher Taschenbücher 1441). 1994. Pp. 94. (Kaiser, Gütersloh. Price: DM 14.80/AS 116/SwF 15.60. ISBN 3 579 01441 2)

The purpose of this little book is to further understanding between Jews and Christians by discussing certain words and phrases occurring in the Hebrew Bible and the New Testament that may have been misunderstood by translators. The forty-five examples dealt with are of very unequal importance. They include 'How did Eve get the apple?'; 'Is God male or female?', 'Is organ-playing forbidden in the Bible?', 'Are Jews really God's enemies?', and 'How blue is the Red Sea?'. Behind some of the apparently frivolous titles there is often a serious intention.

R. N. WHYBRAY

PENKOWER, YIZHAQ (JORDAN) S.: *nwsh htwrh bktr 'rm-ṣwbh 'dwt ḥdšh (New Evidence for the Pentateuch Text in the Aleppo Codex)* (Bar-Ilan Studies in Near Eastern Languages and Culture). 1992. Pp. 144. (Bar-Ilan University Press, Ramat-Gan. Price: $26.00. ISBN 965 226 129 7)

The Aleppo Codex, which is the basis for the Hebrew University Bible project, now lacks both its beginning (including most of the Pentateuch) and its end, although photographs of a few leaves of Genesis and Deuteronomy exist. The 'new evidence' presented here consists of marginal notes in a printed Pentateuch of 1490 in the library of the Jewish Theological Seminary in New York, which are derived according to handwritten statements at the end of Exodus, Leviticus and Numbers from 'the codex which Ben Asher of blessed memory corrected'. These marginal notes relate only to the books from Exodus to Deuteronomy. P. is able to show by a comparison with the sections of the Aleppo Codex which survive and early references to it that only it can be the source of the notes in question. Further chapters discuss Maimonides' reliance on the Aleppo Codex, the accuracy of its text of the Pentateuch, its relation to Yemenite manuscripts, and additional evidence for the missing portions of the Codex. Photographs of pages of the 1490 edition and comparative tables clarify the argument and conclusions of this study, which is a major contribution to our knowledge of the Masoretic tradition.

G. I. DAVIES

PÉTER-CONTESSE, RENÉ and ELLINGTON, JOHN: *A Handbook on the Book of Daniel* (UBS Handbook Series), 1993. Pp. viii, 365. (United Bible Societies, New York. Price: $8.95. ISBN 0 8267 0126 4)

This Handbook, following the format of the earlier volumes of the series, concentrates on exegetical material useful for translators, providing possible solutions for problems in translation related to language and culture. The Revised Standard Version and Today's English Version are presented in parallel columns in bold type, normally verse by verse, followed by comments and discussion. The book has a Selected Bibliography aimed at readers interested in further study of Daniel and a Glossary of terms that are technical from an exegtical or linguistic viewpoint.

P. W. COXON

RICHTER, WOLFGANG (ed.): *Biblia Hebraica transcripta. 1 und 2 Samuel* (Münchener Universitätsschriften: Arbeiten zu Text und Sprache im Alten Testament 33/5). 1991. Pp. vi, 585. (EOS Verlag, St Ottilien. Price: DM 63.00/AS 480. ISBN 3 88096 585 4)

RICHTER, WOLFGANG (ed.): *Biblia Hebraica transcripta. 1 und 2 Könige* (Münchener Universitätsschriften: Arbeiten zu Text und Sprache im Alten Testament 33/6). 1991. Pp. vi, 569. (EOS Verlag, St Ottilien. Price: DM 63.00/AS 480. ISBN 3 88096 586 2)

RICHTER, WOLFGANG (ed.): *Biblia Hebraica transcripta. Jesaja* (Münchener Universitätsschriften: Arbeiten zu Text und Sprache im Alten Testament 33/7). 1993. Pp. vi, 433. (EOS Verlag, St Ottilien. Price: DM 48.00/AS 370. ISBN 3 88096 587 0)

RICHTER, WOLFGANG (ed.): *Biblia Hebraica transcripta. Jeremia* (Münchener Universitätsschriften: Arbeiten zu Text und Sprache im Alten Testament 33/8). 1993. Pp. 497. (EOS Verlag, St Ottilien. Price: DM 58.00/AS 440. ISBN 3 88096 588 9)

RICHTER, WOLFGANG (ed.): *Biblia Hebraica transcripta. Ezechiel* (Münchener Universitätsschriften: Arbeiten zu Text und Sprache im Alten Testament 33/9). 1993. Pp. vi, 433. (EOS Verlag, St Ottilien. Price: DM 48.00/AS 370. ISBN 3 88096 589 7)

RICHTER, WOLFGANG (ed.): *Biblia Hebraica transcripta. Kleine Propheten* (Münchener Universitätsschriften: Arbeiten zu Text und Sprache im Alten Testament 33/10). 1993. Pp. vi, 357. (EOS Verlag, St Ottilien. Price: DM 43.00. ISBN 3 88096 590 0)

RICHTER, WOLFGANG (ed.): *Biblia Hebraica transcripta. Psalmen* (Münchener Universitätsschriften: Arbeiten zu Text und Sprache im Alten Testament 33/11). 1993. Pp. vi, 589. (EOS Verlag, St Ottilien. Price: DM 78.00/AS 660. ISBN 3 88096 591 9)

RICHTER, WOLFGANG (ed.): *Biblia Hebraica transcripta. Ijob, Sprüche* (Münchener Universitätsschriften: Arbeiten zu Text und Sprache im Alten Testament 33/12). 1993. Pp. vi, 389. (EOS Verlag, St Ottilien. Price: DM 48.00/AS 400. ISBN 3 88096 592 7)

RICHTER, WOLFGANG (ed.): *Biblia Hebraica transcripta. Megilloth* (Münchener Universitätsschriften: Arbeiten zu Text und Sprache im Alten Testament 33/13). 1993. Pp. vi, 253. (EOS Verlag, St Ottilien. Price: DM 34.00/ AS 280. ISBN 3 88096 593 5)

RICHTER, WOLFGANG (ed.): *Biblia Hebraica transcripta. Daniel, Esra, Nehemia* (Münchener Universitätsschriften: Arbeiten zu Text und Sprache im Alten Testament 33/14). 1993. Pp. vi, 341. (EOS Verlag, St Ottilien. Price: DM 42.00/AS 350. ISBN 3 88096 597 8)

RICHTER, WOLFGANG (ed.): *Biblia Hebraica transcripta. 1 und 2 Chronik* (Münchener Universitätsschriften: Arbeiten zu Text und Sprache im Alten Testament 33/15). 1993. Pp.vi, 491. (EOS Verlag, St Ottilien. Price: DM 68.00/AS 570. ISBN 3 88096 595 1)

Earlier volumes of this series were reviewed in *B.L.* 1992, p. 56 and 1994, p. 48. The present reviewer has compared R.'s division into short lines with his own similar work on some of the books of the prophets. There are considerable differences between the two sets of results. Overall it is difficult to see the value of publishing such an extensive series, but since the volumes are available they may be useful to some.   K. J. CATHCART

RÖSEL, MARTIN: *Übersetzung als Vollendung der Auslegung. Studien zur Genesis-Septuaginta* (Beihefte zur Zeitschrift für die alttestamentliche Wissenschaft 223). 1994. Pp. viii, 290. (de Gruyter, Berlin–New York. Price: DM 138.00. ISBN 3 11 014234 1; ISSN 0934 2575)

The main part of this book consists of a translation, with quite detailed commentary, of the Septuagint translation of Gen. 1–11. Included in the course of this is a comparison of the terminology employed by the translator of the Creation narrative with that used by Plato in the *Timaeus*, and a discussion of the Septuagint chronology in Gen. 5 and 11. A final section deals with some wider questions of the Septuagint translation of Genesis as a whole (e.g. the translation of certain theologically significant terms, and geographical data). This is a very welcome contribution to Septuagint studies.

S. P. BROCK

STEC, DAVID M.: *The Text of the Targum of Job. An Introduction and Critical Edition* (Arbeiten zur Geschichte des Antiken Judentums und des Urchristentums 20). 1994. Pp. ix, 129, 339*. (Brill, Leiden–New York–Köln. Price: fl. 144.00/$82.50. ISBN 90 04 09874 7; ISSN 0169 734X)

S. aims to produce a critical edition of Targum Job which lists all the readings of every known accessible manuscript and to consider the relationship of the texts to each other. He selects Ms Vatican Biblioteca Apostolica Urbinas I as the base text. His decision not to produce an eclectic text is dictated by the presence of multiple Targums. S. therefore gives us a text supplied with very generous apparatus set out as simply and clearly as circumstances permit. He has been very largely successful in bringing order to an immensely complex enterprise, and his meticulous attention to detail is apparent at every turn. In the Introduction, he discusses the previous attempts to produce a critical edition before discussing the printed editions and describing the manuscripts. He agrees with F. J. Fernández Vallina that the textual witnesses fall into four distinct groups, whose relationship to one another may be depicted diagrammatically (p. 84). From this, S. concludes that the earliest written form of Tg. Job must itself have displayed considerable textual variation.

With regard to the Targum's multiple translation of several verses, he agrees in principle that the original copyist of Tg. Job worked from two or three manuscripts and noted in the margin of his copy those texts which differed from what he was taking as his 'base text'. These were then incorporated into the main text (sometimes at different points) by later copyists. There is indeed a mass of information to hand for the textual critic in this volume, and students of Targum owe S. a debt of gratitude for accomplishing this mammoth task so thoroughly.   C. T. R. Hayward

TALSHIR, ZIPORA: *The Alternative Story of the Division of the Kingdom. 3 Kingdoms 12:24 A–Z* (Jerusalem Biblical Studies 6). 1993. Pp. 319 (Eng.), 7 (Heb.), 8 (appendix). (Simor, Jerusalem. Price $27.00. ISBN 965 242 006 9)

This book is the English translation and revision of the original Hebrew study (1989). The Greek 'Alternative Story' (AS) describes Jeroboam's revolt and the secession of the northern tribes but adds some intriguing details. T.'s meticulous analysis attempts to go beyond earlier research on the phenomenon, and her complete retroversion into Hebrew is so smooth that a Hebrew *Vorlage* appears most likely. The close parallels between the 'Alternative Story' and Kings lead T. to conclude that the former does not represent an independent historical source, nor does it stem from pre-Deuteronomic text. Rather, it is a literary reworking of material similar to that found in Hebrew Kings, being in genre a type of historical midrash. As for the Greek text, it is an integral part of the Old Greek of the *gg* section of 3 Kingdoms. T. refrains from offering any particular date or motive for the composition of the 'Alternative Story' but does suggest with admirable caution that it may reflect conflict between the returned exiles and local enemies: there are some 4th-century, possibly Samaritan, coins bearing the name Jeroboam, which may be the title of a local governor. But as she points out, the denigration of Jeroboam in the 'Alternative Story' differs only in detail, not in degree, from that in Masoretic text. Altogether a useful study.

A. G. SALVESEN

VERBRUGGE, VERLYN D. (ed.): *NRSV Harper Study Bible. Expanded and Updated.* Study helps written by Harold Lindsell. 1991. Pp. xii, 1914, 183 (concordance) + 6 maps. (Zondervan, Grand Rapids MI. Price: $35.99. ISBN 0 310 90203 7)

This handsome presentation volume, whose use seems to be envisaged as a kind of 'Family Bible', is a most curious hybrid. The text is that of NRSV, consciously up-to-date in its eschewal of 'linguistic sexism' and of 'thee' and 'thou'. Each biblical book is provided with a short introduction and with commentary notes, and these, by contrast, are written from a rigidly conservative standpoint, upholding, for example, Mosaic authorship of the Pentateuch and the historical reliability of Daniel. At times the tension between text and notes becomes almost comic (Deut. 34; Isa. 7:14). The Apocrypha is not included, but a brief concordance of the Old and New Testaments is appended. The volume as a whole is intended to replace the *RSV Harper Study Bible* of 1964 (not noticed in *B.L.*).   R. J. COGGINS

Vetus Latina. Die Reste der altlateinischen Bibel nach Petrus Sabatier neu gesammelt und herausgegeben von der Erzabtei Beuron. 11/2: *Sirach (Ecclesiasticus).* Herausgegeben von Walter Thiele. 5. Lieferung: Sir 7,30–11,35. 1993. Pp. 321–400. (Herder, Freiburg. N.P. ISBN 3 451 00428 3; ISSN 0571 9070)

This fifth fascicle continues this excellent edition on its way.   J. BARR

Vetus Latina. Die Reste der altlateinischen Bibel nach Petrus Sabatier neu gesammelt und herausgegeben von der Erzabtei Beuron. 12:*Esaias.* Herausgegeben von Roger Gryson. 10. Lieferung: Is. 35, 5–39,8; Appendice: Un agraphon apparenté à *Isaïe* 31,9. 1993. Pp. 721–96. (Herder, Freiburg. N.P. ISBN 3 451 00478 X; ISSN 0571 9070)

Within the high standard of this edition, special interest will attach to the *agraphon* 'cursed is everyone who does not raise up seed in Israel' (or the like), reported as related to 31:9 but absent from standard texts of the Bible. The evidences for this text, and the text itself in its varied forms, conclude (pp. 783–95) the first portion of the presentation of Isaiah. A separate volume commences with ch. 40 (see below).

J. BARR

Vetus Latina. Die Reste der altlateinischen Bibel nach Petrus Sabatier neu gesammelt und herausgegeben von der Erzabtei Beuron. 12 (Pars II): *Esaias.* Herausgegeben von Roger Gryson. 1. Lieferung: Introduction: Les manuscrits. 1993. Pp. 797–880. (Herder, Freiburg. N.P. ISBN 3 451 00121 7; ISSN 0571 9070)

Vetus Latina. Die Reste der altlateinischen Bibel nach Petrus Sabatier neu gesammelt und herausgegeben von der Erzabtei Beuron. 12 (Pars II): *Esaias.* Herausgegeben von Roger Gryson. 2. Lieferung: Introduction: Les manuscrits (suite et fin) Is 40, 1–41, 20. 1994. Pp. 881–960. (Herder, Freiburg. N.P. ISBN 3 451 00122 5; ISSN 0571 9070)

The presentation of the Book of Isiah in this magnificent edition will have a somewhat peculiar form when it is complete. It had been expected that the entire work could be done in 800 or 900 pages; but in fact 800 have been reached at the end of ch. 39, and so a second part here begins with 40:1. Not only so: but the introduction at the start of the first fascicle, though it analysed the various *types* of textual tradition and gave a preliminary *listing* of manuscripts, did not provide a thorough examination of the latter. The new volume thus begins with a detailed introduction, almost 100-pages long, to the Latin manuscripts of the whole. The actual presentation of the text resumes in the second fascicle, at p. 899 of the whole.

J. BARR

5. EXEGESIS AND MODERN TRANSLATIONS

BOESE, HELMUT. (ed.): *Anonymi Glosa Psalmorum ex traditione seniorum. Teil II: Psalmen 101–150* (Vetus Latina: Aus der Geschichte der Lateinischen Bibel 25). 1994. Pp. 24*, 287 + 4 plates. (Herder, Freiburg. N.P. ISBN 3 451 22682 0; 0571 9070)

The first volume of this work has already been reviewed (*B.L.* 1993, p. 47). In Teil II, besides an Introduction dealing with the sources of the *Glosa*, and a description of the manuscripts used, there are Corrigenda, Addenda and Annotationes to Parts I and II.

R. B. SALTERS

BOOIJ, TH.: *Psalmen III (81–110)* (De Prediking van het Oude Testament). 1994. Pp. 327. (G. F. Callenbach, Nijkerk. Price: fl. 99.50. ISBN 90 266 0734 2)

The two previous volumes on Psalms in this series were by N. A. van Uchelin (not, apparently, reviewed in the *B.L.* although volume 2 on Psalms 41–80 (1977) was mentioned as received in 1978). The work has been taken over by Th. Booij and offers a cautious and balanced approach. Most of the

Psalms discussed are dated in the post-exilic period, exceptions being 93, 96, 98 and 99, which are tentatively connected with a festival, including law-giving, in the month of Tishri, and 110 which is dated to the earlier monarchy. Our lack of knowledge of pre-exilic temple usage is noted, and there is a justifiable reluctance to press Psalms into inappropriate form-critical catego-ries in cases where the content does not warrant this. The careful attention to text-critical and philological detail is characteristic of the series as a whole.

J. W. Rogerson

Bovati, Pietro and Meynet, Roland: *Le Livre du prophète Amos* (Rhétorique Biblique 2). 1994. Pp. 443. (Cerf, Paris. Price; Fr. 220.00. ISBN 2 204 05076 8)

Bovati, Pietro and Meynet, Roland: *La fin d'Israël. Paroles d'Amos* (Lire la Bible 101). 1994. Pp. 238. (Cerf, Paris. Price: Fr. 98.00. ISBN 2 204 04867 4; ISSN 0588 2257)

Commentaries on the book of Amos have for the most part engaged in detailed redaction-critical analysis, confident that the final form of the book conceals many different layers, whose identity can in principle be established. Here by contrast a radically different approach can be found, based on a rhetorical-critical analysis; historical and redaction criticism are regarded as destructive of the artistry underlying the finished work. The authors' presup-position is that biblical books are not mere compilations, but genuine compositions from the hand of a single author. Amos 5:1–17 provides the starting-point; often thought of as a mélange of material from a variety of periods, links are instead found with other parts of the book which demon-strate a genuine overall unity. Thus the whole book is drawn into an elaborate overarching structure; three sequences are described, each being subjected to more detailed analysis. Even the first two verses, usually treated as a detachable introduction, fall within this overall pattern. It should be said that this is not done in a particular conservative interest, wishing to establish that the whole book of Amos comes from Amos himself; indeed, historical issues play only a very small part in the discussion. Though one of the authors is Italian, one can fairly say that this is a very French book, as against the German influence of other approaches. At the exegetical level, however, the approach is less revolutionary; much that is said here could have been found in commentaries using traditional approaches.

The second volume is in effect a briefer and simplified version of the first, based on the same working assumptions, but with the detailed discussion of rhetorical analysis omitted; for theoretical justification readers of the second volume are referred to the first.

R. J. Coggins

Breneman, Mervin: *Ezra, Nehemiah, Esther* (The New American Com-mentary 10). 1993. Pp. 383. (Broadman and Holman, Nashville TN. Price: $27.99. ISBN 0 8054 0110 5)

Miller, Stephen R.: *Daniel* (The New American Commentary 18). 1994. Pp. 348. (Broadman and Holman, Nashville TN. Price: $27.99. ISBN 0 8054 0118 0)

This new commentary series has the subtitle, An Exegetical and Theo-logical Exposition of Holy Scripture, NIV Text, and is intended to represent 'the finest in contemporary evangelical scholarship, and lends itself to the practical work of preaching and teaching'. It also 'assumes the inerrancy of Scripture'. The first approach will no doubt be greeted with pleasure by many readers, but the second claim may well alienate some of the same people (though at least the editors are honest about their stance). As might be expected, the dogma of inerrancy is most apparent in the commentary on Daniel, in which a persistent apologetic for the text is compounded by a polemic against critical scholarship. Within these self-imposed limits there is no doubt useful material to be gleaned by preachers and teachers. Indeed, the writer on Ezra-Nehemiah-Esther seems to be more free about citing standard critical works, even if for his conclusions he quickly dashes back to the security of the conservative fold. Perhaps critical scholarship should ask in a more searching way why so much of the popular commentary writing seems to be churned out by evangelical presses.

L. L. GRABBE

BRENNER, MARTIN L.: *The Song of the Sea: Ex 15:1–21* (Beihefte zur Zeitschrift für die alttestamentliche Wissenschaft 195). 1991. Pp. viii, 193. (de Gruyter, Berlin–New York. Price: DM 88.00. ISBN 3 11 012340 1; ISSN 0934 2575)

This is an uncompromising argument for the post-exilic dating of the 'Song of Moses'. The parallels in language with other sections of the Hebrew Bible are carefully plotted to show that the Song is steeped in the language of D and Dtr but is itself 'post-Deuteronomistic' (there is influence from Deutero–Isaiah). In particular, the Song, based on the traditional victory song, is a 'proto-apocalyptic' product of the Sons of Asaph, while the framework is the work of the Levitical instructors. Perhaps that is as far as one can safely go. The development of the argument to identify the Song as a processional psalm composed after the rebuilding of the walls of Jerusalem by Nehemiah in 444 rests on a number of problematical connections, e.g. that the Pentateuch was introduced in its final form by Ezra and that Ezra preceded Nehemiah. One might have expected a fuller engagement with the linguistic side of the Cross-Freedman argument. There are some puzzling statements: e.g. 'The Levitical singer is styled the sister of Aaron. It is these Levites who considered themselves to be brothers of the priests' (p. 180).

W. JOHNSTONE

BRENNER, ATHALYA (ed.): *A Feminist Companion to Judges* (The Feminist Companion to the Bible 4). 1993. Pp. 242. (Sheffield Academic Press. Price: £16.50/$24.50. ISBN 1 85075 462 4)

This collection of essays is divided into five sections. The first, on 'Women and (Hi)story' examines the relational and functional terms in which women are presented in the book of Judges (L. Klein), the significance of the book when read as the work of a female author (A. J. Bledstein), the role models for women in the book (L. Klein), and how women in Judges weere understood by rabbinic exegetes (L. L. Bronner). The second section has two essays on the question of the authorial or dominant point of view in Judges 4–5 (Brenner and F. van Dijk-Hemmes). The third section offers two feminist readings of the story of the daughter of Jephthah (E. Fuchs and J. C. Exum). The fourth has two essays on Manoah's wife and the significance of her namelessness (Y. Amit and A. Reinhartz). The fifth has three essays on the Levite's wife in Judges 19–21 (K. Jones-Warsaw, P. Kamuf and M. Bal). Throughout, the essays are written in the context of the apparent centrality of women in the book of Judges, a centrality which is, however, belied by the manner of their presentation. Most are unnamed (although the significance of this is differently estimated), and over a third are designated as outsiders in relation to the narrator's community. The essays by Brenner, Exum and Kamuf have previously appeared.

A. D. H. MAYES

BRENNER, ATHALYA (ed.): *A Feminist Companion to Samuel and Kings* (The Feminist Companion to the Bible 5). 1994. Pp. 286. (Sheffield Academic Press. Price: £16.50/$24.50. ISBN 1 85075 480 2)

This volume is a combination of the stimulating, the provocative and the tendentious. Perception of their relationship will depend on the reader's viewpoint! The sixteen essays (a few published previously) fall under five headings together with introduction and epilogue. Part I discusses the liminality and anonymity of women in biblical historiography (Shargent and Reinhartz); Part II focuses on Hannah, in relation to Elkanah (Amit), as victim and 'social redeemer' (Klein) and as participant in cultic activity (Meyers). Of particular interest in Part III Women and Monarchs, is the reading of 1 Samuel 25 as Abigail's story (Bach), the inclusion of Talmudic discussion of David and his women (Valler), and Fontaine's reflections on the importance of wisdom in the shaping of these narratives. Part IV addresses the disputed role of the *gᵉbîrâ* (Ben-Barak), with essays on Maacah (Spanier) and Jezebel (Pippin). Part V offers a 'female' reading of the Elijah cycle (Tarlin), a dual interpretation of 2 Kings 4:8–37 (van Dijk-Hemmes, to whose memory the book is dedicated) and discussion of Huldah, prophet of Yahweh or Asherah? (Edelman). The volume concludes with a brief examination of women's status in the Persian period, specifically at Elephantine and in Ezra-Nehemiah (Eskenazi).   G. I. EMMERSON

BRENNER, ATHALYA (ed.): *A Feminist Companion to Exodus to Deuteronomy* (The Feminist Companion to the Bible 6). 1994. Pp. 269. (Sheffield Academic Press. Price: £16.50/$24.50. ISBN 1 85075 463 2)

The question of the grouping of these books is addressed in a concise but powerful introduction by B. who sees their underlying theme as being a multi-facet 'inauguration myth'. The question asked is that of the role played by women within this phase in Israel's history and the ideology that motivates this portrayal. There are three main parts around which the articles are arranged encompassing various ways in which women are portrayed and involved in these books. The first part examines the situation of the 'suppressed' daughters. The second part (Social Status and Female Sexuality) brings to the fore that women's sexuality is 'owned' by (male) society in its hermeneutical implications for today's questions. The last part is in the form of a dialogue in which various articles respond to each other and engage in a lively hermeneutic debate. Worth reading is A. Bach, a midrash on Miriam's song in Exodus 15:19–21 — a constructive reclamation. This volume reaffirms the bleak statement that women's lives are viewed exclusively from a patriarchal perspective, even and including texts like Exodus 1–4, Numbers 27 and 36, or Deuteronomy 5. It is however — like its predecessors — rich in ideas and thus well worth consulting.   A. JEFFERS

BRISMAN, LESLIE: *The Voice of Jacob. On the Composition of Genesis* (Indiana Studies in Biblical Literature). 1994. Pp. xx, 122. (Indiana University Press, Bloomington-Indianapolis; distributed in the UK by the Open University Press, Buckingham. Price: £20.00. ISBN 2 253 31264 7)

B. rejects the generally accepted documentary hypothesis, arguing that Genesis was composed by one author, whom he calls Jacob (the Jahwistic material), who revised the work of his predecessors (i.e. P and E) whom he designates as Eisaac. B.'s approach is literary rather than historical or sociological, and he explores issues of intertextuality. For example, he argues that Gen. 6:5–7 is Jacob's reaction to the Eisaac story of creation since he quotes the verb used in Gen. 1:1 for creation (6:7). Jacob explores the sorrow of God, in contrast to the casual mention of evil in Eisaac. In the story of Joseph Eisaac has the brothers simply throw Joseph into the pit, whereas Jacob has a midrashic addition which has them observing a passing caravan of Ishmaelites, and listening to Judah's alternative plan to sell Joseph. Whilst B. offers a refreshing and imaginative approach to the text, he is not always convincing, and there still remains evidence that J was the earliest of the sources.

P. J. HARLAND

BURKERT, WALTER and STOLZ, FRITZ (eds): *Hymnen der Alten Welt im Kulturvergleich* (Orbis Biblicus et Orientalis 131). 1994. Pp. 136. (Universitätsverlag, Freiburg (Schweiz); Vandenhoek & Ruprect, Göttingen. Price: SwF 38.00/DM 44.00/AS 343. ISBN (Universitätsverlag) 3 7278 0929 9; (Vandenhoeck & Ruprect) 3 525 53766 2)

This little volume is based on papers read at a one-day conference in Zürich of Swiss societies for Oriental antiquity and the study of religions in 1991. The intention is to provide an informative survey of hymns in various cultures for the furtherance of comparative studies. Six cultures are treated in turn: Greek (Burkert), Sumerian and Akkadian (D. O. Edzard), Egyptian (J. Assmann), Hittite (G. Wilhelm), Indo-Iranian (E. Tichy), Hebrew (H. Spieckermann), and there is a concluding discussion (F. Stolz). Each writer provides a bibliography. The non-biblical chapters especially are important and enlightening.

J. H. EATON

Calvin's Old Testament Commentaries, vol. 18: *Ezekiel I (Chapters 1–12)*. Translated by D. Foxgrover and D. Martin. 1994. Pp. xiii, 322. (Paternoster, Carlisle; Eerdmans, Grand Rapids MI. Price: £21.99/$34.99; paper £14.99/$24.99. ISBN (Paternoster) 0 85364 598 1; paper 0 85364 599 X; (Eerdmans) 0 8028 2468 4; paper 0 8028 0751 8)

Calvin's Old Testament Commentaries, vol. 20: *Daniel I (Chapters 1–6)*. Translated by T. H. L. Parker. 1993. Pp. xii, 300. (Paternoster, Carlisle; Eerdmans, Grand Rapids MI. Price: $34.99; paper $24.99/£14.99. ISBN (Paternoster) 0 85364 572 8; paper 0 85364 573 6; (Eerdmans) 0 8028 2451 X; paper 0 8028 9750 X)

There has long been a need to replace the ageing tomes of the Calvin Translation Society: their prose style is now almost as obscure to the modern undergraduate as Calvin's Latin, and their editorial shortcomings owe much to the Society's intention of conscripting Calvin into the struggle against the 'German Neologians' of the early 19th century. The project to translate afresh all Calvin's Old Testament 'commentaries' (lectures dictated to adolescents for the most part) is therefore welcome, and these two well-produced volumes are a credit to the enterprise, also providing a first-rate set of indices of names, subjects, biblical references, and non-English words. The translations are generally clear and idiomatic, though it was puzzling to see Calvin's characteristic *dominator Jehovah* rendered both 'Sovereign Yahweh' and 'Lord Yahweh' on the same page (*Ezekiel I*, p. 166), when the latter might have been reserved for the more conventional *dominus Jehovah*. Otherwise, the repetitions and inconsistencies to be expected of *viva voce* lectures are allowed to show through in these translations. We should be grateful to Calvin's most recent editors and translators, but we should also be grateful to his original stenographers, who got down *everything*. How else would we know that Calvin finally ended one lecture on Ezekiel, presumably to the relief of his hearers, with 'I see that I cannot finish; I think the clock must be wrong'?

D. V. N. BAGCHI

CAQUOT, ANDRÉ and ROBERT, PHILIPPE DE: *Les Livres de Samuel* (Collection Commentaire de l'Ancient Testament 6). 1994. Pp. 656. (Labour et Fides, Geneva. Price: Fr 78.00, ISBN 2 8309 0703 5)

The interpretation of these books is greatly dependent on theories of compilation. This documentary postulates three stages. The original work comprised the material identified by Rost together with a history of the rise of the monarchy, and was the work of an Elide author or circle closely acquainted with David. It has rightly been said to be Israel's first genuine work of history. After the division of the kingdom it was revised by a Zadokite writer in legitimation of the Davidic dynasty. The final, Deuteronomistic, redaction is basically that proposed by Noth, though the possibility of later recensions of it (not clearly to be defined) is recognized. This commentary is critical in its methods but relatively conservative in its conclusions. The authors reject reductionist views like those of Garbini; but they make a distinction between the Deuteronomistic ideology of the last redactor and the 'petite histoire' in which many authentic details of daily life, politics and religion of the period of the early monarchy are preserved.   R. N. WHYBRAY

CARSON, D. A., *et al.* (eds): *New Bible Commentary. 21st Century Edition*. 1994 (4th ed.). Pp. xviii, 1455. (Inter-Varsity Press, Leicester–Downers Grove, IL. Price: £32.99. ISBN (UK) 0 85110 648 X; (US) 0 8308 1442 6)

This revised and reset fourth edition, quoting the NIV instead of the RSV, and for which 'God has called into being a new international team of writers', presents 80 per cent of totally new articles, with the rest being completely rewritten. Following the standard format of a one-volume commentary on the Protestant canon, there are also six pages of notes on the Apocrypha, the Pseudepigrapha, and the Dead Sea Scrolls. The editors aim to aid 'the individual Christian and the whole professing church today . . . to know, love and submit to the Bible as the Word of God'. The book is generally conservative in perspective: patriarchal ideas found in the biblical text, or in secondary literature, are not critiqued, nor are literary critical methods described, nor are salty humour or erotic innuendo explained. However, the volume does not follow a completely literalist approach, nor are all the (all-but-one male) contributors of one theological hue. Contradictions in the text are likely to be noted, may be described as 'puzzling' (pp. 332, 982) but are considered 'unlikely' to overturn the religious beliefs of the editors and implied readers. The volume's strengths are its compactness, ease of use (it lies open without springing shut again), clarity of print and layout, and sensible and accessible organization of material.   H. A. MCKAY

COLLINS, JOHN J.: *Daniel* (Hermeneia). 1993. pp. xxxvi, 499. (Fortress, Minneapolis. Price: $46.00. ISBN 0 8006 6040 4)

The appearance of this thorough and judicious commentary, five years after Goldingay's (*B.L.* 1990, pp. 54–55), and during the early stages of Koch's (*B.L.* 1988, p. 60), furnishes the student of Daniel with (almost) three excellent and different commentaries (after a number of indifferent ones: Delcor, Lacocque). Collins' work is historical-critical, solid, up-to-date and its judgements shrewd and usually convincing. The translation is limpid, often conveying the tenor, not just the sense, of the original. The commentary pays full attention to the Greek versions, incorporating the Greek 'additions' and printing the translation of the highly variant Old Greek of ch. 5 alongside the MT. As one would expect from C., generic and compositional matters are

fully discussed, and the Qumran material regularly, though not systematically, introduced. History of interpretation is included, and (to allow A.
Yarbro Collins to participate), a long section on Daniel's influence on the
New Testament. Collins is less sensitive to literary and theological matters
than Goldingay (but both miss the comic wordplay in 5:6, 12, 16 involving *qtr*
+ *šr'*.) The bibliography is extensive, though with some inexplicable gaps
(e.g. Rowland's *Open Heaven*). This commentary is indispensable to the
biblical scholar.

P. R. DAVIES

COURSE, JOHN E.: *Speech and Response. A Rhetorical Analysis of the
Introductions to the Speeches of the Book of Job (Chaps. 4–24)* (Catholic
Biblical Quarterly Monograph 25). 1994. Pp. vii, 184. (Catholic Biblical
Association, Washington, D.C. Price $8.50. ISBN 0 915170 24 8)

This monograph sets out to fulfil a modest task. Its aim is to overturn the
commonly accepted theory that the friends and Job in the dialogue section fail
to respond to one another. C. does a detailed analysis of the introductions to
the speeches of the friends and Job in order to demonstrate that there are
subtle links in terms of genre, recurrent words, roots and themes between the
speeches that follow on from one another in the three speech cycles. He also
notes links with the book's prologue notably in the introductions of the first
cycle. For each introduction to a speech C. provides a translation of the text
followed by clearly argued sections on form and rhetorical analysis followed
by an overview. When treating chs 22–24, C. only studies those portions
which provide him with evidence of a response pattern, a method which has a
circular feel. The analysis, whilst it achieves what it sets out to do, does not go
as far as it might. He fails to pick up the irony of much of what Job says in his
speeches and does not do justice to recent study in this area. Furthermore,
attention to chs 25–37 might well have added to the scope and interest of his
work which is limited in its range and thus of interest more to the specialist
than to the student.

K. J. DELL

CURTIS, ADRIAN H. W.: *Joshua* (Old Testament Guides). 1994. Pp. 89.
(Sheffield Academic Press. Price: £5.95/$9.95. ISBN 1 85075 706 2; ISSN
0264 6498)

This is a good little general introduction. The author sets Joshua in its
literary context and goes on to deal with the content, composition, the Joshua
stories and their setting. He discusses the role of archaeology in interpreting
the book and its historical reliability. After assessing history, geography and
theology he ends by looking at the book as literature. The information is
up-to-date and the various current opinions regarding the so-called conquest
and the emergence of Israel are noted. There is an annotated select list of
commentaries on the book. Each chapter has its own list of further reading,
mostly in English though some works in German are cited. The student and
general reader will find this a useful introduction to the book of Joshua and to
its place within the wider context of the deuteronomistic history and Old
Testament theology generally.

J. R. DUCKWORTH

DÖRRFUSS, ERNST MICHAEL: *Mose in den Chronikbüchern. Garant theok-
ratischer Zukunftserwartung* (Beihefte zur Zeitschrift für die alttestamentliche Wissenschaft 219). 1994. Pp. xiii, 302. (de Gruyter, Berlin–New York.
Price: DM 148.00. ISBN 3 11 014017 9; ISSN 0934 2575)

After a general introduction D.'s work falls into two main parts. The first
is a historical study of the concept of theocracy and its interpretation, and is a

useful compilation on a subject that has too often been treated polemically and without real interest, as the supposed opposite of eschatology; even Plöger's seminal work did not define it. D. argues that the concept is necessary to theological discourse on a God of power and might. The second part provides historical-critical analysis of all the Moses passages in Chronicles, concluding that most of the references are secondary (2nd century) and, by presenting Moses in the wilderness as the true mediator of cultic practice and law, implicitly relativize the importance of Israel's kings and of the temple in Jerusalem, and express a longing for the rule of God himself. This is 'theocratic expectation'; D. does not accept either that Chronicles had no eschatology or that it has a purely concrete (Davidic) hope reflecting early 4th-century circumstances. Questions arising concern the social and historical circumstances of the Moses redaction (Jerusalemite? reacting against Maccabean developments?), and whether comparable findings might emerge from Ezra/Nehemiah or the Books of Kings.   K. J. A. LARKIN

EMMERSON, GRACE (ed.): *Prophets and Poets. A Companion to the Prophetic Books of the Old Testament.* 1994. Pp. 301. (The Bible Reading Fellowship, Oxford; Albatross Books, Sutherland, Australia. Price: £8.99. ISBN (B.R.F.) 0 7459 2599 5; (Albatross) 0 7324 0906 3)

Some series of daily Bible readings have looked to well-known scholars for their authors, but it is a pity that these often valuable publications are normally ephemeral. The present volume happily preserves from the B.R.F.'s 'Guidelines' series such commentary on all the prophetic books, treated either entire or in selections. Paul Joyce, for example, writes on Amos and Third Isaiah, Harry Mowvley on Ezekiel, John Barton on Hosea and Habakkuk, John Rogerson on Jeremiah, Jonah and Micah, John Sawyer on Haggai and Zechariah, Grace Emmerson on Obadiah, Nahum and Malachi, Rex Mason on Daniel. This will be a useful book where commentary is required in one volume on the essential prophetic texts and where there is need for scholarly knowledge put simply.   J. H. EATON

ESLINGER, LYLE: *House of God or House of David. The Rhetoric of 2 Samuel 7* (Journal for the Study of the Old Testament Supplement 164). 1994. Pp. 118. (Sheffield Academic Press. Price: £22.50/$35.00. ISBN 1 85075 481 0; ISSN 0309 0787)

Following on from two earlier works (*B.L.* 1989, p. 72; 1990, p. 73) E. handles the question of the apparent conflict between the 'conditional' Sinaitic covenant and the 'unconditional' Davidic covenant. He approaches the issue from a study of the rhetoric of 2 Samuel 7: the verbal parrying whereby God grants to David an unwelcome innovation (the temple), but not on his terms, just as earlier he had granted a king to Israel, but not on their terms. In this way the conditionality of the Sinai covenant is preserved. Structurist interpreters, especially Fokkelman, come in for much praise; historical critics, especially Rost, for much criticism. An unusual feature in a monograph is an excursus in which the debate between the author and one of his sparring partners, A. F. Campbell (on the question of multiple editions of DtrH), is continued by both scholars by response and counter-response. Despite the inclusion of a chapter on 'Biblical Echoes of 2 Samuel 7', no serious attention is given to 1 Chronicles 17, which might throw some light on the question of how a work can be both composite and coherent.

W. JOHNSTONE

FOHRER, GEORG: *Psalmen* (De-Gruyter-Studienbuch). 1993. Pp. ix, 255. (de Gruyter, Berlin–New York. Price: DM 58.00. ISBN 3 11 013927 8)

This contribution to a series for students provides translation and commentary for a selection of thirty-five psalms. There are ten pages of introduction and ten concluding pages summarizing theological features. The selection is said to illustrate the religion around the 5th century and to represent the types at home in that period. The commentary is fairly thorough and avoids technicality. The translation is supported by footnotes which give literal renderings and information about adopted emendations and the supposed glosses that have been omitted from the translation (but the significant 104:35a–b has been omitted without acknowledgement). The work is well-organized and a model of clarity. Some of the views so firmly presented to the students, however, are decidedly questionable, as for example the presentation of Psalm 93 as dependent on a theoretical monotheism attributed to Deutero-Isaiah.

J. H. EATON

FRANKE, CHRIS: *Isaiah 46, 47, and 48: A New Literary Critical Reading* (Biblical and Judaic Studies from the University of California, San Diego 3). 1994. Pp. x, 293. (Eisenbrauns, Winona Lake, IN. Price: $32.50. ISBN 0 931464 79 X)

Over half the text works through the words of Isaiah 46–48 *seriatim*; the balance is taken up with matters of structure and composition. F. contends that each of these chapters is a well-formed composition and appeal to redactional layering is not necessary to explain their structure. Two guides especially point the way: D. N. Freedman (syllable counting), and J. Muilenberg (rhetorical criticism). The textual notes are detailed and orientated to vocabulary, although stylistic comment occasionally surfaces. It is not always clear whether a unified reading of these poems is an *assumption* which F. sets out to prove (cf. pp. 20 and 77) or rather something to be *discovered* about them (cf. p. 262); the former seems more likely. Freedman and Muilenberg have both been highly influential, though some might contend they have reached their 'sell-by' date. Some of F.'s judgements on other scholars' work, especially Kugel and Alter on Hebrew poetry, seem misplaced. The most recent items in the bibliography date from 1987. In spite of these reservations, F.'s careful textual analysis makes the book mandatory reading for any involved in the study of Second Isaiah.

D. J. REIMER

FRITZ, VOLKMAR: *Das Buch Josua* (Handbuch zum Alten Testament I/7). 1994. Pp. ix, 258. (Mohr, Tübingen. Price: DM 68.00. ISBN 3 16 146089 8)

This fresh commentary replaces Noth's path-breaking volume of 1938/53 in the HAT series, and is dedicated to his memory. 'In tradition and composition Joshua proves to be a late work.' Against Noth, who had identified in the first half of the book the contribution of a pre-deuteronomistic 'collector', Fritz finds that the earliest draft already bears the stamp of an idea developed within deuteronomistic theology, and contains no tradition earlier than the state. In addition to many disparate supplements, he identifies two further editorial contributions: his RedD corresponds closely to Smend's DtrN, while his RedP speaks for itself. F. has taken independent and up-to-date interest in the topographical issues raised by the second half of Joshua. On text-critical issues, F. retains Noth's preference for the MT. Very many minor MT pluses over against Septuagint are recognized as late gloses, but no systematic account is offered of major MT pluses. The verdict on Auld's larger claims is still in preparation. 'Despite the fact that the Greek preserves many readings that are preferable to MT, Septuagint as a whole offers a text neither better than nor different from the familiar Hebrew, but rather further development of it.' Beyond this summary we are directed to the still incomplete dissertation of F.'s assistant, C. den Hertog.

    A. G. AULD

GLEDHILL, TOM: *The Message of the Song of Songs. The Lyrics of Love* (The Bible Speaks Today). 1994. Pp. 254. (Inter-Varsity Press, Leicester-Downers Grove IL. Price: £8.99. ISBN 0 85110 967 5)

Not as conservative a writer as series and publisher might suggest, G. attempts 'to view the Song primarily as a literary poetic exploration of human love'. In so doing, he refuses to discern any linear development in the Song, allowing it repetitiveness, ambiguity and vagueness — like all good poetry. Unafraid of the explicit sexuality of the Song, G. suggests its best context is that of a wedding celebration. Wisely, he refuses to use the Song as 'a moral social tract', preferring to see it as 'a celebration of love in all its dimensions' — while allowing that even such celebrations may have much to say about human relationships. There is much that is sensible and useful for readers of all persuasions, but not everyone would accept that the Song is about only love and sex *within* betrothal and marriage. And G.'s claim that God is everywhere assumed in the Song sounds a bit like special pleading — it could be said that the Deity's absence from the Song is saying that intense human passion can block out consideration for anything other than the object of one's desire — even consideration for God!

    C. H. KNIGHTS

GÓMEZ ARANDA, MARIANO: *El comentario de Abraham Ibn Ezra al Libro del Eclesiastés (Introducción, traducción y edición crítica)* (Testos y Estudios 'Cardenal Cisneros' de la Biblia Políglota Matritense 56). 1994. Pp. cxxii, 220, 128* (Heb.). (Instituto de Filología del CSIC, Madrid. N.P. ISBN 84 00 07402 5)

Given the importance of Ibn Ezra's commentary on Ecclesiastes as his earliest dated prose composition, written in Italy in 1140, and as a fine example of his grammatical, philosophical and polemical exegesis, this critical edition is a welcome addition to current literature on the intriguing Spanish commentator. The text is based on British Library MS Add. 27298 (catalogued as late 12th-century Franco-German) and is accompanied by an apparatus indebted to seventeen other codices in European libraries. The editor offers descriptions and critical assessments of these, as well as of seventeen others excluded from the apparatus, and attempts to explain the relationship between the manuscripts. The translation is carefully presented and generously annotated and there are six reproductions of folios from various manuscripts. Also included are brief treatments of Ibn Ezra's life and work, earlier Jewish exegesis, and the commentator's methods, style and sources, as well as detailed bibliography and indexes.

    S. C. REIF

GRYSON, ROGER and DEPROOST, P.-A. (eds): *Commentaires de Jerome sur le Prophete Isaie. Introduction. Livres V–VII* (Vetus Latina: Aus der Geschichte der lateinischen Bibel 27). With the collaboration of J. Coulie, E. Crousse, and V. Somers. 1994. Pp. 470–872. (Herder, Freiburg. N.P. ISBN 3 451 21947 6; ISSN 0571 9070)

This book forms the second volume of the series which will offer a full critical edition of Jerome's *Commentary on Isaiah*. The first volume, with its impressive introduction, was reviewed in *B.L.* 1994, p. 60. The high standard of editing apparent in that first volume is maintained here. The introductory essays to this book include detailed analysis of the manuscripts and pioneering work on the textual tradition of Books 5–7. There is also a significant and very valuable treatment of Origen's critical signs obelus and asterisk as they feature in Jerome's works, particularly in his commentaries on the Prophets.

C. T. R. HAYWARD

HACKING, PHILIP: *Isaiah. Free to Suffer and to Serve* (Crossway Bible Guides). 1994. Pp. 213. (Crossway Books; distributed by Inter-Varsity, Nottingham. Price: £5.99. ISBN 1 85684 082 4)

This simple paperback is aimed at Christian Bible study groups of a conservative evangelical persuasion. The Book of Isaiah, assumed to be an authorial unity, is divided into twenty-two sections, with brief (and often quite penetrating) questions for discussion. The book has no scholarly pretensions, but should serve its intended purpose.

R. J. COGGINS

HAGELIA, HALLVARD: *Numbering the Stars. A Phraseological Analysis of Genesis 15* (Coniectanea Biblica, Old Testament Series 39). 1994. Pp. 252. (Almqvist & Wiksell, Stockholm. Price: SEK 204.00. ISBN 91 22 01591 4)

H. does not investigate the source critical questions of Genesis 15 but focuses on the Masoretic Text at its face value. The chapter is divided into two units; 15:1–6 which describes Abraham's belief in God, and 15:7–21 where the theme is of the promise of the land. The study focuses on the relation in vocabulary, phraseology, context, and theological kinship between Genesis 15 and other parts of the Old Testament such as 2 Sam. 7, 1 Kgs 3, 2 Kgs 17:1–23 and Isa. 7:1–17. Similarities are also noted with late pre-exilic or exilic prophets. H. sets Genesis 15 in the context of Deuteronomism where it has its literary origin. Whilst recognizing that it contains early traditions, he dates the literary product around or after the exile. The discussion finishes with the main theme of the chapter: God's covenant with Abraham. H.'s exegesis contains many useful insights, though his dating of the chapter may be queried by some. Unfortunately there are a number of misprints including 'Melchizedek the king of Sodom' (p. 128).

P. HARLAND

HESS, RICHARD S. and TSUMURA, DAVID TOSHIO (eds): *'I Studied Inscriptions from before the Flood': Ancient Near Eastern, Literary, and Linguistic Approaches to Genesis 1–11* (Sources for Biblical and Theological Study 4). 1994. Pp. xvi, 480. (Eisenbrauns, Winona Lake IN. Price: $34.50. ISBN 0 931464 88 9)

The aims and format of this series were noted in *B.L.* 1993, pp. 87, 113. The editors have written a three-part introduction on 150 years of comparative studies on Genesis 1–11, the Genesis and ancient Near Eastern stories of creation and the flood, and the genealogies of Genesis 1–11 and comparative literature. The rest of the volume is made of reprinted (and some translated) essays (several of them classics). Part 1 explores ancient Near Eastern and comparative approaches; part 2 concentrates on literary and linguistic approaches. The essays have not been updated in most cases (though W. G. Lambert has added a postscript to his 1965 article on the Babylonian background of Genesis) and some errors have been corrected. This is a well-produced and useful collection at a reasonable price.

L. L. GRABBE

HOUTMAN, CORNELIS: *Exodus.* Vol. 1 (Historical Commentary on the Old Testament). 1993. Pp. xix, 554. (Kok, Kampen. Price: fl. 97.50. ISBN 90 242 6213 5)

This is the English translation of the Dutch original noted in *B.L.* 1987 (p. 50). The commentary includes a fresh translation with detailed exegesis of the Hebrew text and full discussion of grammatical and syntactical problems including references to major grammars. That only 7:13 is reached in 554 pages is due to a long introduction of 213 pages. The introduction, (agreeably?!) light on documentary hypotheses, contains detailed word studies of over fifty common Hebrew words (like *'iš, yâd*), numerals, personal and divine names, and names of peoples, countries and places. Attention is given to historical setting (not seen as of prime importance for the book's basic message) and to the significance of the Exodus event in other books of both Old and New Testaments. Particularly significant is the attention given to flora and fauna — forty-five pages, which examine plants and animals occurring throughout the Hebrew Bible as well as in Exodus — naturalists take note! Excellent bibliographical guidance is given at the close of each section, extending even to 'the southern Sinai route in ecological perspective'! Thus the book is a valuable collection of material for naturalists as well as biblical scholars. We look forward to the remaining volumes.   J. G. SNAITH

Johannes Chrysostomos, Kommentar zu Hiob (Patristische Texte und Studien 35). Edited and translated by Ursula and Dieter Hagedorn. 1990. Pp. xliii, 323. (de Gruyter, Berlin–New York. Price: DM 284.00. ISBN 3 11 012540 4; ISSN 0553 4003)

The commentary on Job by Chrysostom was edited and published (by H. Sorlin) just two years prior to this edition (i.e. in 1988). Why, as one might ask, was this edition embarked upon? The answer to this question is explained by the Hagedorns as a genuine misunderstanding, and this despite their knowledge that Sorlin had been working in the same specific field! It is clear that the Hagedorns are at home in the patristic understanding of Job, having worked on commentaries by Julian the Arian and Olympiodorus of Alexandria. After documenting fully the textual basis for the translation and the layout of the edition, the text and translation follow together with a critical apparatus. The layout is exemplary — the Greek text beautifully set out with the German translation on the opposite page. There are copious and informative endnotes and several indexes including a substantial Greek word index. This edition will be welcomed by patristic scholars, by Job scholars, and by those interested in the history of exegesis.   R. B. SALTERS

JONES, GWILYM H.: *1 & 2 Chronicles* (Old Testament Guides). 1993. pp. 139. (Sheffield Academic Press. Price: £5.95/$9.95. ISBN 1 85075 515 1; ISSN 0264 6498)

In the first half of this book, J. works descriptively through 1 and 2 Chronicles with attention to the structure and major themes of each section; for the genealogies and the account of the united monarchy he works sequentially, while for the history of the divided monarchy he sensibly treats the material more by topic. In the second half of the book, he discusses the Chronicler's sources (cautiously positive) and the use made of them, authorship (levitical; Ezra and Nehemiah are excluded; only a few later additions to the work are accepted) and date (late 5th to mid-4th century), purpose of writing ('an interpretation of history', which allows for the inclusion of various particular suggestions which other scholars have made) and theology. The style of presentation is clear, and full attention is paid to a wide variety of secondary literature. This is a valuable contribution to a most useful series. It is indicative of the vigour with which the books of Chronicles are being studied at present that a major commentary (S. Japhet) and several monographs have appeared since J. completed his work.   H. G. M. WILLIAMSON

KEEL, OTHMAR: *The Song of Songs. A Continental Commentary*. Translator Frederick J. Gaiser. 1994. Pp. ix, 308. (Fortress, Minneapolis. Price $40.00. ISBN 0 8006 9507 0)

There have been no changes to the 1986 German original (*B.L.* 1987, p. 50) except that NRSV generally replaces K.'s own translation of the Hebrew. As before, the strength of this work lies in the line drawings (158 in all) which illustrate the text remarkably, especially as they are located at appropriate places in the commentary, not lumped together at the end. Although not brought up-to-date, the commentary, with its main focus on imagery, is still excellent and K. always provides an explanation for the difficulties he raises. According to K., the Song of Songs comprises forty-two songs of desire, with their closest parallels in Egyptian love poems, though he does make reference to other literature. There is no overall formal structure, and the work can best be understood in terms of its cultural setting. The commentary is intended for the informed non-specialist reader and some Hebrew terms are discussed. A brief bibliography is provided and there is an index.   W. G. E. WATSON

KILIAN, R.: *Jesaja II. 13–39* (Die Neue Echter Bible: Kommentar zum Alten Testament mit der Einheitsübersetzung 32). 1994. Pp. 95–217. (Echter Verlag, Würzburg. Price: DM 28.00/SwF 29.00/AS 219.00. ISBN 2 429 01596 0)

The first volume of this commentary was described and evaluated positively in *B.L.* 1988, p. 60. The present volume has no additional introduction, but starts straight in with ch. 13. K. indicates on several occasions (e.g. pp. 162, 174, and 203–04) that he has changed his mind in the meantime about the authorship of parts of the earlier chapters, and his more radical opinions are apparent throughout the present work. Very little remains of Isaiah's own composition: the oracles against the nations are almost entirely post-exilic, frequent appeal being made to the use of the names of nations as ciphers and to the occurrence of *vaticinia ex eventu*; 28:1–6 is a late addition to (24–)27; ch. 30 in its entirety is exilic or post-exilic, and so on. Only 31:1, 3 seem to be ascribed without qualification to the 8th-century prophet. Perhaps surprisingly, therefore, apart from chapters 34–35, little attention is paid to connections with the later parts of the book of Isaiah. Since it seems to be the policy of this series not to refer to other secondary literature, it is inevitable that some of K.'s conclusions give the impression of being cavalier and dogmatic, but he does supply what justification the limited space at his disposal allows. The comments on the text are concise, but often to the point. Even for those unable to follow K. in all his critical positions, he succeeds in outlining how the book might have been read in the Hellenistic period.

H. G. M. WILLIAMSON

LARKIN, KATRINA J. A.: *The Eschatology of Second Zechariah. A Study of the Formation of a Mantological Wisdom Anthology* (Contributions to Biblical Exegesis and Theology 6). 1994. Pp. 267. (Kok Pharos, Kampen. Price: fl. 69.90. ISBN 90 390 0101 4)

This amply documented and persuasively argued study presents a strong case against the view of O. Plöger and P. D. Hanson that apocalyptic eschatology is a theology of dissidence, pessimistic, dualistic, and detached from history. On the other hand, M. Fishbane's contention that mantic wisdom contributed to apocalyptic eschatology and that 'mantological exegesis' has been used to interpret obscure traditions is given general acceptance (though with some reservations) and carried farther. Taking into account the Masoretic divisions of Second Zechariah, detailed examination is made of 9:1–11:3; 11:4–17; 12:1–13:9; and 14:1–21, which is distinct from the preceding sections. Instances of mantological exegesis, inner-textual exegesis, typology, and other lesser features are noted; and the conclusion is drawn that in Zechariah 9–13 there is a mantological anthology (similar to Amos 7–8; Zechariah 1–6; and Daniel 7–12) constructed, as in Job 28, around an 'adversarial centrepiece', the Shepherd Allegory in 11. Evidence is provided of the links between wisdom and apocalyptic. This is a fine piece of exact scholarship which points the way to further research.

G. W. ANDERSON

LAU, WOLFGANG: *Schriftgelehrte Prophetie in Jes 56–66. Eine Untersuchung zu den literarischen Bezügen in den letzten elf Kapiteln des Jesajabuches* (Beihefte zur Zeitschrift für die alttestamentliche Wissenschaft 225). 1994. Pp. ix, 357. (de Gruyter, Berlin–New York. Price: DM 172.00. ISBN 3 11 014239 2; ISSN 0934 2575)

This Kiel dissertation is an examination of the contents of the last eleven chapters of Isaiah. Chs 60–62 are assigned to the prophet Trito-Isaiah. Three passages are classified as individual texts: 56:1–8, 63:1–6, 63:7–64:11. The remainder, apart from a few later glosses, are assigned to three circles of tradents, of which the first is fairly closely related to the prophet, while the other two are concerned particularly with respectively the cult and social justice. Four characteristics indicate a measure of continuity with the earlier part of Isaiah: the Zion tradition, the Servant tradition, the concept of the 'Holy One of Israel', and the Exodus tradition. The overall thesis is that these chapters are 'learned' prophecy, built on direct exegesis of earlier prophecy which was already regarded as a corpus of sacred texts. Most of the book consists of detailed examination of the individual passages from the particular point of view of their use of earlier 'Scripture', and it will be indispensable to future students of this part of Isaiah.

A. GELSTON

LEEUWEN, C. VAN: *Joël* (De Prediking van het Oude Testament). 1993. Pp. 261. (G. F. Callenbach, Nijkerk. Price: fl 89.50. ISBN 90 266 0318 5)

That such a short book as Joel should merit a commentary of over 250 pages is an indication of the thoroughness with which the author treats the text-critical, philological, and literary problems of Joel, with scrupulous attention to the secondary literature. The book is held to be a unity, composed in the late 7th century by a prophet with close connections with the Jerusalem temple. Overall, the book is divided into seven sections which exhibit what the author calls a concentric structure: a: the land devastated by locusts and plague (1:4–20) b: the advancing army on the day of the Lord (2:1–11) c: call for conversion (2:12–14) d: general gathering for penitence (2:15–17) c[1]: response of God (Heb. 2:18–3:5) b[1]: advancing nations on the day of the Lord (Heb. 4:1–17) a[1]: the land fruitful (Heb. 4:18–21). Further, similar patterns in sections of seven or eight are found at various points in the book. This is a rich source of information for the interpretation of Joel.

J. W. ROGERSON

LEEUWEN, C. VAN: *Obadja* (De Prediking van het Oude Testament). 1993. Pp. 115. (G. F. Callenbach, Nijkerk. Price: fl. 54.50. ISBN 90 266 0328 2)

In this companion volume to the author's commentary on Joel, extensive discussion of the date and authorship of this problematic book reach the following conclusions. The material common to Obadiah 1–9 and Jeremiah 49 is assigned to a common, older source which Jeremiah used more freely than Obadiah while sometimes remaining closer to the original; that is, if the divergencies are not to be explained by development in an oral tradition. Regarding the similarities between Obadiah and Joel priority is given to Joel granted the author's dating of the latter in the late 7th century. Obadiah is seen as a prophet with cultic links who proclaimed salvation to Judah and Jerusalem soon after the tragedy of 587–86. Edom stands, eschatologically, for the enemies of God and his people, whose downfall will be brought about by God's irresistible power.   J. W. ROGERSON

LESCOW, THEODOR: *Das Buch Maleachi. Texttheorie—Auslegung—Kanontheorie* (Arbeiten zur Theologie 75). 1993. Pp. 208. (Calwer, Stuttgart. Price: DM 78.00/SwF 79.50/AS 609. ISBN 3 7668 3224 7)

L. here applies to a particular text the principles of linear and concentric structuring discerned in his *Stufenschema* (*B. L.* 1994, p. 91). It was originally envisaged that this work should form part of the series of Calwer Bibel-kommentare, but the detailed concern with textual structuring made it unsuitable for that purpose. The introduction recapitulates his earlier work, setting out the role of the 'kommunikatives Handlungsspiel' in the context of the 'Stufenschema', and its terminology is found in the introduction to each section. Nevertheless, the work retains many features of a commentary, but it operates at different levels according to the assumed development of the work known as Malachi. The basic text dates from 480 BCE, and this was supple-mented by a sermonic editor *c*. 410, a commentator *c*. 300 and before the final form was reached there were glosses added to the 3rd century. These developments are of importance also for our understanding of the final shaping of the prophetic canon, and the last part of the book is devoted to a discussion of some recent theories of the formation of the Book of the Twelve and to the promulgation of L.'s own ideas, which turn on the themes of *torah* and of the day of the Lord. An appendix is devoted to the significance of *torah* in Jer. 8:8f. A wide-ranging study, therefore, despite its modest dimen-sions, and one that contributes to several contemporary hermeneutical issues.

R. J. COGGINS

MCCOMISKEY, THOMAS EDWARD (ed.): *The Minor Prophets. An Exege-tical and Expository Commentary.* Vol. 2: *Obadiah, Jonah, Micah, Nahum and Habakkuk.* 1993. Pp. xii, 495–908. (Baker, Grand Rapids MI. Price $39.99. ISBN 0 8010 6307 8)

In this volume (for the first see *B. L.* 1993, p. 65) the commentaries are by J. J. Niehaus (Obadiah), J. Baldwin (Jonah), B. K. Waltke (Micah), T. Long-man (Nahum), and F. F. Bruce (Habakkuk). Particular interests of the authors are often evident (e.g. Waltke on syntax, Longman on poetic style, Bruce on Qumran exegesis). After a brief introduction and select biblio-graphy, the commentator's translation and the NRSV are set side by side, although differences of translation tend to be left unexplained. There follows an 'exegesis' and an 'exposition'. In the former textual, lexical, and grammati-cal questions are discussed, with reference to pointed Hebrew. The exposi-tion traces the broader argument of the prophet and seeks to relate it to the rest of the Bible and the contemporary world. Inevitably there is a certain amount of repetition, and the commentary format means that complex questions about how the Bible should be read today cannot be treated adequately. Frequent recourse to technical vocabulary will make reading demanding for those without Hebrew. The critical stance is forthrightly conservative, with little discussion of other points of view. From within this tradition the authors offer a solid and positive treatment.   P. P. JENSON

MARGAIN, JEAN: *Le Livre de Daniel. Commentaire philologique du texte araméen* (Les Classiques Bibliques Beauchesne: Session de Langues Bibliques 4). 1994. Pp. 80. (Beauchesne, Paris. Price: Fr 60.00. ISBN 2 7010 1318 6; ISSN 0183 9977)

This is part of a series aimed at teaching the 'biblical languages' (of which the first three volumes are translated from English). Except for a concise five-page grammatical survey and an index to some main grammatical points, this consists of philological notes to the entire Aramaic section of Daniel. These are mainly of an elementary nature, relating to parsing and basic syntax, but both teachers and students will find it useful. A bibliography of reference grammars and philological studies would have been a useful addition.   L. L. GRABBE

MASON, REX: *Zephaniah, Habakkuk, Joel* (Old Testament Guides). 1994. Pp. 132. (Sheffield Academic Press. Price: £5.95/$9.95. ISBN 1 85075 718 6; ISSN 0264 6498)

The author has already contributed to the same series with a volume *Micah, Nahum, Obadiah* (*B.L.* 1992, p. 80). This book is written with the same useful and balanced appraisal of each of the three prophetic books studied. In the part on Zephaniah there are some interesting pages on 'The Prophetic Corpus in Miniature', and readers will find the chapter on 'The History of Criticism' quite useful with particular attention given to the work of Ben Zvi. In his discussion of the theology and function of the book of Habakkuk, M. urges us to 'view the material in the book as a whole as of cultic origin' but rejects the recent view of Haak that the book is a 'prophetic liturgy complete as it stands'. As far as the book of Joel is concerned, its date 'remains a mystery'. The view that the book is a unity and the work of one person is rejected; and it is argued that 3:1–4:21 (Eng. 2:28–3:31) 'comes from other and later circles'. This short volume serves its purpose well.

K. J. CATHCART

MITCHELL, GORDON: *Together in the Land. A Reading of the Book of Joshua* (Journal for the Study of the Old Testament Supplement 134). 1993. pp. 219. (Sheffield Academic Press. Price: £30.00/$45.00. ISBN 1 85075 409 8; ISSN 0309 0787)

M.'s 'reading of the Book of Joshua' originates in a Heidelberg dissertation. Part I retells 'the narrative of conquest' in five chapters: 'Take possession of the land which the LORD gives you to possess' (1:1–5:15); 'The city and all that is within it shall be devoted to destruction' (6:1–8:29); 'You shall do to the city and its king as you did to Jericho and its king' (8:30–12:24); 'There still remains much land to be occupied' (13:1–22:9); 'And you shall perish quickly from off the good land' (22:10–24:33). Part II presents 'the image of the nations' in three: 'All the occupants of the land'; 'When all the kings heard . . .'; 'And they dwelt in the midst of Israel unto this day'. Then the

Conclusion is briefly stated (pp. 185–90). M. follows Rendtorff's more recent concentration on synchronic analysis of compositional structures and offers much well-informed and attentive reading of Joshua: 'What is the book about?' is his focus, not 'What happened back then?' He is illuminating on several expressions (despite a scatter of Hebrew misprints), but does not probe 'hardened their hearts'; *ḥerem*, which in Welch's view (on Deut. 7:1–5) is dramatic not literal, is expounded 'as a literary device for advocating a strict separation from the nations'. Though he acknowledges that diachronic interests are not excluded, his minimal use of Greek Joshua spoils a number of his points.

A. G. Auld

MURPHY, ROLANDE E., O. CARM.: *Responses to 101 Questions on the Psalms and Other Writings*. 1994. Pp. xii, 129. (Paulist Press, New York–Mahwah NJ. Price: $8.95. ISBN 0 8091 3526 4)

This book, one of a series (cf. *B.L.* 1994, p. 137), seeks to provide a basic introduction to the Writings. The questions range from the sublime (how do you understand God's 'answer' to Job?) to what might almost deserve the description ridiculous (what is your favourite book among the Writings?), from the complex (where can we find the history of Israel after its return to Jerusalem in 539?) to the straightforward (what are the shortest, and the longest psalms?), and sometimes the question is begged (why is the book of Lamentations so boring?). Some of the questions are asked and answered from a specifically Christian perspective, but the Jewish origin of the material is acknowledged and, on the whole, handled sensitively. There is an inevitable patchiness, and it could certainly be argued that Ruth deserves more than two questions! But the reader will have been introduced to a number of issues relevant to the study of the books, and to wider issues such as the nature of the Writings, Apocalyptic, and Wisdom (although surprisingly the question, 'What is the Wisdom Literature?' is not asked explicitly).

A. H. W. Curtis

NOGALSKI, JAMES: *Literary Precursors to the Book of Twelve* (Beihefte zur Zeitschrift für die alttestamentliche Wissenschaft 217). 1993. Pp. ix, 301. (de Gruyter, Berlin–New York. Price: DM 138.00. ISBN 3 11 013702 X; ISSN 0934 2575)

NOGALSKI, JAMES: *Redactional Processes in the Book of the Twelve* (Beihefte zur Zeitschrift für die alttestamentliche Wissenschaft 218). 1993. pp. ix, 300. (de Gruyter, Berlin–New York. Price: DM 138.00. ISBN 3 11 013767 4; ISSN 0934 2575)

These two volumes attempt a redactional study of the Book of the Twelve and aim to make sense of it as a single planned work. N. detects catch-words consistently at the 'seams' of the individual books and uses these to launch his investigation. He argues that they have been deliberately inserted by redactors to create meaningful links between books. In its Masoretic order (which N. accepts as original) the Book is a shaped composition, not a collection of already redacted works. N. concludes that it was constructed from two independent collections, a 'Deuteronomistic corpus' (Hosea, Amos, Micah, Zephaniah) and a 'Haggai-Zechariah corpus' (Haggai, Zechariah 1–8) which were merged, with minimal redactional shaping.

The Deuteronomistic corpus was compiled after 587 to explain the catastrophe. Hopeful eschatological passages were added in the early post-exilic period, together with Haggai-Zechariah 1–8. Later development centred on Joel which, in its present form, was constructed by redactors, probably late in the Persian period, out of already existing material. A 'Joel-related layer' (Obadiah, Nahum, Habakkuk and Malachi) was also incorporated. Jonah and Zechariah 9–14 were adapted and included after Alexander's conquest. A short review cannot do justice to this complex study. It has the weakness of redaction criticism, forced to work with so many unprovable possibilities, but N. is aware of this. Even if he does not convince at every point, there is much illuminating argument. Alas, both volumes display an unacceptable level of careless English and typographical errors.

J. M. DINES

POHLMANN, KARL-FRIEDRICH: *Ezechielstudien. Zur Redaktionsgeschichte des Buches and zur Frage nach den ältesten Texten* (Beihefte zur Zeitschrift für die alttestamentliche Wissenschaft 202). 1992. Pp. ix, 274. (de Gruyter, Berlin–New York. Price: DM 138.00. ISBN 3 11 012976 0; ISSN 0934 2575)

This is a detailed and careful work in traditional historical-critical mode, representing an approach to the book quite different from the 'holistic' reading now favoured by Greenberg and some others. The volume falls into two main sections. The first deals with the development of the book of Ezekiel, focusing particularly on what P. calls the 'Gola(Exile)-Oriented Redaction' (exemplified by chapters such as Ezek. 14 and 24) and on texts dealing with the theme of the 'gathering of the dispersed' (particularly chs 20 and 36). The second examines what are argued to be the earliest texts in the book, specifically Ezek. 15; 17; 18; 19:1–14; 23; and 31. This is a stimulating and well-organized interim report, which whets the reader's appetite for the large commentary on the book of Ezekiel which P. is preparing for the series Das Alte Testament Deutsch.

P. M. JOYCE

RANIERI, A. A.: *Studio grammaticale e semantico del parallelismo in Proverbi I–IX. Un contributo alla comprensione della formula introduttiva dell'istruzione sapienziale* (Studium Biblicum Franciscanum, Thesis ad Doctoratum 337). 1993. Pp. 153. (Pontificium Athenaeum Antonianum Sectio Hierosolymitana Facultatis Theologiae, Jerusalem. N.P.)

From a thesis running to over 250 pages only ch. 3, prefaced by a brief introduction, is presented here. Using techniques developed over the past few decades for the analysis of poetry, which the author first assesses, he examines the introductory formula in the 'invitation to listen' sections of Prov. 1–9. He concludes that a single author was responsible both for the formula and for Prov. 1–3. His presentation is very detailed and closely argued. However, in its truncated form the thesis is difficult to follow (ch. 2, the poetic analysis of Prov. 1–3, is missing and would have been useful) and the constant use of abbreviations does not help. It is to be hoped that eventually the study will be published in full.

W. G. E. WATSON

ROTTZOLL, DIRK U. (ed.): *Rabbinischer Kommentar zum Buch Genesis. Darstellung der Rezeption des Buches Genesis in Mischna und Talmud unter Angabe targumischer und midraschischer Paralleltexte* (Studia Judaica 14). 1994. Pp. x, 539. (de Gruyter, Berlin–New York. Price: DM 198.00. ISBN 3 11 014231 7)

The format of R.'s useful index is similar to the well-known Strack-Billerbeck *Kommentar*. It is primarily a collection of passages from the Mishnah and the two Talmuds, quoted in German translation, which specifically cite passages from Genesis. (Those passages alluding to Genesis verses without citing them are generally omitted.) In addition, the footnotes often have cross references to 'parallel texts' in targumic and midrashic literature.

L. L. GRABBE

SAILHAMER, JOHN: *The NIV Compact Bible Commentary*. 1994. Pp. 608. (Zondervan, Grand Rapids MI. Price: $14.99. ISBN 0 310 51460 6)

Commission a one-author commentary from an *Alttestamentler*, and the Old Testament gets the space it deserves. Commission it from an enthusiast for the Pentateuch as narrative (*B.L.* 1993, p. 68) and that gets lots of space. Commission it from the author of a commentary on Genesis (in a volume of the *Expositor's Commentary* not noted in *B.L.*) and Genesis gets 52 pages; contrast three pages for Job, twelve for Isaiah. The stance is conservative (one Isaiah for the twelve pages), the non-argument is sometimes weak ('we can say with certainly [*sic*] that the Old Testament that we have today is the same as that of Jesus'), the literary approach is often interesting (e.g. on the arrangement of the Psalter), but the quantity of straight paraphrase of the text is a shame.

J. GOLDINGAY

SALTERS, R. B.: *Jonah & Lamentations* (Old Testament Guides). 1994. Pp. 125 (Sheffield Academic Press. Price: £5.95/$9.95. ISBN 1 85075 719 4; ISSN 0264 6498)

This volume fully matches up to the high standard set by others in the series of Sheffield guides. The introductory chapters indicate the wider influence of the books on literature, art and music. The books are then outlined and set within their biblical and Near Eastern context, so far as this is possible. The views of other scholars on the difficult issues of the date, integrity and purpose of Jonah and Lamentations are summarised with scrupulous fairness, but S. also states his own views. 'Didactic story' is the best classification for Jonah and the psalm is not original, being a later scribal composition intended as Jonah's thanksgiving on being delivered onto dry land. The purpose of Jonah is complex, as might be expected from its perennial interest. Lamentations is probably a series of individual laments with a communal intention, written by one person shortly after 586 BCE. A concluding discussion of the theology of the book corresponds to the chapter on Jonah's purpose. The note of vengeance is censured, although discussion of the psychological and pastoral aspects of lament might have provided an additional perspective. S. has written an exemplary introduction that combines clarity and sophistication.

P. P. JENSON

SCHARBERT, J.: *Rut*; HENTSCHEL, G.: *1 Samuel* (Die Neue Echter Bible: Kommentar zum Alten Testament mit der Einheitsübersetzung 33). 1994. Pp. 160 (Echter Verlag, Würzburg. Price: DM 34.00/SwF 35.00/AS 265.00. ISBN 3 429 01597 9)

Like all the other volumes already published in this series of Catholic commentaries, the aim of this combined work on Ruth and 1 Samuel is to provide help for a better understanding of the text of the uniform translation of the Bible. That translation, which is intended for liturgical, preaching and study purposes, is printed in the commentary, and the exposition of it is concise and to the point. Long discussions of exegetical problems are avoided, and the emphasis is on a theological understanding of the text and on its kerygmatic content. The exposition of each of these books is preceded by a short introductory survey of its contents and a selected list of commentaries and other relevant publications.

G. H. JONES

SCHREINER, SUSAN E.: *Where Shall Wisdom Be Found? Calvin's Exegesis of Job from Medieval and Modern Perspectives*. 1994. Pp. x, 264. (University of Chicago Press, Chicago and London. Price: $41.50/£28.75. ISBN 0 226 74043 9)

This interesting study in the history of exegesis compares Calvin's *Sermons on Job* with treatments by Gregory, Maimonides, and Aquinas, and with selected modern readings of Job, where the focus is on such literary works as Kafka's *The Trial* rather than on modern commentators. Taking as her central theme the problem that appearances can be deceptive, S. concludes that assessments of Job's 'perceptual and noetic ability' are directly related to the hermeneutical method adopted: Gregory's allegorical approach produces a Job wise to the redemptive nature of suffering, while Calvin's literal approach portrays a Job with faith in, but little understanding of, the mysterious ways of providence. Despite the nowadays obligatory preoccupation with theory (Foucault is as well represented in the index as Bildad), and a tendency to political correctness so marked that the Calvin scholar François Wendel becomes Françoise, this is a generally well-written book. The central chapters on Calvin are particularly good, illuminated by comparisons with the contemporary expositions of Job by Cajetan, Brenz, and Oecolampadius. But it is surprising that S. does not engage with Bouwsma's assertion that Calvin's 'facile moralism' made him particularly ill-equipped to expound Job. Indeed, the weakness of S.'s study is that no especially strong case is made for making Calvin the pivot of the history of Job interpretation.

D. V. N. BAGCHI

SCHULZ-FLÜGEL, EVA (ed.): *Gregorius Eliberritanus, Epithalamium sive Explanatio in Canticis Canticorum* (Vetus Latina: Aus der Geschichte der Latinischen Bibel 26). 1994. (Herder, Freiburg. N.P. ISBN 3 451 21940 9; 0571 9070)

Gregorius Eliberritanus (in Spain: Elvira) is next to Ambrose the most important witness to the Old Latin text of the Song of Songs. S.-F. broadly examines the textual history of Gregory's commentary analyzing its sources and traditions and revealing connections with other texts. Lastly, the book provides a new edition of the Latin text of the *Epithalamium*, of texts in Origin's Commentary on Galatians and of an anonymous commentary on the Song of Songs possibly from the pen of Gregory. The writing unfolds the salvation history along five major themes: The incarnation of Christ as promise of salvation; the status of the Church and how to preserve it; the nature and work of Christ; the Second Coming as the final destination of history and the Church's pilgrimage through history and its final consummation. For Gregory the incarnation is the central expression of the Christian faith, and his clashes with Arianism are evident in this context. The text is marked by a deep inner piety and a great enjoyment of the use of allegory.

P. W. COXON

SEITZ, CHRISTOPHER R.: *Isaiah 1–39* (Interpretation, A Bible Commentary for Teaching and Preaching). 1993. Pp. xvi, 271. (Westminster/John Knox, Louisville KY. Price: $22.00. ISBN 0 8042 3131 1)

This is an admirable addition to a commentary designed as a resource for those who interpret the Bible in Church. However, given that it takes as read the hypotheses of Second and Third Isaiah, it is hardly a book for absolute beginners. S. offers a reading that 'acknowledges and then moves beyond the historical prophet and canonical presentation in order to recover something of the theological coherence available to precritical readers' (p. 4). In the light of work which shows that First Isaiah underwent a Babylonian redaction, S.

feels the need to provide an apologia for a commentary which only looks at Isa. 1–39. In spite of doubts about a tripartite structure he breaks the commentary down into three sections — 1–12; 13–27; 28–39. S.'s 'final form' approach is least persuasive with 28–39 where the cohesion of the material is difficult to determine. There is a manifest lack of enthusiasm for the quest for the historical Isaiah. Rather, S. pragmatically expounds how the prophet and his message was perceived and reinterpreted by subsequent generations. Indeed, the fact that the 'call' occurs in ch. 6 is taken to indicate that the message has priority over the prophet.   D. J. BRYAN

SELMAN, MARTIN J.: *1 Chronicles. An Introduction and Commentary* (Tyndale Old Testament Commentaries). 1994. Pp. 264. (Inter-Varsity Press, Leicester–Downers Grove IL. Price: £9.50. ISBN 0 85111 847 X)

SELMAN, MARTIN J.: *2 Chronicles. A Commentary* (Tyndale Old Testament Commentaries). 1994. Pp. 265–551. (Inter-Varsity Press, Leicester–Downers Grove IL. Price: £8.50. ISBN 0 85111 848 8)

These two volumes on the books of Chronicles provide a valuable addition to this series of commentaries whose primary aim is to give a full exegesis of the text by working through it by section-by-section. In his Introduction the author has taken into account recent trends in Chronicles studies, concluding that the Chronicler's aim was to offer an interpretation of the Bible as he knew it and not to provide an historical alternative to Samuel-Kings, and that it is to be treated as a separate entity from Ezra-Nehemiah with which it did not share a common aim nor common authorship. The work as a whole is regarded as the Chronicler's own composition, and therefore S. does not allow for minor secondary additions to the work or for a secondary reworking of it. The exegesis of short sections and of individual verses is full and very successful in elucidating the meaning of the text. For a commentary of its size and aim, it has given adequate consideration to current opinion, and one of the strengths of its exegesis is the plentiful cross-references to other parts of Scripture.   G. H. JONES

SNELL, DANIEL C.: *Twice-Told Proverbs and the Composition of the Book of Proverbs*. 1993. Pp. xiv, 146. (Eisenbrauns, Winona Lake IN. Price: $32.50. ISBN 0 931464 66 8)

The author attempts to find a solution to the problem of the composition of Proverbs by means of a single criterion: the frequency and distribution of repeated verses and prhases in the book. Complete with tables and charts, his book is the result of much painstaking work. Every repetition in the book is analysed, classified and assessed. On this basis S. has constructed a comprehensive theory about the chronological order in which the various parts of Proverbs were completed and assembled. One wonders why he has deliberately left out of consideration possible correlations between his criterion and other more familiar criteria such as differences of style and content. As they stand, S.'s observations, though interesting and useful, hardly constitute an adequate basis for his hypothesis.   R. N. WHYBRAY

SPRINKLE, JOE M.: *'The Book of the Covenant'. A Literary Approach* (Journal for the Study of the Old Testament Supplement 174). 1994. Pp. 224. (Sheffield Academic Press. Price: £35.00/$52.50. ISBN 1 85075 467 5; ISSN 0309 0787)

S. argues that a synchronic 'literary approach' to biblical law is both possible and generally superior to heavily source-orientated exegesis. He

76   EXEGESIS AND MODERN TRANSLATIONS

begins by examining the narrative framework of the book of the covenant
whose difficulties he resolves by appeal to synoptic/resumptive repetition in
which the narrator treats one event two times. Detailed analysis of the
legislation follows in which S. argues that the author is using law as a vehicle
for expressing morality, rather than devising a detailed law code. He concludes that the book of the covenant is an artfully crafted unity well integrated
into the Pentateuch regardless of sources.   A. C. J. PHILLIPS

SPURGEON, CHARLES: *Psalms. Volume I* (The Crossway Classic Commentaries). 1993. Pp. xvi, 366. (Crossway Books, Wheaton IL. Price: £7.99. ISBN
1 85684 083 2)

SPURGEON, CHARLES: *Psalms. Volume II* (The Crossway Classic Commentaries). 1993. Pp. xiv, 374. (Crossway Books, Wheaton IL. Price: £7.99.
ISBN 1 85684 084 0)

To J. I. Packer and A. A. McGrath we owe this abridgement of the
commentary on the Psalms by the famous Baptist preacher Charles Spurgeon
(1834–92). Believing in the inspiration of all Scripture, S. was loth to pass over
any passage. The original work, *The Treasury of David*, appeared in seven
volumes from 1869 to 1883, in all some 3,000 pages. The present abridged
edition is of a handy size, clearly printed, and still substantial at around
420,000 words. S. wrote with the style of a lively speaker and with warm
devotion. In this new form, his exposition should reach a wide readership and
be greatly appreciated for its spiritual insights.   J. H. EATON

STOEBE, HANS JOACHIM: *Das zweite Buch Samuelis* (Kommentar zum
Alten Testament 8/2). Mit einer Zeittafel von Alfred Jepsen. 1994.
Pp. 550 + tables. (Gütersloher Verlagshaus, Gütersloh. Price: DM 350.00/
SwF 350/AS 2730. ISBN 3 579 04279 3)

This second part of S.'s Samuel commentary appears more than twenty
years after that on 1 Samuel which itself, although its date of publication was
1973, was apparently already completed in 1967 (*B.L.* 1974, p. 40). The
bibliography of the present volume, however, is reasonably up to date. The
general character of the work was described in the previous review. S. regards
2 Samuel as a distinct composition though it forms part of the Deuteronomistic History; he attributes to it a higher historical value than to 1 Samuel. Of its
major complexes, he regards chs 9–20 as a complete unit: the early chapters of
1 Kings are an integral part of the history of the reign of Solomon. Chs 9–20
are thus not to be regarded as a 'succession narrative' but a celebration of
David's kingship in terms of flight and triumphant return.   R. N. WHYBRAY

THOMPSON, HENRY O.: *The Book of Daniel. An Annotated Bibliography*.
1993. Pp.li, 547. (Garland, New York and London. Price: $84.00. ISBN
0 8240 4873 3)

Over 2,000 items are listed. Those in English have useful brief anno-
tations, though the non-English items less often have them. The heart of the
work is a strictly alphabetical listing. This is followed by a section on the main
journals, with the relevant articles listed in association with each one, and
finally some of the main PhD dissertations. There are indexes of authors
(where out of alphabetical order), citations, and subjects.   L. L. GRABBE

WERLITZ, JÜRGEN: *Studien zur literarkritischen Methode. Gericht und Heil in Jesaja 7, 1–17 und 29, 1–8* (Beihefte zur Zeitschrift für die alttestamentliche Wissenschaft 204). 1992. Pp. x, 351. (de Gruyter, Berlin–New York. Price: DM 138.00. ISBN 3 11 013488 8; ISSN 0934 2575)

In this substantially shortened reworking of a doctoral dissertation on justice and salvation in Isaiah 1–39, the author's terms of reference have been reduced from thirty-nine chapters to a few verses, and the emphasis shifted in the direction of methodology. By zooming in on two short and very well-known passages — one incorporating the Shear Jashub incident and the Immanuel sign, the other, the Ariel poem, considered by some to hold a key position in Isaiah's theology — it is possible to submit the text to a degree of meticulous source and redaction criticism rarely seen in the 1990s. A lengthy first chapter justifies this fragmenting approach, in the course of a critical, hermeneutical study of *alttestamentliche Literarkritik* from Gesenius, Wellhausen, Gressmann, Duhm and the rest down to Kaiser, Wildberger and others in our own day. The other two chapters contain some valuable discussion on every detail of the two pericopes, including some excellent exegesis of isolated words and concepts, and then conclude with a clear account of what is original, what has been added and when.

J. F. A. SAWYER

WESTERMANN, CLAUS: *Lamentations. Issues and Interpretation.* Translated by Charles Muenchow. 1994. Pp. xvii, 252. (T & T Clark, Edinburgh; Fortress Press, Minneapolis. Price: £12.50/$14.00. ISBN (Clark) 0 567 29226 6; (Fortress) 0 8006 2743 1)

This is an English translation of the German original noticed in *B.L.* 1991 (p. 101), a thorough treatment of the book of Lamentations and what has been written about it from the middle of the 19th century until 1985. The book opens with a survey of the history of interpretation (chs 1–2). W. is particularly interested in the way that the majority of interpreters, recognizing no theological significance to the lament genre as such, and convinced of the interpretative centrality of Lamentations 3 within the book, have insisted that the intent of the text must be other than — or at least more than — lamentation (e.g. explanation; admonition). Ch. 3 takes up this issue of the true nature and significance of the lament, calling into question the unreasoned prejudices of many (particularly Christian) exegetes in relation to it, and preparing the ground for the exegesis of Lamentations which follows in ch. 4. The final chapter then develops further the argument about the theological significance. Lamentation, simply *qua* lamentation, has its proper place in the relating of mortal being to God, whether in the Old Testament or in modern Christian piety. This is an excellent monograph, which should be regarded as essential reading for anyone wrestling with Lamentations or biblical laments in general, or working in the area of biblical theology. I. PROVAN

WHYBRAY, R. N.: *The Composition of the Book of Proverbs* (Journal for the Study of the Old Testament Supplement 168). 1994. Pp. 173. (Sheffield Academic Press. Price: £30.00/$45.00. ISBN 1 85075 457 8; ISSN 0309 0787)

W. aims solely to elucidate the process of composition of Proverbs, and his treatment is currently the most thorough there is. He proceeds by analysing the separate histories of each of the main sections of the book, devoting half his space to the intractable sentence literature, which he approaches innovatively by providing a taxonomy of the principles on which the individual proverbs seem to have been loosely arranged, from smaller groupings to larger ones. This complements W's careful historical criticism insofar as the larger organising principles (e.g. the structural use of Yahweh-proverbs) belong to later stages of the book's evolution. It is the formation of groups that has given the sentences a new interpretation and made them 'wisdom literature'. Several partial 'editions' preceded the final one, and the hierarchy of the main sections can be deduced from the headings in the Hebrew (although the sequence of the Septuagint after 24:22 'has never been plausibly accounted for'). However, a great variety of editorial practice is evident, and W. denies that any truly systematic redaction has taken place either within or between the main sections. Proverbs is a compendium of traditional educational material from varied milieus, gathered into a single scroll.

K. J. A. LARKIN

WILLIAMSON, H. G. M.: *The Book Called Isaiah. Deutero-Isaiah's Role in Composition and Redaction*. 1994. Pp. xvii, 306. (Clarendon Press, Oxford. Price: £35.00. ISBN 0 19 826360 0)

In these closely argued pages the author sets out his hypothesis that the message of Deutero-Isaiah never existed as an independent work but was intended from the beginning to be understood in connection with the literary deposit of Isaiah of Jerusalem which formed its theological groundwork. Deutero-Isaiah saw his role in terms of opening a book which had long been closed (8:16f.) and proclaiming an end to judgement. W. also adduces cumulative evidence that Deutero-Isaiah edited the earlier prophecies to bind together the two parts of the book. This redactional material is to be found primarily at the start and finish of sections where older material has been combined with his own composition. Of particular interest is the discussion of ch. 33 which formed the original link between the earlier material and chs 40–55. The author nowhere minimises the inherent difficulties but offers his argument as 'the most economical hypothesis which has yet been advanced'. In the nature of the case this cannot be the final word on the subject, but it is a most valuable stimulus to fresh discussion of a complex matter.

G. I. EMMERSON

WITTE, MARKUS: *Vom Leiden zur Lehre. Der dritte Redegang (Hiob 21–27) und die Redaktionsgeschichte des Hiobbuches* (Beihefte zur Zeitschrift für die alttestamentliche Wissenschaft 230). 1994. Pp. xi, 333. (de Gruyter, Berlin–New York. Price: DM 164.00. ISBN 3 11 014375 5; ISSN 0934 2575)

After surveying the main kinds of approach to the problem of the third cycle of speeches in Job 21–27, the author of this dissertation launches upon his own analysis. He arrives at a theory of three main redactions subsequent to both the original Job and the Elihu expansion. He characterizes these redactions respectively as enhancing the themes of humility, divine majesty, and righteousness. He further argues that these redactions can be traced into the rest of the book. He sets out the reasons for these judgements clearly, but some may feel that this kind of criticism, admirably organized as it is, is rather invasive and manipulative. An impressive feature of the book is a final section which contains an outline structural analysis of the speeches in Job, a tabulation of the views-in-a-nutshell of seventy-four critics, a concordance of the vocabulary of Job, and a bibliography of thirty-six pages.

J. H. EATON

WOLDE, ELLEN VAN: *Words Become Worlds. Semantic Studies of Genesis 1–11* (Biblical Interpretation Series 6). 1994. Pp. xi, 218. (Brill, Leiden–New York–Köln. Price: fl. 70.00/$40.00. ISBN 90 04 09887 9; ISSN 0928 0731)

Ten of the eleven essays in this book have been published before, but they have been revised and, where necessary, translated into English, and the collection forms a satisfactory unity. The first part contains seven chapters on parts of Genesis 1–11, and the second, 'Theoretical Background', discusses semantics, semiotics, exegesis and hermeneutics — this makes demanding reading, and is clearest when illustrated by examples. The English is generally good, though sometimes less than fully idiomatic (e.g. 'third fold' on pp. 4 and 156 instead of 'threefold', and 'Sem' on p. 77 and 'Sinear' on pp. 95 and 99 instead of 'Shem' and 'Shinar'). While not everything in the first part is convincing (e.g. the explanation on p. 57 of Gen. 4:8 on the assumption that the Masoretic text is sound), even those who favour a diachronic approach to the text will find much stimulating and convincing exegesis, especially of Genesis 2–3.

J. A. EMERTON

6.   LITERARY CRITICISM AND INTRODUCTION

ABERBACH, DAVID: *Imperialism and Biblical Prophecy 750–500 BCE.* 1993. Pp. xiii, 122. (Routledge, London–New York. Price: £25.00. ISBN 0 415 09500 X)

A. offers an account of the development of Hebrew prophecy in its golden age, viewed as a reaction to three waves of international imperialism: Assyrian, Babylonian, and Persian. He brings out well the nature of the ancient empires and the way in which 'war is the subject of, or background to, most of prophetic poetry.' (p. 4) Many prophetic texts are quoted, in a vibrant and often striking version that the author has been working on for a couple of decades. His translations were mostly 'done with half an ear, as it were, for oral recitation in a relatively colloquial rhythmic style, this being close to the spirit of the Hebrew original' (p. x). The bibliography not only lists works on the prophets, the Hebrew Bible and the ancient Near East, and imperialism, but also (with less point) English Bible versions and the titles of series of biblical commentaries. It is a beautifully produced book, containing seventeen reproductions of (mainly) Assyrian and Babylonian sculptures and carvings from the British Museum. Neither an academic monograph nor a student text-book, it lacks a ready-made market: hence no doubt the steep price for a book of its length.

B. P. ROBINSON

ALONSO SCHÖKEL, LUIS and BRAVO, JOSÉ MARÍA: *Apuntes de hermenéutica.* 1994. Pp. 169. (Editorial Trotta, Madrid. Price: 1400 ptas. ISBN 84 87699 90 1)

'Hermeneutical Jottings' is an unduly modest title for an often beautifully crafted engagement in the discussion of hermeneutics in its linguistic, social, noetic, emotive, etc. dimensions, presented in lucid detail and then in summary at the end of each section. This slim volume, written from a clearly Roman Catholic standpoint, persuasively raises issues about our understanding of biblical texts that are too often ignored within historical and philological approaches or are only carelessly appropriated by literary criticism (which in general the book clearly defends). Throughout, the Christian Bible not only constitutes an element in the hermeneutical circle but is also used to exemplify processes taking place in that circle/spiral. Ch. 9 is devoted to a wide-ranging critique of how institutionalized academic systems can hold back genuine advances in biblical scholarship (e.g. the compilation of dictionaries, mentioned twice!). The quality and comprehensiveness of the present work suggest that a translation into English be considered.

J. F. ELWOLDE

AUFFARTH, CHRISTOPH: *Der drohende Untergang. 'Schöpfung' in Mythos und Ritual im Alten Orient und in Griechenland am Beispiel der Odyssee und des Ezechielbuches* (Religionsgeschichtliche Versuche und Vorarbeiten 39). 1991. Pp. xii, 655. (de Gruyter, Berlin–New York. Price: DM 228.00. ISBN 3 11 012640 0; ISSN 0939 2580)

The subject of this thorough and well documented study is sacral kingship in archaic Greece in the light of its background in the ancient Near East, and in particular the king's place in a great annual festival. In discussing the Mesopotamian New Year festival and creation concepts in Ugarit and Israel, A. offers a new understanding of the annual festival: it should not be seen as a renewal of a quasi-magical royal power but as an assurance that the king will act justly towards his people and hence is concerned to set limits to royal authority. The third chapter, which will perhaps be of most interest, seeks to show the significance of creation ideas for Israel in exile and of the New Year festival there, with particular reference to the oracles against Tyre and Egypt in Ezekiel. The final and longest section consists of a very interesting examination of the influence of the annual creation festival on the composition of the *Odyssey*. In recent years, the close connections between early Greece and the Near East have been increasingly recognized, and this book provides a valuable and stimulating contribution to the ongoing discussion.

J. R. PORTER

AULD, A. GRAEME: *Kings Without Privilege. David and Moses in the Story of the Bible's Kings*. 1994. Pp. x, 203. (T. & T. Clark, Edinburgh. Price: £16.95. ISBN 0 567 09639 4)

A. has produced a bold work which not only questions one of the domain assumptions of biblical studies since de Wette but also goes against the grain of current trends by arguing for a careful source-critical analysis of Samuel–Kings and Chronicles. He challenges the long held view that the Chronicler used the text of Samuel–Kings. This stimulating study questions the status of Kings and Chronicles as history, arguing that they reflect competing appropriations of an earlier story of the kings of Judah. He argues that Deuteronomy is late and also has been influenced by this common story. The author of Samuel–Kings was no less partisan than the Chronicler when retelling older traditions about Israel and Judah. A.'s theory has wide-ranging implications: the book of Jeremiah influenced the text of Kings and not vice-versa; the book of Kings can be no earlier than this shared text which describes the collapse of the monarchy; it leads to a questioning of the use of the term Deuteronomistic; Kings can no longer be considered the best source for the period of the monarchy which it describes. The complex argument is clearly set out and is carefully and persuasively argued, and will engender considerable debate among biblical specialists of all persuasions.

K. W. WHITELAM

BELLIS, ALICE OGDEN: *Helpmates, Harlots, and Heroes. Women's Stories in the Hebrew Bible*. 1994. Pp. xv, 281. (Westminster/John Knox, Louisville KY. Price: $19.99. ISBN 0 664 25430 6)

This book provides a useful introduction to the main lines of thinking informing feminist biblical interpretation. The Introduction provides some useful attempts at definitions of such terms, as 'womanism', 'feminism', 'feminist hermeneutics', and 'patriarchy': It also contains a brief survey of the history of feminist biblical interpretation and its implications. The second (and most significant) section retells biblical stories about women and outlines some feminist responses to them, assessing both the content and underlying methods of such responses. The final section, 'Reflections', contains a summary and some conclusions. The structure of the book means that the information it imparts is readily accessible to those with little specialist knowledge of the field. In addition, it is written with clarity and contains very little of the highly technical vocabulary sometimes found in feminist writing. A good resource for those beginning study of feminist biblical interpretation.

C. SMITH

BOORER, SUZANNE: *The Promise of the Land as Oath. A Key to the Formation of the Pentateuch* (Beihefte zur Zeitschrift für die alttestamentliche Wissenschaft 205). 1992. Pp. xv, 470. (de Gruyter, Berlin–New York. Price DM 184.00. ISBN 3 11 013505 1; ISSN 0934 2575)

This massive exercise in diachronic literary criticism examines the five passages in Exodus/Numbers where Yahweh is said to have sworn an oath to the patriarchs, in order to decide which approach to the composition of the Pentateuch is to be preferred. B. first outlines four major paradigms of the growth of the Pentateuch, those of Wellhausen, Noth, Van Seters and Rendtorff. She then exhaustively examines five texts, comparing them with each other and their parallels in Deuteronomy. Exod. 13:3–16; 32:7–14; 33:1–3; Num. 14:11b–23a and 32:7–11 all appear to be deuteronomic insertions into their contexts and composed more or less in their canonical order. With the exception of Num. 32:7–11 they are earlier than their parallels in Deuteronomy. B. concludes that her evidence disproves Van Seters' argument that Deuteronomy antedates Exodus–Numbers, and Rendtorff's view of a unified deuteronomic editing of these books. Her findings are closer to Wellhausen than Noth. B. is well aware of the tentativeness of this type of study, and there are many points in it that will not command agreement. And to decide between alternative paradigms of pentateuchal origins on the basis of such a narrow range of texts is questionable.

G. J. WENHAM

BOWMAN, ALAN K. and WOOLF, GREG (eds): *Literacy and Power in the Ancient World*. 1994. Pp. ix, 249. (Cambridge University Press. Price: £37.50/ $59.95. ISBN 0 521 43369 X)

The question of literacy and its significance has recently been given prominence by some biblical scholars. This volume addresses one aspect of the question (the relationship of literacy to power) while still recognizing that others could be raised (e.g. literacy versus orality). The editors give an initial essay to set the context of the discussion and bring together some of the points of the other essays. Most of the essays address a specific cultural entity: Persopolis tablets, Greece, Egypt in the Late to Ptolemaic periods, Rome, early Christianity, late antique Syria, the Byzantine dark ages. (J. Goody and W. J. Ong come in for a good deal of criticism.) Of special interest is the carefully nuanced essay on scribes in Judaea (M. Goodman) which concludes that there is little evidence of a *religious* class of scribes.

L. L. GRABBE

BURDEN, TERRY L.: *The Kerygma of the Wilderness Traditions in the Hebrew Bible* (American University Studies. Series 7: Theology and Religion 163). 1994. Pp. x, 259. (Lang, Frankfurt–Bern–New York. Price: SwF 33.00. ISBN 0 8204 2253 3; ISSN 0740 0446)

Influenced by H. W. Wolff's and W. Brueggemann's 'kerygmatic' approach to the sources of the Pentateuch, B. focuses upon the theological use and significance of the wilderness traditions not only in the Tetrateuch, but throughout the Old Testament. In virtually all examples the traditions are brought to bear on situations that occur in relation to issues involving the land, warranting the general conclusion that 'the wilderness traditions receive their great impetus among the traditions of the Pentateuch because of the theological problems being addressed by biblical writers that were caused by the experience of exile, or a landless condition'. The use made of them by the Deuteronomist, Jeremiah, Ezekiel, and Second Isaiah, as well as writers from the restoration period points to contexts of crisis. That is, the 'constitutive effect of Israel's ancient traditions becomes acutely relevant in periods of transition when the community's identity as a Yahwistic community of faith is threatened'. In this way the 'guidance, protection, and miraculous provisions of God in the wilderness, plus God's confrontation with the people, provide an image unmatched in Israel's history'.

E. W. NICHOLSON

BÜTTNER, GERHARD and MAIER, JOACHIM: *Maria aus Magdala-Ester-Debora. Modelle für den evangelischen und katholischen Religionsunterricht Sekundarstufe 1* (Calwer Materialien). 1994. Pp. 91 + 4 transparencies. (Calwer, Stuttgart. Price: DM 29.80/SwF 30.80/AS 233. ISBN 3 7668 3269 7)

This German secondary school teacher's guide to introducing three female biblical characters to a new generation of both Protestant and Catholic youngsters makes use of some innovative teaching methods, e.g. dramatizations, and of some modern biblical scholarship, e.g. investigating characters as role models. The book remains firmly within the conservative evangelical fold, and the role models and stereotypes portrayed in the illustrations do not win approval from this reader.

H. A. McKAY

CARROLL, ROBERT P. and HUNTER, ALASTAIR G. (eds): *Words at Work: Using the Bible in the Academy, the Community and the Churches. Essays in Honour of Robert Davidson.* 1994. Pp. xvii, 155. (Trinity St Mungo Press, Faculty of Divinity, University of Glasgow. Price: £10.00. ISBN 0 952231 0 7)

The fact that these essays eventually appear *faute de mieux* as an in-house, desk-top publishing venture is perhaps appropriate to their occasional (ephemeral in the best sense) nature. Many are the reflections of 'practitioners' (ministers, teachers, broadcasters) on the contemporary *aporia* over the use of the Bible, though the most fun is Robert Carroll's apologia for Mrs Thatcher's 'Sermon on the Mound'; even if the tongue is in the cheek, a powerful point is made. The fact that the essays are longer on *aporia* than on solutions no doubt well matches Professor Davidson's own 'courage to doubt'. Their best sign of hope, perhaps, is their testimony to the enthusiasm for the Bible which Professor Davidson was capable of inspiring — or rather, which the Bible is capable of inspiring when we can get people to 'read the text' (see Heather McKay's piece on how she learnt to find 'pleasure in the Bible').

J. GOLDINGAY

CLIFFORD, RICHARD J.: *Creation Accounts in the Ancient Near East and in the Bible* (Catholic Biblical Quarterly Monograph 26). 1994. Pp. xiii, 217. (Catholic Biblical Association, Washington, D.C. Price: $9.00. ISBN 0 915170 25 6)

The author, a Hebraist with Ugaritic and a little Akkadian, after a brief introduction on the topic and its modern literature, gives a detailed account of Sumerian evidence (based mainly on J. J. A. van Dijk), a similarly detailed account of Akkadian material (using J. Bottéro and others), then a much briefer and more synthetic account of Egyptian textual evidence. The following chapters on Canaanite and Old Testament literature (the latter divided into Gen. 1–11, the Psalms, Is. 40–55 and wisdom texts) are more discussion of the problems than presentation of the evidence. The question whether the Ugaritic Baal cycle is a cosmogony is left open. In the biblical material, creation is often seen as a process begun with the creation of the universe and man, but continuing in the selection and development of the chosen nation. The author is well read and has many stimulating observations to make. The Mesopotamian material is occasionally wrong and not quite up to date, but generally offers a reliable account.
                                                                W. G. LAMBERT

CRENSHAW, JAMES L.: *Old Testament Story and Faith. A Literary and Theological Introduction*. 1992 (1986). Pp. viii, 472. (Hendrickson, Peabody MA. Price: $19.95. ISBN 0 943575 91 5)

This introduction for beginning students seeks to do justice to the literature and theology of the Old Testament in terms of story and faith. After a brief survey of the history from Egypt to the Roman period to provide a sound religious setting for the various books, the discussion follows the order of the books in the Hebrew Bible before helpfully turning to the Deutero-canonical literature and tracing the development from cherished religious writings to a canon of scripture. A useful bibliography of English works is followed by a series of brief but helpful appendices covering subjects as varied as apocalyptic and some significant inscriptions and texts. Students, beginners or otherwise, will benefit greatly from this introduction. Popularly written and wearing its undoubted scholarship lightly, it is informative without ever being condescending, attractively produced and well illustrated.

                                                                R. DAVIDSON

CRYER, FREDERICK H.: *Divination in Ancient Israel and its Near Eastern Environment. A Socio-Historical Investigation* (Journal for the Study of the Old Testament Supplement 142). 1994. Pp. 367. (Sheffield Academic Press. Price: £45.00/$67.50. ISBN 1 85075 353 9; ISSN 0309 0787)

C. has produced an excellent study of a much-neglected subject and shows the importance of divination (and 'magic' in general) to Israelite society. After a chapter on the methodology of historical and sociological knowledge, he devotes a chapter to the anthropological study of magic in general and another specifically to the work of E. Evans-Pritchard. These are followed by a long chapter on the various sorts of divination in Mesopotamia and a short one on Egypt. Another long chapter surveys the different methods of divination known from the Old Testament literature, followed by another chapter on the question of how writers made use of the variety of divinatory practice for literary purposes. I have only one reservation: in his correct emphasis on the fact that divination had an important epistemological function in society beyond mere prediction, C. occasionally even denies any predictive function at all (pp. 188–89). I am not sure that the ancients would

84   LITERARY CRITICISM AND INTRODUCTION

have expressed it that way. But this is a small point. C.'s valuable study
deserves a significant place among studies on Israel's history and society.

L. L. GRABBE

DARR, KATHERYN PFISTERER: *Isaiah's Vision and the Family of God*
(Literary Currents in Biblical Interpretation). 1994. Pp. 280. (Westminster/
John Knox, Louisville KY. Price: $21.99. ISBN 0 664 25537 X)

This is a study based on the author's twin convictions, shared by the
present reviewer and a rapidly increasing number of other biblical interpreters, that 'sequential readers of Isaiah discover unfolding themes, motifs,
etc., likely to be overlooked in the course of purely pericopal readings', and
that metaphors are important as strategic language, inviting readers to
'particular perceptions of reality' (p. 11). After a useful chapter on method,
D. examines the imagery of the rebellious child, 'the ways women are'
(dependence, vulnerability, haughtiness, sexuality, etc.), and female per-
sonifications of cities in Isaiah 1–39 and 40–66, constantly illuminated by
biblical and extra-biblical cross-references. Then, picking out a proverb
uttered by Hezekiah at a critical moment in the history of Judah (37:3), there
is a final chapter on childbirth imagery in Isaiah, especially 26:17–18 and
66:1–16, as an expression of trust in God's strength and readiness to deliver.
In such a comprehensive literary reading of Isaiah, one might have expected
at least a mention of the young woman in 7:14 (showing up the king's lack of
faith?), and of Lilith and another family scene in 34:14f (NRSV). But there is
much good and original interpretation here, even of some of the most familiar
passages in the Bible. The volume is a credit to the excellent new series.

J. F. A. SAWYER

DICOU, BERT: *Edom, Israel's Brother and Antagonist. The Role of Edom
in Biblical Prophecy and Story* (Journal for the Study of the Old Testament
Supplement 169.) 1994. Pp. 227. (Sheffield Academic Press. Price: £30.00/
$45.00. ISBN 1 85075 458 6; ISSN 0309 0787)

D. analyses the prophetic and pentateuchal texts presenting Edom as
Israel's enemy or brother or both. He agrees with earlier studies that Edom's
connection with Esau and Seir is relatively late, resulting from Edomite
expansion west of the Wadi Arabah in the late monarchic period. At the root
of the prophetic oracles on Edom is Edom's supposed conduct in 587 BCE (in
fact less hostile than alleged), which first surfaces in cultic lamentations for
Jerusalem's fall. The earliest oracles (Jer. 49:9–10a, 14–16; Ezek. 35:5, 9)
treat Edom on the same level as other nations. A secondary development
after 552 BCE (Jer. 49:7f, 10b, 12f; Ezek. 35:1–36.15; Obad. 1–14, 15b; 15a,
16–18), turns Edom into a special and *typical* opponent, a representative of
Israel's enemies. A third stage associates and compares Edom with Babylon
for wickedness (cf. Jer. 49:17–21, Isa. 34, Obad. 19–21). While the prophets
are concerned with the destruction of Israel and the nations, Genesis (cf.
pp. 160–66), is concerned with their origins and does not need to present
Edom as hostile for ever; hence Esau is reconciled with Jacob. D. thus rejects
an early origin for Edom's hostility with Israel, but if there is nothing in the
Pentateuch or the prophets of any relevance for the pre-exilic relationships of
Edom and Israel/Judah, we are still left with references in DrtH to serious
hostilities in the monarchic period. I find it hard to believe that these earlier
hostilities had no influence on later attitudes to Edom. However, this is
certainly a most original and important study.   J. R. BARTLETT

DOORLY, WILLIAM J.: *Obsession with Justice. The Story of the Deutero-nomists.* 1994. Pp. viii, 166. (Paulist Press, New York–Mahwah NJ. Price: $12.95. ISBN 0 8091 3487 X)

This is apparently intended as a first introduction to the study of the Deuteronomistic History. It is very simply and lucidly written, with regular charts used to lay out clearly the substance of the view presented. The Deuteronomistic History is understood to have had its first edition, based on primary sources, in the reign of Josiah, this king being presented as the counterpart to Joshua at the beginning of the History. The work was then subsequently revised in a new exilic edition and finally in what the author refers to as the canonical edition. For each of these stages of development the author provides a discussion of the content, historical background and theology. Despite the simplicity of the presentation, the book covers much of the best of modern scholarship on the subject, perhaps too much given the nature of the readership for which the book is evidently intended.

A. D. H. MAYES

DUGUID, IAIN M.: *Ezekiel and the Leaders of Israel* (Supplements to Vetus Testamentum 56). 1994. Pp. xi, 163. (Brill, Leiden–New York–Köln. Price: fl. 100.00/$57.25. ISBN 90 04 10074 1; ISSN 0083 5889)

This explores the attitudes expressed towards the various different leadership groups within Judean society: the monarchy, the priests and Levites, the prophets, and the lay leadership (including $z^e q\bar{e}n\hat{i}m$, $\hat{s}\bar{a}r\hat{i}m$ and other ruling classes.) The thesis is advanced that there is a coherent attitude taken towards these leadership groups throughout the book: those singled out for the most reproach in Ezekiel's critique of the past are marginalized in his plan for the future, while those who escape blame are assigned positions of honour. It is not, argues D., simply a matter of tinkering with the status of a single group in society, but rather there is advanced a radical and complete restructuring, designed to avoid repetition of the sins of the past. This is a carefully executed and well-presented piece of historical-critical scholarship. For the most part, the text is interpreted as it stands, tensions and all. He argues that Ezekiel is substantially a unity, deriving from the exilic age. The present reviewer would have welcomed a fuller discussion of these issues. Nevertheless, the volume is to be welcomed as a valuable contribution.

P. M. JOYCE

EATON, JOHN: *Interpreted by Love: Expositions of 40 Great Old Testament Passages.* 1994. Pp. 160. (Bible Reading Fellowship, Oxford. Price: £5.99. ISBN 0 7459 2588 X)

In this small volume E. draws upon the exegetical skills widely demonstrated elsewhere to feed a most valuable series of meditative reflections on Scripture, owing something in spirit to the Ignatian tradition. Passages are carefully selected from almost the full range of the Old Testament, taking in poetry from the Psalter, Ecclesiastes and the Song of Songs, as well as many narrative sections. A large proportion of the expositions are framed with modern stories briefly told, and (though never articulated explicitly) there is a good deal of hermeneutical insight implicit here. The author carries his learning very lightly, making passing references to the history of interpretation and to the proposals of modern biblical scholars; a short section of notes at the end of the book offers bibliographical guidance. This very accessible book is admirably suited to its intended readership. P. M. JOYCE

EXUM, J. CHERYL: *Fragmented Women. Feminist (Sub)versions of Biblical Narratives*. 1993. Pp. 223. (Trinity Press International, Valley Forge PA. Price: $14.95. ISBN 1 56338 018 8)

This is the American edition of the book reviewed in *B.L.* 1994, p. 85.

ED.

EXUM, J. CHERYL and CLINES, DAVID J. A. (eds): *The New Literary Criticism and the Hebrew Bible*. 1993. Pp. 276. (Trinity Press International, Valley Forge PA. Price: $18.00. ISBN 1 56338 079 X)

This is the American edition of the collection reviewed in *B.L.* 1994, p. 86.

ED.

FISCHER, IMTRAUD: *Die Erzeltern Israels. Feministisch-theologische Studien zu Genesis 12–36* (Beihefte zur Zeitschrift für die alttestamentliche Wissenschaft 222). 1994. Pp. xii, 396. (de Gruyter, Berlin–New York. Price: DM 148.00. ISBN 3 11 014232 5; ISSN 0934 2575)

The author of this excellent work wishes to show that we should not speak of 'Patriarchal Narratives' but of 'Ancestral Narratives'. The women who figure in Gen. 12–36, 38 were not just passive characters but people who played key roles in the unfolding drama of the ancestors of Israel. Her thorough and closely argued study makes us aware of many features of these chapters that have often escaped commentators. F. discusses birth announcements (e.g. Gen. 17:15–21; 18:1–15), birth narratives (e.g. 21:1–7; 25:19–26), *toledot* (e.g. 11:27b–31; 25:12–18), genealogical lists, and notices of the begetting, bearing, and naming of children. She devotes a chapter to the socio-cultural circumstances in which women of the ancient Near East lived. The main section of her work studies the *Preisgabeerzählungen* (Gen. 12:10–20; 20:1–18; 26:1–11) and the stories of Hagar. This careful and balanced study will surely find a place of honour among feminist interpretations of Genesis.

M. MAHER

FISHBANE, MICHAEL: *The Garments of Torah. Essays in Biblical Hermeneutics* (Indiana Studies in Biblical Literature). 1992. Pp. xi, 155. (Indiana University Press, Bloomington and Indianapolis; distributed in the UK by Open University Press, Buckingham. Price: £25.00; paper £8.99. ISBN 0 253 32217 0; paper 0 253 20752 5)

This collection of nine essays, produced during more than a decade, focus on biblical hermeneutics from within the Hebrew Bible to Buber's *Moses*. They offer support of F.'s claim that 'if we reinvent the story forever, we may continue to live'. In Part I, three deal with the Hebrew Bible and illustrate the midrashic/exegetical process at work before the status of 'closed literary corpus' was reached. In Part II, two indicate how the exegetical choices of ancient scholars created both interpretation and culture within Hebrew and, later, Jewish society. Part III has four contributions on modern hermeneutics: two on Buber, one on Rosenzweig and one retelling the methods of medieval exegesis. The book's conclusion explores the 'notion of a sacred text'. F. writes lyrically — almost lovingly — about his subjects and the reader has to be enough in sympathy with that stance to enjoy his evaluations on the ongoing interpretation of the Hebrew scriptures.

H. A. MCKAY

FUCHS, GISELA: *Mythos und Hiobdichtung. Aufnahme und Umdeutung altorientalischer Vorstellungen.* 1993. Pp. 319. (Kohlhammer, Stuttgart–Berlin–Köln. Price: DM 89.00/SwF 91.00/AS 694. ISBN 3 17 012498 6)

F. argues that myth permeates the book of Job and shapes its intention. Yet the distinctiveness of the Old Testament belief in one God is retained. F. undertakes a thorough examination of the *Chaoskampf* myth in mainly Babylonian, Ugaritic and Hittite sources and follows this by an analysis of its general influence on Job. She finds such influence to be more extensive than previous scholars have claimed, finding a surprising number in short passages such as Job 6:4 and 18:5. She also finds influences from other myths such as those of the 'Primal Man' and 'World Tree'. Mythical influence is regarded by F. as the key to unlock the Job poem. She finds particular use of myth at climatic points in Job's laments and accusations and in the sharpness of the antagonism between Job and God. She finds the supreme interest of the author of Job, more than that of other writers in the Old Testament, in using the primal forms of myth to express complex experiences and the diversity of life. This is a thorough and interesting doctoral dissertation from the Evangelical Faculty of the University of Bonn under the supervision of W. Schmidt.

K. J. DELL

GARCÍA MARTÍNEZ, F.; HILHORST, A.; RUITEN, J. T. A. G. M. VAN; WOUDE, A. S. VAN DER (eds): *Studies in Deuteronomy in Honour of C. J. Labuschagne on the Occasion of his 65th Birthday* (Supplements to Vetus Testamentum 53). 1994. Pp. xii, 305. (Brill, Leiden–New York–Köln. Price: fl. 160.00/$91.50. ISBN 90 04 10052 0; ISSN 0083 5889)

It is wholly appropriate that a Festschrift for C. J. Labuschagne should be devoted to the book of Deuteronomy on account of that scholar's deep exegetical involvement with it. The subject of monotheism is consequently well represented among the eighteen essays. Particularly welcome is that several are concerned with the historical origin and literary structure of the book and with its wider impact on Jewish and Christian thinking. Great changes in the evaluation of the rise of the Deuteronomic movement have taken place: Now an exilic, or early Persian, time of origin for much of what is found in the law-book is widely canvassed. Moreover the literary unity of the central law code is no longer convincingly sustainable. So there is very much for the general reader to take note of in this collection, besides its special interest for the student of Deuteronomy.

K. A. Deurloo, Hilhorst, and van Ruiten all contribute stimulating reconsiderations of the subject of monotheism, the first in its historical setting and the last two in aspects of Christian and Jewish exegesis respectively. J. W. Wevers also relates to the theme in examining the Septuagint translation of the Tetragrammaton. Of quite special interest is the essay by F. E. Deist examining 'The Dangers of Deuteronomy' in the light of its use and abuse in the South African social and political context. To mention these is not to neglect the other contributions to this fine collection.

R. E. CLEMENTS

GARRETT, DUANE A.: *An Analysis of the Hermeneutics of John Chrysostom's Commentary on Isaiah 1–8 with an English Translation* (Studies in the Bible and Early Christianity 12). 1992. Pp. 258. (Edwin Mellen, Lewiston–Queenston–Lampeter. Price: $69.95/£39.95. ISBN 0 88946 612 2; (series) 0 88946 913 X)

The text-centred exegesis of those church fathers traditionally classified as 'Antiochene' has more to offer most modern exegetes than other patristic modes of commentary, so that an English translation and study of this important work by John Chrysostom is welcome. G. seems adequately equipped in Greek and Hebrew; less so, unfortunately, in knowledge of indispensable publications: A critical edition with French translation appeared in 1983 (*Sources Chrétiennes* 304). This makes out-of-date both the old text which Migne reprinted and Montfaucon's discussion of why it ends where it does. The author's treatment of the 'Antiochene school' is also weakened by limited knowledge of modern editions (e.g. of Diodore and Theodore), of the Syriac commentators (who are among the finest representatives of this exegetical method), and of studies in language other than English. However, despite all grounds for criticism, this work will help to make Chrysostom more accessible to students.   R. P. R. MURRAY

GILLINGHAM, S. E.: *The Poems and Psalms of the Hebrew Bible* (The Oxford Bible Series). 1994. Pp. xiii, 311. (Oxford University Press. Price: paper £10.95. ISBN 0 19 213242 3; paper 0 19 213243 1)

Here is a thoroughgoing attempt to describe for the non-specialist the poetry of the Hebrew Bible and to understand it primarily in the contexts of the life, literature, and liturgy of ancient Israel, though wider contexts such as poetic interpretation in general and theology are not ignored. After detailed treatments of the relationship between poetry and prose, metre, and parallelism, G. turns to the poetry of the Hebrew Bible outside the Psalter. This she classifies under the headings Law Poetry, Wisdom Poetry, and Popular Poetry; Prophetic Poetry; and Cultic Poetry (though this term is used rather loosely, e.g. including literary compositions using cultic forms). Particular attention is paid to the Psalter, where, in addition to considering the roles of the psalmists, poetic devices in the psalms, and the types of poem in the Psalter, issues concerning the nature of the Psalter as a whole and its interpretation are discussed. G. is to be applauded for taking seriously the importance of appreciation as well as understanding. A very welcome addition to a useful series.   A. H. W. CURTIS

GLATT, DAVID A.: *Chronological Displacement in Biblical and Related Literatures* (Society of Biblical Literature Dissertation Series 139). 1993. Pp. xii, 220. (Scholars Press, Atlanta. Price: $44.95; member price $29.95; paper $29.95 ($19.95). ISBN 1 55540 817 6; paper 1 55540 818 4)

This uses the term chronological displacement to refer to a situation where an author or editor intentionally transfers an episode from its original chronological context into a different setting. He takes chronology to be the linchpin of historical writing and concludes that any intentional deviation indicates an ideological or thematic motivation or an attempt to achieve a more effective historical composition. His working hypothesis when approaching biblical texts is that sequence differences between Chronicles and Samuel–Kings are conscious displacements by the Chronicler. All of the cases in Chronicles are instances of antedating, reflecting ideological and thematic concerns and the historiographical sophistication of the Chronicler. The final chapter deals with examples of displacement which can only be assumed on the basis of internal evidence. He recognizes that this is a loose sense of the term 'displacement' to refer to presentation of an event which the author/editor suggests is sequentialy inaccurate. G. attempts to show that the move from cases of displacement where there are different sources to cases where the evidence is internal provides an empirical model for placing the speculation on firmer grounds. He is aware of the subjectivity of many of his conclusions, although he does not consider newer literary approaches which might offer considerably different explanations of such displacements.

K. W. WHITELAM

GOLDINGAY, JOHN: *God's Prophet, God's Servant. A Study in Jeremiah and Isaiah 40–55* (Biblical Classics Library). 1994 (1984). Pp. 160. (Paternoster Press, Carlisle. Price: £1.99. ISBN 0 85364 604 X)

This is an unrevised reprint of the book reviewed in *B.L.* 1984, p. 80.

ED.

GOLKA, FRIEDEMANN W.: *Die Flecken des Leoparden. Biblische und afrikanische Weisheit im Sprichwort* (Arbeiten zur Theologie 78). 1994. Pp. 176. (Calwer, Stuttgart. Price: DM 58.00/SwF 59.50/AS 453. ISBN 3 7668 3275 1)

This is a version for German readers of Golka's *The Leopard's Spots*, published in 1993 (*B.L.* 1994, p. 87). The contents are identical apart from a few minor changes in the preface and bibliography.

R. N. WHYBRAY

GREENSPAHN, FREDERICK E.: *When Brothers Dwell Together. The Pre-eminence of Younger Siblings in the Hebrew Bible.* 1994. Pp. xi, 193. (Oxford University Press. Price: £22.50. ISBN 0 19 508253 2)

G.'s object is to account for the prevalence of stories in which a younger sibling gains success in conflict with or in preference to an older one. The first half of the book investigates the law and custom of inheritance in Israel and other cultures. It concludes that there was no fixed law based on birth-order in ancient Israel, but that, while all the sons would inherit, fathers had discretion in favouring one son; $b^e kor$ does not necessarily refer to birth-order, but to this parental preference. The second half discusses the literary motif from various points of view. G. relates it to other motifs of the success of the unlikely, such as the barren woman; he suggests that this is appropriate to the theology of the Bible which attributes success to God's choice, and that it reflects 'Israel's' perception of herself as undeserving. The motif itself is more ambiguous than appears at first sight, since it has many different motivations in the stories where it appears. There is an immense range of learning in this book, but it is innocent of literary theory and disfigured with some absurd mistakes.

W. J. HOUSTON

HALPERIN, DAVID J.: *Seeking Ezekiel. Text and Psychology.* 1993. Pp. xv, 260. (Pennsylvania State University Press, University Park PA. Price: $35.00/ £30.00; paper $16.95/£13.95. ISBN 0 271 00947 0; paper 0 271 00948 9)

H. has revived the hypothesis of Ezekiel's mental illness. He attempts to use the text as the basis for nothing less than the psychoanalysis of the man Ezekiel, and presents an account of the whole text in these terms. Giving particular attention to Ezek. 8:7–12, and to chs 16, 23, and 24, he postulates an Ezekiel dominated by a pathological dread and loathing of female sexuality. The study is based on a close reading of and detailed discussion of the Hebrew text, which is in some respects conservatively handled. However, H.'s very detailed picture of Ezekiel's inner life ventures far beyond what, on any showing, the available data could justify. In this H. fails to take seriously the critique of such a procedure made decades ago. The scant personal details found in this ancient text are an insufficient basis for a project as bold as a psychoanalysis. Another problem is that he fails to complement psychological enquiry with other kinds of question, showing no sensitivity to sociological, literary or theological issues. H. is very 'literalistic' in his treatment of the text, which is used with much confidence as a historical source for Ezekiel's life, both outer and inner; his study is thus lacking in any real sense that Ezekiel is a work of literature. Psychological insights, if carefully handled, have a great deal to contribute to the task of biblical interpretation. Unfortunately, H.'s book will only serve to give such work a bad name.

P. M. JOYCE

HEATON, E. W.: *The School Tradition of the Old Testament* (The Bampton Lectures for 1994). 1994. Pp. xiii, 208. (Clarendon Press, Oxford. Price: £25.00. ISBN 0 19 826362 7)

H. acknowledges that it has not proved possible to pin down either the wise as a social group, or the wisdom tradition, in Israel. However, he regards it as highly implausible that there were no schools or libraries in Israel and prefers not so much to argue that they did exist as to take their existence for granted and to demonstrate what good sense such an assumption makes. H. first examines the nature of ancient schooling, from the evidence of Ben Sira and of Israel's neighbours (particularly Egypt), then discusses continuities in content and literary genre between Ben Sira and Proverbs, Job and Ecclesiastes, and more controversially between the school tradition and the prophets and 'story writers'. It is fair to say that the work of Fishbane on inner-biblical exegesis has opened up the question of how, in concrete terms, texts grew and were preserved, and that the activity of scholars provides a plausible answer. It is perhaps more difficult to endorse H.'s larger (and flattering!) claim that it is the radicalism of the teachers that informs and supports the greater radicalism of the prophets, and that school and seminary should be seen as the two main, counterbalanced sources of all Israel's traditions.

K. J. A. LARKIN

HENNINGS, RALPH: *Der Briefwechsel zwischen Augustinus und Hieronymus und ihr Streit um den Kanon des Alten Testaments und die Auslegung von Gal. 2,11–14* (Supplements to Vigiliae Christianae 21). 1994. Pp. xi, 395. (Brill, Leiden–New York–Köln. Price: fl. 175.00/$100.00. ISBN 90 04 09840 2; ISSN 0920 623X)

This is a precise and detailed discussion of the exchange of correspondence between Augustine and Jerome, offering a rigorous analysis of its history, form, and content. H. agrees that the letters fall into two groups, representing two periods of scholarly activity separated by approximately ten years. The first group, dated between 395 and 405, deals with the canon of the Old Testament, exegesis of Gal. 2:11–14, and the 'ceremonial law'; the second, from the years 405 to 419. Readers will find the section on the Old Testament canon of interest. H. shows Jerome's indebtedness to earlier views of canon expressed by Greek Fathers. More especially, Jerome's dependence on Jewish sources is emphasized, in contrast with Augustine's continuing support for the Septuagint as the Bible of the Church. But the divergent views of the two Fathers in respect of Jews and Judaism is crucial, in H.'s estimate, to proper understanding of their different assessment of the Septuagint.

C. T. R. HAYWARD

HILL, CHARLES: *The Scriptures Jesus Knew. A Guide to the Old Testament.* 1994. Pp. xviii, 232. (E. J.Dwyer, Newtown NSW, Australia. Price: (US)$12.95. ISBN 0 85574 365 4)

This is intended for those who have yet to encounter the Old Testament in any depth, and to whom therefore the greater part of Scripture remains literally a closed book. Written with a Roman Catholic constituency in mind, it includes the 'deutero-canonical' books, making the point that during Jesus' lifetime the canon of Scripture was not yet fixed. At the beginning, the author deals with some basic questions of historical and cultural background, and gives an example of how to read a short prophetic book. Each of the following twelve chapters suggests a text for study, a biblical topic and a theological theme; the final chapter looks at further ways of encouraging an interest in the Old Testament. There are good reading lists, and a glossary and biblical and general indices are provided. This would be an excellent book for an adult study group, and could also be a resource for teachers in school. My only reservation is that the connection between the prescribed biblical topic and theological theme is not always clear.   E. B. MELLOR

HILL, ROBERT C.: *Breaking the Bread of the Word. Principles of Teaching Scriptures* (Subsidia Biblica 15). 1991. Pp. xiv, 184. (Pontifical Biblical Institute, Rome. Price: Lire 22,500. ISBN 88 7633 5969)

Addressed mainly to Catholic institutions set up for the training of ministers and teachers this book will prove to be a useful tool to any reader engaged in the teaching of Scriptures especially to adults. Its author has written this volume after years spent in training teachers for teaching religion. His basic thesis in this book: it is not enough to train ministers of the Word to read the Bible and understand its message; we ought to train them also the art of passing on that knowledge to their students whether at school, church pew or Sunday School. His main concern is teaching (Catholic) adults how to use and read Scripture. The book consists of two parts. In Part One Hill studies which theological principles should guide the 'ministry of the Word' (pp. 1–87). One realizes immediately that the author views Scripture not simply as a cultural artefact of the past but as the written Word of God addressing mankind in their own situation. In Part Two (pp. 89–156) H. focuses on the art of teaching the Bible, mainly to adults. Though he moves within the Catholic tradition H.'s perspective is ecumenical; his book will benefit anyone who would like to make the Christian Community grow through preaching and teaching.   A. ABELA

HOUTMAN, CEES: *Der Pentateuch. Die Geschichte seiner Erforschung neben einer Auswertung* (Contributions to Biblical Exegesis and Theology 9). 1994. Pp. xxii, 472. (Kok Pharos, Kampen. Price: fl. 79.90. ISBN 90 390 0114 6; ISSN 0926 6097)

This thorough history of pentateuchal criticism appeared in Dutch in 1980 (see *B.L.* 1981, p. 72). This German edition mentions more recent discussions in new footnotes and in fresh material at the end of some chapters. As there has been so much debate on the Pentateuch in the last decade, it is a pity that H. does not devote more space to evaluating recent work. May we hope that one day an English edition will allow him to do so.

G. J. WENHAM

HOWARD, DAVID M., JR: *An Introduction to the Old Testament Historical Books*. 1993. Pp. 394. (Moody, Chicago. Price: $21.99. ISBN 0 8024 4127 0)

This introduction to Joshua, Judges, Ruth, 1–2 Samuel, 1–2 Kings, 1–2 Chronicles, Ezra, Nehemiah and Esther opens with a general introduction to historical narrative before moving on to a book-by-book analysis which combines attention to standard critical questions with discussion of message, theme and theology, and purpose. It is addressed to a conservative Christian readership, but interacts fairly well with a broader range of scholarship. It is disappointing, however, that having paid so much attention to *narrative* matters in chapter 1, the author should have allowed apologetics with regard to *history* to occupy so disproportionate a place in the rest of the book. It is difficult to see how this will help many readers better to read the biblical texts — the hope expressed by the author in the first chapter. In general, in fact, there is an insufficient sense in this book of the complexity of the relationship in the biblical narrative texts between history, art, and theology.

I. PROVAN

HUSSER, JEAN-MARIE: *Le songe et la parole. Etude sur le rêve et sa fonction dans l'ancien Israël* (Beihefte zur Zeitschrift für die alttestamentliche Wissenschaft 210). 1994. Pp. xii, 302. (de Gruyter, Berlin–New York. Price: DM 158.00. ISBN 3 11 013719 4; ISSN 0934 2575)

H. has produced an important study of a subject greatly neglected in Old Testament study. Individual chapters are devoted to the main biblical texts, as well as to the Deir 'Alla Balaam inscription and to dream texts at Ugarit and in the Gilgamesh epic. H. demonstrates the importance of the use of dreams as a compositional device in various literary narratives. He also refutes the idea that dreams were generally frowned on in the biblical text; on the contrary, dreams were an important means of acquiring knowledge according to both prophetic and wisdom texts. My only reservation is H.'s attempt to deny that 'visions' had a visual element; rather, the line between vision and dream is not always a clearcut one.

As a footnote, the original print run of the book was defective, with several lines duplicated and others omitted on many pages. The publisher has acted with commendable speed in printing a corrected edition. However, if anyone has obtained a copy soon after publication, they should check that they have the corrected version; the publisher will replace any of the original defective copies.

L. L. GRABBE

JEPPESEN, KNUD; NIELSEN, KIRSTEN; and ROSENDAL, BENT (eds): *In the Last Days. On Jewish and Christian Apocalyptic and its Period*. 1994. Pp. 261. (Aarhus University Press. Price: DKK 248. ISBN 87 7288 471 1)

This Festschrift for Benedikt Otzen has twenty essays, as well as an appreciation and bibliography of the honoree, including: Gnosticism, Jewish apocalypticism, and early Christianity (P. Bilde), a note on Zech. 14:4–5 (E. Nielsen), a Judeo-Persian Daniel apocalypse (J. Asmussen), martyrdom as apocalypse (J. Balling), Hippolytus and Theodoret on Daniel (S. Hidal), the role of the devil in the *Apocalypse of Sedrach* (K. Nielsen), von Rad's views on apocalyptic re-examined (M. Sæbø), Mowinckel's thesis on eschatology in Brueggemann's adaptation (E. Holt), from prophetism to apocalyptic (N. Lemche), prophecy at Qumran? (H. Barstad), popular wisdom in Qohelet (B. Rodendal), is Job a scapegoat? (S. Holm-Nielsen), the cosmic wedding and brief life on earth (H. Jensen), Gen. 4:26 (K. Jeppesen), Hellenism in archaeology (J. Strange), the Hasmonean palaces (I. Nielsen), dating biblical Hebrew and the Hebrew of Daniel (F. Cryer), and self-awareness in Christian study of the Old Testament after the Holocaust (G. Dahm).

L. L. GRABBE

KAISER, OTTO: *Grundriss der Einleitung in die kanonischen und deutero-kanonischen Schriften des Alten Testaments. Band 2: Die prophetischen Werke*. 1994. Pp. 198. (Mohn, Gütersloh. Price: DM 68.00. ISBN 3 579 00053 5)

KAISER, OTTO: *Grundriss der Einleitung in die kanonischen und deutero-kanonischen Schriften des Alten Testament. Band 3: Die poetischen und weisheitlichen Werke*. 1994. Pp. 163. (Mohn, Gütersloh. Price: DM 68.00/ SwF 69.30/AS 531. ISBN 3 579 00054 3)

This is the second volume of a revised and enlarged Introduction to the Old Testament (for Vol. 1 see *B.L.* 1993, p. 89). There were ecstatic and mantic prophets in Israel in parallel with other ancient Near Eastern peoples, but the prophetic narratives have all been heavily coloured by Deuteronomists in order to draw lessons for the exiles. The treatment of Isaiah is familiar from K.'s most recent versions of his commentary. Second Isaiah ('the jewel of the prophetic collection') shows signs of editing by disciples to explain the delay in the fulfilment of the promises, while an even later redaction limited the fulfilment to the faithful only. Jeremiah also manifests the three-fold (post-exilic) structure of all the prophetic books; judgement against Israel/Judah, deliverance for Israel and judgement of the nations. Ezekiel (dealt with by K.-F. Pohlmann) shows a later two-stage editing of the prophet's words, one favouring the exiles of the 597 deportation and the other a (later) pro-Diaspora redaction, to which have been added the apocalyptic-type oracles against the nations. The treatment of the smaller books is briefer and mainly limited to the very useful task of reporting recent scholarly investigation, mostly of a redaction-critical nature.

With this third volume K. completes the major rewriting of his earlier Introduction. After a glimpse at other poetry he turns to the Psalms to which he adds the five apocryphal psalms, the Prayer of Manasseh and the Psalms of Solomon. Brevity characterizes this section, but the attention to the history of modern study, the full bibliographies and the succinct comments make this as useful as the other volumes. And in addition to the analytical character of much traditional biblical criticism he always finds room for comment on the final canonical form, so that, for example, the setting of a torah and a messianic Psalm at the beginning of the Psalter shows later generations the conditions for entering the messianic age. The Wisdom section opens with a statement on the forms and setting of Wisdom literature in the ancient Near East and the circles from which it came. To Proverbs, Job and Koheleth are added sections on Ben Sira and the Wisdom of Solomon. A brief final section considers matters of canon, inspiration and the formation of the Hebrew Scriptures. There is a select index of subjects and biblical references for the three volumes but, alas for a work of this kind, not one of modern authors. The list of *corrigenda* for Vols 1 and 2 will need supplementing for this one, not least for the mis-spelling of *unergründlicher* on p. 93.   R. MASON

KAISER, WALTER C., JR, and SILVA, MOISÉS: *An Introduction to Biblical Hermeneutics. The Search for Meaning*. 1994. Pp. 298. (Zondervan, Grand Rapids MI. Price: $24.99. ISBN 0 310 53090 3)

Although the authors see themselves as representing two distinctive positions within the American conservative evangelical world, readers would be more struck by what they have in common: understanding the Bible is first a grammatico-historical (but not historical-critical) task, and then an applicatory one. Ch. 1 includes one-page summaries of the work of figures such as Gadamer and Ricoeur, but the book is not preoccupied by that consciousness of the essential historicity of our work as interpreters. It believes in authors', not readers', meaning and is concerned to offer guidance on how we ascertain the original sense of narrative, poetry, gospels, epistles, and prophecy. Then security is shattered by chs 13 (which reintroduces Gadamer and Ricoeur from a much more positive angle) and 14 (which presents an implicity related and thought-provoking 'case for Calvinistic hermeneutics'). There did seem a very sharp tension between these chapters and the preceding ones.

J. GOLDINGAY

KESSLER, MARTIN (ed.): *Voices from Amsterdam. A Modern Tradition of Reading Biblical Narrative* (Society of Biblical Literature Semeia Studies). 1994. Pp. xxiv, 168. (Scholars Press, Atlanta. Price: $44.95; paper $29.95. ISBN 1 55540 896 6; paper 1 55540 897 4)

This fascinating collection of Dutch voices contains a brief but informative introduction to the Amsterdam tradition by K. (whose work on Jeremiah I have always found to be most useful), tracing the Jewish influences (as befits the city where the great Spinoza lived and worked) of Juda L. Palache (a professor in Amsterdam from 1924 to 1940, when the Germans of the Third Reich removed all Jews from public service) and the Buber-Rosenzweig approach to biblical hermeneutics on the Amsterdam school. Palache was followed by M. A. Beek (1946–74) and K. A. Deurloo (1974–). So there are echoes and traces of seventy years of Amsterdam voices in this volume. The section on methodological essays includes Palache's inaugural address, along with essays by Beek (on the study of Hebrew literature), Deurloo (on Cain and Abel), Klaas A. D. Smelik (on approaches to Hebrew narrative), and Rochus Zuurmond (on a critical hermeneutic). Three studies on Genesis are included: Frans H. Breukelman on Gen. 6:1–4; Deurloo on routes and localities in Gen. 11:27–25:11 and on Gen. 22. The final section consists of Aleida G. van Daalen on Exodus 3, and Beek on Joshua and on David and Absalom. The whole volume contributes significantly to those voices currently heard objecting to the critical sclerosis of much of contemporary biblical *Wissenschaft*. A volume well worth listening to and I heartily recommend it.

R. P. CARROLL

KLEIN, CHRISTIAN: *Kohelet und die Weisheit Israels. Eine formgeschichtliche Studie* (Beiträge zur Wissenschaft vom Alten und Neuen Testament 132 = Folge 7, Heft 12). 1994. Pp. 227. (Kohlhammer, Stuttgart. Price: DM 79.00/AS 616/SwF 80.90. ISBN 3 17 012497 8)

Since the advent of the form-critical approach to Old Testament study there have been attempts to isolate *Gattungen* in the book of Kohelet, but the attempts have usually focused on a passage here and a verse there. K., taking his cue from a remark by von Rad, tries to be more comprehensive. After an introduction, he discusses the nature of the Old Testament *mašal*; and follows this with a discussion of the Old Testament wisdom *Kunstspruch* and its relationship to the proverb. Having set the scene, as it were, K. tackles a form-critical analysis of the book of Kohelet, at first isolating and classifying Kohelet's sayings and the various forms to be found there, and offering a classification table (p. 121); and then showing that extended passages may be considered larger *mešalim*: 1.4–11; 1.12–2.26; 3.1–15; 4.13–16; 9.13–10.3; 11.7–12.7, eventually raising the question of the possibility of classifying the entire book as a *mašal*. The final chapter is a discussion of the place of Kohelet in the wisdom of Israel. This book is stimulating and will provoke further research, but it is not entirely convincing, and it is marred by too many mistakes in the Hebrew.

R. B. SALTERS

KREITZER, LARRY J.: *The Old Testament in Fiction and Film. On Reversing the Hermeneutical Flow* (The Biblical Seminar 24). 1994. Pp. 243. (Sheffield Academic Press. Price: £12.50/$18.95. ISBN 1 85075 487 X)

Many of us who study, teach and/or preach the Bible are lamentably ignorant of the extent to which the Bible has influenced modern literature, both written and cinematic. K. has set himself the task of starting to remove that ignorance. In 1993, he tackled *The New Testament in Fiction and Film*. Now he has turned his attention to the Old Testament or, at least, to parts of it, and to how those parts have influenced selected novels and films: he looks at Job and Jonah in *Moby-Dick*, Cain and Abel in *East of Eden*, Genesis 1–2 in *Frankenstein*, Qoheleth in *A Farewell to Arms* and the Decalogue in two films, C. B. DeMille's *The Ten Commandments* and Kieslowski's *Decalogue*. Admittedly only a small selection from an absolutely vast subject, one which needs whole libraries to cover completely! K. is opening up an important area for biblical studies, and does so in an easy and accessible style. Not everyone will agree with all that he says, and whether he has completely succeeded in 'reversing the hermeneutical flow' is open to debate, but there is no doubt that all will enjoy reading this book and will 'have their reading of, and appreciation for, the Old Testament documents enhanced' (p. 223).

C. H. KNIGHTS

McEVENUE, SEAN: *Interpretation and Bible. Essays on Truth in Literature*. 1994. Pp. 187. (Liturgical Press, Collegeville MN. Price: $12.95/£11.99. ISBN 0 8146 5036 8)

This book is a collection of some of M.'s lectures (many of them already published) on understanding the Bible from the point of view of the late Bernard Lonergan's philosophy of imagination and his method in theology. As Lonergan did not write directly on the Bible, these essays attempt to apply his insights, so M.'s project might be categorized as part biblical hermeneutics and part biblical *Wirkungsgeschichte*. The book is divided up into sections on 'The Affirmation of Truth in the Bible', 'Truth in Literature', 'Examples of Interpretation in this Mode', and 'Preaching based on Old Testament Texts'. Within these sections are numerous essays, many of them full of interest, on current debates on the Bible as literature and as scripture, especially in relation to M.'s own interests in the Pentateuch and the Bible in Catholic liturgy. Much insight and much irritation with modern writers on the Bible are to be found in this collection. I enjoyed and liked this book, especially M.'s emphasis on the text as literature: 'Once one begins to treat the texts as literary texts, then the scholarship of the past two centuries ceases to be a problem. Rather, it becomes a precious contribution.' (p. 176). I recommend it to every reader concerned with 'making sense' of the Bible today.

R. P. CARROLL

MAGONET, JONATHAN: *A Rabbi Reads the Psalms*. 1994. Pp. viii, 200. (SCM, London. Price: £12.95. ISBN 0 334 01364 X)

Following the author's *A Rabbi's Bible* (*B.L.* 1992, p. 126), this new book has also grown out of actual teaching, in dialogue with both students and colleagues (among whom the reviewer gladly acknowledges a great debt to him); but also out of M.'s work of translation of Psalms for the Reform

Synagogue's Prayer Book. This new volume contains more precisely focused exegesis of passages than its predecessor, but always with the same mixture of learning, penetrating insight and delightful light touches. The Psalms dealt with are 145, 92, 23, 25, 19, 22; those in which the epithet 'Maker of heaven and earth' occurs (115, 121, 124, 134, 146); 90 and 73. M. notes patterns of key words and particles, which become clues to structure and then to deeper insights; often these are then shown to have been noted long ago by Ibn Ezra, Rashi, or Radak. The choice of psalms here shows a particular (though balanced) interest in various forms of chiastic structure and in illustrating how attention to structure often reveals deeper meanings. A pleasing feature is the appendix giving full Hebrew texts of the Psalms studied; this also can help some readers to decode the transliterations of Hebrew words in the text!

R. P. R. MURRAY

MARCH, W. EUGENE: *Israel and the Politics of Land. A Theological Case Study*. Foreword by Walter Brueggemann. 1994. Pp. xiii, 104. (Westminster/ John Knox, Louisville KY. Price: $12.99. ISBN 0 664 25121 8)

Nearly half this brief study comprises an even-handed introduction to the peoples of contemporary Israel and to the history of the land since New Testament times. It then goes on to consider the theological and ethical issues related to land as these apply to that particular land. It offers as a 'guiding vision' the premises of God the creator and human beings as God's earth-keepers, with the right and responsibility to live in *shalom* on their land. A strength and a weakness is that its perspective applies to any people's land. If one excludes the view that Old Testament prophecy is literally fulfilled in contemporary Middle Eastern events, there is no way in which special theological significance attaches to this particular land, and it questions whether even Judaism needs Israel. I was surprised that an avowedly Reformed Christian stance adopts this position, given that tradition's emphasis on the theological significance of the Jewish people as well as M.'s own stress on the this-worldliness of the gospel.

J. GOLDINGAY

MEIER, SAMUEL A.: *Speaking of Speaking. Making Direct Discourse in the Hebrew Bible* (Supplements to Vetus Testamentum 46). 1992. Pp. xvi, 383. (Brill, Leiden–New York–Köln. Price: fl. 175.00/$100.00. ISBN 90 04 09602 7; ISSN 0083 5889)

In Biblical Hebrew prose, direct discourse is consistently 'marked', almost always with some form of the verb *'amar*, which always occurs before the direct discouse. Poetry often leaves direct discourse 'unmarked', frequently does not employ the verb *'amar*, and commonly positions the mark of direct discourse (e.g. 'Thus said Y'.) within or following the direct discourse. Within prose, M. claims to detect different preferences in different books, or even within sources in the same book, for formulae for introducing direct discourse (for example, 'he spoke and said', *wydbr w'mr* in Leviticus). As for divine speech, he notices an 'aggressive concern' to mark it in exilic and post-exilic texts, by contrast with the more casual marking in earlier texts. But even there, the use of speech markers is rather unpredictable, and it is unwise to assume that, for example, n'm Yhwh is a signal of closure in a prophetic oracle. There is patient and systematic work here, but the harvest is, predictably, rather meagre. And fundamental categories like prose, poetry and even 'direct discourse', as well as assumptions about dating texts, need further consideration.

D. J. A. CLINES

MILLARD, MATTHIAS: *Die Komposition des Psalters. Ein formgeschicht-licher Ansatz* (Forschungen zum Alten Testament 9). 1994. Pp. ix, 290. (Mohr, Tübingen. Price: DM 168.00. ISBN 3 16 146214 9; ISSN 0940 4155)

The flurry of interest in the shape and shaping of the Psalter which has marked recent American research is here taken up in a German dissertation. The study has three main parts. First, the concern is with the literary context of the individual psalm, for example where there is a series of clearly related psalms. Second, groups of psalms such as the Korah collections are examined form-critically as a unit, and patterns such as lament–oracle–hymn running through the block are traced and examined in their variations. Third, the history of the development of the Psalter is reconstructed with special attention to the early form of the Elohistic collection and the construction of the Psalter in the Persian period. The study is rounded off with consideration of the place of the Psalter in the canon and its role as a book of prayer. This is altogether a useful discussion, based on wide reading.   J. H. EATON

NICCACCI, ALVIERO: *La casa della sapienza. Voci e volti della sapienza biblica*. 1994. Pp. 186. (Edizioni San Paolo, Milan. Price: Lire 24,000. ISBN 88 215 2758 1)

The author begins by contrasting Lady Wisdom and Dame Folly, with their respective invitations and promises. Then from the practical wisdom of Proverbs via Job down to Sirach and the Wisdom of Solomon he presents the theology of Old Testament wisdom culminating in Jesus, incarnate Wisdom, the voice and face of the invisible God. The author's interest in biblical wisdom literature flows from an interest in ancient Egyptian literature which it surpasses. He illustrates his presentation of biblical wisdom with numerous line drawings from Egyptian art and sculpture. The book is part of a series, Narrare la Bibbia, aimed at a popular readership who will learn of the problem wrestled with in the book of Job, the stance of Qoheleth, love as the force of life in the Song of Songs, and the search for wisdom that runs through the literature into the New Testament.   J. R. DUCKWORTH

OLSON, DENNIS T.: *Deuteronomy and the Death of Moses. A Theological Reading* (Overtures to Biblical Theology). 1994. Pp. xvi, 191. (Fortress, Minneapolis; SCM, London. Price: $14.00/£10.50. ISBN 0 8006 2639 7)

My appreciation of this broad-brush reading of Deuteronomy is reflected in the fact that I kept wanting to interrupt and say 'That's interesting, couldn't you elaborate it a bit?' or 'That's a bit of an exaggeration, isn't it?' or 'Oh, come off it'. He offers much illumination on the book's structure and function, even if he tends to claim too much for the finality of his understanding and to treat an illuminating partial insight as total objective truth (e.g., the stress on the motif of Moses' death as underlying the book as a whole). In other words, it's a more readerly read of Deuteronomy than he acknowledges. One giveaway is the way Deuteronomy's concerns nicely coincide with ours — chs 7–10 confront the gods of miltarism, materialism, and moralism. I liked his emphasis on the triumph of God's grace in Deuteronomy (compare J. G. McConville's: *B.L.* 1994, p. 111) but that's my readerly perspective on his readerly perspective . . . Diachronic considerations are not ignored, but they do not contribute much to the argument.   J. GOLDINGAY

PARDES, ILANA: *Countertraditions in the Bible. A Feminist Approach*. 1992. Pp. x, 194. (Harvard University Press, Cambridge MA–London. Price: £23.95/$29.95; paper £10.25/$15.50. ISBN 0 674 17542 5; paper 0 674 17545 X)

This is an attractive and somewhat novel approach to feminist biblical interpretation. P. sets herself against two common feminist stances which she regards as false: that represented by Phyllis Trible, who seeks to 'depatriarchalize' biblical texts, and its opposite, found in Esther Fuchs, who stresses only the patriarchal presuppositions of the biblical writers. Instead she argues for an appreciation of the 'heterogeneity of the Hebrew canon', and a recognition that many different 'socio-ideological horizons' are present in the text. After commenting on six interpretations of Eve (Elizabeth Cady Stanton, Simone de Beauvoir and Kate Millett, Trible, Fuchs, Mieke Bal, and Harold Bloom), she discusses in turn Genesis 3, Rachel, Zipporah, Ruth, the Song of Songs, and Job's wife. In each case features which present women in a favourable light are set alongside patriarchal attitudes, cultural norms and values. She also utilizes Freudian psychology to assist her interpretations. Both as an exposé of the very different ways feminists read a biblical text, and as a positive exposition of the selected passages, this is an important contribution to both feminist studies and biblical interpretation.

C. S. RODD

PARKER, T. H. L.: *Calvin's Old Testament Commentaries*. 1993 (1986). Pp. ix, 239. (T. & T. Clark, Edinburgh; Westminster/John Knox, Louisville KY. Price: £12.50/$16.99. ISBN (Clark) 0 567 29242 8; (Westminster) 0 664 25490 X)

P. has performed a sterling service by his many studies of Calvin's exegetical, expository, and homiletic work. Together, they offer a lucid picture of the other Calvin, the Calvin who wrote (and preached and lectured) much more than the *Institutes*. This study, first published in 1986 and now in its second UK and first US edition, is a worthy addition to that series. Since the new edition contains no substantive changes, there is little to add to the review which appeared in *B.L.* 1987, p. 73 (apart from noting the peculiar fact that typographical errors have been introduced on p. 38 which were not present in the first edition!). It is a pity that P. has not taken the opportunity offered by a second edition to compare Calvin's methods of exegesis and exposition, however cursorily, with those of his contemporaries and of medieval prdecessors — particularly since the book is intended for general readers. But the book remains so readable and informative as it stands that it would be ungrateful to ask for more.

D. V. N. BAGCHI

PERDUE, LEO G.; SCOTT, BERNARD BRANDON; and WISEMAN, WILLIAM JOHNSTON (ed.): *In Search of Wisdom. Essays in Memory of John G. Gammie*. Foreword by James Barr. 1993. Pp. xviii, 318. (Westminster/John Knox, Louisville KY. Price: $24.99. ISBN 0 664 25295 8)

Although the title of this volume indicates a general intention to investigate concepts of wisdom found in a wide variety of texts, it consists of a collection of disparate essays in which its various authors, specialists in their respective fields, have gone their own ways. There is neither a general introduction nor a concluding editorial attempt to draw together the diverse strands of the wisdom theme. After an initial chapter on the concept of God in Old Testament wisdom (J. L. Crenshaw), the remaining fourteen chapters discuss respectively wisdom in the work of the Chronicler (J. Blenkinsopp), the Book of the Twelve (R. C. Van Leuuwen), the Psalter (S. Terrien), Job (Perdue), Proverbs (C. R. Fontaine), Qoheleth (M. V. Fox), Ben Sira (A. A. di Lella), Wisdom of Solomon (D. Winston), apocalypticism (J. J. Collins),

Q and the *Gospel of Thomas* (S. J. Patterson), Mark (R. Horsley), Matthew (Scott), Paul (E. E. Johnson), and the Apocalypse of John (T. Pippin). In one of these (Chronicles) the author was hard put to discover anything that could properly be called wisdom. Some of the chapters are mainly summaries of the present state of scholarship, but there is also original material here.

R. N. WHYBRAY

PERLITT, LOTHAR: *Deuteronomium-Studien* (Forschungen zum Alten Testament 8). 1994. Pp. viii, 271. (Mohr, Tübingen. Price: DM 178.00. ISBN 3 16 146154 1)

The fifteen studies contained here have all been previously published, but many of them in Festschriften which may easily be overlooked. They are all in some way connected with the book of Deuteronomy and well repay study as carefully researched and argued expositions of specific themes. The topics covered include Moses as Prophet, Sinai and Horeb, Israel as a Nation of Brothers, Deut. 6:20–25, The Septuagint of Deut. 1:12, Giants in the Land in Those Days, Gospel and Law in Deuteronomy and Hebraismus — Deuteronomismus — Judaismus. The method is that of a close textual analysis, critical evaluation of source material and historical origin, and a thorough exposition of the significance of the text or theme. The general reader will probably feel the lack of any presentation of the author's understanding of the overall place of Deuteronomy in critical research to give an introduction, although much of this is implied in the studies.

Throughout these essays provide a valuable guide to the wealth that literary-critical and form-critical method have to offer in understanding the complex nature of Deuteronomy.

R. E. CLEMENTS

POLAK, FRANK: *hsypwr bmqr'. bhynwt b'yṣwb wb'mnwt [Biblical Narrative. Aspects of Art and Design]* (Biblical Encyclopaedia Library 11). 1994. Pp. 31*, 481. (Bialik Institute, Jerusalem. N.P.)

This is an important and wide-ranging book which seeks to apply the results of modern literary studies (up to 1988) to the interpretation of the Bible. The author covers many topics, ranging from oral transmission and folk-lore studies through narrative style and plot to larger questions such as authors and readers. Following a general introduction about the nature of story in general and biblical story in particular, the author discusses linguistic style, the composition of stories, and the formation of larger narratives before turning to authors and readers. An interesting and important chapter then discusses the relation between literary and historical-critical methods, and while the author's views incline towards the conservative, he affirms the importance of diachronic readings. (For non-readers of Hebrew, P. has an article on this in the *Amsterdamse Cahiers* (1988). A short concluding history of literary study leaves much to be desired, and matters such as deconstruction are touched on only briefly. However, the book as a whole is marked by comprehensiveness, fairness and sensitivity. The excellent indexes enable readers to find topics and biblical passages easily. A translation into English would be worth consideration.

J. W. ROGERSON

100   LITERARY CRITICISM AND INTRODUCTION

POLZIN, ROBERT: *Moses and the Deuteronomist. A Literary Study of the Deuteronomic History. Part One: Deuteronomy, Joshua, Judges* (Indiana Studies in Biblical Literature). 1993 (1980). Pp. xiii, 232. (Indiana University Press, Bloomington and Indianapolis; distributed in the UK by the Open University Press, Buckingham. Price: £27.50; paper £13.99. ISBN 0 253 34554 5; paper 0 253 20848 3)

This is an unaltered paperback reprint of the volume reviewed in *B.L.* 1982, p. 70.

ED.

POLZIN, ROBERT: *Samuel and the Deuteronomist. A Literary Study of the Deuteronomic History. Part Two: 1 Samuel* (Indiana Studies in Biblical Literature). 1993 (1989). Pp. ix, 297. (Indiana University Press, Bloomington and Indianapolis; distributed in the UK by the Open University Press, Buckingham. Price: £27.50; paper £13.99. ISBN 0 253 34552 9; paper 0 253 20849 1)

POLZIN, ROBERT: *David and the Deuteronomist. A Literary Study of the Deuteronomic History. Part Three: 2 Samuel* (Indian Studies in Biblical Literature). 1993. Pp. x, 245. (Indiana University Press, Bloomington and Indianapolis; distributed in the UK by Open University Press, Buckingham. Price: £35.00. ISBN 0 253 34553 7)

These are the middle volumes of a projected four-volume series on the Deuteronomistic History (for the first, see above). Part Two, which first appeared in 1989 and is now issued in paperback, has not so far been noted in *B.L.* In the introduction to this volume P. weighs in against representative commentators and monographers whose literary excavative preoccupations have lashed their attentions to reconstructed 'pre-texts' of their own creation rather than the only text that actually exists, here described as the 'real text'. The Bakhtin-influenced discussion of the 'real text' maintains the high level of discourse of the first volume, with many sharp observations on the narrative artistry of the Deuteronomist who is essentially an author, and not just the redactor of so many modern accounts of the Deuteronomistic History. Thus, while the warnings about the perils of reconstructing sources are justified, P.'s assumption of a plenipotentiary Deuteronomist writing in the exile becomes the basis of its own set of assumptions about historical context and referents ('in these plaintive words [*sc.* in 1 Sam. 28:15], it is not especially difficult to hear the voice of Israel in exile . . .' [p. 220]).

Part Three does not offer the lively introductory banter of the earlier volumes and is less concerned to interact with contemporary writings in the main text, 'to allow my version of the story in 2 Samuel to speak for itself' (p. ix). P.'s concern with levels of meaning in texts remains and, though there is a distinct air of the over-wrought about some of the discussion, he writes brilliantly on the interrelationships between texts, whether within Samuel or within the larger Deuteronomistic work which his series assumes.

R. P. GORDON

RABINOWITZ, ISAAC: *A Witness Forever. Ancient Israel's Perception of Literature and the Resultant Hebrew Bible* (Occasional Publications of the Department of Near Eastern Studies and the Program of Jewish Studies, Cornell University 1). Edited with afterwords by Ross Brann and David I. Owen. 1993. Pp. xvii, 148. (CDL Press, Bethesda MD. Price: $20.00. ISBN 1 88305 302 1)

The volume comprises a manuscript left by Rabinowitz at his death, together with a bibliography of his writings, a reminiscence, and a brief biography. It offers an attempt to describe how words and the literary process were understood in ancient Israel and to draw some conclusions about the Hebrew Bible as a whole. Words were believed to have 'extra-communicative properties and potencies' (p. 4) and represented the 'inner, specific characters of their respective realities' (p. 10). Reading was a speech-act intended to accomplish an effect. Written words were the inscriptional form of their referents, and the act of writing fixed the words so that they became a living witness. Rabinowitz then considers and illustrates some of the consequences of such perceptions. The final chapter considers the literary unity of the Hebrew Bible as 'the word-essence of the God-man-natural order' (p. 120), but perhaps goes too far in suggesting that this was the conscious aim of the assemblers and compilers. It makes a pleasant change to be asked to think about what those who produced the Hebrew Bible may have thought they were doing!

A. H. W. CURTIS

REVENTLOW, HENNING GRAF: *Epochen der Bibelauslegung. Band II: Von der Spätantike bis zum Ausgang des Mittelalters.* 1994. Pp. 324. (Beck, Munich. Price: DM 58.00. ISBN 3 406 34986 2)

Vol. I was reviewed in *B.L.* 1992, p. 23. Vol. II opens with a long chapter on the great 4th- and 5th-century exegetes: Theodore of Mopsuestia, Didymus the Blind, Jerome, Ambrose, John Cassian and Augustine (the weighting on the Latin side is curious: no mention of Cyril of Alexandria or Theodoret). Ch. 2 cover the 6th to 9th centuries with Gregory the Great, Isidore of Seville, Bede, Alcuin and John Eriugena. Ch. 3 discusses the importance of the Catenae and Glosses and that of the Sententiae and Quaestiones, before considering Abelard, Rupert of Deutz, Hugo of St Victor, Joachim of Fiore, Thomas Aquinas and Bonaventure. Ch. 4 looks briefly at the main trends in medieval Jewish exegesis, focused on Rashi and Ibn Ezra. The final chapter traces Jewish influence on late medieval Christian writers, especially Nicholas of Lyra, and ends in the late-14th century, with John Wyclif.

J. M. DINES

REVENTLOW, HENNING GRAF; HOFFMAN, YAIR; and UFFENHEIMER, BENJAMIN (eds): *Politics and Theopolitics in the Bible and Postbiblical Literature* (Journal for the Study of the Old Testament Supplement 171). 1994. Pp. 216. (Sheffield Academic Press. Price: £30.00/$45.00. ISBN 1 85075 461 6; ISSN 0309 0787)

The papers which comprise this volume were read at meetings between the Department of Bible of Tel Aviv University and the Faculty of Protestant Theology of the University of Bochum. To say that the subject matter is important is to make a cult of understatement, for the place of power politics in the shaping of the biblical literature is apparent on almost every page of the Bible. Studies of the biblical texts themselves deal with the hidden polemic in the final chapters of Judges, tensions in the picture of David representing both 'the divine legitimation of royal authority' and 'the king's responsibility for the use and abuse of his power', Paul's promise of the victory of Christ over the cosmic powers and John's vision contrasting Babylon and New Jerusalem, a contrast Wengst sees as sadly lost later by the Church to the detriment of subsequent Jewish–Christian relations. The implications for the modern politics both of Israel and of 'Christendom' are enormous, though only hinted at here and there. Not only is the variety of themes of interest but also the complementary variety of approaches between Israeli and European scholars. A volume to savour.

R. MASON

RYKEN, LELAND and LONGMAN III, TREMPER (eds): *A Complete Literary Guide to the Bible*. 1993. Pp. 528. (Zondervan, Grand Rapids MI. Price: $29.99. ISBN 0 310 51830 X)

This collection of essays, designed as a counter to Alter and Kermode's *The Literary Guide to the Bible* (*B.L.* 1990, p. 64), is divided into four parts. Introductory essays on the literary study of the Bible and its main genres are followed by two sections in which most of the Old and New Testament books are dealt with individually. The final part links the Bible to contemporary literary culture. The claimed completeness of the guide is certainly hard to square with the lack of separate essays on Ezekiel or Jeremiah. The editors also consciously adopt a particular and therefore incomplete view of what constitutes literary criticism. The avowed aim is to marry literary approaches to the Bible with the theology of Evangelical readers. Within these parameters, there is much in the individual essays that is thought-provoking. Particularly interesting are the contributions from practising novelists, notably Chaim Potok. Readers would do well to be aware, however, of the range of possibilities of literary interpretation which are not dealt with in this volume.   H. S. PYPER

SCHÄFER-LICHTENBERGER, CHRISTA: *Josua und Salomo. Eine Studie zu Authorität und Legitimität des Nachfolgers im Alten Testament* (Supplements to Vetus Testamentum 58). 1995. Pp. xii, 424. (Brill, Leiden–New York–Köln. Price: fl. 190/$108.75. ISBN 90 04 10064 4; ISSN 0083 5889)

Essentially the author's 1992 Heidelberg *Habilitationsschrift*, this is in three main parts. The first (pp. 16–106) opens by exploring the concepts authority and legitimacy, then notions of succession. It next reviews Deuteronomy's teaching on God's authority and the political system, concentrating on the laws relating to king and prophet: a separation of powers *in nuce*. The second (pp. 107–224) reviews the Joshua traditions in the Bible under four headings: war-hero; scout and successor; Joshua in Deuteronomy; the successor, his task, and the Torah. The third (pp. 225–355) reviews the portrait of Solomon in 1 Kings 1–11, including the relationship of the two figures. The short conclusion (pp. 356–74) sketches the results: Joshua was successful because he orientated himself not by Moses' person, but by the norm granted to Moses and transmitted in written form by Joshua; Solomon was a failure because he conformed neither to what was exemplary in his father nor to the Torah which David had specifically commended to him. Much of the so-called Deuteronomistic History comes under S.-L.'s scrutiny in this thoroughly argued and often very illuminating study.   A. G. AULD

SCHMIDT, LUDWIG: *Studien zur Priesterschrift* (Beihefte zur Zeitschrift für die alttestamentliche Wissenschaft 214). 1993. Pp. viii, 281. (de Gruyter, Berlin–New York. Price: DM 134.00. ISBN 3 11 013867 0; ISSN 0934 2575)

Basically, this detailed study sets out to prove that P was originally an independent written source, with its own particular outlook. To demonstrate this, the author analyses three blocks of material. The first consists of the priestly texts in Exod. 1–14. The second is the four priestly 'murmuring' stories, which S. views as forming two pairs of contrasts: the quail-manna narrative where Yahweh shows benevolence and the story of the scouts where he punishes, with the similar pattern of punishment in the case of the 250 men and benevolence in the case of water from the rock. The third section discusses the priestly accounts of the deaths of Moses and Aaron and the appointment of Joshua: P had no account of the occupation of Canaan, because for P only the lifetime of Moses was the period of fundamental significance for Israel. Although P is an independent composition, it uses the pre-priestly literary version of events in the first two above sections and the Deuteronomistic presentation in the third. S.'s work is an example of the revival of the Wellhausian spirit characteristic of much recent German Old Testament scholarship. Within its own terms of reference, it presents a strong case: those who do not share the author's pre-suppositions may not find it quite so convincing.

J. R. PORTER

SCHNECK, RICHARD, S. J.: *Isaiah in the Gospel of Mark, I–VIII* (BIBAL Dissertation Series 1). 1994. Pp. xii, 339. (BIBAL Press, Vallejo CA. Price: $19.95. ISBN 0 941037 28 2)

In a dissertation of rather uneven quality, S. considers those passages in Mark 1–8 in which the Bible Societies' Greek New Testament detects quotations of or allusions to Isaiah (he adds a small number not noted there, and occasionally addresses alleged parallels with other prophets). Exegesis, sometimes rather discursive, of these passages frames exploration of their use of the Isaianic and other prophetic texts in question. In several cases S. revives and expands the hypothesis that Mark had access to a collection of Testimonia. He also tries to show that the author of the Marcan text, once pointed by the tradition towards a verse in Isaiah, found himself able to make structural and theological use of a number of elements in that verse's context (S. attributes much of this work to a 'catechist or . . . preacher' who knew the Masoretic text, p. 72: the Hebrew text forms the basis of most of what S. says, and at least once the pre-Marcan tradent is assumed to know the Isaiah Targum, pp. 129–32). Few of the new parallels S. finds between Mark and Isaiah are, however, solid enough to bear the weight he puts on them. He has interacted widely with previous work, but his own contribution fails to inspire confidence.

C. J. A. HICKLING

SCHÜSSLER FIORENZA, ELISABETH (ed.), with the assistance of S. Matthews: *Searching the Scriptures. Volume 1: A Feminist Introduction.* 1994. Pp. xiii, 397. (SCM, London. Price: £17.50. ISBN 0 334 02556 7)

SCHÜSSLER FIORENZA, ELISABETH (ed.), with the assistance of Ann Brock and Shelly Matthews: *Searching the Scriptures. Volume 2: A Feminist Commentary.* 1994. Pp. xiii, 525. (SCM, London; Crossroad, New York. Price: £20.00/$49.50. ISBN 0 8245 1424 6)

These are a fascinating collection of essays illustrating the range and diversity of feminist interpretation, much of it grounded in practical experience of using the Bible in preaching and non-academic study groups. The horizons of feminism are widened to address not only questions of gender but of class and race and there is much that is fresh and stimulating. Cady Stanton's work of last century is commemorated but criticized too for its white middle class ethos, hence the editor's introductory essay, 'Transforming the Legacy of *The Woman's Bible*'.

The twenty-four essays of volume 1, whose contributors represent ecumenical and multiracial scholarship, fall into four sections concerned respectively with (1) biblical interpretation in various socio-historical contexts (European, black American, Cuban and African); (2) creating feminist frames of meaning in place of the patriarchal; (3) rethinking critical methods, literary, sociological and anthropological; and (4) feminist approaches to preaching and Bible study in the context of black and white churches. Diverse approaches to the Hagar story demonstrate how social forces influence the reading of texts: the primary significance for black American women is her slavery, for Latin Americans her poverty, for Africans polygamy, for Asians the loss of cultural identity. It is to be hoped that so stimulating a work will reach beyond the feminist constituency. Volume 2 is concerned mainly with Christian texts, canonical and non-canonical. The chapters of particular relevance treat of the Wisdom of Solomon, Judith, the Sibylline Oracles and the Testament of Job.

G. I. EMMERSON

SEIDEL, BODO: *Karl David Ilgen und die Pentateuchforschung im Umkreis der sogenannten Älteren Urkundenhypothese. Studien zur Geschichte der exegetischen Hermeneutik in der Späten Aufklärung* (Beihefte zur Zeitschrift für die alttestamentliche Wissenschaft 213). 1993. Pp. xii, 357. (de Gruyter, Berlin–New York. Price: DM 158.00. ISBN 3 11 013833 6; ISSN 0934 2575)

For two centuries Karl David Ilgen's name has remained but a footnote in the history of Pentateuchal research — Eichhorn's successor at Jena who isolated two 'Elohists' in Genesis but whose findings published in 1798 made no impact and had to be more successfully rediscovered by H. Hupfeld more than half a century later. Perhaps if Ilgen had remained in his chair at Jena his name would have gained a more illustrious place in the history of biblical studies. He left Jena in 1802 for a post as a school master. In a biographical chapter S. discusses the reasons for such a move. He describes also Ilgen's considerable unpublished works, of which he edits and published as an appendix his source analysis of Exodus 1–12 ('Zur Geschichte der Israeliten unter Diktatoren'). The main interest of S.'s study, however, focuses upon Ilgen's work within the intellectual context of the late Enlightenment, with special emphasis upon the emergence of historical thinking in biblical criticism, and upon Ilgen's book itself, its hermeneutical presuppositions and literary conclusions, and its analysis of Genesis. S. deserves our thanks for this interesting and fascinating book, which has all the signs of having been a labour of love.

E. W. NICHOLSON

SIMKINS, RONALD A.: *Creator and Creation. Nature in the Worldview of Ancient Israel.* 1994. Pp. xii, 306. (Hendrickson, Peabody MA. Price: $14.95. ISBN 1 56563 042 4)

In keeping with various trends of recent years this book plays down the role of history as a sphere of divine activity in the Old Testament. The author rather focuses on the sphere of nature and considers the various attitudes towards it in different parts of the Old Testament: mastery-over-nature, harmony-with-nature, and subjugation-to-nature. Thus, for example, the royal theology of Jerusalem reflects both the mastery-over-nature and the harmony-with-nature orientation, while the Yahwist and Priestly writers are held to advocate harmony-with-nature. The book of Job, on the other hand, reflects an experience of subjugation-to-nature, an attitude found also in some prophetic books, though the latter also envision God's new creation when the land will be restored as a new Eden. In general this is an interesting and valuable study. It sets Israel's creation theology in its ancient Near Eastern background and emphasizes the continuity between them, and is also concerned that the Bible should be able to contribute to the current discussion about the modern environmental crisis.

J. DAY

STIENSTRA, NELLY: *Yhwh Is the Husband of his People. Analysis of a Biblical Metaphor with Special Reference to Translation.* 1993. Pp. 252. (Kok Pharos, Kampen. Price: fl. 59.90. ISBN 90 390 0103 0)

In her investigation into the biblical metaphor of Yhwh as the husband of his people, S. has attempted to combine three areas of research — metaphor, biblical exegesis, and translation. After a survey of modern theories on metaphorical concepts, in which it is concluded that metaphor is a matter of concept as well as of language, the author gives some indication of how to apply the insights of modern metaphor theory to biblical examples. She turns to biblical exegesis in her two sections on the marriage metaphor, one on the book of Hosea and the other on literature before and after Hosea, but they are preceded by a general introduction to Israelite marriage. A unified set of metaphorical concepts is found in the book of Hosea, most of them direct derivatives from the marriage metaphor. It is further demonstrated that the metaphor played a very important role in the Old Testament from the time of the pre-exilic prophets onwards. Turning to the translation of the metaphor, is claimed that distance in time and culture can be bridged if we can be sensitive to the concepts involved; the metaphor can in this way be preserved in modern translations of the Bible.

G. H. JONES

TERTEL, HANS JÜRGEN: *Text and Transmission. An Empirical Model for the Literary Development of Old Testament Narratives* (Beihefte zur Zeitschrift für die alttestamentliche Wissenschaft 221). 1994. Pp. x, 311. (de Gruyter, Berlin–New York. Price: DM 152.00. ISBN 3 11 013921 9; ISSN 0934 2575)

This is a dense and complex study of Assyrian Royal Annals, with some discussion of Samuel–Kings and the biblical Chronicler's editorial methods, and an application of the results to 1 Kings 22:1–38 and 1 Kings 20. The English is at times awkward. The aims are stated as an examination of various internal criteria for the identification of redactional intervention in Old Testament narratives and the investigation of the applicability of some empirical models (p. 18). As a first principle of his study T. assumes the unity of a biblical text and single authorship until the opposite can be demonstrated and argues at length against most biblical scholars. So his book is very much a polemical work as well as an interesting exploration of some Assyrian annalistic texts imagined to provide an appropriate empirical model. The final section on the application of the results is mostly devoted to disagreeing with various scholars on the two selected texts from 1 Kings. Having waded through such immense detail I was left with the impression that the hidden agenda of the monograph was a 'saving the appearances' defence of a theologically conservative reading of the biblical narrative.

R. P. CARROLL

VALERIO, KAROLINA DE: *Altes Testament und Judentum im Frühwerk Rudolf Bultmanns* (Beihefte zur Zeitschrift für die neutestamentliche Wissenschaft 71). 1994. Pp. xiv, 454. (de Gruyter, Berlin–New York. Price: DM 172.00. ISBN 3 11 014201 5; ISSN 0171 6441)

This Erlangen dissertation concentrates on the development of Bultmann's thinking on the Old Testament in the period up to his interaction with Barth and Heidegger in the 1920s. Among influential teachers, colleagues, and friends, Gunkel stands out, though mention should be made of Hölscher and Baumgartner, and among Jewish scholars Hans Jonas. V. pays close attention to Bultmann's writings as a student, and also to his preaching and reviews, in which she sees themes that will develop later: the similarity of the human situation as Old Testament/Judaism and New Testament see it, the 'historicity' of God's involvement with humanity, and the novelty of the Christian faith's new perspective, with the consequent ambivalence of the 'new' faith's relationship to the 'old'. From the 1930s Bultmann went on to write a number of stimulating but perhaps undervalued pieces on the Old Testament's significance which, if one does not like their presuppositions or conclusions, still drive one to work at alternatives.

J. GOLDINGAY

VAN SETERS, JOHN: *The Life of Moses. The Yahwist as Historian in Exodus–Numbers* (Contributions to Biblical Exegesis and Theology 10). 1994. Pp. xvi, 524. (Kok Pharos, Kampen. Price: fl. 79.90. ISBN 90 390 0112 X; ISSN 0926 6097)

This work represents the culmination of V.S.'s reconstruction of the growth of the Pentateuch. Here he completes the exposition of ideas first mooted in *Abraham in History and Tradition* (*B.L.* 1976, p. 62) and further developed in *Prologue to History* (*B.L.* 1993, p. 45). He argues that the Yahwist is the major writer responsible for the narrative from Exodus to Numbers. V.S. of course accepts that P supplemented J with much legal and other material. He argues against the fissiparous approach of traditional source criticism, holding that the material in these books is more homogeneous than often supposed. He denies that J is based on old traditions or developed over a long period. It was written in the exile as a preface to the deuteronomistic history. V.S. draws attention to parallels with late prophetic material (e.g. call narratives) and Near Eastern texts (e.g. itineraries, Deir Alla texts) to validate his late datings. He argues that parallels with Deuteronomy (e.g. the golden calf story) are better explained by J using D than *vice versa*. This is an important book to note, as it challenges standard theories. Whether it will have as much impact on critical views of Exodus–Numbers as his 1975 work has had on Genesis remains to be seen.

G. J. WENHAM

WASHINGTON, HAROLD C.: *Wealth and Poverty in the Instruction of Amenemope and the Hebrew Proverbs* (Society of Biblical Literature Dissertation Series 142). 1994. Pp. xi, 242. (Scholars Press, Atlanta. Price: $29.95; paper $19.95. ISBN 0 7885 0072 4; paper 0 7885 0073 2)

W. dates Amenemope conventionally to about 1100 BCE; however, he emphasizes that it arose at a time during the late Rameside period which was characterized by economic disruption and corruption in the royal administration. This helped to shape Amenemope's approach to wealth and poverty. W. argues that Proverbs arose in a similar milieu, in the village society of Persian Judaea (even though some pre-exilic material may be present). The 'democratization of wisdom' was already well advanced in Amenemope which gave it an outlook compatible with the compilers of Proverbs; it is with regard to the poor that the perspective of Proverbs is most like the ancient Near East texts, especially Amenemope. W.'s thesis is interesting and clearly presented, but why must Proverbs have been compiled by 'lay leaders' of the Persian community?

L. L. GRABBE

WATSON, DUANE F. and HAUSER, ALAN J.: *Rhetorical Criticism of the Bible. A Comprehensive Bibliography with Notes on History and Method* (Biblical Interpretation Series 4). 1994. Pp. xx, 206. (Brill, Leiden–New York–Köln. Price: fl. 110.00/$63.00. ISBN 90 04 09903 4; ISSN 0928 0731)

This useful volume is organized in two main sections dealing with the Old and New Testaments respectively. Both sections consist of an introductory essay outlining the history and methodology of rhetorical criticism which sets the scene for the ensuing bibliographies. The Old Testament bibliographies begin with a listing of general and methodological articles, followed by separate listings on the four main sections of the Old Testament plus the Apocrypha. Each of these divisions begins with a section on general topics, followed by bibliographies specific to each biblical book, The New Testament section contains extensive bibliographies on Greco-Roman rhetoric, modern rhetoric and selected topics in New Testament rhetoric, including the Jewish heritage, in addition to studies of the individual books. There is no index of authors or of topics, but items are included under more than one heading if this seems appropriate. Despite its usefulness, there are some surprising omissions and inconsistencies.

H. S. PYPER

WATSON, FRANCIS: *Text, Church and World. Biblical Interpretation in Theological Perspective*. 1994. Pp. viii, 366. (Eerdmans, Grand Rapids MI; T. & T. Clark, Edinburgh. Price: $34.99/£24.95. ISBN (Eerdmans) 0 8028 3774 3; (Clark) 0567 09700 5)

During the period of predominance of the historical-critical method, any association with systematic theology has come to be regarded with grave suspicion, as a reversion to pre-Enlightenment world views. In this very ambitious study W. challenges that assumption, arguing that the propriety of reading the whole Bible within the ecclesial community can be upheld in the light of much modern (and, more specifically, post-modern) literary theory. He engages in detailed dialogue with a number of theorists. Though full of thought-provoking material the first two parts of the book ('The Autonomous Text' and 'Theology and Post-Modernism') are at times extremely opaque. The argument becomes much clearer in Part 3, where he engages very fruitfully with the dilemma faced by Christian feminists confronted by texts which are apparently irredeemably androcentric. The last part tries, again in an extremely interesting and provocative way, to draw together theology, hermeneutics and exegesis. W. is a New Testament scholar, and so much of his discussion relates to that field, but he is familiar with Old Testament study and has plenty of Old Testament illustrations. His work should be read both for its serious challenge to the assumptions of historical-critical study, and for its theoretical contribution to the on-going debate on interpretation.

R. J. COGGINS

WESTERMANN, CLAUS: *Die Geschichtsbücher des Alten Testaments. Gab as ein deuteronomistisches Geschichtswerk?* (Theologische Bücherei 87). 1994. Pp. 150. (Chr. Kaiser, Gütersloh. Price: DM 38.00. ISBN 3 579 01810 8)

Two main strands intertwine through this study from the Heidelberg emeritus. The one concentrates attention on difficulties noted over the years with Noth's hypothesis of a Deuteronomistic History. The other offers a fresh classification of the discrete kinds of material found in the historical books: a *form*engeschichtliche study of Exodus to Kings of a sort never before offered. Each book had its own history, and was separately edited in the period after Jerusalem's collapse. Over against Rendtorff on the Pentateuch regretting that Noth had not stayed with his earlier model of a creative historian dependent on sources already committed to writing, W. appears to be pursuing the traditions in Joshua to Kings to their earliest beginnings. W.'s volume seems to have been many years in the making. Its review of more recent research, from Jenni (1961) to O'Brien (1989), closes with approval of Fohrer's 1979 rejection of the Deuteronomistic History hypothesis which he had read once his own study was basically complete; and several significant studies of the last decade and a half are passed over in silence. This reader is more sympathetic to critical review of the Dtr hypothesis than relentless pursuit of genealogies, itineraries, and commands, towards better interpretation nearer the light of the events themselves.

A. G. AULD

WHITE, J. BENTON: *Taking the Bible Seriously. Honest Differences about Biblical Interpretation.* 1993. Pp. xii, 177. (Westminster/John Knox, Louisville KY. Price: $12.99. ISBN 0 664 25452 7)

For a British reader the interest in this book may lie chiefly in its account of issues in the battle between 'fundamentalism' and 'modernism' in the USA. It again illustrates the difference between the American and the British profiles of such debates (e.g. the role of creationism, the Schofield Bible, and dispensationalism). The book contains a number of oddities, such as its definitions of form criticism and of hermeneutics, the 5th-century setting of Daniel, and the statement that the Roman Catholic Church fixed the scriptural canon in the 4th century. It does not take up the question whether the issues it considers may look very different if modernity is becoming a thing of the past. Although its tone is more eirenic than many such works, it will provide further material for the needed PhD on the critical anxiety about fundamentalism in the late 20th century.

J. GOLDINGAY

WÜRTHWEIN, ERNST: *Studien zum deuteronomistischen Geschichtswerk* (Beihefte zur Zeitschrift für die alttestamentliche Wissenschaft 227). 1994. Pp. vii, 220. (de Gruyter, Berlin–New York. Price: DM 138.00. ISBN 3 11 014269 4; ISSN 0934 2575)

This volume brings together a number of essays and articles previously published in various journals and Festschriften between 1962 and 1989. It also contains three hitherto unpublished studies: observations on the so-called Deuteronomistic history work, Abimelech and the destruction of Shechem in Jud. 9, and tradition and theological redaction in 1 Kings 17–18. Most of the other material here will already be well-known to, and highly valued by, Old Testament specialists but it is good to have these contributions to the discussion of the Deuteronomistic History by a veteran scholar all assembled in a single collection for future students.

J. R. PORTER

ZUCKER, DAVID J.: *Israel's Prophets. An Introduction for Christians and Jews.* 1994. Pp. xiv, 208. (Paulist Press, New York–Mahwah NJ. Price: $11.95. ISBN 0 8091 3494 2)

This is a brief introductory work. Its main interest for the general reader will lie in the contrast between Christian and Jewish traditions of interpretation. After general comment on the role of prophets in Israelite society and a brief survey of pre-classical prophecy, discussion turns to the later prophets, outlining their historical background, main themes, and interpretation in the New Testament and in Jewish sources, concluding with brief comment on a minimal number of selected passage. Inevitably it suffers from the limitations of attempting this enterprising task in so small a compass, although this is redeemed to some extent by the occasional references to scholarly works for further study.

G. I. EMMERSON

7. LAW, RELIGION, AND THEOLOGY

AGUS, AHARON R. E. and ASSMANN, JAN (eds): *Ocular Desire/Sehnsucht des Auges* (Yearbook for Religious Anthropology). 1994. Pp. 187. (Akademie Verlag, Berlin. Price: DM 68.00. ISBN 3 05 002646 4)

The papers printed here arise from a colloquium on the 'Apprehension of the Divine: Theological Structuring of the Sense of Reality' held at Bar-Ilan University in 1990, with the ultimate title of the collection taken from a phrase of Augustine's. The subject is explored in essays relating to ancient Egypt (Assmann), midrashic hermeneutic (D. Boyarin), Gnosticism, Paul, and the rabbis (Agus) through Augustine and later thinkers to Heidegger.

L. L. GRABBE

ALBERTZ, RAINER: *A History of Israelite Religion in the Old Testament Period. Volume 1: From the Beginnings to the End of the Monarchy.* Translated John Bowden. 1994. Pp. xvi, 367. (SCM, London. Price £20.00. ISBN 0 334 02553 2)

ALBERTZ, RAINER: *A History of Israelite Religion in the Old Testament Period. Volume 2: From the Exile to the Maccabees.* Translated John Bowden. 1994. Pp. vii, 369–740. (SCM, London. Price: £20.00. ISBN 0 334 02554 0)

This is the English translation of the German original reviewed in *B. L.* 1993, p. 101.

ED.

BARR, JAMES: *Biblical Faith and Natural Theology. The Gifford Lectures for 1991 Delivered in the University of Edinburgh.* 1993. Pp. xii, 244. (Clarendon Press, Oxford. Price: £30.00; paper £11.50. ISBN 0 19 826205 1; paper 0 19 826376 7)

B. challenges the characteristic denial of natural theology in modern Protestant theology. Defining natural theology as that which is rooted in the very fact of our humanity he seeks to demolish Karl Barth's and all later Barthianism's no to natural theology, arguing inter alia that it is based on unsound and in some cases ludicrous exegesis of biblical texts. Natural theology is shown to be a part of the biblical tradition in the New Testament, intertestamental Jewish sources, and the Old Testament. The modern discussion of natural theology is then reopened in terms of religion and tradition, the image of God, science, language, parable and scripture. A concluding chapter discusses natural theology and the future of biblical theology. The critique of opposing views is trenchant and provocative, the argumentation incisive and well documented. Systematic theologians and philosophers of religion will find much to interest them. Although the lecture format may have precluded this, from the standpoint of biblical studies a fuller discussion of the place of natural theology 'within the Old Testament' and its contribution to the future of biblical theology would have been welcome.

R. DAVIDSON

BAUER, JOHANNES B., in collaboration with Johannes Marböck and Karl M. Woschitz (eds): *Bibeltheologisches Wörterbuch.* 1994 (4th, fully revised edn). Pp. 621. (Verlag Styria, Graz–Wien–Köln. Price: DM 175/SwF 175/AS 1225. ISBN 3 222 12256 3)

The 4th, completely revised edition, has contributions by a number of well-known contemporary scholars, mostly from German-speaking universities (but H. Cazelles also contributes). For example, E. Otto writes on

Dekalog, Gerechtigkeit (AT), and *Gesetz (AT)*; H. V. Kieweler, on *Armut/ Reichtum (AT)* and *Bund (AT)*; and O. Wahl, on *Stadt*. The bibliographies, although short, generally give some recent studies. It appears, however, that some entries were written for previous editions and have not been updated (e.g. the long article on *Reich Gottes* and other articles by R. Schnackenburg and B.'s own many entries).

L. L. GRABBE

BILDE, PER; ENGBERG–PEDERSEN, TROELS; HANNESTAD, LISE; and ZAHLE, JAN (eds): *Religion and Religious Practice in the Seleucid Kingdom* (Studies in Hellenistic Civilization 1). 1990. Pp. 269. (Aarhus University Press. Price: DKK 211.00/$35.16. ISBN 87 7288 322 7)

This collection arose from a Danish research project on the Hellenistic period. Eleven papers from an international conference explore various aspects of religion in the Hellenistic period. Articles of particular interest concern the continuity from the Achaemenid Empire to the Seleucid period (P. Briant), temple states in Asia Minor (S. Isager), Hellenization in relation to the Maccabean revolt (N. Hyldahl), the emergence of Jewish identity in both religious and ethnic terms in Maccabean Palestine (S. Cohen), and Jewish apocalypticism as a reaction to crisis (B. Otzen). Other essays are on the subjects of how 'Western' writers described the peoples of the East, temple architecture, religious motifs on coins, the survival and modification of Zoroastrianism in the Seleucid period, and the cult of the goddess Atartagis.

L. L. GRABBE

BOVATI, PIETRO: *Re-Establishing Justice. Legal Terms, Concepts and Procedures in the Hebrew Bible* (Journal for the Study of the Old Testament Supplement 105). Translated by Michael J. Smith. 1994. Pp. 478. (Sheffield Academic Press. Price: £47.50/$71.00. ISBN 1 85075 290 7; ISSN 0309 0787)

This study first appeared in Italian a few years ago, based on the author's 1985 doctoral thesis (to some extent supplemented since); its translation into English is very welcome. The author has collected and painstakingly analysed a wealth of material relating to legal procedure as reflected in the Bible. Part I deals with the *rib*, conceived as a two-party controversy settled by the parties themselves without judicial intervention, with chapters on 'The Juridical Dispute in General', 'The Accusation', 'The Response of the Accused', and 'The Reconciliation'. Part II deals with 'Judgement' (*Mishpat*), where the dispute is submitted to third-party adjudiction, with chapters on 'Judgement in Court: General Elements and Vocabulary', 'The Acts and Procedures Preceding the Debate', 'The Debate', 'Sentence and Execution (The End and Aim of a Trial)'. The two-part division of the book reflects an important distinction for our understanding of biblical law. The author, however, eschews any attempt to provide a history of the relationship between private settlement and adjudication, but rather offers a 'synchronic' account, one stressing the theological implications of the procedures (encapsulated in the title): justice is a matter not merely of desert, but of re-integrating the parties with each other and the community. Both the discussion and extensive apparatus will be of considerable value to future researchers.

B. S. JACKSON

BRIN, GERSHOM: *Studies in Biblical Law. From the Hebrew Bible to the Dead Sea Scrolls* (Journal for the Study of the Old Testament Supplement 176). Translated from the Hebrew by Jonathan Chipman. 1994. Pp. 309. (Sheffield Academic Press. Price: £45.00/$67.00. ISBN 1 85075 484 5; ISSN 0309 0787)

In the first part of his book, B. examines some general problems in biblical law, including essays on double laws; the formula 'if he shall not (do)', and the problems of sanctions; caring for the poor; the uses of 'or' in legal texts; biblical laws in the Dead Sea Scrolls. In the second half of his collection, B. examines the legal aspects of the first-born, both religious and civil. He begins with a general discussion of the development of biblical laws of the first-born before examining the provisions on clean animals, unclean animals and humans, and concludes with essays on the laws of inheritance of the first-born, and the first-born and the inheritance of the monarchy. The essays in this collection, some previously published, are both well-argued and perceptive and constitute a valuable contribution to biblical law studies.

A. PHILLIPS

DEARMAN, J. ANDREW: *Religion and Culture in Ancient Israel*. 1992. Pp. xvi, 281. (Hendrickson, Peabody MA. Price: $19.95. ISBN 0 943575 90 7)

D. defines the subject of this textbook as the interaction of religion and culture in ancient Israel. It falls into two parts. The first is historical: 'a sketch of Israelite religion according to the biblical storyline and in light of extra-biblical sources.' The second studies four distinct expressions of religion in the Hebrew Bible — Deuteronomy, the 'pre-exilic prophets', wisdom, and apocalyptic (mainly Daniel) — and categorizes them in a way derived from the typology of H. Richard Niebuhr (*Christ and Culture*). As a survey of recent research, the book is useful, and its bibliographical materials are particularly valuable. D.'s own insights are also thought-provoking. But the book suffers from having no single argument, and the relation between the two parts is never spelt out. The 'biblical storyline' and 'extrabiblical sources' are combined in a most uneasy fashion in Part One, so that one is never clear whether one is reading a commentary on the biblical histories or a history of Israelite religion. In the second part, an opportunity for a thorough reading of the texts against their cultural background is largely missed: a conventional Introduction would contain most of what is said.   W. J. HOUSTON

DIETRICH, WALTER and KLOPFENSTEIN, MARTIN A. (eds): *Ein Gott allein? JHWH-Verehrung und biblischer Monotheismus im Kontext der israelitischen und altorientalischen Religionsgeschichte* (Orbis Biblicus et Orientalis 139). 1994. Pp. 618. (Universitätsverlag, Freiburg (Schweiz); Vandenhoeck & Ruprecht, Göttingen. Price: DM 146.00/SwF 125.00/AS 1138. ISBN (Universitätsverlag) 3 7278 0962 0; (Vandenhoeck & Ruprecht) 3 525 53774 3)

The twenty-eight essays in English and German (one in French) here arose out of a conference in Bern in 1993. D. gives an intoduction. The next section looks at the Religious History and Historical Context: note N. P. Lemche who asks whether 'Israelite religion' can be spoken of anymore. The Archaeological and Epigraphic Finds include Kuntillet 'Ajrud (A. Meshel) and aniconism (T. Mettinger). Under YHWH and the Divine World of Canaan are essays in the subject by J. Day and M. Smith, as well as specific ones on Yahweh and 'his asherah' (J. Hadley), Yahweh and the sun divinity of Jerusalem (O. Keel/C. Uehlinger), and Yahweh in the role of Baalšamem (H. Niehr). The next section is on the One and Female Religion, including essays on traces of the goddess in Hosea (M.-T. Wacker) and female

112   LAW, RELIGION, AND THEOLOGY

spirituality in the Psalms and domestic cult (E. Gerstenberger). This is
followed by the Step from the Many to the One, with essays on Hosea 12 (A.
de Pury), the Baal concept in Hosea (J. Jeremias), and the Decalogue
prohibition against images and foreign gods (O. Loretz). The section on the
One in Multiple Manifestations includes essays on the goddess in Proverbs
1–9 (M. Klopfenstein) and monotheism and angelology (K. Koch).

L. L. GRABBE

DIJK-HEMMES, FOKKELIEN VAN and BRENNER, ATHALYA: *Reflections on
Theology and Gender.* 1994. Pp. 107. (Kok Pharos, Kampen. Price: fl. 49.90.
ISBN 90 390 0111 1)

The contents of this volume reflect its origins — as a group of papers
presented at a study day to inaugurate a women'sstudies research programme.
It contains six paper, including an outline of the proposed programme (by
D.-H.) and a theoretical piece on feminist use of concepts of gender (by
Braidotti). Korte discusses the birth of Aphrodite and her connection with
Cyprus. The other papers cover biblical material. Van Henten, using 'reader-
response' methods, compares Judith with Moses in a less than convincing
essay. Heijerman (using a similar approach) attempts to rehabilitate the
'strange' woman of Proverbs 7 by discussing her in turn as 'mother's rival';
'men's scapegoat'; and 'needy woman'. The strongest paper in the collection
is that of B. It considers the use of the 'marriage metaphor' in Jeremiah as
both propaganda and pornography. Most challenging is her comparison of the
use of sexual imagery in the prophets with *The Story of O*, which disturbs both
by its content and its execution. This book is for those with some familiarity
with the methods and concerns of feminist biblical interpretation.

C. SMITH

FELDTKELLER, ANDREAS: *Im Reich der Syrischen Göttin. Eine religiös
plurale Kultur als Umwelt des frühen Christentums* (Studien zum Verstehen
fremder Religionen 8). 1994. Pp. 333. (Gütersloher Verlagshaus. Price:
DM 148.00/AS 1155/SwF 148.00. ISBN 3 579 01790 X)

This is a schematic study, based on a good knowledge of the religious
cultures in first-century Syria, of how religions interact with one another.
Constituting the theoretical part of the author's dissertation 'Das entstehende
Heidenchristentum im religiösen Umfeld Syriens zur Prinzipatszeit', this
volume is intended for a wider audience of scholars concerned with Religions-
wissenschaft in general. (The other part is to be published under the title
'Identitätssuche des syrischen Urchristentums — Mission, Inkulturation und
Pluralität im ältesten Heidenchristentum').

S. P. BROCK

GERTZ, JAN CHRISTIAN: *Die Gerichtsorganisation Israels im deuteronomi-
schen Gesetz* (Forschungen zur Religion und Literatur des Alten und Neuen
Testaments 165). 1994. Pp. 256. (Vandenhoeck & Ruprecht, Göttingen.
Price: DM 84.00/SwF 85.50/AS 655. ISBN 3 525 53847 2)

Recent literary- and historical-critical studies of the laws in Dt. 12–26
have felt compelled to abandon the conclusion that they form a single
coherent and unified whole. This excellent dissertation seeks to contribute
towards a fuller understanding of the problems by examining closely those
passages, chiefly Deuteronomy 16:18–17:13, 19:1–13, 15–21, 21:1–9 and
25:1–3, which presuppose, or provide for, a system of legal administration. A
body of professional judges and law officials (16:18) appear alongside elders

(21:2) and the cities of asylum presuppose cult-centralization. Differing systems appear to operate side by side. The provision for asylum can be seen as either a practical necessity in the wake of Josiah's reform, or as a highly theoretical exilic innovation. If the turning-points for changes in legal administration can be traced, then the laws reflecting them can be set in a probable chronological order. G. faces the problems honestly and cautiously, proposing as the most likely development an original fundamental reform in Josiah's time, demanding cult-centralization, and instituting professional judges. The appearance of elders alongside these is taken as most likely occurring during the social and political upheavals of the exile. In general G. sees the provisions as serious attempts to deal with practical realities, without ruling out some features of legalistic theorizing.   R. E. CLEMENTS

GOSSAI, HEMCHAND: *Justice, Righteousness and the Social Critique of the Eighth-Century Prophets* (American University Studies. Series 7: Theology and Religion 141). 1993. Pp. xii, 351. (Lang, Frankfurt–Bern–New York. Price: SwF 40.00. ISBN 0 8240 2029 8; ISSN 0740 0446)

G. examines the meaning and use of *ṣdq* and *špṭ* in the ancient Near East and the Old Testament, and *mišpāṭ* in the Old Testament. He concludes that both *ṣdq* and *mišpāṭ* are to be understood not as an objective norm but in the wider context of relationship, both divine-human and human-human. This is confirmed in their use by the 8th-century prophets in pointing to the cultic, economic and financial perversions in Israelite society. Absence of *ṣdq* between Yahweh and Israel leads to loss of *mišpāṭ* in all areas of Israelite life. G. assumes a Mosaic convenantal background to 8th-century prophecy though this is not strictly necessary for his thesis. He rightly recognizes that much of the ills in 8th-century Israelite society were not necessarily illegal, but a corrupt cult inevitably leads to social and juridical injustice.   A. PHILLIPS

GRESCHAT, HANS-JÜRGEN (ed.): *Mündliche Religionsforschung. Erfahrungen und Einsichten* (Marburger Studien zur Afrika- und Asienkunde, Serie C: Religionsgeschichte Band 1). 1994. Pp. 113. (Dietrich Reimer, Berlin. Price: DM 36.00/SwF 37.00/AS 281. ISBN 3 496 02532 8)

This book is about personal encounter with people of contemporary faith communities as a method of research in *Religionswissenschaft*. Its relevance to Old Testament study is at most indirect.   W. J. HOUSTON

GUNNEWEG, ANTONIUS H. J.: *Biblische Theologie des Alten Testaments. Eine Religionsgeschichte Israels in biblisch-theologischer Sicht*. 1994. Pp. 255. (Kohlhammer, Stuttgart. Price: DM 34.00/SwF 36.00/AS 272. ISBN 3 17 012199 5)

Professor Gunneweg died in 1990 while still at work on this book, which has been completed from his notes by his widow and by M. Oeming. These circumstances probably explain a certain unevenness in the finished work, especially its very cursory treatment of the later period (eight pages on the whole wisdom tradition, three pages on eschatology and apocalyptic). It is also that rarity, a learned German work with no footnotes. The main concern is to explore the inter-relation between studying the history of Israel's religion with historical-critical assumptions, and a theological appraisal. To the latter end the earlier chapters discuss the New Testament re-use of the various Old Testament themes. After an introduction dealing with the previous history of the discipline, and in particular with the debate between 'biblical theology' and the 'history of religion', the treatment is broadly historical, with separate chapters devoted to different periods, that on the monarchy being much the longest. Many individual sections of the book are worthy of attention; regrettably the inevitable lack of awareness of the most recent literature and areas of controversy (e.g. concerning Israel's origin, or the place of covenant) gives the work as a whole a somewhat dated air.   R. J. COGGINS

HENSHAW, RICHARD A.: *Female and Male. The Cultic Personnel: The Bible and the Rest of the Ancient Near East* (Princeton Theological Monograph Series 31). 1994. Pp. xiii, 385. (Pickwick, Allison Park PA. Price: $52.00. ISBN 1 55635 015 5)

This work is the result of many years of painstaking scholarship. The author evidently had some difficulty in defining the limits of the material he has assembled. He decided to restrict the period to the pre-Alexandrian ancient Near East. He concentrates particularly on female cultic personnel, while noting that these are rare in the Hebrew and Ugaritic texts, but common in Mesopotamia. His method is to assemble the primary source material, which is arranged mainly according to the titles used for various cultic officiants. He attempts a classification of the Mesopotamian cultic personnel into five categories: chief functionaries, musicians and dancers, diviners and magicians, officiants related to sexuality and fertility, and officiants auxiliary to the main cult. Copious references are given to the secondary literature of scholarship as well as to the primary source material, while the author himself provides detailed notes on the material listed. A short introduction draws attention to some of the wider issues raised. Old Testament scholars will be able readily to identify the sections immediately relevant to their discipline, but the rich collection of comparative material will enable this to be set in the wider context of the ancient Near East. This will long remain a valuable resource for scholarship.   A. GELSTON

HESS, RICHARD S.; WENHAM, GORDON J.; and SATTERTHWAITE, PHILIP E. (eds): *He Swore an Oath. Biblical Themes from Genesis 12–50* (Tyndale House Studies). 1994 (2nd edn). Pp. 222. (Paternoster, Carlisle. Price: £10.99. ISBN 0 85364 609 0)

The papers in this book were delivered at the 1993 meeting of the Tyndale Fellowship in Cambridge, and are dedicated to Professor D. J. Wiseman. T. D. Alexander writes on Abraham and the New Testament doctrine of justification by faith. J. Goldingay examines the role of Abraham in Isaiah 41. R. Hess compares Gen. 15:8–21 and the Alalakh texts which speak of the slaughtering of animals, and K. Kitchen relates Gen. 12–50 to the Near Eastern World of the 2nd millennium. B. McConville examines the meaning of Gen. 14 and its relation to other passages, and A. Millard writes on 'Abraham, Akhenaten, Moses and Monotheism' to demonstrate that monotheism could have existed in the 2nd millennium. T. Mitchell offers a paper on shared vocabulary in the Pentateuch and the book of Daniel, and R. W. L. Moberly in 'Christ as the Key to Scripture' looks at Genesis 22 to suggest ways in which a Christological reading of the Old Testament might be undertaken. D. Pennant writes on Gen. 32, and G. Wenham concludes the book by exploring hidden agendas of the Pentateuchal commentator. This is a stimulating collection of essays which tackles major issues of Genesis, and would be useful for scholar and preacher alike.   P. J. HARLAND

HUBBARD, ROBERT L., JR: JOHNSTON, ROBERT K.; and MEYE, ROBERT P.
(eds): *Studies in Old Testament Theology. Historical and Contemporary
Images of God and God's People.* 1992. Pp. 333. (Word, Dallas. Price:
$17.99. ISBN 0 8499 0865 5)

This collection of essays by fourteen scholars is presented in honour of Dr
David Hubbard on the occasion of his 65th birthday. After four personal
tributes to Dr Hubbard, there are papers on method in the study of the Old
Testament from Robert Hubbard Jr, Elizabeth Achtemeier and Daniel
Fuller. David Clines, Frederic Bush and Walter Kaiser look at aspects of the
Pentateuch in the next three articles. John Watts, Leslie Allen and Carl
Armerding contribute essays on the prophets. The canonical pattern is
completed by contributions from Roland Murphy, John Goldingay and
Robert Johnston on the Writings. Finally Richard Mouw offers a discussion of
how the life of ancient Israel serves as a resource for the Christian community's vocation on the world, and William Dyrness writes about contemporary
environmental issues from the perspective of Hosea 2. The articles are written
from a conservative standpoint, with each writer being keen to offer readings
of the text which are applicable to the work of the contemporary church. This
is a stimulating book which contains interesting material for both scholar and
preacher.
                                                              P. J. HARLAND

JANZEN, WALDEMAR: *Old Testament Ethics. A Paradigmatic Approach.*
1994. Pp. 240. (Westminster/John Knox, Louisville KY. Price: £19.99. ISBN
0 664 25410 1)

J.'s concern is to read the Old Testament in a way that will be fruitful for
Christian ethics, following an avowedly 'canonical' approach. He makes
paradigms rather than laws or principles central to his account (while not
neglecting these) in order to include prophecy, wisdom, and narrative texts as
well as legal material. The result is a constructive and comprehensive account
of Old Testament ethics, rather similar in style to C. J. Wright's *Living as the
People of God*, which J. discusses along with other recent works. Not much
attention is paid to the problems modern readers have with aspects of Old
Testament ethics; nevertheless, this is a useful book.   J. BARTON

KOCH, ROBERT: *Die Bundesmoral im Alten Testament.* 1994. Pp. 92.
(Lang, Frankfurt–Bern–New York. Price: SwF 17.00. ISBN 3 631 46976 4)

This book, intended to give moral theologians a biblical basis for their
work, can best be described as a popular presentation of views that were held
with greater certainty a generation ago than they are now. Beginning from
Eichrodt's conviction that the covenant is fundamental to understanding Old
Testament theology, the author expounds briefly the texts that exhibit
covenant morality and practice, with comparisons also drawn from the
ancient Near East. Texts covered include the Ten Commandments, Deuteronomy, Micah 6:1–8, Isaiah 1:2–3, 10–20, Genesis 15, Exodus 24:1–11 and
Psalm 50.   J. W. ROGERSON

MATHYS, HANS-PETER: *Dichter und Beter. Theologen aus spätalt-
testamentlicher Zeit* (Orbis Biblicus et Orientalis 132). 1994. Pp.. x, 386.
(Universitätsverlag, Freiburg (Schweiz); Vandenhoeck & Ruprecht, Göttingen. Price: SwF 110.00/DM 132.00/AS 1033. ISBN (Universitätsverlag)
3 7278 0931 0; (Vandenhoeck & Ruprecht) 3 525 53767 0)

This argues that pray-ers and poets were the systematic theologians of
the Old Testament's younger sections. M. believes that these prayers and

hymns provide evidence for the late, canonizing stages of the Hebrew Bible. The post-exilic prayers of Nehemiah, Ezra and Daniel form the foundation for M.'s argument, as their late date and systematic nature is widely granted. Although these poems have mostly to do with systematic constructions of *Heilsgeschichte* (a notion flavouring much of the book), poets also considered God's character systematically (e.g. the wisdom psalms). A 'canonical approach' is in evidence throughout. As traditions became authoritative and were brought together, their rough edges needed systematizing, and this was provided by these independent poetic compositions. Several prayers/psalms, for instance, control the reading of the passages in which they are embedded (e.g. Hannah's song and David's psalm in 1 Sam. 2 and 2 Sam. 22). Though some will find M.'s findings on canon flawed or unconvincing , his exegeses of texts provide good examples of inter-textual studies, although this is not the context in which they are offered

D. J. REIMER

MATSUSHIMA, EIKO (ed.): *Official Cult and Popular Religion in the Ancient Near East. Papers of the First Colloquium on the Ancient Near East — The City and its Life held at the Middle Eastern Culture Center in Japan (Mitaka, Tokyo), March 20–22, 1992.* 1993. Pp. 224. (C. Winter, Heidelberg. Price: DM 80.00. ISBN 3 8253 0031 5)

Most of the twelve essays printed here concern religion in the ancient Near East, though there are also essays on Japanese popular belief, modern Iranian popular belief, and early Sassanian art: exorcism and private cult in Mesopotamia (J. Bottéro), the interpretation of the Ugaritic funerary text KTU 1.161 (D. Tsumura), Asherah in Israelite religion (Y. Ikeda), sacred marriage in early Mesopotamia (J. Cooper), lucky and unlucky days (hemer-ologies) (A. Livingstone), popular concerns reflected in Mari theophoric names (I. Nakata), the roles of the minor gods in Mesopotamia (A. Finet), private piety in Sumer (D. Edzard), and divine statues in Mesoptamia (Matsushima). Edzard gives a summation, and opening and closing addresses are also included.

L. L. GRABBE

MUFFS, YOCHANAN: *Love and Joy: Law, Language, and Religion in Ancient Israel.* 1992. Pp. xxvii, 240. (Jewish Theological Seminary of America; distributed by Harvard University Press, Cambridge MA and London. Price: $35.95/£23.95. ISBN 0 674 53931 1)

Eight articles are collected in this book, six previously published. They are: 'Who Will Stand in the Breach?: A Study of Prophetic Intercession' (original in Hebrew in *Torah Midreshet*, 1984); 'As a Cloak Clings to its Owner: Aspects of Divine/Human Reciprocity', exploring the metaphor of Jer. 13:11 (new); 'A History of Mesopotamian Religion' (*Numen* 1978); 'Abraham the Noble Warrior. Partiarchal Politics and Laws of War in Ancient Israel' (*JANES*, 1973); 'The Permitted and the Prohibited in Early Rabbinic Literature: The Route DRK, "To Be Empowered"' (new); the last two chapters, from the Morton Smith Festschrift 1975 and *JANES* 1979, explore aspects of 'Love and Joy as Metaphors of Willingness and Spontan-eity in Cuneiform, Ancient Hebrew, and Related Literatures'. The strength of these studies lies in the discussion of specific examples of the inter-penetration of legal and religious ideas and terminology. Prominent among the religious themes discussed is the relationship between collective and deferred punishment, and the notion of a 'personal god'. Though the original studies are not updated, the value of the collection is enhanced by indices of subjects, authors (termed Authorities!), terms, and sources. A valuable collection.

B. S. JACKSON

NAVARRO, ENRIQUE FARFAN: *El Desierto Transformado. Una imagen deuteroisaiana de regeneración* (Analecta Biblica 130). 1992. Pp. 304. (Editrice Pontificio Istituto Biblico, Rome. Price: Lire 35,000. ISBN 88 7653 130 0)

In this study of Isaiah 41:17–20, N. argues that the passage is not referring to the return of Israel from the exile, but is an allegory of the regeneration of Israel. The people who have been punished under Assyria, who are poor and needy and are likened to a desert, will be revived by their creator to a luxuriant, flourishing life, which will be marked by knowledge of God. 41:17–20 do not mention a march or a new exodus, but rather the attention is focused on a new Israel which is to be created. In order to support his case N. offers a detailed analysis of the vocabulary, structure and the history of interpretation of the passage. There are twenty-two tables which illustrate how particular words are employed in the Old Testament. He examines how scholars have given figurative and literal studies of the text. N. has produced a thorough, well presented and stimulating study.   P. J. HARLAND

NEEF, HEINZ-DIETER: *Gottes himmlischer Thronrat. Hintergrund und Bedeutung von* sôd JHWH *im Alten Testament* (Arbeiten zur Theologie 79). 1994. Pp. 96. (Calwer, Stuttgart. Price: DM 28.00/SwF 29.00/AS 219. ISBN 3 7668 3288 3)

This study, an expanded form of an inaugural lecture at the University of Tübingen, has three main sections. After a brief review of various Old Testament passages which speak of divine beings accompanying Yahweh, the author discusses the evidence for divine assemblies in Ugaritic, Phoenician, and Aramaic religions. Then the incidence and etymology of *sôd* is examined, followed by a description of the various meanings and renderings of the term in the Old Testament, the Septuagint, the Targum, and the Qumran literature. At the end, a New Testament perspective on the divine assembly in Rev. 4:1–11 is considered. N.'s work must be judged somewhat disappointing, promising more than it actually provides. It is a useful collection of material but it says little that is new. Much of it is not directly concerned with Yahweh's heavenly council but rather with the word *sôd* in general: we miss any real attempt to bring out the significance of the divine assembly for Israel's religion. Nor is the author's presentation of a chronological development of the meaning of *sôd* likely to prove very convincing.   J. R. PORTER

NELSON, RICHARD D.: *Raising Up a Faithful Priest. Community and Priesthood in Biblical Theology.* 1993. Pp. xiv, 192. (Westminster/John Knox, Louisville KY. Price: $19.99. ISBN 0 664 25437 3)

The Bible's view of priesthood entails nurture and care of the community; but the logic of the priestly office was lost in the Christian framework, as the community itself comes to share this role. So argues N. in this stimulating work of biblical theology. N. uses language of the 'culture map' to locate within Israelite society the role and function of the priesthood and rehearses some of the historical debate about its development. A synthetic picture of priests as teachers and sacrificers emerges from a wide range of biblical texts. Theological implications are teased out in a separate chapter, before four priestly 'visions' receive focused attention (Ezek. 40–48, Zech. 1–8, 'P', and Chonicles). N. carries this Old Testament picture into an examination of priestly notions in Hebrews and 1 Peter. The conclusion relates this study to modern Christian ministry. Much can be welcomed in this positive approach to priesthood, but there is a confusing message as well. The critique of 'priestly religion' affirmed on p. 102 compromises N.'s larger argument, and

118   LAW, RELIGION, AND THEOLOGY

the book's conclusion reverses the positive flow as Jesus 'obliterates', 'annihi-
lates', 'revolutionizes' and 'demolishes' the priestly office (pp. 170–71). Still,
thoughtful engagement with N.'s study will provide useful stimulus for the
church communities where this work finds its natural home.   D. J. REIMER

OEGEMA, GERBERN S.: *Der Gesalbte und sein Volk. Untersuchungen zum
Konzeptualisierungsprozess der messianischen Erwartungen von den Mak-
kabäern bis Bar Koziba* (Schriften des Institutum Judaicum Delitzschianum
2). 1994. Pp. 351. (Vandenhoeck & Ruprecht, Göttingen. Price: DM 98.00/
AS 765/SFr 99.50. ISBN 3 525 54201 1)

O. is far from the first to collect and study the various texts on messianism, even in recent times (cf. *B. L.* 1989, pp. 140–41; 1993, p. 75); however,
he does so with conscious attention to the methodological problems involved.
His aim is to understand the messianic texts in their historical context. He well
illustrates that there is no consistent 'messianic concept' but rather a great
variety of views which seem to be related to the historical situation in which
the particular text arose. Only a few biblical passages appear more than once
in the sources, but even those (e.g. Isaiah 11 and Daniel 7) are not given a
consistent interpretation. One constant that O. does find are two main
concepts of the Messiah, as a priest-king and as a warrior-judge. In addition to
O.'s analysis of all relevant texts, readers will appreciate the tables (e.g.
pp. 291–301) which summarize and make conveniently available some of the
main results of his study. This is likely to become the definitive treatment of
the subject to the time of Bar Kokhba, rightly replacing older works such as
that of J. Klausner.
                                                            L. L. GRABBE

OTTO, ECKART: *Theologische Ethik des Alten Testaments* (Theologische
Wissenschaft 3/2). 1994. Pp. 288. (Kohlhammer, Stuttgart–Berlin–Köln.
Price: DM 39.80/SwF 39.80/AS 311. ISBN 3 17 008923 4)

Breathtaking in its breadth and depth, this book will become an essential
reference work for all concerned with biblical law and ethics. An introductory
chapter reviews previous works. Ch. 2 reviews the material in Exod. 2–23,
parallel ancient Near Eastern legal material, early parts of Deuteronomy and
P, as well as narrative texts reflecting pre-exilic practice. Ch. 3 sums up the main
thrusts of Egyptian, Mesopotamian, and biblical wisdom texts. Ch. 5 discusses
the particular contributions of Deuteronomy and P. Ch. 6 looks briefly at the
contribution of Daniel. Each section is headed by excellent bibliographies. O.
shows himself thoroughly at home in the details of Near Eastern and biblical
law, but at the same time he offers an integrating view of the biblical texts.
Obviously many details of his interpretation are open to question, but there are
three areas where more discussion would have been helpful. First, there is very
little said about Jewish interpretation and use of the law. Second, O. hardly
uses the opening chapters of Genesis as a key to biblical law and ethics, though
they provide a lens through which the whole Torah may be viewed. Third, O.
never investigates the stance of the biblical narrators in the historical books as
opposed to their actors. But these are quibbles.
                                                            G. J. WENHAM

PEDERSEN, SIGFRED (ed.): *New Directions in Biblical Theology. Papers of
the Aarhus Conference, 16–19 September 1992* (Supplements to Novum
Testamentum 76). 1994. Pp. xiii, 290. (Brill, Leiden–New York–Köln. Price:
fl. 155.00/$88.75. ISBN 90 04 10120 9; ISSN 0167 9732)

The Institute for New Testament of the Aarhus theological faculty
celebrated the fiftieth anniversary of the faculty by holding two conferences,

one of which is represented in this volume of papers, dedicated to Poul Nepper-Christensen. They are all focused on the issue of 'biblical theology', which here refers to the relationships between the Old and New Testaments. Nearly all the contributors are in fact New Testament scholars, and the majority of contributions concern the links of particular parts of the New Testament with the Hebrew Bible. The papers are introduced by the editor, who underlines the theme of continuity and discontinuity running through many of them. There are thirteen papers, seven in English and six in German. Kirsten Nielsen offers a characteristically thought-provoking piece on 'Old Testament Metaphors in the New Testament'. But many of the other essays are well worth the attention of Old Testament scholars, at any rate of those among them who are concerned for the effective life of the Old Testament within the Christian Church.

W. J. HOUSTON

SAMUELSON, NORBERT M.: *Judaism and the Doctrine of Creation*. 1994. Pp. xi, 362. (Cambridge University Press. Price: £40.00/$54.95. ISBN 0 521 45214 7)

This is an attempt at an integrated understanding of creation in the context of Jewish tradition and philosophy, Greek philosophy, and modern physics. The original study has been split into two books (for the first, see *B. L.* 1993, p. 68). In this volume, Part 1 interacts with F. Rosenzweig's *Star of Redemption*. Part 2 takes into account Jewish tradition, especially as interpreted by medieval philosophers and commentators. Part 3 looks at creation in Genesis and in Plato's *Timaeus*. Part 4 considers the question from the point of view of modern physics and philosophy. This is mainly a contribution to modern Jewish philosophy.

L. L. GRABBE

SCHMIDT, BRIAN B.: *Israel's Beneficent Dead. Ancestor Cult and Necromancy in Ancient Israelite Religion and Tradition* (Forschungen zum Alten Testament 11). 1994. Pp. xv, 400. (Mohr, Tübingen. Price: DM 158.00. ISBN 3 16 146221 1; ISSN 0904 4155)

Going against recent trends, S. argues that the Israelite belief in seeking to the dead for supernatural help and knowledge was quite late, a foreign introduction in the post-Manasseh period as a result of a prolonged period of social crises caused by Assyrian domination. One of the most useful contributions is S.'s set of definitions and distinctions which shows, e.g. that 'cult of the dead' does not have to imply worship of or belief in the power of the dead. He examines the cult of the dead in Syria-Palestine from Ebla through Mari and Ugarit to the Hebrew Bible where all passages which have been interpreted as examples of consulting the dead for aid or foreknowledge are studied in detail. Some doubts remain as to whether S. has successfully dismissed all arguments for an early belief in the beneficent dead in Israel, but any attempt to maintain this view must now deal with his impressive study.

L. L. GRABBE

SINGER, KARL H.: *Alttestamentliche Blutrachepraxis im Vergleich mit der Ausübung der Blutrache in der Türkei. Ein kultur- und rechtshistorischer Vergleich* (Europäische Hochschulschriften. Series 23: Theology 509). 1994. Pp. 283. (Lang, Frankfurt–Bern–New York. Price: SwF 32.00. ISBN 3 361 47301 X; ISSN 0721 3409)

The practice of blood-revenge in ancient Israel has left a legacy in the Old Testament. This valuable dissertation, prepared under the guidance of

Professor B. Lang of Paderborn, examines the biblical evidence for the practice and draws further illumination for understanding how it operated by comparing it with the similar custom in Turkey until relatively recent times. S. gives close attention to Gideon's vengeance for his murdered brothers (Jgs. 8:18–21), Joab's killing of Abner (2 Sam. 2:18–23) and Amaziah's vengeance against his father's murderers (2 Kgs. 14:5f.). The significant features, supported by the comparative data, reveal the importance of the background of vengeance killing in a clan ethos and the strong efforts, with the introduction of state legislation, to put an end to the practice. At the same time — and equally operative — was the decaying motivation for it once the ethos and organizational structure of society on a clan basis was eroded. Certainly this offers a valuable insight into the early moral life of Israel and why the development of law was so prominent a feature within it. R. E. CLEMENTS

SMITH, RALPH L.: *Old Testament Theology. Its History, Method, and Message.* 1993. Pp. 525. (Broadman and Holman, Nashville. Price: $32.99. ISBN 0 8054 1606 4)

The aim of this book is to provide university and seminary students with a textbook that both describes what others have said and done about Old Testament theology and also offers a model of the way in which the theological materials may be organized, interpreted and appropriated. Ch. 1 traces the story of Old Testament theology from biblical times to the present, and ch. 2 with the nature and method of Old Testament theology. Chs 3 to 11 then present the theology according to what is described as a systematic-thematic approach: the emphasis is upon variety of theological themes rather than upon one central theme as organizing principle, and upon a systematic, rather than a chronological approach to the subject matter. The themes selected are 'the knowledge of God'; 'election and covenant', 'who is a God like Yahweh?'; 'what is mankind?'; 'sin and redemption'; 'worship'; 'the good life', 'death and beyond'; and 'in that day'. This is a well-written book from a broadly conservative and evangelical perspective. Its author is well-informed, keeps his aim in mind, and writes clearly. It would be a useful book for students beginning Old Testament studies and interested in reading the Old Testament within the framework of Christian theology. I. PROVAN

TAYLOR, J. GLEN: *Yahweh and the Sun. Biblical and Archaeological Evidence for Sun Worship in Ancient Israel* (Journal for the Study of the Old Testament Supplement 111). 1993. Pp. 308. (Sheffield Academic Press. Price £40.00/$60.00. ISBN 1 85075 272 9; ISSN 0309 0787)

This is a tightly argued and well-documented Yale dissertation, which surveys firstly all the relevant archaeological, and secondly the textual evidence. Firstly the Taanach cult-stand is examined, and argued to represent alternating forms of Yahweh and Asherah. Whether the evidence supports such specific interpretation is perhaps doubtful. The *lmlk* jar seals are then examined, in the light of the iconography of Horus. Since the winged disk and falcon motifs are often explicitly *royal* motifs in Egypt, it seems at least as likely that this is the reason for their borrowing. The various horse-figurines from Palestinian sites are discussed, and a negative assessment made. The orientation of a number of temples is considered, Yahwistic personal names examined, and a cautious position maintained on each issue. An exhaustive treatment is then offered of all biblical evidence, from toponyms to historical and poetic texts, and it is argued that in some instances, at least, a case can be made for the identification of Yahweh and the sun. It has to be admitted that much of the linking of solar symbolism and iconography with Yahweh is circumstantial. The theophany language of the celestial rising of heavenly bodies and the eastward orientation of the temple, for instance, could also be used as the basis for an argument for Yahweh's lunar nature, and the significance of the gender of *šemeš*, which obviously has a bearing on the meaning of Psalm 19, is not considered. The question of Yahweh's relationship with the sun remains open: the present work is valuable in giving an up-to-date assessment of the main arguments.   N. Wyatt

WALTON, JOHN H.: *Covenant. God's Purpose, God's Plan.* 1994. Pp. 192. (Zondervan, Grand Rapids MI. Price: $14.99. ISBN 0 310 57751 9)

Avowedly written from an Evangelical Christian biblical-theology perspective, this book is likely to have only limited appeal to those who do not share this approach to the Bible. W.'s proposals that the various covenants in the Bible (both Testaments) are essentially revelatory and are phases of *the* Covenant are both intriguing ones, but they fail to take adequate account of all the data — possible ancient Near Eastern parallels are discussed in a mere one and a half pages; the covenant with Noah is specifically excluded from discussion (p. 47); and the whole of the post-exilic period, up until the time of Jesus, is dismissed as a 'transition' between God's covenant with David and the New Covenant (p. 51). Add to this the assumptions that the biblical story is historically accurate and that Daniel was written in the 6th century, and the very conservative orientation of this book becomes clear. Its concern is really more with the relationship between the Old Covenant and the New Covenant, and its implications for Christians today, and with the role the written Torah may play in Christianity, than with providing an in-depth analysis of the covenant(s) in the Hebrew Bible. The result is a book with a number of interesting ideas, which are neither fully worked out, nor very coherently presented.   C. H. Knights

WEIGL, MICHAEL: *Zefanja und das 'Israel der Armen'. Eine Untersuchung zur Theologie des Buches Zefanja* (Österreichische Biblische Studien 13). 1994. Pp. vi, 329. (Österreichisches Katholisches Bibelwerk, Klosterneuburg. Price: DM 49.20/SwF 41.70/AS 330. ISBN 3 85396 085 5)

The first section of this book consists of a detailed study of the text of the book of Zephaniah section by section. Each considers matters of translation, text, delineation of the unit, literary criticism, structure and diachronic analysis, with a final summarizing paragraph. In general W. takes a fairly conservative approach to the composition and redaction of the book. Most of it goes back to the prophet, not only in substance but in its present three-fold arrangement, and the prophet is also most likely to have been responsible for the 'universalization' of the original attacks on Jerusalem to be found in such passages as 1:2–3, 17–18a. A second section then examines more fully the composition of the book in the light of the preceding textual study. In the third section W. turns to an examination of the theology of Zephaniah, a theology defined almost entirely in terms of Yahweh's concern for the poor. The contrast between the rich and powerful of the city with the 'poor of the land' is fully discussed, any 'spiritualising' of the concept of the poor being vigorously denied. The full radical nature of Zephaniah's preaching is emphasized, although the hope for their salvation lies in Yahweh's action rather than in any active revolution of theirs. This is a most valuable addition to Zephaniah studies, taking full note of recent scholarship but making an original contribution of its own.   R. Mason

WOODS, FRED E.: *Water and Storm Polemics Against Baalism in the Deuteronomic History* (American University Studies. Series 7: Theology and Religion 150). 1994. Pp. 171. (Lang, Frankfurt–Bern–New York. Price: SwF 26.00 ISBN 0 8204 2111 1; ISSN 0740 0446)

The central argument is that there are a considerable number of passages in the Deuteronomic history in which Yahweh's power over water or in the storm are to be understood as embodying an implied polemic against the Baal cult. For the most part, however, W.'s arguments are extraordinarily weak and unconvincing. Whilst the anti-Baal polemic contained in 1 King 18 is abundantly obvious and the poetic storm theophany imagery in 2 Sam. 22 (= Ps. 18) doubtless derives ultimately from Baal, there seem to be no good grounds at all for supposing that conscious polemic against Baalism has influenced many of the other passages. One requires more clear and concrete evidence before one can affirm, say, that allusions to Yahweh's parting of the Red Sea or River Jordan (Josh. 2:9–11, 4:23–5:1) contain deliberate polemic by the Deuteronomist against the cult of Baal. This book also shows many signs of carelessness in its bibliographical citations, for the names of scholars are often misspelled and foreign accents are frequently missing. The author's command of the literature in languages other than English is also poor.

J. DAY

ZOBEL, KONSTANTIN: *Prophetie und Deuteronomium. Die Rezeption prophetischer Theologie durch das Deuteronomium* (Beihefte zur Zeitschrift für die alttestamentliche Wissenschaft 199). 1992. Pp. x, 267. (de Gruyter, Berlin–New York. Price: DM 108.00. ISBN 3 11 012838 1; ISSN 0934 2575)

This is a slightly revised version of a dissertation presented at the University of Hall-Wittenberg. It is concerned with the adoption and development of fundamental theological themes in the book of Deuteronomy which appear earlier in the eighth-century prophets. The mehod is form-critical and tradition-historical, and the subject itself harks back to a theme that at one period commanded wide support. The themes examined are those of the divine love for Israel, seen as a development from that of human married love, the notion of seeking God and that of Israel as a divine theocracy, expressed through the institutions of kingship (Deut. 17:14–20), civil judges (Deut. 16:18–20) and the prophets (Deut. 18:9–22). Z. sees the influence of Hosea in particular in Deuteronomy, but also traces themes from Amos, Micah and Isaiah in the book. The approach is largely that of a history of theological motifs, but interprets the innovative and reactionary work of the pre-exilic prophets as having been shaped and co-ordinated in the Deuteronomic movement into a restoration programme for the exilic age. That this movement was heavily steeped in prophetic ideas has largely fallen to the side in recent study in favour of following through developments of laws and legal administration so the thesis has a worthwhile contribution to offer.

R. E. CLEMENTS

8.   THE SURROUNDING PEOPLES

Archaeologische Mitteilungen aus Iran. Vol. 25. 1992. Pp. 378 + 78 plates. (Dietrich Reimer, Berlin. Price: DM 175.00/AS 1365/SwF 175.00. ISSN 0066 6033)

As expected in an archaeological annual, most of the articles discuss archaeology and building activity from various historical periods in Iran. While many of these may not be of direct interest to Old Testament scholars, a number of the essays are of potential interest: I. Medvedskayar discusses 8th–7th-century Median sites. R. Schmitt writes on the Darius inscription 'Susa e'. M. Dandamayev asks whether Eanna was destroyed by Darius I. Following earlier studies, M. Heltzer addresses the problem of taxation in Achaemenid Judah, including specific reference to Nehemiah 5.

L. L. GRABBE

BAGNALL, ROGER S. and FRIER, BRUCE W.: *The Demography of Roman Egypt* (Cambridge Studies in Population, Economy and Society in Past Time 23). 1994. Pp. xix, 354. (Cambridge University Press. Price: £35.00/$49.95. ISBN 0 521 46123 5)

The heart of this excellent study is a compilation of about 300 actual family census records from the first three centuries of the Common Era. To the data of these are applied the standard demographic methods and techniques developed by social historians for a variety of societies and historical periods. The authors are very conscious of the limitations of their data. Nevertheless, they are able to draw some reasonable conclusions about the population of Egypt. For one thing, Josephus' often-quoted figure of about eight million, allegedly based on census data, is probably about twice as large as the actual figure of about four to five million. L. L. GRABBE

BERNBECK, REINHARD: *Die Auflösung der häuslichen Produktionsweise* (Berliner Beiträge zum Vorderen Orient 14). 1994. Pp. 387 + xxxi tables. (Reimer Verlag, Berlin. Price: DM 80.00/SwF 81.00/AS 624. ISBN 3 496 02525 5)

This lengthy book was the author's doctoral thesis over household production in prehistoric periods in Mesopotamia. The work is not simply a report of collected data reflecting types of household production, but it also takes theoretical positions on the early development and evolution of society. The data itself is essentially archaeological, referring to methods of irrigation, agriculture, building remains, and ceramics. The theoretical chapters, based in the first instance upon Marx, deal with questions of subsistence levels of nourishment, as well as family structures, such as the number of married women in a family. The book also studies climatic patterns and the ecology of pre-historic northern Mesopotamia. The new theory identifies a distinction between 'household' and 'tributary' production, representing mathematical models of subsistence agriculture and exchanges of goods, and comparisons are made with other societies, such as Turkey and Mexico. The book is full of technical data and is a useful resource for understanding the current theories on early development of society in the Near East. M. J. GELLER

BICKEL, SUSANNE: *La cosmogonie égyptienne. Avant le Nouvel Empire* (Orbis Biblicus et Orientalis 134). 1994. Pp. 346. (Universitätsverlag, Freiburg (Schweiz); Vandenhoeck & Ruprecht, Göttingen. Price: SwF 98.00 ISBN (Universitätsverlag) 3 7278 0950 7; (Vandenhoeck & Ruprecht) 3 525 53769 7)

In the past, much attention has been devoted to ancient Egyptian views of the orgins of our world and universe in the wealth of texts of the New Kingdom to Roman period (*c.* 1550 BC to 300 AD). But now, B. has interrogated the Pyramid Texts (3rd millennium BC) and especially the Coffin Texts (*c.* 2200–800 BC) for Egyptian views, *c.* 2500–1700 BC. She deals in turn with the intitial abyss (Nun), the initial creator, the god Atum, and modes of creation. Then with the son of the Creator (any of the gods Shu, Ptah, Hapi and Heka), responsible for the rest of creation (gods, humanity, etc.) and its continuance, then on mankind, entry of evil, and possible world's end. A briefer second part reviews the situation that we have numerous mythical allusions in funerary and other texts, but no mythic narratives in this early epoch. Of special interest to Old Testament scholars should be the section on the creative word (in Egypt long before *logos*). Before the New Kingdom, the role of first creator belonged exclusively to Atum; other gods also took on this role from then on. An elegantly-articulated and useful volume.

K. A. KITCHEN

BROOKE, G. J.; CURTIS A. H. W.; and HEALEY J. F. (eds): *Ugarit and the Bible. Proceedings of the International Symposium on Ugarit and the Bible. Manchester, September 1992* (Ugaritisch-Biblische Literatur 11). 1994. Pp. xii, 472. (Ugarit-Verlag, Münster. N.P. ISBN 3 927120 22 7)

Of the twenty-four papers from the Manchester symposium collected here, some eighteen impinge directly on Old Testament studies, and several offer updatings of the various debates that Ugaritic studies have engendered in the biblical field. A. Curtis examines Dahood's impact on Psalm research; A. A. da Silva, comparative cosmology; L. Davey, echoes of Anat in the Bible; and J. Day asks questions of the supposed common assumptions of the two religious worlds. J. A Emerton looks at the linguistic legacy of Ugaritic in Hebrew; T. Fenton, at poetics and mythopoetics; while D. Fleming examines sweat as a literary motif. J. Gibson re-examines elements of West Semitic kingship', L. Grabbe considers the appropriateness of the term 'Canaanite' in Old Testament and Ugaritic scholarship; and R. Hess discusses topography and boundaries. P. Hughes surveys the computer software market in Semitic studies; K. Koch, the real targets of biblical prophetic diatribes against other cults; J. C. de Moor considers a possible source for the Job tradition; while G. Del Olmo Lete examines the 'Canaanite' dimension in Israelite religion. M. S. Smith discusses myth as a literary category in Ugarit and the Bible; W. G. E. Watson compares formulaic introductions to speech; and N. Wyatt looks at the theogony motif in the two traditions. Other papers are given by W. Jobling, M. E. J. Richardson, W. H. van Soldt, J. Tropper, E. Ullendorff, and M. Yon.

N. WYATT

BRUNNER-TRAUT, EMMA (ed.): *Die grossen Religionen des Alten Orients und der Antike.* 1992. Pp. 176. (Kohlhammer, Stuttgart–Berlin–Köln. Price: DM 25.00/SwF 26.30/AS 195. ISBN 3 17 011976 1)

This little volume gives an introduction to some of the major religions of the ancient Near East: Egyptian (B.-T.), Mesopotamian (W. Röllig), Syrian-Canaanite (K. Koch), Zoroastrianism (H. Gaube), Greek and Roman (K. Hoheisel), Gnostic-Manichaean (A. Böhlig). B.-T.'s introduction takes the form of questions and answers about religion in antiquity.

L. L. GRABBE

BUTLER, E. M.: *The Myth of the Magus.* 1993 (1948). Pp. xiv, 282. (Cambridge University Press. Price £7.95/$10.95. ISBN (paper) 0 521 43777 6)

A first glance at this republished tome invites the reaction, 'Oh no! Not all that myth-and-ritual nonsense rehashed!' Persevere, dear reader, for though as a *B.L.* devotee you will be looking for the latest thing in intertextuality in Old Testament studies, here is an entertaining and witty survey of the Magus motif, perhaps somewhat stretched at times, to include Moses and Solomon, from its Zoroastrian origins through Faust and beyond, down to Mme Blavatsky and her discoveries, and even Rasputin. There is nothing like an interdisciplinary study of this kind to prick the bubble of pomposity we blow up to contain our own studies. Moses' magic is averred to be 'dark of hue', which the author explains as meaning that 'whoever wrote or edited the epic of Exodus was on the wrong side of the magical fence' p. 34). As for Solomon, for all his much-vaunted wisdom, 'Love and death proved to be beyond his control He could not arrest the course of fate and was ignorant of its established decrees. More humiliating still, he had not the wherewithal to satisfy the hunger of a single whale, let alone its seventy thousand kin' (p. 40). That is those two prigs cut down to size. What more need one say?

N. WYATT

CANTARELLA, EVA: *Bisexuality in the Ancient World*. Translated by Cormac Ó Cuilleanáin. 1994 (1992). Pp. xii, 284. (Yale University Press, New Haven and London. Price: £8.95 (paper). ISBN 0 300 04844 0; paper 0 300 05924 8)

This is a paperback edition of a book published in hardback in 1992 and originally published in Italian in 1988. The author draws on legal texts and inscriptions as well as literary texts to discuss the role of bisexuality in ancient Greece (primarily classical Athens) and Rome from the archaic period to the late empire. The term 'bisexuality' is used to encompass all forms of homosexuality — passive and active, between men and between women. The most original section of the book is the analysis of Roman legal views. The condemnation of homosexuality in the Judaeo-Christian tradition is dealt with sensibly and clearly on pp. 191–210; the discussion of the attitudes expressed in the Hebrew Bible is unexceptionable, but nothing novel emerges.

M. D. GOODMAN

CASSON, LIONEL: *The Ancient Mariners: Seafarers and Sea Fighters of the Mediterranean in Ancient Times*. 1991 (2nd ed.). Pp. xviii, 246. (Princeton University Press, Princeton NJ. Price: £32.50/$52.50; paper £12.50/$17.95. ISBN 0 691 06836 4; paper 0 691 01477 9)

C. has revised and up-dated his 1959 edition (note, e.g. ch. 3, 'Excavating under Water'). He begins with early Egyptian, Minoan and Mycenaean seafaring, and vividly retells the stories of Wenamon and Jason before moving to the Mediterranean of Homer, the Phoenicians (with a side glance at Solomon) and the Greek colonists. C. includes a picture of a sailing ship apparently without oars, probably a Phoenician *hippos*, on a seal described as an 8th–7th centuries Hebrew seal (pl. 26; from Avigad, *BASOR* 246 [1982], 59–61); Wallinga, who argues that there are no pre-6th century representations of ships which are purely sailing ships, unfortunately does not discuss this interesting iconographic evidence (*B.L.* 1994, p. 42). The heart of the book is given to the maritime power of the Greeks, the Hellenistic world, and the Romans; the last pages briefly review the Byzantine world. C. excels at explaining the details of ship construction or maritime fraud for ignorant and honest landlubbers, but some of this is done even better, with sharper photographic illustrations, in his *Ships and Seafaring in Ancient Times* (British Museum Press, 1994).

J. R. BARTLETT

CIVIL, MIGUEL: *The Farmer's Instructions. A Sumerian Agricultural Manual* (Aula Orientalis Supplementa 5). 1994. Pp. xiii + 268; XVI plates. (Editorial Ausa, Sabadell, Barcelona. N.P. ISBN 84 88810 03 2)

The core of this critical edition of an 18th-century BC Sumerian manual on farming comprises 109 lines of text from tablets from Nippur, supplemented by tablets from elsewhere. The manual is essentially practical, with a mythological element only in the introduction, and covers a range of farming techniques over the agricultural year. Civil's commentary spills over into separate discussions on levees, ditches and dikes, on oxen, agricultural tools and on furrows. Additonal material on farming is provided from letters and other texts from about the same period. No hand copies are given as the author prefers reading from photographs, supplied at the end of the volume. There are also indices and a bibliography. Although not of direct interest for the Old Testament the *Farmer's Instructions* is in many ways of great significance not least as the earliest known example of the genre.

W. G. E. WATSON

CLARK, GILLIAN: *Women in Late Antiquity. Pagan and Christian Lifestyles.* 1994 (1993). Pp. xix, 159. (Clarendon Press, Oxford. Price: paper £9.95. ISBN 0 19 872166 8)

C. has put together a fascinating collection of material documenting the life of women in the 3rd to 6th century CE. In her own words this is very much a 'patchwork' of attitudes and information. In such a broad area as the Roman Empire there were many variations both in legal terms and in attitudes in the treatment of women. Apart from the problems caused by geography there are the usual questions of interpretation of texts written by men, mostly belonging to a patriarchal class-ridden society. The sources are taken from patristic, legal, and medical texts and aim to convey a complete picture of the public and private lives of women. Although sometimes one may feel overwhelmed by the sheer wealth of information, many questions arise. The book explores the complex relationship between Roman law and Christian attitudes and the nature of the changes in attitudes, conjuring up a vivid picture of what it was like to be a woman in late antiquity.   A. JEFFERS

COPENHAVER, BRIAN P.: *Hermetica. The Greek* Corpus Hermeticum *and the Latin* Asclepius *in a New English Translation, with Notes and Introduction.* 1992. Pp. lxxxiii, 320. (Cambridge University Press. Price: £50.00/ $74.95. ISBN 0 521 36144 3)

Up to now the only English translations of the *Corpus Hermeticum* have been based on obsolete texts. The basic corpus (including the *Asclepius* but not the Nag Hammadi texts, the Stobaeus *Excerpts*, the Armenian *Definitions*, or the Vienna fragments) is translated from the standard Nock/ Festugière text. The seventy-page introduction and bibliography and more than 160 pages of notes to the translation make this a most useful tool. For a recent critical discussion the *Corpus*, Fowden's monograph is important (p. 129 below).   L. L. GRABBE

CORNELIUS, FRIEDRICH: *Geschichte der Hethiter, Mit besonderer Berücksichtigung der geographischen Verhältnisse und der Rechtsgeschichte.* 1992 (1976). Pp. xiv, 378 + 48 plates and 2 maps. (Wissenschaftliche Buchgesellschaft, Darmstadt. Price: DM 79.00/SwF 80.00/AS 616. ISBN 3 534 06190 X)

It is somewhat exaggerated to claim, as this study does, to be the 'first comprehensive' history of the Hittites. After all, O. R. Gurney's *The Hittites* has been in print since 1952 and has been periodically reprinted with revisions (1954, 1981, 1990). The amount of text is roughly comparable, but the two books have different emphases. Gurney devotes more space to aspects of the culture, whereas C. gives more space to the political history. C. also well documents his study in endnotes, while Gurney often does not even identify the source of his many quotes (in translation) of Hittite texts. C.'s book also benefits from his expertise on geographical matters. It was also last updated in 1976, the year of the author's death.   L. L. GRABBE

DECKER, WOLFGANG and HERB, MICHAEL: *Bildatlas zum Sport im Alten Ägypten. Corpus der bildlichen Quellen zu Leibesübungen, Spiel, Jagd, Tanz and verwandten Themen: Teil 1. Text; Teil 2. Abbildungen* (Handbuch der Orientalistik, Erste Abteilung: Der Nahe und Mittlere Osten, Band 40). 1994. Pp. xx, 1009 + 450 plates. (Brill, Leiden–New York–Köln. Price: fl. 650.00/$371.50. ISBN 90 04 09974 3 (set); ISSN 0169 9423)

This pair of volumes, monumentl in bulk, scope and price, presents as full a collection as possible of all the data from Ancient Egypt that might be considered to mention or depict any kind of sporting activity (including also board-games, dancing, hunting), or which (even in ritual) might be a reflex of such activity. The text of the work is in eight major divisions (I–VIII) through which run twenty chapters (lettered A to T). Much of the first four divisions, usually involving the king, are mainly cult scenes, and not sport at all, but such acts as striking or throwing a ball might have had their origin in some ancient game — hence their inclusion here. In the other four divisions, we have real sports and pastimes: for example, wrestling, archery, single-stick combat, juggling, ball-catching piggyback, acrobatics, water-sports, hunting, or board-games (distant ancestors of chess and draughts). Dancing (as of the *Muu*) is sometimes ritual (which does not really belong here) rather than for entertainment. In casting their net as widely as possible, the authors may have included too much. But this vast, well-illustrated repertoire will be a valuable reference-work for anyone studying sport and games in the biblical world.

K. A. KITCHEN

DI VITO, ROBERT A.: *Studies in Third Millennium Sumerian and Akkadian Personal Names. The Designation and Conception of the Personal God* (Studia Pohl: Series Maior 16). 1993. Pp. xii, 327. (Editrice Pontificio Istituto Biblico, Rome. Price: Lire 25,000. ISBN 88 7653 601 9)

This is a careful catalogue and analysis of personal names in Sumerian and Old Akkadian texts with source, date, name-types and some translations given (pp. 23–81, 128–247). It shows what can be learned about the specific character and concept of a personal god among the Semitic inhabitants of the very earliest period of the 3rd millennium BC in the Middle East. In popular piety various deities are unquestionably designated as guaranteeing the individual's well-being, protection and intercession. The references to IL/EL, *ilum*, etc., as 'my/his god' invite study of the later chief deity of the Canaanite pantheon and of all later Hebrew personal names with theophoric elements. This is an essential reference work.   D. J. WISEMAN

DUNCAN-JONES, RICHARD: *Money and Government in the Roman Empire*. 1994. Pp. xix, 300 (Cambridge University Press. Price: £45.00/ $79.95. ISBN 0 521 44192 7)

Since the publication of his first book, *The Economy of the Roman Empire: Quantitative Studies* (2nd edn, 1982). D.-J's technique is to lay out the statistical evidence from the Roman world in graphs and tables, to which he attaches cautious conclusions in a tone so clear and straightforward that the importance of their implications sometimes almost escapes the reader. The bulk of this new study is a quantitative analysis of a huge number of coin hoards from the first three centuries of the Roman empire. Discussion of the currency profiles and metal contents reveals much about the use of money in the Roman economy and the minting of coin by the state. The text is clear and cogent but sometimes technical; D.-J. generally writes for scholars rather than undergraduate students. The exception lies in Part I of the book. From the discussion here (pp. 1–63), readers will gain particular insight of the economics of empire. D.-J. provides a compelling account of the extent to which the Roman state attempted to control the economy, and the more limited extent to which it succeeded. Throughout the book D.-J. uses much comparative evidence from other societies and balances the testimony of literary sources against the evidence from papyrological and archaeological finds. The economy of the Roman empire is better known than that of any other ancient state. This book is thus an exercise in historical method of immense importance for all students of antiquity.

M. D. GOODMAN

ESCHWEILER, PETER: *Bildzauber im alten Ägypten. Die Verwendung von Bildern und Gegenständen in magischen Handlungen nach den Texten des Mittleren und Neuen Reiches* (Orbis Biblicus et Orientalis 137). 1994. Pp. x, 384 + 26 plates. (Universitätsverlag, Freiburg (Schweiz); Vandenhoeck & Ruprecht, Göttingen. Price: DM 132.00/SwF 110.00/AS 1033. ISBN (Universitätsverlag) 3 7278 0957 4; (Vandenhoeck & Ruprecht) 3 525 53772 7)

In essentials, this book surveys the use actually made by the ancient Egyptians of drawings and images-in-the-round in performing magical acts, which formed a part of their religious and medical practice. It therefore includes numerous citations (in transliteration and translation) of texts that refer to the preparation and use of drawings and figurines, and goes into detail on the utilisation of these physical aids in particular magical enactments. From the use of actual, separate drawings and figurines, the Egyptians moved towards simply including images of these along with the texts in their papyri. Bibliography, indexes and a selection of illustrations complete the work. Mainly useful to Egyptologists, but a convenient source for others to see Egyptian magic at work, if they need to.

K. A. KITCHEN

FALES, F. M. and POSTGATE, J. N. (ed.): *Imperial Administrative Records, Part I: Palace and Temple Administration* (State Archives of Assyria 7). 1992. Pp. xliii, 259 + 11 plates. (Helsinki University Press. Price: $65.00; paper $49.50. ISBN 951 570 112 0; paper 951 570 111 2)

The administrative tablets from Nineveh edited in this book were written between the accession of Sargon II to the fall of Nineveh, i.e. 721–612 BC. The texts, mostly hitherto unedited, constitute lists of personnel at the Assyrian court, as well as accounts of commodities such as metals and textiles, in addition to the acounts of the royal banquets and offering lists of foodstuffs to the temples. Of particular interest to biblical scholars are texts mentioning place names from Palestine and the vicinity, such as Ashdod, Megiddo, Dor, and others, from which places or commodities originated. Another insight to be gathered from the banquet accounts is what types of foods were actually eaten, and one notices the almost complete lack of any dairy products (milk or cheese) on the menus, as well as from the temple offering lists. This agrees with the lack of milk products given as offerings in the Jerusalem temple as well. Such lists may help explain the taboo in Jewish law against mixing meat and dairy foods, since the latter were not foods of preference in antiquity, which suggests a more realistic explanation than the reason normally given based upon Ex. 23:19.

M. J. GELLER

FOWDEN, G.: *The Egyptian Hermes. A Historical Approach to the Late Pagan Mind* (Mythos). 1993 (reprint of 1986 edn with new preface). Pp. xxv, 244. (Princeton University Press, Princeton NJ. Price: £9.95/$17.95. ISBN 0 691 02498 7)

The book, written in a limpid style, has three parts. In Part I, the origin of Hermetic literature is shown to be in the Ptolemaic period, when the Greeks absorbed Egyptian ideas. Part II, 'The Way of Hermes', is the longest and explains that Hermetism can be best understood as a form of religion for which the evidence of Zosimus of Panopolis and of Iamblichus of Apamea is shown to be more significant than previously thought. Part III briefly describes the evidence for the Egyptian and Greek setting of Hermetism. In a short appendix the earliest testimonies to the name 'Hermes Trismegistus' are assessed. A map, bibliography and index are provided. The relevance of this work to Old Testament studies is only tangential.

W. G. E. WATSON

GARDNER, JANE F: *Being a Roman Citizen*. 1993. Pp. viii, 244. (Routledge, London–New York. Price £35.00. ISBN 0 415 00154 4)

This learned study of the rights and duties of Roman citizens in private life uses the dry rules of Roman civil law to investigate how Roman citizens actually lived. Recent epigraphic discoveries, especially texts from Pompeii which show commercial law in action at Puteoli, demonstrate that such rules were indeed followed even in detail, at least by some Romans sometimes. John Goodman used ingenuity to investigate in detail the legal disabilities of a freedman, children (even after they have reached adulthood), independent women, disgraced men, and handicapped citizens. The resulting book is not always easy reading but it is full of interest.

M. GOODMAN

HAAS, VOLKERT: *Geschichte der hethitischen Religion* (Handbuch der Orientalistik: Erste Abteilung, Der Nahe und Mittlere Osten: Band 15). 1994. Pp. xxi, 1031 + 137 plates and 1 map. (Brill, Leiden–New York–Köln. Price: fl. 460.00/$263.00.ISBN 90 04 09799 6; ISSN 0169 9423)

H. has given a definitive handbook on Hittite religion in its widest sense from Neolithic times to about 1150 BCE. He includes treatment of the main myths, the cosmogony, the place of the king, tombs and burial, and the ancestor cult, as well as the local and national divinities and cults and the many festivals. He also has a chapter on magic and on rituals to do with cursing. The introductory chapter gives a historical overview to orient the reader. The study is richly documented from original sources in the footnotes. There is an extensive bibliography and indexes on historical names (personal, divine, geographical) and subjects, but sadly no index of modern authors. Considering that this splendid study will be consulted not only by Hittite specialists but by many others with an interest in Hittite religion, rather more than a scant page should have been devoted to the question of sources.

L. L. GRABBE

HANDY, LOWELL K.: *Among the Host of Heaven. The Syro-Palestinian Pantheon as Bureaucracy*. 1994. Pp. xvii, 218. (Eisenbrauns, Winona Lake IN. Price: $27.50. ISBN 0 931464 86 6)

H.s aim is a simple one: because the governmental system took the form of the city-state, the key to the culture's religion may lie in the city-state structures. Recognizing that a single model is not likely to explain the whole of the religion, nevertheless H. thinks some of the characteristics and activities of the gods may be understood in terms of bureaucratic structure (pp. 4–5). After surveying the (meagre) sources and the correct methodology for their use (ch. 2), the heart of the book (chs 3–6) surveys the various deities and what is known of each under the headings of authoritative, active, artisan, and messenger deities. H. concludes there was a multi-tiered hierachy (with at least four layers) of gods which closely corresponds to the hierarchy of aristocracy, royal servants, royal labourers, and private slaves. As well as reflecting each other, the divine and human hierarchies were also parts of a single cosmic hierarchy. The fact that scribes would have seen themselves as belonging to the 'royal labourer' group might suggest why the artisan gods (their divine counterparts) are pictured in some cases as more clever and competent than the authoritative and active gods — the heavenly counterparts to their own human superiors!

L. L. GRABBE

HÖLBL, GÜNTHER: *Geschichte des Ptolemäerreiches. Politik, Ideologie und religiöse Kultur von Alexander dem Grossen bis zur römischen Eroberung*. 1994. Pp. xxxii, 402 + 3 maps. (Wissenschaftliche Buchgesellschaft, Darmstadt. Price: DM 78.00/SwF 79.00/AS 609. ISBN 3 534 10422 6)

This book arises out of the needs of teaching. Since the publication of E. Bevan's *History of Egypt under the Ptolemaic Dynasty* in 1927, there has been no general overview of Ptolemaic history. H. provides this in commendable fashion, with his references focusing on the most recent secondary studies. However, the system of references could not be more cumbersome: these are given in endnotes at the back of the book, with only the chapter numbers to show which are which; but the literature in the notes is in abbreviated form, and the reader must go to the front of the book to find it listed. Both author and publisher should be ashamed of such a senseless arrangement.

L. L. GRABBE

HOERTH, ALFRED J.; MATTINGLY, GERALD L.; and YAMAUCHI, EDWIN M. (eds): *Peoples of the Old Testament World*. Foreword by Alan R. Millard. 1994. Pp. 400. (Baker, Grand Rapids MI. Price: $19.99. ISBN 0 8010 4383 2)

This well-produced volume contains thirteen essays which provide a useful survey of what is known about various peoples of the ancient Near East, most of whom were in contact with ancient Israel. The peoples covered include Sumerians (W. R. Bodine), Babylonians (B. T. Arnold), Assyrians (W. C. Gwaltney), Persians (E. M. Yamauchi), Hittites (H. A. Hoffner), Canaanites and Amorites (K. N. Schoville), Phoenicians (W. A. Ward), Arameans (W. T. Pitard), Philistines (D. M. Howard), Egyptians (J. K. Hoffmeier), Ammonites (R. W. Younker), Moabites (G. L. Mattingly), and Edomites (K. G. Hoglund). Special attention has been given to the 'significant new archeological and historical data' which have been gathered since the publicaion of Wiseman's *Peoples of Old Testament Times* (*B.L.* 1974, p. 81). The footnotes are particularly useful, though the reviewer found no mention of S. Parpola and K. Watanabe, *Neo-Assyrian Treaties and Oaths* (*B.L.* 1993, p. 126). The recommended reading (S. A. Pallis and C. H. Gordon) for a history of the decipherment of the cuneiform languages is not good and should be replaced by M. Pope, *The Story of Decipherment* (1975) and the recent publications of P. T. Daniels. This book can be recommended for teacher and student alike.   K. J. CATHCART

HUNGER, HERMANN (ed.): *Astrological Reports to Assyrian Kings* (State Archives of Assyria 8). 1992. Pp. xxix, 384 + 15 plates. (Helsinki University Press. Price: $80.00/$59.50. ISBN 951 570 131 7; paper 951 570 130 9)

The 567 texts in the book represent a new edition of R. Campbell Thompson's *The Reports of the Magicians and Astrologers of Nineveh and Babylon I–II*, (1900), with the addition of a number of subsequently identified texts edited here for the first time, with photos of many of the unpublished tablets. The book gives a clear impression of applied 'science' in use at the Assyrian court, since the tablets are reports to the king which quote directly from a large collection of celestial omens known as *Enūma Anu Enlil*, but applying the omens to the current situation at court between the years 708–648 BC. The reports are divided between Assyrian and Babylonian scholars, and it is noteworthy that the latter writers occasionally appended to their reports to the king personal complaints or requests, since they had no other means of access, while Assyrian scholars might append advice to the king, reflecting their greater familiarity at the court as advisers to the king. The book offers a brief but useful introduction to the texts, followed by transliterations and translations, with indices consisting of an Akkadian glossary, personal and geographical names, and a subject index.

M. J. GELLER

ISAAC, BENJAMIN: *The Limits of Empire. The Roman Army in the East.* 1993 (1992 rev. edn). Pp. xiv, 510 + 4 maps. (Clarendon Press, Oxford. Price: paper £19.95. ISBN 0 19 814925 2)

This revisionist study of the nature of the Roman frontier in the eastern empire down to the rise of Islam has had an immense influence on ancient historians since its first publication in 1990. Its main thesis, that Rome had no grand strategy for defending the frontier, has been widely accepted. The second edition (*B.L.* 1993, p. 121), with a ten-page postscript referring mostly to new bibliography, is here issued in paperback. It will be of great servce in putting the activities of the Roman state in the region into the context of the Near East as a whole. It should now be read in conjunction with Fergus Millar, *The Roman Near East* (p. 133 below).   M. D. GOODMAN

KELLENS, JEAN: *La religion iranienne à l'epoque achéménide. Actes du Colloque de Liège 11 décembre 1987* (Iranica Antiqua Supplément 5). 1993. Pp. vii, 135. (Peeters/Departement Orientalistiek, Leuven. Price: BEF 900. ISBN 90 6831 329 0)

Of the eight papers published here, several are of potential interest to readers: P. Briant argues that the ritual of the succession of Achaemenid kingship was more complex than often realized. B. Jacobs examines the development of the symbol of Ahura Mazda, arguing that it shows an original solar deity which has become assimilated to Ahura Mazda in the Iranian pantheon. H. Koch traces the geographical location of cult places, personnel, and divinities as represented in the Persepolis tables. J. Wiesehöfer studies religious relations in early Hellenistic Persis.   L. L. GRABBE

Koch, Klaus: *Geschichte der ägyptischen Religion. Von den Pyramiden bis zu den Mysterien der Isis.* 1993. Pp. 676. (Kohlhammer, Stuttgart–Berlin–Köln. Price: DM 129.00/SwF 130.00/AS 1006. ISBN 3 17 009808 X)

Despite many good studies on Egyptian religion or aspects of it, K. notes that there is no treatment which shows its development from the beginning to its displacement by Christianity. In this work he attempts to fill this gap, showing both what is continuous and what changes over the centuries. Each chapter is followed by the major textual sources (where limited), a brief bibliography of secondary studies, and a set of endnotes. K. freely admits that he has depended on standard collections and translations for his data, but though not an Egyptologist, he has studied with specialists and has freely drawn on the advice of various well-known Egyptologists.   L. L. Grabbe

Krings, Véronique: *La civilisation phénicienne et punique. Manuel de recherche* (Handbuch der Orientalistik: Erste Abteilung, Der Nahe und Mittlere Osten: Band 20). 1995. Pp. xx, 923 + 64 plates. (Brill, Leiden–New York–Köln. Price: fl. 435/$248.75. ISBN 90 04 10068 7; ISSN 0169 9423)

Over thirty scholars contribute to this compendium which, S. Moscati explains, reviews the present state of knowledge in order to be a tool, hitherto unavailable, for further study of the Phoenicians. The first section, 'Sources' has surveys of the relevant texts in various ancient languages, then of material remains. Part II, 'Introduction to the Civilisation', includes chapters on language and script (M. G. Amadasi-Guzzo and W. Röllig), on the onomasticon (F. Israel), religion (C. Bonnet and P. Xella), attitudes to life (S. Ribichini), politics and society (S. F. Bondi) and arts and crafts, history and trade. Part III describes each region touched by the Phoenicians, from Lebanon to Morocco, with a summary of the sites, some with plans, and current opinions about them. The bibliography covers over fifty pages in small type. Drawings, plans and maps illustrate a few chapters, although unevenly, with the plates showing sites, monuments, sculptures, seventy-nine coins, but not seals or pottery. This is almost an encyclopaedia, but it lacks a subject index to enable readers to trace references to a topic like *tophet*. Biblical material is introduced wherever appropriate, with cautious acceptance (e.g. 'it would be hypercritical . . . to deny any relations between Tyre and, at least, Solomon', G. Bunnens, p. 226). The volume gathers an enormous amount of information from very diverse sources and will serve long as the basic reference work about Israel's culturally influential neighbour.   A. R. Millard

Leick, Gwendolyn: *Sex and Eroticism in Mesopotamian Literature.* 1994. Pp. xvi, 320. (Routledge, London–New York. Price: £45.00. ISBN 0 415 06534 8)

This book is more serious than the title suggests. The author has suggested some interesting new interpretations of Sumerian and Akkadian literary texts, from the perspective of love and sex. She offers new insights into the Sumerian myths of Enki and Ninhursag and Enlil and Ninlil, as well as some of the Sumerian love songs, combined with a reasonable appraisal of the goddess Inanna's role in such literature. Leick's discussion of sacred prostitution offers some new suggestions towards clarifying the ambiguities, although her chapter defining 'liminal sexuality' is unconvincing. The role of sexuality in both black and white magic is thought provoking, and deserves further analysis. The role of sexuality in myths of cosmology is clearly described. The main weaknesses in the book are admitted by the author, resulting from her lack of training in Sumerian (although she is familiar with Akkadian). The philological discussions would be more easily followed if transliterations of the main texts were available in the book, since in some cases the latest editions of texts were not used. Nevertheless, despite these limitations, the book represents an intelligent and thorough discussion of the material, and merits attention.

M. J. GELLER

LIPINSKI, E.: *Dictionnaire de la civilisation phénicienne et punique.* 1992. Pp. xx, 502 + 16 plates. (Brepols, Turnhout. Prece BEF 3953. ISBN 2 503 50033 1)

In an academic market increasingly beset with encyclopaedic works, this volume deserves an honoured place. Eighty-seven specialists in all branches of Phoenician and West Semitic studies have produced over one thousand articles covering every aspect of Phoenician and Punic culture from its 2nd-millennium antecedents down to Roman times, and from Mesopotamia to Portugal. Copious monochrome illustrations and plans, together with a small section of colour plates, show all manner of iconographic and architectural detail. Entries are fully cross-referenced, with both immediate bibliography and reference to larger bibliographical sources. Much of the material contained here may be of peripheral interest to *B.L.* readers, but it enriches the general background enormously, provides authoritative treatments of many Phoenician issues impinging on the Old Testament world, and at times contributes directly to matters of biblical scholarship. This volume should be in every research library.

N. WYATT

LUGINBÜHL, MARIANNE: *Menschenschöfungsmythen. Ein Vergleich zwischen Griechenland und dem Alten Orient* (Europäische Hochschulschriften. Series 15: Classics 58). 1992. Pp. 296 + 10 plates. (Lang, Frankfurt–Bern–New York. Price: SwF 25.00. ISBN 3 261 04533 7)

The author points out that, while myths from different cultures about the creation of the world have often been collected and examined, there has so far been no cross-cultural study of myths about the creation of humanity which, in the view of many scholars, constitutes a distinct *Gattung.* L.'s work thus seeks to fill a gap, and she has produced a competent and comprehensive survey of both the resemblances and the differences in this area between Greece and the ancient Near East. Her first section is concerned with anthropogenic myths in Mesopotamia and accounts of the creation of humanity in the Old Testament and in Egypt. Turning to Greece, she notes a basic difference with the Near East. While the latter is concerned with the creation of humanity in general, the social and political structure of the former meant that the earliest myths dealt only with the emergence of human beings in a particular area or social group. Only later, and as a result of Near Eastern influences, did a universal anthropogeny arise, reaching its full development in the speculations of Greek philosophy. One might question whether so clear a distinction can really be drawn and perhaps too much reliance is placed on van Dijk's three-fold classification of myths, but the clarity of the exposition is to be commended.

J. R. PORTER

MILLAR, FERGUS: *The Roman Near East 31 BC — AD 337.* 1994. Pp. xxix, 587. (Harvard University Press, Cambridge MA and London. Price: $45.00/ £35.95. ISBN 0 674 77885 5)

M.'s excellent study covers the geographical area between the Taurus Mountains of Asia Minor and Egypt, extending as far east as Mesopotamia.

As he points out, the main sources are epigraphic, not only Greek and Latin but also Semitic. M. has not only consulted various specialists for advice in particular areas of his study but has also spent a good deal of personal effort to work in languages not normally associated with a classicist. Part I is a historical survey of the East as a part of the Roman empire. Part II is laid out geographically, focusing on the individual regions. A good section of the book impinges on Judaea and Jewish history, including ch. 10 on Judaea to Syria Palestine and a good section of ch. 2 on the history 31 BC to AD 74. This book makes an important companion to previous studies on the Hellenistic Near East edited or written by S. Sherwin-White and A. Kuhrt (*B.L.* 1989, p. 37; 1994, pp. 128–29).

L. L. GRABBE

Mari. Annales de Recherches Interdisciplinaires. Tome 5. 1987. Pp. 737, including numerous figs and ills. Tome 6. 1990. Pp. 682, including numerous figs and ills. Tome 7. 1993. Pp. 417, including numerous figs and ills. (Éditions Recherche sur les Civilisations, A.D.P.F., Paris. Prices: Fr. (vol. 5) 452.00; (vol. 6) 395.00; (vol. 7) 280.00. ISBN (vol. 5) 2 86538 176 5; (vol. 6) 2 86538 204 0; (vol. 7) 2 86538 238 9)

See *B.L.* 1986, p. 107, for this journal. The three further volumes continue to put out a vast amount of important new information and documents about Mari and related matters. In these three, readers may be particularly interested in the find of a small number of tablets from Mari roughly contemporary with the big Ebla archive (D. Charpin in 5, with supplement in 6); a Mari-style 'prophecy' addressed to a king of a city in the Diyala valley contemporary with the major Mari archives (M. deJong Ellis in 5); and two major contributions to the topic of the battle between the storm god and the sea (in 7). J.-M. Durand publishes the Mari letter in which king Yaḥdun-Līm is told of a 'prophecy' of Hadad of Aleppo that he would be victorious, being given the weapons with which Hadad had defeated the Sea. The discussion is stimulating, but brief and dogmatic. To accompany this letter, P. Bordreuil and D. Pardee edit, translate and comment on the Ugaritic passages dealing with the battle between Baal and Yam.

W. G. LAMBERT

MILLER, PATRICIA COX: *Dreams in Late Antiquity. Studies in the Imagination of a Culture*. 1994. Pp. xii, 273. (Princeton University Press, Princeton NJ. Price: $39.50/£30.00. ISBN 0 691 07422 4)

This book demonstrates the importance of dreams to the thought world of antiquity (cf. also the study of Husser [p. 92 above]), not just among magicians and peripheral figures but also among philosophers and theologians. Special credence was placed in dreams as a source of esoteric knowledge. (Cicero's skepticism was an isolated exception.) Part I focuses on the images and concepts relating to dreams, including ancient theories about dreaming and principles of dream interpretation. Part II is composed of essays on individual Greco-Roman dreamers (though most of these discussed happen to be Christians). M. sees dreams as a type of ancient semiotics: 'dreams functioned as occasions for formulating coherent understandings as well as for giving articulate expression to perceptions of self and world' (pp. 251–52).

L. L. GRABBE

MILLARD, ALAN, with a contribution by Robert Whiting: *The Eponyms of the Assyrian Empire 910–612 B.C.* (State Archives of Assyria Studies 2). 1994. Pp. xvi, 153 + 20 pls. in line. (The Neo-Assyrian Text Corpus Project, Helsinki. Price: $36.50. ISBN 951 45 6715 3, ISSN 1235 1032)

The precise chronology of the whole of the ancient Near East before 600 BC depends on Assyrian evidence. So far back as 1800 BC (and no doubt earlier) the Assyrians dated years by the name of an official who held the title *līmu* for one year. The king and highest officers of state held this rank in turn, and lists of their names and titles were complied and preserved. The list can be reconstructed for the years 910–649. Some copies offer also a brief historical entry for each year, one of which is an eclipse of the sun, now fixed astronomically to 763. Despite the importance of this material, the last edition (of 1938) depended on old and sometimes doubtful copies of the tablets and fragments. This new work gives a full critical edition of the list with English translation and explanatory material. It also gathers other material naming *līmus*. Generally this is a reliable work, but while the majority of tablets and fragments were recopied, those in Berlin were only collated from photographs and those in Ankara not at all.   W. G. LAMBERT

O'CONNOR, DAVID and SILVERMAN, DAVID P. (ed.): *Ancient Egyptian Kingship* (Probleme der Ägyptologie 9). 1995. Pp. xxxiii, 347. (Brill, Leiden–New York–Köln. Price: fl. 180.00/$103.00. ISBN 90 04 10041 5; ISSN 0169 9601)

The papers printed here arise out of a symposium in Denver in 1987, though it was only subsequent to the conference that a decision was made to request the oral addresses to be turned into papers for print — hence the delay in publication. In addition to an introduction by the editors, there are chapters on legitimation of Egyptian kingship (J. Baines), its nature (Silverman), its origins (Baines), its concept during the Eighteenth Dynasty (D. Redford) and the Nineteenth Dynasty (W. Murnane), the programmes of the royal funerary complexes of the Fourth Dynasty (Z. Hawass), and the royal palace in the New Kingdom (O'Connor). For those interested in the question of 'divine kingship', it is addressed in the introduction and in the chapter on the nature of Egyptian kingship (pp. xxii–xxvi, 49–87).

L. L. GRABBE

PARPOLA, SIMO (ed.): *Letters from Assyrian and Babylonian Scholars* (State Archives of Assyria 10). 1993. Pp. xxxix, 421. (Helsinki University Press. N.P. ISBN 951 570 169 4; paper 951 570 168 6)

The letters of Assyrian scholars to the Late Assyrian kings were edited by P. in 1970 (*B.L.* 1972, p. 64), and his detailed commentary on them appeared in 1983 (*B.L.* 1984, p. 115). These letters are now reissued in revised form together with similar letters from Babylonian scholars, not previously available in a reliable edition. The commentary is not repeated, though there is some relevant matter in the concise Introduction and in the notes. However, the view that according to 'Mesopotamian Wisdom' 'God created the universe as a mirror of his existence and man as his image' and the related new doctrine of the *Tree of Life* (note the capitals) are not generally accepted by Assyriologists. Otherwise this is a major and indispensable work for understanding official Assyrian mentality and the processes of Assyrian government during the later Hebrew monarchy.   W. G. LAMBERT

136   THE SURROUNDING PEOPLES

PEDEN, A. J.: *The Reign of Ramesses IV*. 1994. Pp. xxvi, 130. (Aris & Phillips, Warminster, Wilts. Price: £15.00/$29.95. ISBN 0 85668 622 0)

This compact, handy volume renders account of a less-famous Egyptian pharaoh, the man that succeeded Ramesses III (of Sea Peoples fame) in about 1150 BC. Ramesses IV reigned little more than six years, but without colour and variety in the sources for his rule. P. gives a systematic outline in eight chapters, on the king's family background (his father was assassinated), his accession-day and age at death, data on Egypt's foreign relations and the mining of copper at Timna, turquoise in Sinai, and stone in Hammamat; then, a survey of the royal buildings, a cross-section of the officials and clergy of the reign, conclusions, and translations of thirteen of the most interesting inscriptions and papyri from this time, plus four plans and index. For ox-drawn wagons used in the desert, the same West-Semitic word is used as for the same means of desert transport in Numbers 7:3–8, namely *'agala(t)*. A chief workman receives two silver vessels 'from Ascalon'. And the theological attitudes in the king's great stelae from Abydos are well worth study. The work is well-documented, concise and easy to use.   K. A. KITCHEN

PENGLASE, CHARLES: *Greek Myths and Mesopotamia. Parallels and Influence in the Homeric Hymns and Hesiod*. 1994. Pp. xii, 278. (Routledge, London–New York. Price: £40.00. ISBN 0 415 08371 0)

The theme of this book is a promising one, in the train of the substantial work of scholars such as M. C. Astour, W. Burkert, P. Walcot, M. West, and others. The author discusses various myths of the deities Inanna (Ishtar) and Ninurta, with emphasis on their journeys, which he considers to symbolize the acquisition of power. He then turns to myths of the origins of Apollo, Demeter, and Aphrodite, and to the journey traditions of Hermes and Zeus, before treating Pandora, Prometheus (compared with Enki) and Athena. It is to the Mesopotamian tradition that these Greek myths bear the closest relationship. The *prima facie* case seems compelling, although no account is taken of the well-documented relationship of West Semitic evidence of early Greek thought. The matter of the actual means of transmission also remains problematic. We should more plausibly suppose mediation through Phoenician or Anatolian channels, now largely lost. On the apparently exclusive claim of the book, for all its close textual analysis, the verdict must remain 'not proven' until these further issues are clarified. But the author does right in highlighting connections that deserve further scrutiny.   N. WYATT

POMEROY, SARAH B.: *Xenophon, Oeconomicus. A Social and Historical Commentary, with a New English Translation*. 1994. Pp. xii, 388. (Clarendon Press, Oxford. Price: £50.00. ISBN 0 19 814082 7)

Along wityh the Pseudo-Aristotelian *Oeconomicus*, Xenophon's work is an important source for data on the ancient economy. P. uses the Oxford text of E. C. Marchant but gives her own translation, along with a lengthy introduction and a detailed commentary. P. is particularly interested in how women are portrayed in Xenophon's treatise.   L. L. GRABBE

REDFORD, DONALD B.: *Egypt, Canaan and Israel in Ancient Times*. 1992. Pp. xxii, 488. (Princeton University Press, NJ. Price: paper $16.95. ISBN (paper) 0 691 00086 7)

The book reviewed in *B.L.* 1993, p. 43, is now available in paperback.   ED.

RICH, JOHN and SHIPLEY, GRAHAM (eds): *War and Society in the Roman World* (Leicester–Nottingham Studies in Ancient Society 5). 1993. Pp. xii, 315. (Routledge, London–New York. Price: £35.00. ISBN 0 415 06644 1)

This is the fifth volume in the fine series of studies produced by contributors to seminars organized jointly by the Classics Departments of Leicester and Nottingham Universities. Twelve distinguished ancient historians discuss the different ways that warfare affected Roman society from the Republic to the late Empire. The topic is important, since Romans placed an extraordinarily high valve in military success, a fact which goes a long way to explain the expansion of their empire. Among the chapters of most interest for the impact of Rome on Jewish history are the contributions by Adam Ziolkowski (on how the Romans sacked cities) and by Greg Woolf (on the 'Roman peace'); both authors stress the force and brutality of the Roman state, in peace as well as war.
                                                                    M. GOODMAN

RICHARDSON, JOHN: *Roman Provincial Administration* (Inside the Ancient World). 1994 (1976). Pp. 88. (Duckworth, London. Price: £6.95. ISBN 0 86292 128 7)

This is part of a series aimed at sixth-form students but written by specialists in the specific subject area. It gives a clear introduction to the main aspects of Roman administration, including a useful glossary of the main terms. The principal lack is references or bibliography which would allow the non-specialist to follow up areas of interest.
                                                                    L. L. GRABBE

RUDICH, VASILY: *Political Dissidence Under Nero. The Price of Dissimulation.* 1993. Pp. xxxiv, 354. (Routledge, London–New York. Price: £35.00. ISBN 0 415 06951 3)

While avoiding drawing contemporary parallels, the author's own experience as a dissident in the former Soviet Union has obviously shaped his interest in the tensions between conviction and necessity which faced the politically articulate in the particular circumstances of Nero's rule. His attempt to write a 'historical psychology' which maps the interplay between the drive of historical necessity or particularity and the dilemma of universal values and personal conviction through the behaviour of the individuals involved results in a vivid and strong narrative; engagement with scholarly debate and details of interpretation are reserved for the extended note to each chapter which replaces detailed footnotes. The few references to Judaism and Christiantity suggest that for R. they represent a dissent rooted in a very different, apolitical, other-worldly or eschatological ethos even if the responses they generated sometimes appear similar. Readers will therefore await with interest the author's promised monograph on 'themes of ethnic, religious and cultural dissent among the Christians, the Jews, and the Greeks'.
                                                                    J. LIEU

SASSOON, JOHN: *From Sumer to Jerusalem. The Forbidden Hypothesis.* 1993. Pp. 128. (Intellect, Oxford. Price: £14.15. ISBN 1 871516 42 0)

On the basis of the propositions (a) that in Genesis 11:2 the 'they' who are described as having come to Shinar (Sumer and Akkad) from the east were the Hebrews; and (b) that at the time of the destruction of the Third Dynasty of Ur, the Sumerians 'could not stay in Sumer and survive as Sumerians because here they would all be finally absorbed by the Akkadians ... Where would they go? ... North was the way to go; Haran their immediate aim' (p. 76); and acceptance of the throw-away speculation of S. N. Kramer that Shem refers to the Sumerians, the author concludes that the Hebrews of the Old Testament were Sumerians from Mesopotamia. On this assumption he offers a commentary on Genesis 11:1–9 which he designates 'An Outline History of Sumer in the Bible'. In general the author is aware that 'Semitic' (for instance) is a purely linguistic classification (p. 81), but this is hardly observed elsewhere in the book, where there is no clear distinction between linguistic and ethnic terminology. The sub-title 'The Forbidden Hypothesis' refers to the suggestion that the 'scholarly establishment' ignores or discounts it out of deference to Jewish susceptibilities. It is, however, simply unconvincing.

T. C. Mitchell

SCHWEIZER, ANDREAS: *Seelenführer durch den verborgenen Raum. Das ägyptische Unterweltsbuch Amduat*. Mit einem Vorwort von Erik Hornung. 1994. Pp. 240. (Kösel, Munich. Price: DM 39.80. ISBN 3 466 36411 6)

This very elegantly produced little book is simply a Jungian psychologist's personal interpretation of the Egyptian religious composition *Am Duat*, to be found in the tombs of the pharaohs of the 18th–20th Dynasties (*c*. 1550–1070 BC). That composition takes the path of the sun-god through the twelve hours of the night, from when he sinks below the western horizon to his triumphant rebirth daily in the east to sail the skies once more — a destiny to be shared by the deceased king. This encounter of two such radically different writers 3,000 years apart is intriguing, but remains little more than a curio. *Am Duat* is best studied in the able and authoritative editions and translations by Erik Hornung, the expert in this genre.

K. A. Kitchen

SMITH, MARKS S.: *The Ugaritic Baal Cycle. Volume 1: Introduction with Text, Translation and Commentary of KTU 1.1–1.2* (Supplements to Vetus Testamentum 55). 1994. Pp. xxxvi, 446 + 47 plates. (Brill, Leiden–New York–Köln. Price: fl. 210.00/$120.00. ISBN 90 04 09995 6; ISSN 0083 5889)

This is the first study of the Ugaritic Baal myths on such a scale, and in commentary format. It follows in the best tradition of biblical commentary, with an exhaustive survey of scholarly opinion and general theoretical issues. A lengthy introduction covers such topics as the tablet and column order, genre, transmission-history, grammatical features, and history of interpretation. Each column is then presented in transliteration, with translation (sometimes a vocalized text), periodic discussions on prosodic matters, and philological and exegetical commentary. The author's views are always temperate and balanced, and his handling of alternative positions eirenic and entirely fair. There are excursi on the *Marzeah*, divine dwellings, and Athtar. The discussion is wide-ranging and thorough in its consideration of conflicting views, and the reconstruction of KTU 1.1 v, for instance, is original and impressive, debunking once and for all the theory of El's deposition. The bibliography is up-to-date and comprehensive.

The plates are of the high-resolution photographs of the tablets in sections by Bruce and Kenneth Zuckerman, and are the finest quality so far published. These act as a useful yardstick for the analysis offered, though at times (particularly with KTU 1.2 iii) they merely highlight the intractability of the raw materials. A number of minor errors have slipped in. Some signs have been misread in spite of the photographs. The name Burkert is consistently misspelt, I suspect on cacographic grounds. In the table on p. 17, right hand centre, read 'Athtar triumphant'.

N. Wyatt

SODEN, WOLFRAM VON: *The Ancient Orient. An Introduction to the Study of the Ancient Near East.* Translated by Donald G. Schley. 1994. Pp. xx, 262 + 1 map. (Eerdmans, Grand Rapids MI; Gracewing, Leominster. Price: $14.99/£12.99. ISBN (Eerdmans) 0 8028 0142 0; (Gracewing) 0 85244 252 1)

This is an English rendering of the original German *Einführung in die Altorientalistik*, the Italian rendering of which is dealt with in *B.L.* 1991, p. 130.   W. G. LAMBERT

SOLDT, W. H. VAN: *Letters in the British Museum. Transliterated and Translated* (Altbabylonische Briefe in Umschrift und Übersetzung 12). 1990. Pp. x, 155. (Brill, Leiden–New York–Köln. Price: fl. 62.00/$35.43. ISBN 90 04 09208 0; ISBN 0065 6593)

SOLDT, W. H. VAN: *Letters in the British Museum. Transliterated and Translated. Part 2* (Altbabylonische Briefe in Umschrift und Übersetzung 12). 1994. Pp. x, 163. (Brill, Leiden–New York–Köln. Price: fl. 85.00/$48.75. ISBN 90 04 09948 4; ISSN 0065 6593)

It was F. R. Kraus, the Professor of Assyriology in Leiden University, who first had the vision to provide a series of collections of these letters in translation and transliteration more than thirty years ago. Old Testament scholars — linguists, historians and sociologists alike — who really want to know what was going on in Old Babylon and its environs cannot neglect primary sources such as these. V.S. has prepared English translations from tablets which for many of the decades of this century rested untouched in London in the care of the British Museum. He began with the archives of some travelling salesmen, some of whom seem to have gone westwards to Anatolia to trade textiles for tin and who became relatively wealthy citizens of the Patriarchal age. Some letters were sent officially from Hammurabi himself and testify to what must have been the usual concerns of a king of that time: seeing that civil engineering projects were carried out properly, locating personnel who had gone absent without leave, issuing reminder notices for unpaid tax bills, ensuring that the land was being correctly farmed. The letters are not sorted according to subject matter; V.S. adopts the practice of following the order of the Museum's registration system. The reader of both volumes thus encounters an unbelievably rich variety of human interest situations which long to be indexed and classified. Each of them contains 200 letters; another is on its way.   M. E. J. RICHARDSON

TEISSIER, BEATRICE: *Sealing and Seals on Texts from Kültepe kārum Level 2* (Publications de l'Institut historiques–archéologique néerlandais de Stamboul 70). 1994. Pp. xiv, 280. (Nederland Instituut voor het Nabije Oosten, Leiden. Price: fl. 75.00. ISBN 90 6258 070 X; ISSN 0926 9568)

This work, which owes much to K.R. Veenhof, studies seals and sealing among the Assyrian merchant archives from Cappacocia in the 19th century BC. It relates the seal-impressions on clay tablets to persons named in the inscriptions on them, and seeks to explain in which texts they were used, etc. It does not study the various artistic styles of the seals, the author's actual speciality. Within these limits it is an important work, though the drawings of seal-impressions given are mostly those of previous scholars, of varying standards of precision.   W. G. LAMBERT

Texte aus der Umwelt des Alten Testaments. Band 3: *Weisheitstexte, Mythen und Epen*; Lfg. 3: *Mythen und Epen II.* By Kark Hecker, W. G. Lambert, Gerfrid G. W. Müller, Wolfram von Soden, and Ahmet Ünal. 1994. Pp. 360–865. (Mohn, Gütersloh. Price: DM258.00/AS 2013/SwF. 258.00. ISBN 3 579 00075 6)

The book is a useful compendium of myths and epics in German translation from originals mostly in Akkadian and Hittite. There is no obvious basis for the present grouping of texts, except that they generally reflect ancient cosmology. The texts reflect well-known creation myths (e.g. *Enūma eliš*, *Atramhasis*, *Kumarbi*, and *Telepinu*), as well as netherworld myths (e.g. *Ishtar's Descent*, *Nergal and Ereshkigal*), and the Gilgamesh Epic. Other genres include rituals and medical texts which reflect mythological motifs, although the reason for the inclusion of some of the Hittite(-Hurrian) texts is not clear. Nevertheless, the translations are reliable and provided with brief but helpful notes. An important duplicate for one of the texts ('die Kosmologie des *kalû*-Priesters' — p. 604f.) has recently appeared in E. von Weiher, *Spätbabylonische Texte aus Uruk IV* (1993), no. 141, indicating that the so-called cosmology is actually part of a prayer for the welfare of the country. The major Akkadian literary texts mentioned above (e.g. *Gilgamesh*, *Atramhasis*, *Ishtar's Descent*, *Nergal and Ereshkigal*, and *Enūma eliš*) are also available in recent translations in English, by Stephanie Dalley (*B.L.* 1990, p. 119), Benjamen Foster (*B.L.* 1994, p. 120), and Rene Kovacs.

M. J. GELLER

TREGGIARI, SUSAN: *Roman Marriage*. Iusti Coniuges *from the Time of Cicero to the Time of Ulpian.* 1993 (1991). Pp. xv, 578. (Clarendon Press, Oxford. Price: paper £19.95. ISBN paper 0 19 814439 5)

This is the paperback issue of T.'s huge study, originally published in 1991, of the practicalities of Roman marriage. Her discussion of marriage, from first steps to final separation by divorce or death, is firmly based upon the injunctions of the legal texts and the exhortations of moralizing philosophers, but she is most concerned to get behind the texts to see how marriages actually worked. The concentration on literary evidence makes T. conclusions more applicable to the better-off than to the rest of Roman society; the bias is only partially corrected by quotations from inscriptions. The book is an eminent example of a flood of new studies of the family in the classical world, but Treggiari differs from most others in the field in her sparing use of comparative sociological and anthropological material.

M. D. GOODMAN

WALLACE-HADRILL, ANDREW: *Augustan Rome* (Classical World Series). 1993. Pp. xii, 105. (Bristol Classical Press (Duckworth), London. Price: £6.95. ISBN 1 85399 138 4)

This enthusiastic essay on the city of Rome under Augustus by the current editor of the *Journal of Roman Studies* should do much to bring some major current debates in the history of the early empire to the attention of sixth-formers and first-year undergraduates. W.-H. skillfully and accessibly evokes the atmosphere of the city after Actium, interweaving the artistic and literary images of the period with his discussion of the realities of power. Of particular interest to readers may be his analysis of the claims to divinity made on Augustus' behalf (Ch. 6).

M. D. GOODMAN

WORTHINGTON, IAN (ed.): *Ventures into Greek History*. 1994. Pp. xxvi, 401. (Clarendon Press, Oxford. Price: £45.00. ISBN 0 19 814928 X)

This fine volume is a collection of articles in honour of the distinguished ancient historian Nicholas Hammond. The topics selected reflect the dedicatee's own main academic interests: the study of literary sources for the history of Greece in the classical and Hellenistic periods and problems in the hisory and archaeology of Macedonia in the 5th and 4th centuries. Hammond's own scholarship has had an overwhelming impact in these areas since the publication of his first article in 1932, not least in setting a trend for friendly debate over many issues. The varied contributions to the book show a striking willingness to continue the debate.   M. D. GOODMAN

ZAIDMAN, LOUISE BRUIT and PANTEL, PAULINE SCHMITT: *Religion in the Ancient Greek City*. Translated by Paul Cartledge. 1994 (1992). Pp. xx, 278. (Cambridge University Press. Price: £35.00/$59.95; paper £13.95/$19.95. ISBN 0 521 412625; paper 0 521 42357 0)

This is a reprint of the 1992 translation of a general introduction to ancient Greek religion first published in French in 1989. The main aim of the book is to encourage study of ancient polytheism from a non-Christianizing perspective by concentrating on religion in the context of social systems rather than the individual soul. The point is emphasized by extensive quotations from primary sources. The value of this approach is widely recognized among ancient historians, but still cannot be stressed too strongly to students, particularly when, like most readers of the *B.L.*, they are primarily concerned with the Judaeo-Christian tradition. Paul Cartledge has done an excellent job in clarifying some of the more obscure elements of the original French.

M. D. GOODMAN

9. APOCRYPHA AND POST-BIBLICAL STUDIES

ANDERSON, GARY A. and STONE, MICHAEL E. (eds): *A Synopsis of the Books of Adam and Eve* (Society of Biblical Literature Early Judaism and Its Literature 5). 1994. Pp. xi, 76. (Scholars Press, Atlanta. Price: $24.95; paper $14.95. ISBN 1 55540 963 6; paper 1 55540 964 4)

A. and S. have provided a textual companion to S.'s earlier work in the same series, *A History of the Literature of Adam and Eve* (*B.L.* 1993, p. 96). The five principal traditions of the *Life of Adam and Eve* are presented in parallel columns: Greek and Latin in the original, the Armenian in English (from S.'s *Penitence of Adam* [1981]), the Georgian in French (from J.-P. Mahé's corrected contribution to *Studies in Gnosticism and Hellenistic Religions* [1981]), and the Slavonic in German (from V. Jagič's 1893 article 'Slavische Beiträge zu den biblischen Apocryphen'). The Greek text is that prepared by M. Nagel for use in A.-M. Denis' *Concordance*; the Latin has been freshly provided by W. Lechner-Schmidt. Although the materials are presented in a far more comprehensible way than in R. H. Charles (ed.), *Pseudepigrapha*, and in a more comprehensive fashion than in J. H. Charlesworth (ed.), *Pseudepigrapha 2*, the editors offer no stemma to explain the interrelations of the various versions. Readers are left to ponder the diversity for themselves, but are somewhat aided in the task by the allocation of new overarching pericope numbers. This useful compendium contains several minor mistakes, e.g. Lechner-Schmidt (p. xi); *hēmin* for *hēmōn* (29:7, p. 1); Mahé's correction is not incorporated at 13:2 (p. 11).

G. J. BROOKE

BASSER, HERBERT W. (ed.): *Pseudo-Rabad: Commentary to Sifre Deuteronomy* (South Florida Studies in the History of Judaism 92). Pp. xliv (Eng.), 342 (Heb.). (Scholars Press, Atlanta. Price: $109.95; member price $74.95. ISBN 1 55540 925 3)

What is here being made available to scholars is a late medieval commentary on a tannaitic midrash, in an eclectic edition prepared by B. on the basis of manuscripts in Oxford and New York and accompanied by a photographic reprint of L. Finkelstein's *Sifre on Deuteronomy* (1939), and by the editor's brief textual and exegetical notes. In addition to these Hebrew texts, there is an English introduction in which Basser attempts to illustrate (with some difficult examples) how halakhic midrash relates to mishnaic and talmudic material and how the interpretation of rabbinic traditions is a coherent and ongoing process. He also identifies some of the characteristics of the commentary being edited (promising more treatment later) and points out the arguments against an attribution to Rabbi Abraham ben David of Posquières (Rabad). Even allowing for the fact that the 'work is meant for scholars . . . in Rabbinic Literature' (p. xliii), the presentation is not always lucid, the literary chronology will be seen as controversial, and the proof-reading could have been more careful.

S. C. REIF

BELL, RICHARD H.: *Provoked to Jealousy. The Origin and Purpose of the Jealousy Motif in Romans 9–11* (Wissenschaftliche Untersuchungen zum Neuen Testament: 2. Reihe 63). 1994. Pp. xxii, 471. (Mohr, Tübingen. Price: DM 118.00. ISBN 3 16 146091 X; ISSN 0340 9570)

Two sections of this impressive thesis, accepted at Tübingen, will be of interest. Pp. 8–24 survey, with appropriate discussion, all the evidence for the meanings of *qn'* in the Hebrew Bible, and add examples from Qumran and the rabbinic literature. *Parazēloō* in the Septuagint is then treated in the same detailed fashion (pp. 27–34). Ch. 7 extensively studies Deuteronomy 32 and its history of interpretation: the latter takes in not only *Sifre Deuteronomy* (to which B. ascribes great importance) but also the Targums and the Samaritan literature.

C. J. A. HICKLING

BORNHÄUSER, HANS and MAYER, GÜNTER (eds): *Die Tosefta. Seder II: Moëd, 3: Sukka–Jom tob–Rosch ha-Schana* (Rabbinische Texte: Reihe 1). 1993. Pp. viii, 196. (Kohlhammer, Stuttgart–Berlin–Köln. Price: DM 280.00/ AS 2184/SwF 278.00. ISBN 3 17 012694 6)

This is a further volume in a long-running series established by Gerhard Kittel and K. H. Rengstorf. It offers a translation of three tractates of the Tosefta, with footnotes but without the original Hebrew. Though the translations are carefully done, and the notes useful, the underlying philosophy of the series is beginning to look very dated. The introductions are perfunctory and the notes are for the most part discrete glosses illuminating discrete problems of philology and archaeology in the text. The agenda which dominates current discussion of the Tosefta is effectively ignored. Thus there is no analysis of the overall structure, literary problems or argument of the tractates, and the question of their relationship to the Mishnah and to the Bible features hardly at all. It is, perhaps, indicative that the only work of Jacob Neusner cited in the bibliography is his *Life of Rabban Yohanan ben Zakkai* (1970)! His more recent studies of Mishnah-Tosefta are conspicuous by their absence, as is much important Israeli writing on the same literature.

P. S. ALEXANDER

BROOKE, GEORGE J., with FLORENTINO GARCÍA MARTÍNEZ (eds): *New Qumran Texts and Studies*. *Proceedings of the First Meeting of the International Organization for Qumran Studies, Paris 1992* (Studies on the Texts of the Desert of Judah 15). 1994. Pp. vii, 328 + 9 plates. (Brill, Leiden–New York–Köln. Price: fl. 145.00/$83.00. ISBN 90 04 10093 8; ISSN 0169 9962)

Volumes of essays on the Scrolls now contain publications of new texts from the expanded editorial community. In the first part of this volume (Texts), we are offered a fragment of 4Q265 (community laws) by J. Baumgarten; an Apocryphon of Jeremiah (4Q385[B]) by D. Dimant; a textual comparison of the Psalms scrolls by P. W. Flint; a report on 4QBerakhot (4Q286–290) by B. Nitzan; two notes on 4QJosh[a] by A. Rofé and E. Ulrich; a review of the still unpublished texts by E. Tov; and a report on 4QJubilees[g] (edited with J. Milik) by J. C. VanderKam. The contents of the second part (Studies) are: Isaiah 40:3 and the 'wilderness' in the 4QS fragments by Brooke (arguing for a real wilderness experience); the orthography of some verbal forms in 1QIsa[a] by J. Cook; J. Kampen on the Matthean divorce texts (*porneia* = *zenut* as relates to sectarian allegiance); H.-W. Kuhn on the significance of Qumran texts for Galatians (German with English summary and bibliography); A. Lange on computer-aided transcription with reference to the Scrolls (recommended as a clear explanation); E.-M. Laperrousaz on methods of dating the Copper Scroll (3Q15) (its contents are treasures of Bar Kokhba); G. W. Nebe on wisdom texts from the Cairo Geniza and their relation to Qumran and the Essenes (German, and comes to no definite conclusion); the *millu'im* (ordination rites) in the Temple Scroll by L. H. Schiffman; 11QT 29's 'covenant like Jacob's' and the 'new covenant' of Jeremiah by D. D. Swanson (on 'new covenant' the Temple Scroll differs from the *yaḥad*); and non-initial perfects and imperfects in the *Hodayot* by L. Vegas Montaner (French). There are plates of the new fragments, and indices. B. has edited and typeset with his usual great care.   P. R. DAVIES

BROOKE, GEORGE J.; SCHIFFMAN, LAWRENCE H.; and VANDERKAM, JAMES C. (EDS): *Dead Sea Discoveries. A Journal of Current Research on the Scrolls and Related Literature*. Vol. 1/1. 1994. Pp. 1–148. (Brill, Leiden–New York–Köln. Price: fl. 98.00/$56.00 p.a. ISSN 0929 0761)

Founded to meet the recent increase of interest in manuscript finds in the Judaean Desert, this new journal seeks to convey the significance of texts found at Qumran, Wadi Daliyeh, Masada and Bar Kokhba caves to a wider readership. The first issue, however, is devoted entirely to the Qumran scrolls with lengthy articles on rewritten bible, *pesharim*, New Jerusalem texts, role of messiah, and an index of passages (Genesis–Kings) found among the 'biblical' fragments. Compared to *Revue de Qumrân*, it emphasizes themes and a broader sweep of the subject area, and it also includes a substantial book review section.   T. H. LIM

CHARLESWORTH, JAMES H. and WEAVER, WALTER P. (ed.): *The Old and New Testaments. Their Relationship and the 'Intertestamental' Literature* (Faith and Scholarship Colloquies Series). 1993. Pp. xvii, 140. (Trinity Press International, Valley Forge PA. Price: $13.50. ISBN 1 56338 062 5)

This collection of symposium papers has as its centrepiece a disproportionately long, discursive, semi-popular essay by C. himself on various aspects of the question why Christians retain the Old Testament. In an introduction

144   APOCRYPHA AND POST-BIBLICAL STUDIES

his co-editor reports salient passages from the discussion which followed these pieces when first given. In the remaining three papers, Bernhard Anderson reflects on both Jewish and Christian faith as centring on the retelling of history, J.-J. Carey considers some issues connected with Jewish apocalyptic, and R. F. Johnson, in a more text-focused contribution, offers a detailed analysis of the Fourth Servant Song.

C. J. A. HICKLING

CHILTON, BRUCE: *Judaic Approaches to the Gospels* (University of South Florida International Studies in Formative Christianity and Judaism 2). 1994. Pp. xii, 321. (Scholars Press, Atlanta. Price: $79.95. ISBN 1 7885 0001 5)

Seven out of twelve of the items in this collection have been published elsewhere, four are accepted for publication in other volumes, and one, 'Eight Thesis (*sic*) on the Use of Targums in Interpreting the New Testament', is peculiar to this book. The range of C.'s expertise and interest is indicated by the titles: 'John the Purifier'; 'God as "Father" in the Targumim, in Non-Canonical Literatures of Early Judaism and Primitive Christianity, and in Matthew'; 'The Son of Man: Human and Heavenly'; 'Forgiving at and Swearing by the Temple'; '"Do not do what you hate": Where there is not Gold, there might be Brass. The Case of the Thomean Golden Rule'; '[hōs] phragellion ek schoiniōn (John 2:15)'; 'Typologies of Memra and the Fourth Gospel'; 'Romans 9–11 as Scriptural Interpretation and Dialogue with Judaism'; 'The Epitaph of Himerus from the Jewish Catacomb of the Appian Way'; 'Prophecy in the Targumim', and 'Recent and Propective (*sic*) Discussion of *mêmra*'. Vigorous and challenging in his approach, C. has established a reputation for bringing startling new insights to his chosen subjects; and he has many useful and valuable things to say. It is therefore unfortunate that some of the papers (e.g. those on 'God as Father' and 'Son of Man') betray a streak of unnecessary polemic against scholars whose views he does not accept.

C. T. R. HAYWARD

COHEN, SHAYE J. D. (ed.): *The Jewish Family in Antiquity* (Brown Judaic Studies 289). 1993. Pp. 167. (Scholars Press, Atlanta, GA. Price: $40.95; member price $26.95. ISBN 1 55540 919 9)

This volume, of the collected papers of the Hellenistic Judaism section of the 1990 and 1991 annual meetings of the society of Biblical Literature and of 'the offspring of the papers', comprises: Introduction by C., Part One, Assumptions and Problems: 'Family/ies in Antiquity: Evidence from Tannaitic Literature and Roman Galilean Architecture' (M. Peskowitz); Part Two, Parents, Children, and Slaves: 'Parents and Children in the Jewish Family of Antiquity' (O. L. Yarbrough); 'Parents and Children: A Philonic Perspective' (A. Reinhartz); 'Jewish Mothers and Daughters in the Greco-Roman World' (R. S. Kraemer), and 'Slavery and the Ancient Jewish Family' (D. B. Martin); Part Three, Rabbinic Law: 'Reconsidering the Rabbinic *ketubah* Payment' (M. Satlow); and Part Four, By Way of Comparison: Some Greek Families: 'Some Greek Families: Production and Reproduction' (S. B. Pomeroy). There is a short subject index, but there is no bibliography, bibliographic details being given in the footnotes of each paper. Each paper is well supported by detailed footnotes encompassing the full range of ancient sources and secondary literature. Overall the collection supplies a rich source for the minutiae of daily life in the varied cultural environments of Hellenistic Judaism.

H. A. McKAY

COHEN, SHAYE J. D. and FRERICHS, ERNEST S. (eds): *Diasporas in Antiquity* (Brown Judaic Studies 288). 1994. Pp. iii, 130. (Scholars Press, Atlanta. Price: $39.95; member price $24.95. ISBN 1 55540 918 0)

This interesting collection of four papers has a theme, and it is a central one for all post-exilic Jewish history — 'how dispersed peoples maintain a sense of self-identity and a measure of communal cohesion' and yet manage to adapt to their environments. The specific reference is to the Greco-Roman world, with two studies on Hellenistic Egypt, and two of the Roman milieu. C. himself asks how recognizable Jews were in antiquity. He concludes that women were not at all so, males only (and probably almost universally) by circumcision; though it is scarcely clear, he opines, in what circumstances the latter could be useful, outside the gymnasium, or the aberrant investigations of the emperior Domitian. Thus, diaspora Jews seem to have melted physically into their environments. Ramsay Macmullen writes suggestively on 'The Unromanized in Rome', exploring with a sharp eye to geography and the realities of life less familiar activities of the poorer quarters of the imperial city — especially loading corn into the great warehouses. The ethnic mix of the Janiculum quarter, and within it the Jewish element, receive attention. J. Mélèze-Modrzejewski discusses 'How to be a Jew in Hellenistic Egypt', reminding us that prior to Roman interference, Jews were part of the class of Hellenes. S. Honigman offers bold hypotheses, linking the Jewish onomastics of Ptolemaic Egypt to shifting cultural attitudes among the Jews: not so much Hellenism, as their own homeland, the broader Semitic milieu, and, above all, the reading of the Bible. The observation that the names of the patriarchs are notably more popular in Egypt than in Palestine should be followed up.

T. RAJAK

COOK, EDWARD M.: *Solving the Mysteries of the Dead Sea Scrolls. New Light on the Bible.* 1994. Pp. 191. (Zondervan, Grand Rapids MI; Paternoster, Carlisle. Price: $12.99/£6.99. ISBN 0 310 38471 0; (Paternoster) 0 85364 542 6)

Here is yet another popular book on the scrolls. C. assumes little or no knowledge on the part of his readership. The first four chapters cover the history of publication and non-publication and provide some details about personal entanglements not to be found in other similar works. Three further chapters deal with the problems surrounding the identification of the authors of the so-called sectarian scrolls. The Essene hypothesis is preferred but with some reservations largely because of the discrepancies between the texts from Qumran and the classical sources. Here C.'s own presentation is old fashioned, since he is largely content to lump the various sectarian texts together, and he works only with 1QS when discussing the Manual of Discipline and CD for the Damascus Document. MMT is referred to in relation to Sadduccean theories, but only a few of the other recently available texts are mentioned at this point. Although there is a short appendix on the significance of the scrolls for the Old Testament, the subtitle is really only justified because of the extended treatment of the messianism of the scrolls in relation to the New Testament. Here the concern is with new texts and the stress is on the distinctiveness of Jesus as the Son of God, the same title in 4Q246 taken as a reference to an archvillain (as Milik) or antichrist (Flusser). The brief discussion of 4Q541 is particularly thought-provoking: perhaps the anointed priest of frag. 9 is the priest of the fourth jubilee (cf. TLevi 17:5), not the final messianic high priest.

G. J. BROOKE

CORRENS, DIETRICH (ed.): *Die Mischna: Text, Übersetzung und ausführ-liche Erklärung*, III.5: *Giṭṭin, Scheidebriefe*. 1991. Pp. x, 188. (de Gruyter, Berlin–New York. Price: DM 158.00. ISBN 3 11 012464 5)

The latest instalment of this project to provide a complete edition, translation and commentary on the Mishnah in German follows exactly the pattern of the earlier volumes. The volume is well produced, the translation accurate and the notes painstaking. The work will doubtless be of use in initiating students to the Mishnah. But the project has been running now for so long that it is caught in a time-warp. Even the most recent volumes show little awareness of current work on the Mishnah and could have been written fifty years ago.

P. S. ALEXANDER

CROWN, ALAN DAVID: *A Bibliography of the Samaritans* (American Theological Library Association Bibliographical Series 32). 1993 (2nd edn). Pp. xviii, 376. (Scarecrow Press, Metuchen NJ and London. Price: $39.50. ISBN 0 8108 2646 1)

The first edition appeared in 1985 (not reviewed in the *B.L.*). The need for a new edition, and its expansion in so short a time, amply attests the growth of Samaritan studies. C. lists more than 3,500 separate items, in alphabetical order by author. The subject of each item is indicated by a number or numbers which are keyed to a detailed subject index. There is also an alphabetical list of short titles. An important tool for all interested in Samaritan studies.

L. L. GRABBE

DERRETT, J. D. M.: *The Victim. The Johannine Passion Narrative Re-examined*. 1993. Pp. xvi, 300. (Peter I. Drinkwater, Shipston-on-Stour, Warwicks. Price: £18.50. ISBN 0 9466 43 43 1)

D. proposes that John's text represents a retelling of the passion tradition in terms of eight overlapping themes (scripture, king, prophet, betrayal, persecution, power, Passover and Messiah), each of which resonates signifi-cantly with the Old Testament and its contemporary interpretations within Judaism. While D.'s immense learning is beyond dispute and cannot fail to impress, the question of whether his approach constitutes a realistic interpre-tation of John's text remains. Confident that anything and everything was grist to John's mill, that disanalogy rules and coincidences are deliberate, D. proceeds to an exegesis of the passion narrative which is often wilful, to say the least. To take one example (p. 23) we learn, with reference to Luke 22:43, John 12:29, 3 Macc. 6:18–19 and a snippet from Homer, that what Judas and company actually *saw* at Jn 18.6 was an angelic vision which genuine disciples would not need to see, The subject of angels is introduced here by D., and *not* John. Another difficulty is that the issue of historicity in relation to John's text seems not to have been thought out properly. While on the one hand D. is clear that John cannot be taken strictly as a historian (2, 90–91), on the other he sees no problem in entering into the psyche of John's characters. This is not to say that there is nothing of value here. Quirky it may be, but D.'s argument is always in lively style, of fresh perspective, and often thought-provoking. Nevertheless, such gleanings are harvested at a price.

W. E. SPROSTON

EFROYMSON, DAVID P.; FISHER, EUGENE J.; and KLENICKI, LEON (eds): *Within Context. Essays on Jews and Judaism in the New Testament.* Forewords by Irwin J. Borowsky and L. Klenicki. 1994. Pp. xii, 160. (Liturgical Press, Collegeville MN. Price: $11.95. ISBN 0 8146 5033 3)

This collection of essays is specifically intended for 'the literate but not fully biblically trained Catholic teacher'(!) in the wake of *Nostra Aetate*, and builds on an earlier set of 'Guidelines on the catechetical presentation of Jews and Judaism in the New Testament' (= *Within Context*, included as an appendix in this volume). The essays cover the now standard areas: the unacceptability of past models (M. Boys); the presentation of Judaism in the Synoptic Gospels, and in John (P. Cunningham, U. v. Wahlde); the historical questions of first century Judaism, of Jesus's opponents, and of his death (A. Saldarini, Efroymson, Fisher); Paul's attitude to the Law and to the Jewish people (T. Callan). They draw heavily on recent scholarship in the area, making it accessible to their readers rather than breaking new ground, and close with questions for discussion or reflection. There is probably still a need for a book popularizing what has now become familiar in scholarly circles, and this volume could be used by non-Catholic study groups, but the danger is that it all appears far too straight forward, obscuring the issues of canon and authority, and the serious theological re-thinking that is still demanded.

J. M. LIEU

EILBERG-SCHWARTZ, HOWARD: *The Savage in Judaism. An Anthropology of Israelite Religion and Ancient Judaism.* 1994 (1990). Pp. xii, 290. (Indian University Press, Bloomington; distributed in the UK by the Open University Press, Buckingham. Price: £15.99. ISBN 0 253 31946 3)

E.-S. applies recent insights from anthropology to show the survival within Judaism of many 'savage' elements also known from 'primitive' religions. In some ways, this is a polemical book, but it is clear that there is an audience who needs to be convinced since there has been much resistance to the idea that Judaism can be compared with 'primitive' religions. For those familiar with recent applications of anthropology to Old Testament study, however, much of the conceptualization here will be familiar. Part I is devoted to the general ideas of anthropology and to overcoming resistance to his investigation. Part II is the core of the book, a series of studies (some already published) on such subjects as circumcision, fluid symbolism (menstruation, blood, semen), impurity, and animal metaphors. The path trod by Frazer and Robertson Smith is once again open.

L. L. GRABBE

ELMAN, YAAKOV: *Authority and Tradition: Toseftan Baraitot in Talmudic Babylonia.* 1994. Pp. xiv, 328. (Ktav, Hoboken NJ. Price: $39.50. ISBN 0 88125 426 6)

Anyone reasonably familiar with current literary criticism of early rabbinic literature will be aware that the usual assumption that the Tosefta reflects a late tannaitic or early amoraic milieu is challenged by the major variations that exist between the tannaitic traditions cited in the Babylonian Talmud and those that deal with the same subject, in parallel fashion, in the Tosefta. E.'s careful analysis of the *Pisha/Pesaḥim* texts in the two major sources pinpoints their linguistic and literary divergences and evaluates earlier interpretations of the overall evidence. His important findings are that the Tosefta as now constructed was not used as a source by the redactors of the Babylonian Talmud and that all *baraitot* were accorded equal authority. 'Toseftan' *baraitot*, in oral form, circulated independently or in clusters, some of which were eventually included in the Tosefta, and Babylonian material exists in the Tosefta in its authoritative form. The dating and literary history of that form therefore require reassessment (taking due account of recent linguistic theories) and Epstein's 'proto-Tosefta' hypothesis has to be abandoned.

S. C. REIF

FELDMEIER, REINHARD and HECKEL, ULRICH (eds): *Die Heiden. Juden, Christen und das Problem des Fremden* (Wissenschaftliche Untersuchungen zum Neuen Testament 70). 1994. Pp. xviii, 449. (Mohr, Tübingen. Price: DM 288.00. ISBN 3 16 146147 9; ISSN 0512 1604)

With an introduction by M. Hengel, this collection of essays examines the presentation of the subject of the 'Gentiles/heathen' in three sections: early Jewish literature, early Christian literature, and (a single essay) the polemic about Epicurianism in Roman literature. The essays in the first section consider the subject in 2 Kings 5:19 (P. Marinković), Philo of Alexandria (N. Umemoto), the pseudo-philonic treatise *De Jona* (F. Siegert), and Qumran (R. Deines). H. Lichtenberger writes on the sacredness of the land and life; A. M. Schwemer, on the haggadic tradition of Elijah as an Arab; B. Ego, on the rabbinic interpretation of the Ninevite repentance; and F. Avemarie, on Edom as a surrogate for Rome in early rabbinic literature.

L. L. GRABBE

FILORAMO, GIOVANNI: *A History of Gnosticism*. Translator Anthony Alcock. 1992 (1990). Pp. xx, 268. (Blackwell, Oxford. Price: £12.95. ISBN 0 631 15756 5; paper 0 631 18707 3)

F. has given a good overall survey of the history of Gnosticism. Considering that there are many aspects of Gnosticism still very much debated, F.'s treatment is generally balanced, even if not everyone will agree with all his interpretations. He devotes a certain amount of attention to the Jewish content of the Gnostic texts. References are generally good, though the use of endnotes instead of footnotes is annoying, and there is a general but rather incomplete bibliography (nothing by B. Pearson, though an item or two do appear in the notes). The translator is evidently not acquainted with biblical scholarship and gives such renderings as 'Jahweh'.

L. L. GRABBE

GOODBLATT, DAVID: *The Monarchic Principle: Studies in Jewish Self-Government in Antiquity* (Texte und Studien zum Antiken Judentum 38). 1994. Pp. xii, 336. (Mohr, Tübingen. Price: DM 188.00. ISBN 3 16 146176 2)

G. argues that the principle of one-man rule was the dominant view during both the Second Temple period and the rabbinic period. During the Second Temple period, except for the brief period of Herodian rule and Alexandra Salome's reign, the rule was by the high priest. With the destruction of the temple in 70, the leadership shifted from priestly to lay governance in both Palestine (the patriarchate) and Babylon (the exilarch). G. also denies the existence of the Sanhedrin as an institution before 70. Here I think he tries to explain away too much. He is certainly right that the attempt to project back the rabbinic picture is misguided, but the existence of an on-going institution of some sort — e.g., an advisory board to the high priest but perhaps with some powers of its own — is consistent with the facts known. Accepting the existence of such an institution would not affect G.'s overall thesis. He argues his case well and has made a significant contribution to the study of early Judaism.

L. L. GRABBE

GOODMAN, MARTIN: *Mission and Conversion. Proselytizing in the Religious History of the Roman Empire*. 1994. Pp. xiv. 194. (Oxford University Press. Price: £25.00. ISBN 0 19 814941 7)

Hard on the heels of L. H. Feldman's gigantic 1993 survey (*B.L.* 1994, p. 136) presses G.'s own contribution. His hypothesis is twofold. (a) Early Christian proselytization was indebted to neither pagan nor Jewish antecedents. In fact there was no Jewish proselytization prior to the third century CE. (b) Nor are the origins of early Christian proselytization to be found in theology or christological speculation but rather in the internal wrangles about admitting Gentiles into the church. Following some Jewish methods of argumentation, G. claims that what was *permitted* might be raised to the level of *desirability* (170, 173), i.e. not only could Gentiles be admitted, but they should be and so should be evangelized. The seven chapters that propound hypothesis (a) are full of good things, always engaging with the vigorous current debate and, with queries here and there, highly likely. One impression, however, is that G.'s touch is slightly less sure when it comes to New Testament matters. But hypothesis (b) seems less likely than one that takes seriously the view that Jesus, 'the friend of publicans and sinners', did not cease to influence his movement once it burst upon the world beyond Palestine.

J. L. NORTH

GOODMAN-THAU, EVELINE and SCHULTE, CHRISTOPH (eds): *Das Buch Jezira/Sēfer Yeṣîrā* (Jüdische Quellen 1). In der Übersetzung von Johann Fredrich von Meyer, mit Nachworten von Moshe Idel und Wilhelm Schmidt-Biggemann. 1994. Pp. ix, 64. (Akademie Verlag, Berlin. Price: DM 48.00. ISBN 3 05 002313 9)

It is difficult to understand what purpose is served by the publication of this book, consisting, as it does, almost entirely of a reprint of the original German edition and translation by von Meyer (1830). The early printed editions and translations have only antiquarian value; proper academic study of the text must start from Grünwald's edition in *Israel Oriental Studies* 1 (1971), pp. 132–77, and Nehemiah Alloni's edition of the Geniza scroll in *Temirin* 2 (1981), pp. 9–29. Scholars of Jewish mysticism will be interested only in the short six-page appendix by Moshe Idel on 'Das Buch Jezira in der jüdischen Tradition' and, to a lesser extent, that of Wilhelm Schmidt-Biggemann on 'Das Buch Jezira in der christlicher Tradition' (pp. 45–64).

A. P. HAYMAN

GRABBE, LESTER L.: *Judaism from Cyrus to Hadrian*. 1994 (1992). Pp. xxxv, 722. (SCM, London. Price: £25.00. ISBN 0 334 02578 8).

This is the British edition of a landmark book (*Book List* 1993, p. 135), which in less than two years has made itself an indispensable guide to students, teachers and (often enough) scholars. Two volumes have become one sizeable but well-produced and surprisingly convenient paperback (even if not quite at convenient price). Second Temple Judaism is a vast and rapidly increasing field of scholarship, covering the later Old Testament books at one end, the formation of Rabbinic culture at the other. This is the right moment for an analytical synthesis. Comparison with the 'new Schürer' is unavoidable, and readers will be interested to note that G. covers all the post-exilic biblical literature and related Iranian and Mesopotamian sources. Furthermore, G.'s distinctly modern approach complements Schürer's admirably and perhaps deliberately. The focus is always wide before it becomes narrow, and history is understood in terms of issues and problems, socio-economic and cultural as much as political and religious. Very much of our own time is

150   APOCRYPHA AND POST-BIBLICAL STUDIES

the way in which the author makes the reader wholly aware of the purpose and goals of each and every enquiry. The unusual structure, with its separate sections of sources, overview, issues, studies, problems and syntheses (described by the previous reviewer) may generate some initial confusion; but among its other advantages is that of allowing the sap to be extracted from scholarly controversies and of placing them in an intelligible context, teasing out their implications. G.'s own observations are bracing: 'the sweeping summary statement is perhaps the bane of Josephus scholarship. Josephus is — or is not — reliable. He is — or is not — a good historian . . .' (p. 11). Here students find the invitation to enquire further which they do not get from Schürer's apparent impassivity. G.'s achievement is to have combined all this vigour with faultless methodological rigour. A topic is not addressed before the primary sources for it have been displayed and analysed. Bibliographies are full but not overloaded, masterpieces of intelligent selectivity; and there is an additional and very useful bibliography at the back. With this carefully thought-out handbook, G. has given a huge impetus not only to the understanding of this period but to future research.

T. RAJAK

HALPERN-AMARU, BETSY: *Rewriting the Bible. Land Covenant in Post-biblical Jewish Literature.* 1994. Pp. xi, 189. (Trinity Press International, Valley Forge, PA. Price: $15.00. ISBN 1 56338 091 9)

H. analyses the treatment of the biblical concept of a promised land in four 'rewritten bible' texts: *Jubilee, The Testament of Moses, Pseudo-Philo* and the *Jewish Antiquities* of Josephus, drawing comparisons with the biblical promise of eternal possession of the land, thematically connected with covenant, eschatology and a special relationship with the deity. *Jubilees* re-focuses future hopes on a restored creation; the *Testament of Moses* maintains that the promise of God to Israel and the nation's ownership of the land are secure in a way that transcends time; in *Pseudo-Philo* the descend-ants of the Patriarchs will own the land — though their continued faith might be less certain; and Josephus extends the concept 'land' to include the Diaspora and prioritizes loyalty to Torah above loyalty to the Land. Each writer re-defines the biblical promise from a distinct perspective; all down-grade the importance of the land but retain the other themes.

H. A. McKAY

HECKEL, ULRICH: *Kraft in Schwachheit: Untersuchungen zu 2. Kor 10–13* (Wissenschaftliche Untersuchungen zum Neuen Testament: 2 Reihe 56). 1993. Pp. x, 391. (Mohr, Tübingen. Price: DM 118.00. ISBN 3 16 146061 8; ISSN 0340 9570)

Boasting concerning oneself (*Sich-Rühmen*) is an important idea in the passage H. has chosen for study, and he devotes pp. 159–72 to *(en)kau-chasthai* in the Septuagint and to Jeremiah 9:22 and its *Wirkungsgeschichte* in Judaism. The use of this verb in the verse from Jeremiah is, for H., the key to understanding this section of 2 Corinthians (pp. 210–14).

C. J. A. HICKLING

HERRMANN, KLAUS (ed.): *Massekhet Hekhalot. Traktat von den himm-lischen Palästen. Edition, Übersetzung, und Kommentar* (Texte und Studien zum Antiken Judentum 49). 1994. Pp. xi, 363, 103* (Heb.). (Mohr, Tübingen. Price: DM 168.00. ISBN 3 16 146150 9)

This doctoral dissertation completed under Peter Schäfer contains an edition, translation and commentary on a text not included in Schäfer's original *Synopse zur Hekhalot-Literatur* (1981). *Masseket Hekhalot* is one of the latest of the Hekhalot texts. As for its date, H. can only narrow the gap between Scholem's date of 7th to 8th century CE and Grünwald's date of 1150–1250. He sets the limits between the 9th century and the beginning of the 12th, and raises the possibility that it passed through Spanish kabbalistic circles before being handed on to the *haside ashkenaz*. H.'s commentary confirms the view that the Hekhalot tradition developed on two trajectories, one (to which it belongs) stripping out the magical element which was such an important element in the earlier tradition, the other concentrating on the magic and displacing the original mystical component of desiring 'to see the King on his throne'. But *Masseket Hekhalot* has also lost interest in the tradition of the ascent to the Merkavah. The book is likely to be of interest primarily to scholars specializing in the study of the Hekhalot texts and the transposition of Jewish mystical traditions from their original eastern home to medieval Europe.

A. P. HAYMAN

HERZER, JENS: *Die Paralipomena Jeremiae. Studien zu Tradition und Redaktion einer Haggada des frühen Judentums* (Texte und Studien zum Antiken Judentum 43). 1994. Pp. xi, 252. (Mohr, Tübingen. Price DM 158.00. ISBN 3 16 146307 2; ISSN 0721 8753).

This study of Paralipomena Jeremiou tries to show its unity and thoroughgoing consistency. H. argues for the direct literary dependence of ParJer on 2 Baruch. Together with some further scriptural exegesis by the author, as in the pro-Samaritan parts of ParJer 8, this literary relationship is sufficient to explain most of the features; no other sources need be proposed, the author also composing the letters found in ParJer 6 and 7. The literary coherence of the work is displayed in its principal aim of reflecting the hopes of some Jews for the heavenly Jerusalem. This aim derives from dialogue with questions that arose amongst Jews in the years 125–32 CE, after Hadrian's building of Aelia Capitolina but before the Bar Kokhba revolt, and can be aligned with those forms of early Judaism critical of the emergent revolutionary political messianism. The Christian postscript in ParJer 9 replaced the original ending; H. suggests this reflects Johannine circles of the mid-2nd century CE. By proposing that ParJer was originally composed in Greek, H. further disagrees with much of the emerging consensus. It is helpful to have a monograph which takes the final form of the text this seriously, but H. has moved too far away from those whose handling of the history of traditions is more subtle and in so doing he somewhat undermines the value of his own contribution.

G. J. BROOKE

HIMMELFARB, MARTHA: *Ascent to Heaven in Jewish and Christian Apocalypses*. 1993. Pp. xii, 171. (Oxford University Press. Price: £25.00. ISBN 0 19 508203 6)

H. aims to offer a thematic study of 'the entire body of Jewish and Christian ascent Apocalypses' from the *Book of Watchers* down to *3 Baruch*. It is a welcome continuation of the trend away from preoccupation with eschatology in this field. Even so, the exclusion of Revelation was surprising. H. provides good evidence that priestly speculation played a role in the early apocalypses, especially in tracing the roots of ascent back to the book of Ezekiel, in the depiction of heaven as a temple served by angelic priests, and in the various descriptions of the hero's transformation into an angel in terms of priestly investiture. She also shows that wider concerns from the Graeco-Roman world played a role, especially when arguing that the inclusion of

Platonic elements in *2 Enoch's* account of creation is evidence of a 1st-century
CE Egyptian provenance (pp. 84–86). Finally, a good case is made for
regarding these apocalypses as scribal products. However, H.
too quickly
dismisses the possibility that genuine experience underlies them. If the
prominence of scribes as heroes is an example of 'authorial self-
consciousness' (p. 99), why should the same not apply to the more conspicuous claims to visionary experience?

D. J. BRYAN

HORST, PIETER W. VAN DER: *Hellenism–Judaism–Christianity. Essays on
Their Interaction* (Contributions to Biblical Exegesis and Theology 8). 1994.
Pp. 300. (Kok Pharos, Kampen. Price: fl. 69.90. ISBN 90 390 0106 5; ISSN
0926 6097)

H. has produced another collection of essays (cf. *B.L.* 1993, p. 137), all
but one of the sixteen previously published. Essays include the subjects of
Samaritans and Hellenism; images of women in early Judaism; Exodus 22:23
(27) in the Septuagint; Ezekiel 20:25 in early Judaism and Christianity; the
cosmic conflagration in Hellenism, early Judaism, and early Christianity;
silent prayer; and hieroglyphs as secret symbols in antiquity.   L. L. GRABBE

JONES, GARETH LLOYD: *Lleisiau o'r Lludw. Her yr Holocost i'r Cristion.*
1994. Pp. 210 (Gee, Dinbych. Price: £9.50. ISBN 0 7074 0246 8)

Although this book does not fall directly within the field of Old Testament study, it is of interest to all concerned with the Jewish background of
Jesus. Its title means 'Voices from the Dust. The Challenge of the Holocaust
to the Christian', and one of the topics under discussion is the possibility that
some New Testament sayings gave rise to anti-Semitism. The volume originated with J.'s course in Bangor on 'The Church and the Jews — from
Persecution to Dialogue', but it has been written with a wider audience in
mind. Different attitudes towards Jews are reviewed, and the periods covered
are the Early Church, the Middle Ages, the Protestant Reformation, the rise
of Zionism, and after Auschwitz. The book is written well and catches one's
interest from beginning to end. Judicious references to sources appear in
footnotes, but it is unfortunate that it lacks a bibliography.   G. H. JONES

KOLARCIK, MICHAEL: *The Ambiguity of Death in the Book of Wisdom
1–6. A Study of Literary Structure and Interpretation* (Analecta Biblica 127).
1991. Pp. xii, 208. (Éditrice Pontificio Istituto Biblico, Rome. Price:
Lire 34,500. ISBN 88 7653 127 0)

The ambiguous message about death in the book of Wisdom has often
been commented on. K. attempts to answer the question by an analysis of the
literary structure of the book. After a survey of previous studies of the
structure (ch. 1), he does his own analysis (ch. 2), which in general is a
refinement of the concentric pattern found by previous investigators. He
deduces from the structure that the argument of Wisdom 1–6 takes the form
of a trial in which the wicked (the accused) become the accusers (of the
righteous). This format allows the author to explore the nature of mortality,
but the 'ambiguity' is only a surface feature: Mortality has the function of
testing but is sinister only when it is the ultimate death of those who reject
God. The final chapter explores this message in the light of modern psychological studies and in the context of Christian hermeneutics.   L. L. GRABBE

KRAEMER, DAVID: *Responses to Suffering in Classical Rabbinic Literature*. 1995. Pp. xv, 261. (Oxford University Press. Price: $49.95. ISBN 0 19 508900 6)

Given that 'rabbinic literature in general and the midrashim in particular are often internally inconsistent' (p. 91), K. is fully justified in using a variety of historical, theological and literary criteria for identifying rabbinic views of national catastrophe, personal suffering and divine justice in the first six centuries CE. Adopting a modified form of Neusner's methodology rather than Urbach's approach, the author cites and analyses a large number of translated texts from Mishnah and Tosefta, halakhic and aggadic midrashim, and the two Talmudim. He demonstrates how they maintain the earlier Jewish notions of punishment for sin, special discipline, future justice, unexplained suffering and the right to challenge the system and argues for a complicated theological history ranging from the idealized Torah-world of the Mishnah, by way of an evolution of tannaitic and amoraic ambivalence and apologetics, to the angry and innovative opinions of the late talmudic rabbis of Babylon ('there is death without sin and there is suffering without transgression', as cited on p. 185). K.'s speculative explanations of the changing viewpoints and their relative chronology will inevitably be controversial but there is no doubt that he has succeeded in compiling an important anthology of rabbinic attitudes and establishing their incontrovertibly complex nature.   S. C. REIF

KRAEMER, ROSS SHEPARD: *Her Share of the Blessings. Women's Religions Among Pagans, Jews, and Christians in the Greco-Roman World* (Oxford Paperbacks). 1993 (1992). Pp. xi, 275. (Oxford University Press. Price: £7.99. ISBN 0 19 508670 8)

This book is the first comprehensive study of women's religions in Greco-Roman antiquity. The thirteen chapters cover devotion to the goddesses of ancient Greece and to Adonis and Dionysos, the Isis cults and those of Roman matrons. The greater part of the book deals with Jewish and Christian material, reconstructing Jewish women's lives according to rabbinic sources and in the Greco-Roman diaspora, and the much debated role of women in early Christianity and in what came to be regarded as heresy. There is good use of primary sources and the author has provided full end notes. Much of the analysis is based on Mary Douglas's theory of 'Grid, Group and Gender' first published in her *Natural Symbols* (1970). There is little here of interest to the Old Testament specialist, but all could profit from reading the perceptive remarks in the introduction which show (with examples!) how male scholars have 'understood' the ancient sources and then translated them in the light of that pre-understanding   M. BARKER

LAPORTE, JEAN: *Eucharistia in Philo* (Studies in the Bible and Early Christianity 3). 1983. Pp. 261. (Edwin Mellen, Lewiston–Queenston–Lampeter. Price: $89.95/£49.95. ISBN 0 88946 601 7; (series) 0 88946 913 X)

Not many studies have been done of Philo's concept of 'thanksgiving', and L.'s is acknowledged as an important one (see the reviews listed in his p. 187, n. 1). It first appeared in French in 1972 and was not updated for the English translation, so the work is now getting on for a quarter of a century old. He examines the concept in the Hebrew and Greek texts of the Old Testament, *the Letter of Aristeas*, and general Greek usage. He emphasizes Philo's influence from the biblical text over and above anything taken from Greek philosophy or even from synagogue usage. The sacrificial cult with its variety of sacrifices and offerings and the regular temple festivals are all interpreted primarily in eucharistic terms. There is also a strong cosmic dimension in Philo's interpretation: for example, the high priest, with his vestments as a model of the universe, gives thanksgiving on behalf of all humanity. Once again, Philo is seen to be an important repertoire of Jewish theological thought, though the extent to which he is only representative of a much wider stream of thought and to what extent he is original is still debated.

L. L. GRABBE

LASSNER, JACOB: *Demonizing the Queen of Sheba. Boundaries of Gender and Culture in Postbiblical Judaism and Medieval Islam* (Chicago Studies in the History of Judaism). 1993. Pp. xv, 281. (University of Chicago Press, Chicago–London. Price: $49.95; paper $19.95. ISBN 0 226 46913 1; paper 0 226 46915 8)

Taking as its starting point the story of the meeting of the Queen of Sheba with King Solomon (1 Kings 10:1–13), L. traces the complex process of its transformation as it is read in postbiblical Judaism and in the Islamic world. The book is divided into six chapters looking at the readings of the story in rabbinic Judaism and in the Qur'an and its associated Islamic literature. The additional details in the postbiblical accounts (e.g. the riddles; the hairy legs of the Queen) emphasize the concept of natural cosmic order (which is hierarchical and patriarchal) and betray the preoccupations of the writers, as do the closely-related issues of gender. The 'Islamization' of this Jewish theme is the object of ch. 5 as the story gains more detail and links Jewish gender issues to Qur'an's message against polytheism. This is a very well-researched book, full of insights, questions and humour.

A. JEFFERS

LEVINSON, PNINA NAVÈ: *Einführung in die rabbinische Theologie* (Die Theologie). 1993 (3rd rev. edn). Pp. xii, 169. (Wissenschaftliche Buchgesellschaft, Darmstadt. Price: DM 39.00/SwF 40/AS 304. ISBN 3 534 08558 2)

This is a very traditional and — for many — a very frustrating book. Despite the title, it really seems to be a summary of traditional teaching for a modern Orthodox Jew. Although many references to rabbinic literature are given (in a prooftexting manner), reference is also often made to medieval and later writers. After an Overview, it is organized according to Teaching about God, Teaching about Humans, Teaching about the World, and (as a supplement to the 1993 reprint) Egalitarian Developments and Feminist Theology. In this last section, for example, the question of women rabbis and cantors is discussed. It may well serve its intended audience, but those wanting a proper critical introduction to rabbinic literature should go elsewhere (e.g. to the Strack/Stemberger *Introduction* [*B.L.* 1992, pp. 130–31; 1994, p. 154–55]).

L. L. GRABBE

LIEU, JUDITH; NORTH, JOHN; and RAJAK, TESSA (eds): *The Jews among the Pagans and Christians in the Roman Empire.* 1994 (1992). Pp. xvii, 198. (Routledge, London–New York. Price: paper £11.99. ISBN (paper) 0 415 11448 9)

This is the paperback edition of the book reviewed in *B.L.* 1993, p. 139.

ED.

LIEU, SAMUEL N. C.: *Manichaeism in Mesopotamia and the Roman East* (Religions in the Graeco-Roman World 118). 1994. Pp. xiv, 325. (Brill, Leiden–New York–Köln. Price: fl. 150.00/$85.75. ISBN 90 04 09742 2; ISSN 0927 7633)

This is a collection of six essays (two co-authored with J. M. Lieu), all but one previously published. All but one of the essays deals with some aspect of the history of Manichaeism in the Eastern Roman Empire. The first essay touches on the references to Judaism in Manichaean texts and discusses whether a Jewish group is being referred to in the damaged passage of the *Cologne Mani Codex* 137–40.   L. L. GRABBE

LIGHTSTONE, JACK N.: *The Rhetoric of the Babylonian Talmud, Its Social Meaning and Context* (Studies in Christianity and Judaism 6). 1994. Pp. xiv, 317. (Published by Wilfred Laurier Press, Ontario, for Canadian Corporation for Studies in Religion. Price: $28.50 (USA). ISBN 0 88920 238 9; ISSN 0711 5903)

Employing tools derived from the social sciences, Lightstone explores the character and function of the Babylonian Talmud against its social and political background in late Sassanian Persia and in contrast to the Mishnah and other early Rabbinic writings from the Land of Israel. The close study and analysis of rhetorical formulae reveals them to be the key both to what the editors of the Talmud were aiming to achieve and to the extraordinary role of the Talmud in the Geonic culture of the early Muslim centuries.

N. R. M. DE LANGE

LUDWIG, MARTINA: *Wort als Gesetz. Eine Untersuchung zum Verständnis von 'Wort' und 'Gesetz' in israelitisch-frühjüdischen und neutestamentlichen Schriften. Gleichzeitig ein Beitrag zur Theologie des Jakobusbriefes* (Europäische Hochschulschriften. Series 23: Theology 502). 1994. Pp. 217. (Lang, Frankfurt-Bern-New York. Price: SwF 25.00. ISBN 3 631 46437 1; ISSN 0721 3409)

The main purpose of this study is to illucidate the 'word' concept in the epistle of James. To do so, L. traces 'word' and 'law' in the Hebrew and Greek texts of the Old Testament, Qumran, Philo, and the New Testament outside James. She finds a theological tradition in Israel and early Judaism (though not in Philo) which equates God's word with his Law. This is taken and developed in James which uses 'word' and 'law' interchangeably, in contrast to Paul and some other New Testament texts (indeed, James may have known Romans and Galatians), though Luke and Revelation have similarities to James.   L. L. GRABBE

MCCARTHY, CARMEL: *Saint Ephrem's Commentary on Tatian's Diatessaron. An English Translation of Chester Beatty Syriac MS 709 with Introduction and Notes* (Journal of Semitic Studies Supplement 2). 1993. Pp. viii, 381. (Oxford University Press. Price: £35.00. ISBN 0 19 922163 4; ISSN 0022 4480)

For *B.L.* readers, the relevance of a patristic Gospel commentary inevitably lies mainly in its handling of Old Testament references. Ephrem's commentary is full of interest for the history of exegesis; most relevant here are his statements of exegetical principles, his use of the Old Testament and the fact that his language is not far removed from that of the Targums. This commentary was once known only in an Armenian version; what is known of the Syriac text now amounts to about 80 per cent of the original. The late

Dom Louis Leloir edited both the Armenian and the Syriac, and also published a French translation of the whole based on both. M. has now rendered a like service in English. It is a careful and accurate version which will help many to appreciate the value of studying Syriac literature. The notes are mainly limited to biblical references with a few other brief explanations. It is a pity that these are so few, for several passages invite comparison with Targum and midrash or both Jewish and early Christian prayers and homiletic literature.

R. P. R. MURRAY

McKAY, HEATHER A.: *Sabbath and Synagogue. The Question of Sabbath Worship in Ancient Judaism* (Religions in the Graeco-Roman World 112). 1994. Pp. xi, 279. (Brill, Leiden–New York–Köln. Price: fl. 125.00/$71.50. ISBN 90 04 10060 1; ISSN 0927 7633)

The subject of this monograph is one, as M. shows, where assumptions abound, often creating a rounded and confident picture which carries a superficial persuasiveness. M., in a confessedly minimalist assessment, treats the various sources (Hebrew Bible, Jewish Literature, Philo and Josephus, Graeco-Roman writers, New Testament, early Christian writers, Mishnah, and the archeological evidence) separately, with careful attention to each agenda and perspective. In so doing she also covers much other ground — the development of the synagogue, so-called pagan 'anti-Semitism'. Some will query a definition of worship in an ancient context which prioritizes singing and prayer, excluding a primary focus on study (well-attested) or even preaching, but given that definition the conclusions reached are nuanced and coherent. The style seems aimed at the student, with discursive engagement with secondary authors and thumb-nail introductions to primary sources, usually discussed via an established English translation. Much of this material is extensive and might still benefit from more detailed analysis in its own right, but this is a useful volume to disabuse both students and scholars of fondly held certainties.

J. LIEU

MASON, STEVE: *Josephus and the New Testament*. 1992. Pp. 248. (Hendrickson, Peabody, MA. Price: $9.95. ISBN 0 943575 99 0)

This welcome, readable book 'was written explicitly for students of the New Testament and its world who want to know how to approach Josephus so that he will shed light on the New Testament texts'. The answer is, not by fragmenting Josephus' writings into little bits of data and isolating 'facts', but by engaging with Josephus' assumptions, intentions and apologetic concerns. Ch. 3 discusses the apologetic aims of his writings (with a good brief examination of the *Life* as a rebuttal of Justus' account, pp. 73–76). Ch. 4 compares treatment of the Herodian family, the Roman governors of Judaea, the high priests, and the Pharisees and the Sadducees in Josephus and the New Testament; ch. 5 focuses similarly on John the Baptist ('Josephus' account . . . forces us to ask whether [he] has not been posthumously adopted by the church in a way that he did not anticipate'), Jesus, and his brother James. Finally, M. argues that the author of Luke–Acts knew something of Josephus' work; in the case of Agrippa I's death, Felix and Drusilla, Agrippa II and Berenice, Luke's narrative 'seems to depend squarely' on Josephus' information. In other cases, disagreements (e.g. the sequence of Theudas and Judas the Galilaean) result from imperfect memory or deliberate schematization. 'Most telling, however, is Luke's presentation of Christianity as a "philosophical school" within Judaism' (p. 224), comparable with Josephus' apologetic presentation of Judaism. A brief chapter on the significance of Josephus for New Testament study, in effect an essay on historiography, concludes an excellent study, and makes a point which applies to all who try to relate biblical to extra-biblical historical sources.

J. R. BARTLETT

MÉCHOULAN, HENRY (ed.): *Los Judíos de España. Historia de una diáspora. 1492–1992*. 1993. Pp. 668. (Editorial Trotta/Fundación Amigos de Sefarad/Sociedad Quinto Centenario, Madrid. Price: 5500 ptas. ISBN 84 87699 61 8)

Originally published as *Les juifs d'Espagne: Histoire d'une diaspora* (Paris: Liana Levi, 1992), this provides a goldmine of information on Jewish — not just Sefardi — history and society throughout the world from the Inquisition to the Holocaust. The recurrent demons of the Sefardim are Catholic France and Spain — in contrast, Jews have generally prospered under the pragmatism that peculiarly distinguished the post-Reformation English-speaking world. Thus, we discover that in Gibraltar, Menorca, and Malta, Jews were generally welcomed under the British and rejected by the French and Spanish. In the USA and its colonial predecessor, as in modern Israel, tolerance led to the disappearance of Spanish-speaking Jews as a distinct socio-religious group. Other samples of what this encyclopaedic volume contains are the following: a synagogue was destroyed in Barbados in 1739; the Jews of Martinique were expelled in 1684; 'Jews' Cove' and 'Jews' Bridge' are found in Haiti; Sarajevo is called Sarai and (by metathesis?) Little Jerusalem; the descendants of Majorca's converted Jews still face discrimination; 19th-century Mexico discovered its own 'falashas', allegedly converted three centuries before; Norway did not accept Jews until 1851 but Denmark allowed them from 1622. The Jews of England, expelled in 1290, are well represented, from the Rodrigo Lopes affair at the court of Elizabeth I to the readmission under Cromwell and to their complete emancipation in the mid-19th century; we discover, for example that the English 'Sefardim' include descendants of immigrants from Baghdad, Mashad, and India. The text of the 1492 decree of expulsion is reproduced, and there are pieces on the kabbalists Meir ibn Gabbai, Solomon Alkabetz, and Joseph Caro, as well as a brief introduction to Judaeo-Spanish in its *djudezmo* (spoken) and *ladino* (literary and liturgical) varieties.

J. F. ELWOLDE

MENDES-FLOHR, PAUL (ed.): *Gershom Scholem. The Man and His Work* (SUNY Series in Judaica: Hermeneutics, Mysticism, and Religion). 1994. Pp. xi, 127. (State University of New York, Albany. Price: $39.50/$12.95. ISBN 0 7914 2125 2; paper 0 7924 2126 0)

This is a slight book. It 'is based on papers read at a memorial meeting held, in accordance with Jewish custom, thirty days after Scholem's death on 20 February 1982' (p. 26). Hence the papers are primarily eulogistic and take no account of the debate over Scholem's work which has developed in the last twelve years. Isaiah Tishby, for example, offers a straight summary of Scholem's views on the Zohar but never mentions at all his well known disagreements with his mentor. Joseph Ben-Shlomo, writing about Scholem's view of Pantheism in the Kabbalah, makes no attempt to respond to, or even mention, Moshe Idel's critique of Scholem on this point (*B.L.* 1989, p. 136). Joseph Dan, however, does mention faults in Scholem's analyses and refers to his controversies with Tishby, but the reader would be better off with Dan's full-scale treatment in his *Gershom Scholem and the Mystical Dimension of Jewish History* (1988). Rivka Schatz, discussing Scholem's views on Hassidism, is the only scholar in this book who really engages with him. I enjoyed reading Malachi Beit-Arié's paper on 'Gershom Scholem as Bibliophile'.

A. P. HAYMAN

MINEAR, PAUL SEVIER: *Christians and the New Creation. Genesis Motifs in the New Testament.* 1994. Pp. xvi, 142. (Westminster/John Knox, Louisville KY. Price: $14.99. ISBN 0 664 25531 0)

Not surprisingly, Paul's Corinthian letters and John's Gospel feature prominently in this study: it is the curse on the earth and creation from the earth that holds the key to Jesus's enigmatic writing on the ground in John 8 and his 'creating' with mud in John 9. The book's first half traces intriguing contacts between Genesis and Luke–Acts, beginning from the Bethlehem shepherds, linked via the shepherds in Ezekiel 34 with figures in Genesis starting with Abel. In the book as a whole, Abel has a prominence which hints that the New Testament is less inclined to separate off Genesis 4 from Genesis 1–3 than is the subsequent Christian tradition (which made me wonder whether the New Testament may have some echoes from the climactic Fall story in Genesis 6). The twice-retired Yale professor thus shows how old (shepherd) dogs can learn and teach new intertextual tricks (though his concept of intertextuality may be a bit fuzzy, appealing as it does to authors' intentions and original readers' horizons as well as to juxtapositions of texts).

J. GOLDINGAY

MOMIGLIANO, ARNALDO: *Essays on Ancient and Modern Judaism.* Edited and with an Introduction by Silvia Berti; translated by Maura Masella-Gayley. 1994. Pp. xxviii, 242. (University of Chicago Press. Price: $24.95. ISBN 0 226 53381 6)

This is a translation of a volume originally published in Italian in 1987, with the exception of a number of pieces that were originally published in English and were translated into Italian for the earlier publication. The twenty-three articles are divided into two groups: Part One focuses on ancient history, with a strong emphasis on Greco-Jewish relations; Part Two looks to the modern age and includes a number of vignettes on individual scholars. Readers interested in the Hellenistic period will find some classic essays conveniently collected here, including 'Daniel and the Greek Theory of Imperial Succession' and 'The Second Book of Maccabees'.

N. R. M. DE LANGE

MOR, MENACHEM (ed.): *Jewish Sects, Religious Movements, and Political Parties. Proceedings of the Third Annual Symposium of the Philip M. and Ethel Klutznick Chair in Jewish Civilization Held on Sunday–Monday, October 14–15, 1990* (Studies in Jewish Civilization 3). 1992. Pp. xxiii, 426. (Creighton University Press, Omaha NE. Price: £26.95. ISBN 1 881871 04 5)

Most of the essays in this collection relate to Jewish religious history and controversy in the modern period and in the contemporary world, with particular emphasis on the situations in the USA and Israel. The first quarter of the volume does, however, raise some important issues in connection with Judaism in the ancient and medieval worlds. On the topic of Samaritanism, there are three contributions: E. B. Whaley examines the complicated nature of various sources and interpretations of Josephus's *Antiquities* 11.297–347; L. H. Feldman demonstrates that the famous historian was ambivalent, sometimes regarding Samaritans as a separate national entity and at other times seeing them as a variety of Jew; and B. Tsedaka expresses his personal conviction that both Judaism and Samaritanism are daughters of the Israelite religion. The assumption of extreme religious conflict between strictly defined Jews and Christians in the first four Christian centuries is justifiably challenged by R. A. Freund who prefers to postulate the existence of various Jewish–Christian sects at odds with both rabbinic Judaism and the early church. A not-wholly-dissimilar situation is speculatively reconstructed by S. M. Wasserstrom with regard to Jewish sectarians in the early Islamic period.

S. C. REIF

MÜLLER, M.: *Kirkens første Bibel, Hebraica sive graece veritas?* 1994. Pp. xvi, 152. (Anis, Frederiksberg. Price DKR 175. ISBN 87 7457 147 8)

In 1992 a new Danish Bible translation was published; in the same year the liturgy of the Danish church was revised and regular Old Testament readings were brought back into the service. On this background the author of 'the first Bible of the Church' has taken up the important question whether the basis for a modern translation authorized to be used in the Lutheran church ought to be the Septuagint as in the old church or the Hebrew Bible, following the Reformed tradition. No definite answer is given, but the author succeeds in giving, as he intends, critical comment on the latter tradition. These problems are of course not specific Danish, and some of the material in this volume has already been published in English (*SJOT* 1989, 1–2; 7/1993).

K. JEPPESEN

MÜLLER, M. and STRANGE, J. (eds): *Det gamle Testamente i jødedom og kristendom* (Forum for bibelsk Eksegese 4). 1993. Pp. 182 (Museum Tusculanums Forlag, København. Price DKR 154. ISBN 87 7289 252 8)

The fourth issue of 'Forum for bebelsk Eksegese' is published to celebrate the twenty-fifth anniversary of the Department of Biblical Exegesis at the University of Copehagen (in its present form). The topics dealt with are related to the old historical and theological problem that the first Christians found it a necessity to maintain both the idea that the Jewish holy scripture 'was still the word of God' and 'at the same time to establish an interpretation, which made an exodus out of Judaism possible' (p. 7); thus, three of the essays deal in very different ways with the relation between Old Testament and New Testament. J. Høgenhaven stresses that the christological readings of Old Testament texts are not without feeling for history in spite of the perspective of salvation history; Lemche moves backwards from the baptism of Jesus to Ps. 2, which he dates to the Hellenistic period; Müller explores the relation to the law in the earliest congregation as described in Luke's writings. G. Hallbäck and J. Strange have made an interesting joint investigation into biblical geography, discussing texts like Gen. 10 and Jub. 8 and 9. H. Ulfgard writes about 2 Baruch, and in the last essay H. Tronier discusses the hermeneutics of Philo and Paul.

K. JEPPESEN

MURPHY, FREDERICK J.: *Pseudo-Philo. Rewriting the Bible.* 1993. Pp. xiv, 322. (Oxford University Press. Price: £35.00. ISBN 0 19 507622 2)

The book falls into three parts: I, Prologue, on narrative criticism as a literary critical tool and its application to Pseudo-Philo's *Liber Antiquitatum Biblicarum*; II, a narrative commentary on the *LAB*; and III, Broader Perspectives on Pseudo-Philo, consisting of three chapters that deal with major characters, themes and 'the real author in historical context'. There is a full bibliography, together with helpful indexes, including a Latin word index (curiously called a 'General Concordance').

S. P. BROCK

MUTIUS, HANS-GEORG VON (ed.): *Jüdische Urkundenformulare aus Marseille in Babylonisch-Aramäischer Sprache* (Judentum und Umwelt — Realms of Judaism 50). 1994. Pp. xiv, 99. (Lang, Frankfurt–Bern–New York. Price: SwF 29.00. ISBN 3 631 46900 4; ISSN 0721 3131)

Three types of documents are translated in this collection of 12th-century CE Hebrew formularies from the south of France. First, eleven documents relating to marriage, the family and personal status (e.g., release from slavery). Then, twenty-eight texts concerning obligations and laws relating to things (e.g. concerning rent) and lastly, seven about the judiciary, adjective law and distraints (e.g. conferring power of attorney). There is a brief introduction, the texts (in translation only) are provided with notes and there are indices and a bibliography.

W. G. E. WATSON

NELSON, PETER K.: *Leadership and Discipleship. A Study of Luke 22:24–30* (Society of Biblical Literature Dissertation Series 138). 1994. Pp. xvii, 330. (Scholars Press, Atlanta. Price: $32.95; paper $21.95. ISBN 1 55540 900 8; paper 1 55540 901 6)

Part One of this study offers 'background perspectives' including 'The History of Israel' (four pages!), 'The Household', 'Jewish Banquet and Meal Traditions' (three pages), 'Reversal Motifs . . . in Jewish Sources' (another very brief survey, but this time a little less superficial) and a longer section on the present state of scholarship about the Farewell Discourse as a genre. This last, with its fairly well-documented footnotes, is the only part of this monograph likely to interest readers of the *B.L.*

C. J. A. HICKLING

NEUSNER, JACOB: *The Mother of the Messiah in Judaism. The Book of Ruth* (The Bible of Judaism Library). 1993. Pp. xxii, 138. (Trinity Press International, Valley Forge, PA. Price: $12.00. ISBN 1 56338 061 7)

Presupposing in the reader a basic understanding of rabbinic midrash, N. sets out to explain the text of Ruth Rabbah as an exemplar of rabbinic reader response criticism in action, understanding it as rabbinic dialogue 'with scripture', God, and the important issues of their day. The rabbis' conception of the 'original' meaning of the text — God's meaning — was undifferentiated from the meaning the rabbis found for themselves. What N. sees as the oft-repeated, though never explicitly stated, message of Ruth Rabbah is indicated by frequent references to the Torah in general, quotations from Torah, and by use of parallels with Genesis Rabbah and Leviticus Rabbah. It is that the outsider (from Moab) generates a Messiah (from the periphery) and that mastery of the Torah accomplishes this miracle. David, the messiah of Judaism, is seen as a sage, a master of both written and oral Torah. At times this reader felt that a page layout similar to that of the Talmud would have aided understanding, for the weaving style of the midrash — at times echoed by N. — demands intense concentration. However, N. mostly employs the typical delivery style of Western biblical scholars in the explanatory sections.

H. A. McKAY

NEUSNER, JACOB: *Rabbinic Judaism. Disputes and Debates, First Series* (South Florida Studies in the History of Judaism 107). 1994. Pp. xvi, 284. (Scholars Press, Atlanta. Price: $79.95. ISBN 1 7885 0006 6)

In this collection of essays and reviews, the first essay surveys the 'American contribution' to scholarship on rabbinic literature, from the European antecedents of the 19th century (such as Geiger and Graetz) through G. F. Moore and eventually to N. himself (along with a section on the Israeli 'competition'). The next four essays review N.'s positions on several topics and set out new hypotheses for debate: the three stages in the formation of rabbinic writings, the Tosefta, the hermeneutics of the law, and a brief summary of the results of his book *The Presence of the Past, the Pastness of the Present. History, Time, and Paradigm in Rabbinic Judaism*. Four chapters review D. Stern, *Parables in Midrash* (1991); H. Shanks (ed.), *Christianity and Rabbinic Judaism* (1992; cf. *B.L.* 1994, pp. 153–54); L. H. Feldman, *Jews and Gentiles* (1993; cf. *B.L.* 1994, p. 136); and Y. H. Yerushalmi, *Zakhor. Jewish History and Jewish Memory* (1982). In his prologue N., in the context of celebrations for the fortieth anniversary of his graduating class, reflects on his own work over the past four decades.   L. L. GRABBE

NEUSNER, JACOB: *Rabbinic Literature and the New Testament. What We Cannot Show, We Do Not Know*. 1994. Pp. xii, 195. (Trinity Press International, Valley Forge PA. Price: $17.00. ISBN 1 56338 074 9)

'What we cannot show, we do not know' could in many ways be considered N.'s motto over the past quarter of a century and more. This volume is not intended as a comprehensive, systematic introduction to the use of rabbinic literature by New Testament students — could such be imparted by a volume so constructed, in any case? Rather, N. has given a collection of writings and reviews which address and illustrate some of the main issues of methodology raised by use of rabbinic literature to interpret the New Testament. It is in the context of this give-and-take that he hopes to bring home to the New Testament student the correct approach. His aim is a positive one, even if at times it proceeds by severe criticism of the work of others. Readers should keep their eyes constantly on the subtitle of the book.

L. L. GRABBE

NEUSNER, JACOB: *Scripture and Midrash in Judaism. Volume One* (Judentum und Emwelt – Realms of Judaism 47). 1994. Pp. 389. (Lang, Frankfurt–Bern–New York. Price: SwF 40.00. ISBN 3 631 46461 4; ISSN 0721 3131)

N. points out that midrash in the early compilations (3rd–4th centuries) took the form of exegeting passages in sequence; in the 5th–6th centuries, not only the exegesis of verses not in sequence but also the demonstration of various concrete doctrines; and in the final range, a systematic setting forth of a single coherent position through exegesis of a sequential order. As a result, he has planned three volumes, each one devoted to one particular form (and chronological period). This first one takes up selections from Sifra and Sifre to Numbers and Deuteronomy. Each writing has an introduction, then a judicious selection of excerpts in English translation. The Preface gives a general introduction to midrash. Volume two will be an anthology of Genesis and Leviticus Rabbah and Pesiqta deRav Kahana; and volume three, of Lamentations Rabbati, Canticles and Ruth Rabbah, and Esther Rabbah I. Many readers would no doubt be grateful if the publisher used larger type in the translation sections.   L. L. GRABBE

NEWSOME, JAMES D.: *Greeks, Romans, Jews. Currents of Culture and Belief in the New Testament World*. 1992. Pp. xiv, 475. (Trinity Press International, Valley Forge, PA. Price: $29.95. ISBN 1 56338 037 4)

N. endeavours to provide a textbook introducing the Jewish history, literature, and theology of the Graeco-Roman period. Although the book is primarily designed for New Testament students, it will also prove helpful to students of the Second Temple period. It is less detailed than Nickelsburg's *Jewish Literature* (*B.L.* 1982, p. 114), but has wider scope. The book is divided into two parts: 'the Hellenistic Period' (from Alexander to 63 BCE) and 'the Roman Period' (down to the end of the Bar Kokhba revolt). This division is not entirely satisfactory and a degree of overlap occurs. N. draws upon recent research in most areas, especially in the chapter on Qumran, and shows good grasp of the issues. However, the chapter entitled 'Apocalyptic' follows the mistake of older scholarship in identifying works as belonging to the 'genre of apocalyptic' (p. 72) because they had certain features such as developed angelology and demonology or the periodization of history (p. 66). Other surprises were that 'the canonization of the Torah' was complete by 400 BCE (p. 103) and the fact that N. never quotes directly from the Mishnah but from citations in the new Schürer.

D. J. BRYAN

NITZAN, BILHAH: *Qumran Prayer and Religious Poetry* (Studies on the Texts of the Desert of Judah 12). 1994. Pp. xxi, 415. (Brill, Leiden–New York–Köln. Price: fl. 130.00/$74.50. ISBN 90 04 09658 2; ISSN 0169 9962)

This book provides a comprehensive study of the character of Qumran prayer and religious poetry. By 'prayer' N. understands texts that were intended for liturgical purposes, and distinguishes between fixed prayer and prayer of the congregation. Fixed prayers served within the Qumran community as a substitute for regular sacrificial worship, and in this category she analyses the *Daily Blessings* (4Q503) and — in much greater detail — the *Prayers for the Festivals* (4Q507–09; 1Q34[bis]) and *Dibre hamme'orot* (4Q504–06). Prayers of the congregation were used on specific cultic occasions, and here N. discusses first blessings and curses (specifically Deut. 28 as a model for the ceremony of entry into the covenant, and Num. 6:24–26 as a textual form underlying several Qumran texts), and then songs of praise. A general discussion of songs of praise in the Bible and at Qumran is followed by a detailed treatment of three different types: eschatological poetry (1QM XIII, XIV, and XVIII); magical poetry (11QPsAp[a]; 4Q510–11); and mystical poetry (the *Songs of the Sabbath Sacrifice*). N. argues that the *Hodayot* are quite different in character from all the preceding material. She maintains that the *Hodayot* are to be understood as religious poetry and were not intended for liturgical use, and she emphasizes the personal concerns reflected in them and their much more overt sectarian character.

M. A. KNIBB

PAPER, HERBERT H. (ED.): *Hebrew Union College Annual*. Vol. 64. 1993 (1994). Pp. vii, 200 (English), 58 (Hebrew). (Hebrew Union College, Cincinnati. Price: $30.00. ISSN 360 9049)

The two carefully researched articles in this issue that are of most interest to biblical scholars are both concerned with 2 Kings 3. P. D. Stern compares the accounts of Israel's war with Moab as presented in 2 Kings 3 and in the Mesha Inscription. He concludes that the latter, though revealing elements of propaganda and other shortcomings, is more historically reliable than the biblical account, which he characterizes as a theological reaction to a lost war and an 'historic fiction'. C. T. Begg compares that same chapter as recorded in the Hebrew, Greek and Aramaic versions with the account of the campaign of the kings of Israel, Judah and Edom given by Josephus in his *Antiquities* 9.29–43. He identifies various divergencies, suggests that Josephus had several text-forms available to him, and explains the historian's minor alterations as motivated by apologetic, literary and stylistic considerations. Also of relevance to students of the Hebrew Bible are the reconstruction of part of Shem Tov Ibn Falaquera's lost Bible commentary by R. Jospe and D. Schwartz and Y. Harel's (Hebrew) study of the 1865 edict of the Aleppo rabbis to destroy the modern commentary by Eliahu Ben Amozeg of Livorno. Other articles touch on the Pseudo-Clementine *Homilies*, Josephus's *Antiquities* 1–4, two Bar Kosiba letters, the *sukkah* in talmudic thought, messianism in medieval Jewish philosophy, and the Hebrew enlightenment in Germany.

S. C. REIF

PARENTE, FAUSTO and SIEVERS, JOSEPH (eds): *Josephus and the History of the Greco-Roman Period. Essays in Memory of Morton Smith* (Studia Post-Biblica 41). 1994. Pp. x, 392. (Brill, Leiden–New York–Köln. Price: fl. 160.00/$91.50. ISBN 90 04 10114 4; ISSN 0169 9717)

The essays in this collection were given at a symposium in San Miniato, Italy, in 1992. Two essays address philological questions (Part I): the *politeia* of Israel (L. Troiani) and *Ioudiaos to genos* and related questions (S. Cohen). Under Part II Sources are discussed Josephus' portrayal of the Hasmoneans compared with 1 Maccabees (L. Feldman), Onias III's death and the founding of the temple at Leontopolis (F. Parente), and Josephus as historian of Rome (M. Hadas-Lebel). Part III Literary and Other Models studies Josephus' portrayal of: Amalek (J. Maier), John Hyrcanus I (C. Thoma), the Essenes (T. Rajak), and Daniel and the Flavian house (S. Mason). Part IV History and Topography has treatments of Jerusalem and the Akra (J. Sievers), Hyrcanus II (D. Schwartz), the Jerusalem temple (L. Levine), and the geographical excurses in Josephus (P. Bilde). Part V Views of the War considers Josephus' actions in Galilee (G. Jossa, S. Schwartz) and asks whether he was lying in the *Life* or in the *War* (U. Rappaport). Part VI concerns Josephus himself, including certain 'dark periods' in his life (G. Hata) and his Roman citizenship (M. Goodman). The collection is dedicated to Morton Smith who not only proposed the colloquium in the first place but whose estate also underwrote a substantial portion of its cost.

L. L. GRABBE

Philo, The Works of: New Updated Edition. Complete and Unabridged. Translated by C. D. Yonge. Updated with foreword by David M. Scholer. 1993. Pp. xx, 918 + 6 maps. (Hendrickson, Peabody MA. Price: $29.95. ISBN 0 943575 93 1)

The Yonge translation of Philo (mid-19th century) was superseded by the Loeb edition; however, it continued to be widely used as a cheap and compact translation and also for translations of some Armenian tractates not in the Loeb edition. The text of the Yonge translation has now been reset and reissued in a one-volume edition with the text corrected to conform to the standard critical text (and newly translated where necessary). The Loeb reference system of numbered paragraphs has also been added to the text, as well as a new set of notes (though these are minimal). David Scholer and Hendrickson Press are to be congratulated for such a useful volume.

L. L. GRABBE

PIETERSMA, ALBERT: *The Apocryphon of Jannes and Jambres the Magicians. P. Chester Beatty XVI (with new Editions of Payrus Vindobonensis Greek inv. 29456 + 29828 verso and British Library Cotton Tiberius B. v f. 87)* (Religions in the Graeco-Roman World 119). Edited with Introduction, Translation and Commentary, with full facsimile of all three texts. 1994. Pp. xvii, 349. (Brill, Leiden–New York–Köln. Price: fl. 170.00/$97.25. ISBN 90 04 09938 7; ISSN 0927 7633)

In the early 1970s P. identified the remains of the Apocryphon of Jannes and Jambres and gave a preliminary English translation. He here provides an edition and translation of the fragments accompanied by an excellent commentary. He also provides new editions of the brief fragments that were already known and are contained in a Vienna papyrus and a British Library Latin manuscript; but regrettably he was not able to include the brief fragments that are found in a Michigan papyrus because this has not yet been published. References to Jannes and Jambres occur in numerous pagan, Jewish and Christian sources, which P. assembles and discusses in his lengthy introduction, and P. Chester Beatty XVI is of importance not least because it provides us with a relatively clear picture of the content and purpose of the apocryphon attached to their names. P. argues that the apocryphon is a Jewish work that was composed in Egypt no later than the 2nd century AD, and possibly as early as the 1st, and that the main concern of the extant fragments is the wilful opposition and stubborn persistence of the book's chief protagonist, Jannes. He also argues convincingly that the story of the two *Egyptian* magicians ultimately derives from the tradition reflected in Damascus Document 5:17b–19 concerning two *Israelite* leaders, Yoḥanah and his brother, who led Israel astray in Egypt, but that Yoḥanah and his brother are not the Jannes and Jambres of the book and the later tradition.

M. A. KNIBB

POINTON, MARCIA (ed.): *The Image in the Ancient and Early Christian Worlds = Art History. Journal of the Association of Art Historians.* Vol. 17/1. March 1994. Pp. 142. (Blackwell, Oxford. Price: £46.00/$83.00 p.a.; £13.99/$19.95 this special issue. ISBN 0 631 194 746; ISSN 0141 6790)

These essays are part of a wider debate, arising out of the death of Kurt Weitzmann and the passing of the age of *Kunstgeschichte*, about how images attain meaning in a particular cultural and historical situation. Of interest to many readers will be the article on the Dura Europas synagogue — contexts, subtexts, intertexts (A. J. Wharton). There are also articles on narrative structure and the Ara Pacis Augustae building, the moving of statues to new contexts in late antique Rome, the images of Saints Peter and Paul, and the apse in St Catherine's monastery at Mount Sinai. There are also review articles and shorter reviews.

L. L. GRABBE

PORTON, GARY G.: *The Stranger within your Gates. Converts and Conversion in Rabbinic Literature* (Chicago Studies in the History of Judaism). 1994. Pp. xiii, 410. (University of Chicago. Price: $29.95. ISBN 0 226 67586 6)

This imposing volume consists of a survey of all the relevant passages in the Mishnah, Tosefta, early Midrashic texts and Talmud, followed by separate chapters on the conversion ritual, marriages between converts and Israelites and other issues concerning the complex relationship between converts and Israelite society. It is the first study to approach the subject in this way, informed by recent insights from the social sciences, and studiously avoiding some of the familiar and rather emotive issues that have perhaps bedevilled earlier studies of the subject. These include the theological debate between Judaism and Christianity on universalism and particularism, the question of Jewish missionary activity (a topic in any case not addressed in the rabbinic literature), and scholars' traditional preoccupation with dating (P.'s approach is synchronic). The study focuses throughout on the opinions and attitudes of the rabbis, rather than on the experience of the converts, and concludes that the convert is 'a marginal being, one who often stands at the edges of both Israelite and non-Israelite society'. Almost half the volume is taken up with notes, bibliography, and indices.   J. F. A. SAWYER

QIMRON, ELISHA and STRUGNELL, JOHN, with contributions by Y. Sussmann and A. Yardeni: *Discoveries in the Judaean Desert. Volume 10: Qumran Cave 4: V Miqṣat Maʿaśe ha-Torah*. 1994. Pp. xiv, 235 + 8 plates. (Clarendon Press, Oxford. Price: £40.00. ISBN 0 19 826344 9)

After much interest — even hype — the famous 4QMMT is finally published. Now all scholars will have access to it, not just those making grand pronouncements about the importance of the document for Jewish history. The *editio princeps* is well-done, for which we can all be grateful. Each separate manuscript and its orthography is discussed before a composite reconstruction with English translation and philological notes is given. A discussion of the language of the scroll follows. The chapter on the literary character and the historical setting is very speculative, much more so than the authors admit. A chapter on the *halaka* has much valuable data from Qumran and rabbinic literature. An appendix gives an English translation of Y. Sussmann's Hebrew article in *Tarbiz* 59 (1989–90), pp. 11–76 (though many of the footnotes are omitted), and two additional appendixes give further observations from each of the editors. In his introduction, S. mentions that the basic text had been reconstructed by 1959, but then proceeds to explain the difficulties with writing the commentary. But since when does one have to have a detailed commentary before publishing a text in preliminary form? S. did find time in his busy schedule to criticize Allegro's 1967 publication. Whatever Allegro's faults, all scholars have been able to study his important texts from Cave 4 and advance the field for more than a quarter of a century. The basic text of MMT could have been made available thirty-five years ago, and we could all have been working on its commentary.

L. L. GRABBE

RABENAU, MERTEN: *Studien zum Buch Tobit* (Beihefte zur Zeitschrift für die alttestamentliche Wissenschaft 220). 1994. Pp. viii, 249. (de Gruyter, Berlin–New York. Price: DM 138.00. ISBN 3 11 014125 6; ISSN 0934 2575)

This study is an interaction with R. Hanhart's critical text and P. Deselaers' commentary, with much attention given to traditio-historical concerns throughout. Ch. 1 discusses the most original text of the book (the tradition represented by Codex Sinaiticus) and provides a literary analysis. Chs 2 and 3 study the admonitions of Tobit 4 and the psalm of Tobit 13. Ch. 4 reconstructs what the assumed base text has to say about Jewish piety (and some aspects of daily life) in the Diaspora. Ch. 5 discusses the various layers added to the assumed base text. Ch. 6 discusses the time (3rd century BCE, though some older material may have been used, and three additional layers were added in the 2nd century) and place (in the area of Samaria, though it was 'judaized' by later redactors). R. gives his own translation of the text, with different type faces showing the various layers according to his analysis.   L. L. GRABBE

REEVES, JOHN C. (ed.): *Tracing the Threads. Studies in the Vitality of Jewish Pseudepigrapha* (Society of Biblical Literature Early Judaism and Its Literature 6). 1994. Pp. xiii, 296. (Scholars Press, Atlanta. Price: $29.95; paper $19.95. ISBN 1 55540 994 6; paper 1 55540 995 4)

This programmatic collection in tradition history and comparative literature is both innovative and intriguing. M. Kister, R. A. Kraft, and S. M. Wasserstrom outline some of the methodological issues in handling the Jewish pseudepigrapha in later Jewish, Christian and Muslim sources respectively. They show that seldom can any direct influence of one text upon another be shown; in place of historical trajectories researchers must generally be content with noting the antiquity and pervasiveness of Jewish exegetical traditions. A fourth study by A. Urowitz-Freudenstein underlines the same point for Pirqe de Rabbi Eliezer. M. Himmelfarb proposes that the echoes of Jubilees in medieval Jewish literature may have occurred through the translation into Hebrew in Byzantine Italy of excerpts of Jubilees that were used independently by the Byzantine chronographers. In similar vein W. Adler investigates Syriac chronography and argues for the transformation of Jubilees by later exegetes. R. investigates the influence of Enochic traditions in Manichaean literature. Comparative analysis is offered by B. L. Visotzky as he assembles traditions that describe talkative palm trees, by J. E. Bowley in collecting together literature attributed to Abraham, and by S. Dalley in pointing out how traces of the Gilgamesh Epic in the Tale of Buluqiya may be explained. The overall range of sources cited in these studies is breathtaking, but the frequent references in them to Genesis and its pseudepigraphic reworkings show, not surprisingly, that certain universally applicable aspects of Judaism's foundational texts had wide appeal in the first millennium CE.

G. J. BROOKE

ROSE, CHRISTIAN: *Die Wolke der Zeugen. Eine exegetisch-traditionsgeschichtliche Untersuchung zu Hebräer 10,32–12,3* (Wissenschaftliche Untersuchungen zum Neuen Testament: 2. Reihe 60). 1994. Pp. xi, 445. (Mohr, Tübingen. Price: DM 128.00. ISBN 3 16 146012 X; ISSN 0340 9570)

In this Tübingen doctoral thesis R. offers an exhaustive study, first of the place of 10:32–12:3 within the structure of Hebrews, and then of both theological and *religionsgeschichtliche* aspects of the content of that section of the document. Some concepts, and more extensively a number of passages in the text, have led him to seek comparable material not only in Hellenistic–Jewish literature but also in the Targums (on which he offers a five-page excursus, pp. 163–69, focused largely on questions of dating) and later Jewish tradition. Thus Habakkuk 2:3f as used at Hebrews 10:37f receives some twenty pages of detailed discussion (pp. 51–72) which draws in some of the Midrashim, and a fairly full history of interpretation of the Genesis material used in Hebrews 11 occupies nearly a third of the whole study. Unsurprisingly, this thoroughgoing engagement with traditions drawn from the Old Testament and Jewish apocalyptic has led R. to reject the view that Hebrews neglects the 'mainstream', eschatologically-orientated Jewish heritage in favour of a Philonic dualism.

C. J. A. HICKLING

RUNIA, DAVID T.: *Philo in Early Christian Literature. A Survey* (Compendia Rerum Iudaicarum ad Novum Testamentum III/3). 1993. Pp. xvi, 422. (Van Gorcum, Assen. Price: fl. 95.00. ISBN 90 232 2713 1)

Although indubitably a Jew, Philo came to be quoted with approval by Christian scholars, who sometimes describe him as a Father of the Church or even a Bishop of Alexandria. How did this conversion come about? The story is told in full for the first time in this wonderfully rich and thorough book. The patristic authors (up to c. AD 400) are scrutinized in systematic order to see what they make of Philo and his ideas, and the work is grounded in a careful presentation of the fruits of previous scholarship rather than in a personal synthesis. The book can thus be consulted from a number of viewpoints that may focus variously on Philo and his reception in the Church, on the patristic authors themselves, or on the arguments of modern scholars. The history of Christian exegesis of the Bible naturally bulks large. The thirty-six-page bibliography is also an index, as it includes references to all the citations of each work in the notes. There are also indexes of biblical and Philonic passages and a comprehensive general index.

N. R. M. DE LANGE

SAFRAI, ZE'EV: *The Economy of Roman Palestine*. 1994. Pp. xii, 500. (Routledge, London–New York. Price: £55.00. ISBN 0 415 10243 X)

Z. covers the period of time from the fall of the Second Temple to the mid-4th century, though there are some sections which discuss the economy during the Second Temple period. Where possible, Z. makes use of archaeological data, but a main source is still rabbinic literature. To some extent Z. discusses the methodological problems with using this (pp. 3–8), though he states that a full discussion is beyond the scope of his treatment (pp. 5, 10). On the contrary, it would seem that the methodological question is central to any such study. To what extent the views of 'the rabbis' give us data about the actual society and economy is a question which cannot be bypassed. To be sure, Z. shows his awareness of this and cites secondary literature which addresses some specific points. Nevertheless, in his actual study, rabbinic citations seem to serve merely as prooftexts for generalized statements rather than as data to be interrogated and interpreted. Z.'s attempt to quantify and turn the data into graphs and charts is impressive, but one cannot help wondering whether in the end it is also 'mountains hanging by hairs' (*M. Ḥag.* 1:8).

L. L. GRABBE

SALDARINI, ANTHONY J.: *Matthew's Christian–Jewish Community* (Chicago Studies in the History of Judaism). 1994. Pp. 317. (University of Chicago. Price: $55.00; paper $17.95. ISBN 0 226 73419 6; paper 0 226 73421 8)

This is an interesting book. S. argues that the Matthean community was part of Judaism, and its opponents were other Jews, not the Jewish community as a whole. He provides a useful corrective to scholarship which has placed this Gospel too far away from Judaism inside the Gentile world. For this purpose, he makes fruitful use of the sociology of groups, as well as conventional New Testament tools, with which he is almost fully conversant. He does not however use identity theory, which would have facilitated sharper analysis, nor Aramaic. This book could also be better written — too much information is scattered in a massive plethora of endnotes. None the less, this should be regarded as required reading for anyone interested in the conflict through which Christianity separated from Judaism, and in the cultural orientation of New Testament writers, not only for specialists in Matthean studies.

P. M. CASEY

168   APOCRYPHA AND POST-BIBLICAL STUDIES

Scott, James M.: *Adoption as Sons of God. An Exegetical Investigation into the Background of HUIOTHESIA in the Pauline Corpus* (Wissenschaftiche Untersuchungen zum Neuen Testament: 2. Reihe 48). 1992. Pp. xv, 353. (Mohr, Tübingen. Price: DM 88.00. ISBN 3 16 145895 8; ISSN 0340 9570)

Part II of this Tübingen dissertation is devoted to 'Adoption in the Old Testament and Early Judaism'. The hitherto standard treatment of the subject by H. Donner is subjected to devastating criticism as being built on flawed premises. Oepke's article on *huiothesia* (*Theological Dictionary of the New Testament*) also needs correction: S. has found very extensive evidence for the practice of adoption in Hellenistic Judaism where, however, other terminology is always used. Going over all the ground very thoroughly on his own account, S. has made an exhaustive and authoritative contribution to our understanding of the social world of Second Temple Judaism. Part III examines successively Galatians 4:5, 2 Corinthians 6:18 (S. argues powerfully for Pauline authorship, pp. 215–20) and Romans 8:15, 23. Old Testament texts are shown to have been extensively in the background of Paul's thought and of its expression, among them those inviting 'Exodus typology' and those which exhibit the Covenant Formula. Of the latter, 2 Samuel 7:14 is of particular importance (pp. 96–117 are devoted to the Hebrew text and its history of interpretation). A number of combined quotations are identified and carefully discussed. This is an impressively thorough study of the background and articulation of a key element in Paul's thought.

C. J. A. Hickling

Segal, Eliezer: *The Babylonian Esther Midrash. A Critical Commentary (Volume 1: To the End of Esther Chapter 1); (Volume 2: To the Beginning of Esther Chapter 5); (Volume 3: Esther Chapter 5 to End)* (Brown Judaic Studies 291–93). 1994. Pp. (vol. 1) xi, 330; (vol. 2) xx, 360; (vol. 3) xx, 308. (Scholars Press, Atlanta. Price: (vol. 1) $49.95; (vol. 2) $56.95; (vol. 3) $49.95. ISBN (vol. 1) 1 55540 996 2; (vol. 2) 1 55540 997 0; (vol. 3) 1 55540 998 9)

S. offers a new translation, accompanied by an extensive commentary, of the Midrash to the Book of Esther which is incorporated into the Babylonian Talmud Tractate *Megillah* 10b–17a. In spite of the fact that this midrash is located in the Talmud, and not, as one might expect, in a homiletic collection, it is arranged along the lines of the classical Palestinian model. It is, S. believes, to a large extent a homiletic midrash which originated in Palestine, but which was transformed into an exegetical-style commentary when it was included in the curriculum of the *yeshivah*. It is very similar to *Esther Rabbah*, and it seems that the two compilations represent different developments of a pool of common material. S. bases his translation on the Yemenite manuscript Columbia University X893 T141. In places where the differences between the textual traditions are very great the different texts are recorded in parallel columns. In other cases variants are listed in the footnotes, although no effort is made to include all variants.

M. Maher

Steck, Odil Hannes: *Das apokryphe Baruchbuch. Studien zu Rezeption und Konzentration »kanonischer« Überlieferung* (Forschungen zur Religion und Literatur des Alten und Neuen Testaments 160). 1993. Pp. xi, 340. (Vandenhoeck & Ruprecht, Göttingen. Price: DM 114.00. ISBN 3 525 53842 1)

The book of Baruch has often been left aside, claims S., as just a collection of secondary citations from earlier writings in the Old Testament. Consequently scholars have not bothered to ask for what purpose such material was assembled. S. seeks to correct this neglect with this comprehensive study in two main sections. First, he gives a fresh translation of Ziegler's Greek text with detailed commentary on the four different parts of the book, devoting attention to the original language and unity of each part. The second section then concentrates on the book as a whole, its origin and purpose. The later Baruch tradition in Judaism and Christianity (including the extensive Syriac tradition) is too wide ranging to be included though there are many references to more contemporary works like the books of Maccabees, the Psalms of Solomon, Sirach and the Qumran texts. The book's purpose is seen against the Diaspora situation, where it was essential to ensure the centrality of biblical tradition — not unlike the purpose behind phylacteries and *mezuzot*. The original language (Hebrew) and the vexed question of literary unity are keenly debated; there is a huge bibliography.   J. SNAITH

STEGEMANN, EKKEHARD (ed.): *Messias-Vorstellungen bei Juden und Christen*. 1993. Pp. 168. (Kohlhammer, Stuttgart. Price: DM 39.80. ISBN 3 17 012202 9)

H. Lichtenberger gives a brief but useful survey of texts relating to Messianic expectations and figures in the Second Temple period. Other essays consider the question in relationship to the theology of Luke, the gospel of John, rabbinic literature, Maimonides, and contemporary Judaism and Christianity and Jewish-Christian dialogue.   L. L. GRABBE

STERN, SACHA: *Jewish Identity in Early Rabbinic Writings* (Arbeiten zur Geschichte des Antiken Judentums and des Urchristentums 23). 1994. Pp. xxxix, 269. (Brill, Leiden–New York–Köln. Price: fl. 150.00/$85.75. ISBN 90 04 10012 1; ISSN 0169 734X)

This book, based on a 1992 Oxford D.Phil. thesis, is concerned with Jewish identity as a topic within the rabbinic writings down to the Arab conquests of the 7th century. It is essentially a study of the rabbinic theology of Israel, and within these parameters it makes interesting reading. The biblical precedents, although they are present in the background, are not specifically studied: the focus is exclusively on the rabbinic sources.

N. R. M. DE LANGE

STEUDEL, ANNETTE: *Der Midrasch zur Eschatologie aus der Qumrangemeinde (4QMidrEschat [a,b])*. *Materielle Rekonstruktion, Textbestand, Gattung und traditionsgeschichtliche Einordnung des durch 4Q174 ('Florilegium') und 4Q177 ('Catena A') repräsentierten Werkes aus den Qumranfunden* (Studies on the Texts of the Desert of Judah 13). 1994. Pp. xi, 237. (Brill, Leiden–New York–Köln. Price: fl. 150.00/$85.75. ISBN 90 04 09763 5; ISSN 0169 9962)

This careful study has two main concerns: a reconstruction by the Stegemann method of the fragmentary remains of 4Q174 (the so-called 'Florilegium') and 4Q177 ('Catena A'), and analysis of the *Midrash on Eschatology* (4QMidrEschat [a,b]). The results of the reconstruction, are convincing. There is no overlap between the two manuscripts, but S. argues that 4Q174 represents the beginning, and 4Q177 th middle, of the work which consisted of three parts: an exegesis of Deut. 33 (A), an interpretation of the promise to David in 2 Sam. 7 (B), and a midrash (the heading used in 4Q174 III, 14) on a selection of psalm passages which appear all to have been drawn from Pss. 1–41 (C). S. argues that 4QMidrEschat is best defined as a thematic midrash with parallels with the (early) pesharim. Its purpose was to maintain within the Qumran community belief in the imminence of the end in the face of delay in its coming. Overall S. makes a strong case, and her work includes many valuable observations. But some questions inevitably remain, not least about the relationship between A, B, and C: S. argues that the link is prophecy, but sees A and B essentially as introductory to C. Also, it may be wondered whether the text can be dated quite so precisely to 71–63 BC.

M. A. KNIBB

SWANSON, DWIGHT D.: *The Temple Scroll and the Bible. The Methodology of 11QT* (Studies on the Texts of the Desert of Judah 14). 1995. Pp. xi, 268. (Brill, Leiden–New York–Köln. Price: fl. 125.00/$71.50. ISBN 90 04 09849 6; ISSN 0169 9962)

S.'s aim is to establish the biblical sources of 11QT and investigate how they are used. Because an examination of the entire Scroll would be impossible, separate chapters look at the Festival Law (18:1–23:1), the King's Law (57:2–59:21), the Purity Law (48:1–51:5), and the Temple Law (4:1–7:15). S. finds that the Scroll is an example of commentary on scripture. In each passage, this takes the form of a base text (with possible alternations) which is then commented on by the use of secondary and supplementary texts which are interwoven with it to clarify, amplify, and focus its meaning. This type of commentary — the use of scripture to comment on scripture rather than the commentator's own words — is apparently unique. As for the dating of the Scroll, S. argues that it is secondary to Chronicles and thus subsequent to those books. Although the Scroll was used by members of Qumran, it lacks the typical polemic and vocabulary of the sectarian documents and thus seems to have originated outside the community and probably earlier than its formation. It looks like a Levitical document.

L. L. GRABBE

SWARTLEY, WILLARD M.: *Israel's Scripture Traditions and the Synoptic Gospels. Story Shaping Story*. 1994. Pp. xv, 367. (Hendrickson, Peabody MA. Price: $17.95. ISBN 1 56563 001 7)

The main thesis of this work is that a number of Old Testament theological traditions have influenced the structure and theology of the Synoptic Gospels. The word 'synoptic' acquires a new meaning when it is applied to the dependence of the three Gospels on common structures and themes derived from Israel's stories about itself. The four traditions under discussion are the Exodus and Sinai traditions, which are connected with the Galilee narrative; the Old Testament Way-Conquest traditions and their influence on the journey narrative of the Gospels; the Temple traditions, which are relevant to the pre-passion narrative; and the Kingship traditions with their impact on the Passion narrative. But in their use of the Old Testament the Gospels show unity and diversity. Although they stand in continuity with the stream of Israel's traditions, there emerges a diversity in the ways in which they transform that material. To conclude his study, S. has a chapter on 'Story shaping Story'. This fascinating study, with its detailed exposition of biblical texts and its full references to current literature, will be of great interest to those concerned with the relationship between the Old and New Testaments and with biblical theology.

G. H. JONES

THIEDE, CARSTEN PETER: *The Earliest Gospel Manuscript? The Qumran Fragment 7Q5 and its Significance for New Testament Studies*. 1992. Pp. 80. (Paternoster Press, Carlisle. Price: £4.99. ISBN 0 85364 507 8)

Chapter 4 of this short collection is a conveniently accessible detailed account of the case for identifying this much-discussed fragment, reproduced and fifteen times enlarged at p. 68, as Mark 6:52f. Ch. 5 reproduces O'Callaghan's proposed identifications of eight further fragments from the same cave. Of these, only one (7Q4?–1 Timothy 3:16–4:3) is selected for a full discussion, and T. goes on to put forward detailed archaeological and other evidence for 'close and natural' contacts between 'the Jerusalem Christians [of the first decade or so] and the Jerusalem Essenes' (pp. 55–62). As with a more recent claim concerning the Magdalen fragment of Matthew, there seems to be a fractionally more than negligible possibility that T. might be right.

C. J. A. HICKLING

TWERSKY, ISADORE AND HARRIS, JAY M. (eds): *Rabbi Abraham Ibn Ezra: Studies in the Writings of a Twelfth-Century Jewish Polymath* (Harvard Judaic Texts and Studies 10). 1993. Pp. v, 170 (Eng.), 48 (Heb.). (Harvard University Press, Cambridge MA and London. Price: $29.95; paper $14.95/ £11.95. ISBN 0 674 74554 X; paper 0 674 74555 8)

Nine hundred years after his birth, Abraham Ibn Ezra continues to fascinate scholars in a variety of Hebrew and Jewish fields, as is again demonstrated in this collection of papers from a recent Harvard conference. Of particular interest to students of the Hebrew Bible are the articles by N. M. Sarna, U. Simon and (in Hebrew) S. Kogut. Sarna sets Ibn Ezra's biblical commentaries in the context of his biography and lifestyle and summarizes, in a useful and at times refreshing manner, his methods, his theories, and his approach to the work of others. The range and nature of 13th- and 14th-century supercommentaries, particularly as reported by Judah Ibn Mosconi, are critically assessed by Simon in a characteristically thorough fashion, and a variety of verses are cited by Kogut to exemplify Ibn Ezra's role as a philologist and to demonstrate his support for traditional cantillation and exegesis as long as they tallied with sound linguistic criteria. In the remaining studies, Y. T. Langermann expertly discusses astrology in Ibn Ezra's philosophy and commentaries; Twersky (in Hebrew) compares his ideas with those of Maimonides and is cautious about drawing conclusions; and Harris traces the use of Ibn Ezra as a model by Jewish and Christian scholars of the modern period.   S. C. REIF

VELTRI, GIUSEPPE: *Eine Tora für den König Talmai. Untersuchungen zum Übersetzungsverständnis in der jüdisch-hellenistischen und rabbinischen Literatur* (Texte und Studien zum Antiken Judentum 41). 1994. Pp. xiii, 289. (Mohr, Tübingen. Price: DM 138.000. ISBN 3 16 145998 9)

This dissertation, presented in the Freie Universität Berlin, offers a thorough analysis of the rabbinic traditions regarding the Septuagint. Its core is a detailed commentary on the list of verses which *Bavli Megillah* 9a–b (and parallels) claims were changed in the Greek translation 'for King Talmai [Ptolemy]'. Close attention is paid, as one would expect in a Berlin dissertation, to problems of text, tradition-history and Sitz im Leben. V. also offers a wide-ranging discussion of the concept of translation in rabbinic literature, which includes the most penetrating discussion which the reviewer has seen of the use of the verb *letargem* in rabbinic texts. This is a model piece of work which throws a flood of light on rabbinic attitudes towards translating the Bible, and which helps to reclaim for Septuagint studies a curious episode in the history of the Greek version.   P. S. ALEXANDER

VERMES, GEZA: *The Dead Sea Scrolls. Qumran in Perspective*. 1994 (revised edn). Pp. xi, 238. (SCM, London. Price: £12.95. ISBN 0 334 02565 6)

The first edition was noted in *B.L.* 1978, p. 135; 1982, p. 121; and the second in 1983, p. 124. The first chapter has now been replaced by one on the Scrolls 1947–94 and other revisions have been made here and there in the text.

ED.

VERMES, GEZA: *Jesus the Jew. A Historian's Reading of the Gospels*. 1994 (5th impression with new preface). Pp. 286. (SCM, London. Price: £12.95. ISBN 0 334 00805 0)

The first edition was reviewed in *B.L.* 1974, p. 93. A new preface discusses its reception and makes some brief comments about two sections which need revision. The text is otherwise a straightforward reprint.   ED.

WISE, MICHAEL OWEN: *Thunder in Gemini And Other Essays on the History, Language and Literature of Second Temple Palestine* (Journal for the Study of the Pseudepigrapha Supplement 15). 1994. Pp. 265. (Sheffield Academic Press. Price: £25.00/$37.50. ISBN 1 85075 460 8; ISSN 0951 8215)

This is a collection of studies, but only two of the six essays here have been published before, and then only in an earlier form. The first studies the Aramaic brontologion 4Q318. The second concerns the high priest Ananias bar Nedebaeus and his and his family's part in the 66–70 revolt, including some interesting speculation on the identity of the Eleazar at Masada (possibly Eleazar bar Ananias, who could also be called the instigator of the revolt). The third considers the possibility of linguistic dating of Aramaic Qumran scrolls, concluding that such 'dating of the Aramaic DSS is an exercise in futility' (p. 151). Essay four is a study of 4QFlorilegium 1:1–13; five, of the annalistic calendar at Qumran (4Q322–24c or 4QMishmarot C[a–f]), arguing that it is a catalogue of events of the Hasmonean period; and six, of the calendar texts 4Q321 and 321[a] (4QMishmarot B[a–b]) and 4Q252. This is a stimulating collection, whatever one thinks of the conclusions.

L. L. GRABBE

10. PHILOLOGY AND GRAMMAR

ANDERSEN, FRANCIS I. and FORBES, A. DEAN: *The Vocabulary of the Old Testament*. 1992. Pp. viii, 721. (Editrice Pontificio Istituto Biblico, Rome. Price: Lire 85,000. ISBN 88 7653 575 6)

This promises to be a valuable resource for those researching into the distribution of Old Testament vocabulary. Word counts are given for the main divisions like Torah and Nebiim, for each biblical book, and for (according to Eissfeldt's analysis) the main Pentateuchal sources. All words are divided into their grammatical categories, including not only nouns and verb, but nouns with the article or suffixes and verbal 'tenses' and derived conjugations; and other parts of speech like adverbs, prepositions and conjunctions. Detailed cross references are supplied to Brown-Driver-Briggs, Mandelkern, and Even-Shoshan, where there is often distributional information, though it is not arranged in such an accessible form. The editors are well aware of the complex theoretical issues involved in ordering the material, and a further volume discussing these in detail is promised. A final assessment will have to await the appearance of this volume, but meanwhile we should be grateful for the selfless labour which has gone into these count tables. The volume is not a substitute for traditional lexica and concordances, but it does things they cannot do and should be an excellent supplement to them. It should go very well in tandem with the new Sheffield dictionary (*B. L.* 1994, p. 159), which seems to me to share its up-to-date approach.

J. C. L. GIBSON

BARTELMUS, RÜDIGER: *Einführung in das biblische Hebräisch: ausgehend von der grammatischen und (text-) syntaktischen Interpretation des althebräischen Konsonantentexts des Alten Testaments durch die tiberische Masoreten-Schule des Ben Ascher.* Mit einem Anhang: Biblisches Aramäisch für Kenner und Könner des biblischen Hebräisch. 1994. Pp. 287. (Theologischer Verlag, Zürich. Price: SwF 42.00. ISBN 3 290 10963 1)

Biblical Hebrew is in fact a late creation of the Massoretes and should be taught synchronically as such without confusing students with diachronic explanations. This is a laudable aim, but B.'s introduction is too tied to the linguistic theories of Wolfgang Richter. Under a teacher familiar with these theories, it should be a very effective tool. It is well arranged and crisply, sometimes laconically, written. Some parts are very good, especially the sections on the particles which amount to a syntax *in parvo*. Those interested in accuracy of linguistic description should certainly have a look at it, but it is much too technical and dense for using in Hebrew lessons to the kind of students I have to teach.

J. C. L. GIBSON

BEN ZVI, EHUD; HANCOCK, MAXINE; and BEINERT, RICHARD: *Readings in Biblical Hebrew. An Intermediate Textbook.* 1993. Pp. xiv, 241. (Yale University Press, New Haven CT and London. Price: £26.00. ISBN 0 300 05573 0)

This textbook is a praiseworthy attempt to help students who have gone through an elementary grammar. There are readings from all the genres in the Hebrew Bible accompanied by copious notes on points of grammar, syntax and pointing. Particular attention is paid to translation techniques and the bearing of linguistics matters on exegesis, with plenty of little exercises and questions (and spaces provided for the answers). There are also comments on historical background and literary devices, so that the book falls roughly between a grammar/syntax and a commentary. There is no doubt that students above first year level require assistance of this kind, but should the supplying of it not be the teacher's task in class? The textbook hopes that it may prove useful to students studying on their own, but it seems to me too detailed for that.

J. C. L. GIBSON

BERGEN, ROBERT D. (ed.): *Biblical Hebrew and Discourse Linguistics.* 1994. Pp. 560. (Summer Institute of Linguistics, Dallas; distributed by Eisenbrauns, Winona Lake IN. Price: $40.00. ISBN 1 55671 007 0)

This collection arose from a conference of mostly working Bible translators but also linguists and biblical scholars which was held in 1993. The twenty-two essays are divided into three sections. Part I Grammatical, Syntactical, and Accent Studies has articles on discourse linguistics and Hebrew grammar, *weqatal* forms, salient features, the Hebrew verbal system, the collision between source criticism and discourse analysis, and the Masoretic accents. Part II Narrative Genre discusses analysis of biblical narrative, direct discourse, genealogies and Genesis, Genesis 27:46, the miraculous grammar of Joshua 3–4, evil spirits and eccentric grammar, and a textlinguistic approach to Jonah. Part III Topics Relating to Nonnarrative Genres addresses rhetorical questions in Job, genre criticism and the Psalms, genre and form criticism in Old Testament exegesis, how to translate Hebrew proverbs, Song of Songs 1:1–2:6, prophetic quotation formulas in Jeremiah, prophetic discourse in Micah, and vision and oracle in Zechariah 1–6. A helpful feature is that each essay is headed by an abstract.

L. L. GRABBE

BEYER, KLAUS: *Die aramäischen Texte vom Toten Meer samt den Inschriften aus Palästina, dem Testament Levis aus der Kairoer Genisa, der Fastenrolle und den alten talmudischen Zitaten. Ergänzungsband.* 1994. Pp. 450. (Vandenhoeck & Ruprecht, Göttingen. Price: DM 198.00. ISBN 3 525 53599 6)

B.'s original volume was reviewed in *B.L.* 1985, p. 150. The new supplement updates that volume in the light of the scholarship of the past decade. New texts are added, and old texts — or the relevant sections — are redone where significant new information has become available. The grammar and lexicon are also updated with supplementary information. Many of the amendments to the section on the history of Aramaic had already been incorporated into the English translation (*B.L.* 1987, p. 122). Ideally, the material of the supplement would have been integrated into the original edition to produce a new edition: as it is, a certain awkwardness is now inevitable in having to look in two places on each item, to see whether and in what way the original has been updated. However, considering the expense of completely redoing — and repurchasing — the first edition, this compromise will be much appreciated.

L. L. GRABBE

BLAU, JOSHUA: *A Grammar of Biblical Hebrew* (Porta Linguarum Orientalium 12). 1993 (2nd edn). Pp. xii, 220. (Harrassowitz, Wiesbaden. Price: DM 78.00/AS 593/SwF 76.00. ISBN 3 447 03362 2)

The first edition of this grammar by a well known Semitist was rather grudgingly reviewed in *B.L.* 1977, p. 116. It is accurate and precise, and has the good idea of basing many of its biblical references and examples on the Joseph stories in Genesis. But it is heavy and is hardly suitable for beginners. Unfortunately, this is hardly a second edition, but a photographic reproduction of the first edition with some ten pages of addenda and corrigenda.

J. C. L. GIBSON

DAWSON, DAVID ALLAN: *Text-Linguistics and Biblical Hebrew* (Journal for the Study of the Old Testament Supplement 177). 1994. Pp. 242. (Sheffield Academic Press. Price: £37.50/$55.00. ISBN 1 85075 490 X; ISSN 0309 0787)

This author aims to provide the Hebraist with an introduction to macro-syntactic theory without getting lost in incomprehensible jargon. He is not averse to using a new and pertinent analogy to make a point, he is clearly a communicator and not just a codifier, and text-linguisticians need to excel as both. He begins by contrasting the different ways some recent scholars have dealt with text-linguistic analysis, commenting on the work of Khan (*B.L.* 1990, p. 147), Longacre (*B.L.* 1992, pp. 77 ff), Eskhult (*B.L.* 1991, p. 152) and Niccacci (*B.L.* 1991, p. 154). Somewhat surprisingly Waltke and O'Connor's work (*B.L.* 1990, pp. 149 ff) is deliberately excluded (cf. pp. 24–28) and Niccacci's work on Micah is not mentioned (*B.L.* 1991, p. 88). His own sample texts are essentially chosen at random. Judges 2 illustrates 'narrative history', Leviticus 14:1–32 'procedures-instructions', and Leviticus

6:1–7:37 embedded material. The analysis of the parallel accounts of the building of the tabernacle affords special insights into his method of working. Finally he embarks on the detailed analysis of his two main texts, the Jephthah story and the book of Ruth, which he uses for 'refining and testing the hypotheses'.   M. E. J. RICHARDSON

GIBSON, J. C. L.: *Davidson's Introductory Hebrew Grammar — Syntax.* 1994. Pp. xi, 229. (T & T Clark, Edinburgh. Price: £19.95. ISBN 0 567 09713 7)

The appearance of a comprehensive study of Biblical Hebrew syntax is a major event in the field of biblical research, and 'Gibson's Davidson' is to be warmly welcomed. Perhaps out of deference towards his famous predecessor, whose *Hebrew Syntax* was first published exactly a century ago, G. has retained much of the original format and style: e.g. paragraphs and 'remarks' instead of numbered chapters, the overall arrangement of topics, an unexpectedly arbitrary use of abbreviations (adj. prep., constr., etc.) and some gratuitous Latin expressions like *ad sensum* and *dativus ethicus*. But in all important respects this is as up to date and scholarly as one could wish. Modern terminology is used, notably QATAL/YIQTOL in preference to Perfect/Imperfect, and occasional reference is made to Ugaritic and other extrabiblical examples unknown to the original author. Important additions include a substantial separate section on the 'Adverb and Adverbial Phrases and Clauses' and another on the 'Infinitive and Participle', as well as new paragraphs on many topics including Quasi-verbals, the particles *'et* and *lĕ*, Compound Sentences and Word-Order. There is also a much expanded 'Index of Subjects' which reveals some of the book's other merits, for example, the author's concern with such crucial matters as emphasis, English usage and poetry.   J. F. A. SAWYER

GREENSPAHN, FREDERICK E. (ed.): *Hebrew Studies. A Journal Devoted to Hebrew Language and Literature.* Vol. 35. 1994. Pp. 249. (National Association of Professors of Hebrew in American Institutions of Higher Learning, published at the University of Wisconsin at Madison. Price: $25.00. ISSN 0146 4094)

This volume has two articles to note: two kinds of sexual relationships in the Hebrew Bible (D. Grossberg) and Chomsky's separation of syntax and semantics (D. Washburn). Other articles are on modern Hebrew and the 'theatre of protest'. There are more than 140 pages of reviews plus two responses to a review of C. Westermann's *Wurzeln der Weisheit* (cf. *B.L.* 1991, p. 102).   L. L. GRABBE

HESS, RICHARD S.: *Amarna Personal Names* (American Schools of Oriental Research Dissertation Series 9). 1993. Pp. xii, 292. (Eisenbrauns, Winona Lake IN. Price: $37.50. ISBN 0 931464 71 4)

This is both an exhaustive index of all personal names occurring in the Amarna documents and, up to a point, a study of them. The names are given in a 'Catalog', and there is also a list of other spellings in use but not adopted in this book with references to the adopted spelling. The Catalog gives not only all occurrences, but comments on the identity of the person(s), analyses the names and translates them (with evidence where needed), and lists occurrences of the same name in other sources (not, however, drawing on I. J. Gelb's massive *Computer-Aided Analysis of Amorite* for this purpose). A brief section of 'Grammatical Analysis' by language is followed by glossaries for West Semitic, Akkadian, Egyptian, Sanskrit, Hurrian, Anatolian and Kassite, and by a list of deities and geographical names occurring in the personal names. This is an extremely conscientious work of compilation, intelligently done, and advancing the study of these names.

W. G. LAMBERT

HOCH, JAMES E.: *Semitic Words in Egyptian Texts of the New Kingdom and Third Intermediate Period.* 1994. Pp. xxi, 572. (Princeton University Press. Price: $65.00/£50.00. ISBN 0 691 03761 2)

This very substantial volume is a major contribution to our understanding and interpretation of the wide variety of Semitic words (mainly Northwest Semitic) to be found in ancient Egyptian texts during the new Kingdom (*c.* 1550–1070) BC) and less often down to *c.*700 BC. In his Introduction H. explains his procedures very clearly; a useful (but not infallible) novelty is his grading of the degree of certainty/uncertainty for the explanations offered. The bulk of the book (15–396) deals with the Semitic words identified under 595 entries — the majority of the interpretations suggested are probably acceptable, although not always. The second part of the book successively studies the traces of Semitic morphology and range of phonology here found — it is instructive to compare this part with D. Sivan, Z. Cochavi-Rainey, *West Semitic Vocabulary in Egyptian Script of the 14th to the 10th Centuries BCE* (*Beer-Sheva* VI, 1992), on these matters. Then H. summarizes the range of Egyptian texts in which the Semitic loanwords appear, and the slippery question of which precise languages/dialects they came from. Finally, he reviews the whole development of the special orthography used by the Egyptians for foreign words ('group writing' or 'syllabic orthography') well but rather concisely. For this task, one needs *all* the data, not only common nouns, and also from all languages involved, *not* only the Semitic group. The work ends with a good set of indexes. It should be stressed that H.'s book is in large measure complementary to that of Schneider (*B.L.* 1993, pp. 127–28) who concentrated on foreign (mainly Semitic) proper names in the Egyptian sources — which are not the object of H.'s study. Place-names are not dealt with by either scholar, nor the non-Semitic languages. Sometimes, H. may be inclined to assume errors by the ancients a little freely; but overall, his volume will be an invaluable help in studying Semitic vocabulary and language-forms as preserved in ancient Egyptian texts.

K. A. KITCHEN

HOFTIJZER, J. and JONGELING, K.: *Dictionary of the North-West Semitic Inscriptions* (Handbook of Oriental Studies 21). 1994. Pp. lxxi, 1266. (E. J. Brill, Leiden. Price: fl. 550/$314.50. ISBN (set) 90 04 09821 6; (vol. 1) 90 04 09817 8; (vol. 2) 90 04 09820 8)

What is officially a new edition of Jean and Hoftijzer's *Dictionnaire* (the last fascicle of which appeared in 1965) at first sight looks like something completely different. But once this tool for scholarship is put to use the old familiar and trustworthy format of the entries proves that these two volumes will be indispensable for today's generation of Hebraists. The judiciously selected but copious references to the secondary literature, the careful classification of dialect types (Ammonite is here), the frequent translation (into English) of problematical passages, all make the book so much more user-friendly than an automatically generated string of lexemes from an electronic database. No material published after 'the beginning of 1991' is included, but the two appendices describe new readings in the Ahiqar narrative (noted by Porten in his third volume of Aramaic documents from Egypt, 1993) and a 'selective glossary' of material from Egypt written in demotic script. The editors have been obliged to take important and often difficult decisions, like treating the language of the Deir Alla inscription separately instead of opting for Aramaic or Canaanite, excluding Ugaritic and Syriac, and construing biradical roots as triradicals. Even though we may not always agree with them, the editors have performed a sterling service for those who want to know about 'non-Biblical Hebrew and Aramaic'.

M. E. J. RICHARDSON

IZRE'EL, SHLOMO: *Amurru Akkadian: A Linguistic Study, Volume 1*, with an Appendix on the History of Amurru by Itamar Singer (Harvard Semitic Studies 40). 1991. Pp. 387. (Scholars Press, Atlanta. Price: $39.95; member price $24.95. ISBN 1 55540 633 5)

IZRE'EL, SHLOMO: *Amurru Akkadian: A Linguistic Study, Volume 2* (Harvard Semitic Studies 41). 1991. Pp. 258. (Scholars Press, Atlanta. Price: $29.95: member price $19.95. ISBN 1 55540 634 3)

Though originating as a thesis, this work emerges after six years' revision as a masterly grammar of the Akkadian of the kingdom of Amurru, in west Syria, in the fourteenth and thirteenth centuries BC, a language known from 18 Amarna letters, 13 from Ras Shamra, and 6 from Boghazköy. The methodology is rigorous, and the author writes from wide knowledge of not only the main dialects of Akkadian, but also of other Akkadian used in the west, and of the native spoken languages of the whole area. Much progress has been made in defining and explaining the features of this scribal language. In addition the basic texts are edited and translated with notes (some based on unpublished collations), and a 60-page 'Concise History of Amurru' by I. Singer is included. Even when one may differ in details on some of the issues, one cannot fail to admire the achievement and to learn much from it.

W. G. LAMBERT

JASTROW, OTTO: *Der neuaramäische Dialekt von Mlaḥsô* (Semitica Viva 14). 1994. Pp. xiii, 195. (Harrassowitz, Wiesbaden. Price: DM 132.00/SwF 132.00/AS1030. ISBN 3 447 03498 X; ISSN 0931 2811)

The Neo-Aramaic dialect from the Turkish village of Mlaḥsô is clearly presented in a form which makes the modern dialect easily available to the reader. The 200–300 families in this Christian village speak Aramaic, which was electronically recorded by the author, and then analysed philologically. Many problems were encountered, such as linguistic contamination from Kurdish and Armenian, but the author also offers comparisons with another Neo-Aramaic dialect, Ṭuroyo, which he has classified as Neo-Western-Aramaic. The book consists of a rather concise traditional grammar giving the morphology, followed by a chrestomathy and two separate glossaries, one of verbal forms and the second a general word index. Both glossaries offer etymological data. The use of this book for biblical scholars or Semitists is not immediately apparent, since the corpus of texts and *Belegstelle* bears no relation to any ancient text. Nevertheless, one of the great difficulties in reading an ancient text is the lack of any living informants to help with linguistic and syntactic problems. Occasionally the modern dialects preserve words or grammatical forms which were the product of oral transmission, and difficult to find in the literature, but none the less represent classical structures in the language.

M. J. GELLER

KELLEY, PAGE H.: *Biblical Hebrew. An Introductory Grammar*. 1992. Pp. xiv, 453. (Eerdmans, Grand Rapids MI. Price: $29.99. ISBN 0 8028 0598 1)

This book was reviewed in *B.L.* 1993, p. 154. This is the current price in dollars.

ED.

KIRAZ, GEORGE ANTON: *Lexical Tools to the Syriac New Testament* (JSOT Manuals 7). 1994. Pp. v, 137. (Sheffield Academic Press. Price: £25.00/$37.50. ISBN 1 85075 470 5; ISSN 0262 1754)

The author, a leader in computer-based lexical aids to the study of the Syriac New Testament, has already produced a Syriac Primer (1985), an electronic synopsis of the Four Gospels and a concordance in six volumes (1993). The present work contains frequency lists of six categories of words, indices (Syriac and English) and a skeleton Syriac grammar contributed by S. P. Brock. The whole should prove a useful tool for students of Syriac, which is more and more becoming recognized as a desideratum in both biblical and patristic studies.

R. P. R. MURRAY

KOEHLER, LUDWIG and BAUMGARTNER, WALTER, subsequently revised by W. Baumgartner and Johann Jakob Stamm, with assistance from B. Hartmann, Z. Ben-Hayyim, E. Y. Kutscher, P. Reymond: *The Hebrew and Aramaic Lexicon of the Old Testament. Vol. I: '-ḥ.* Translated and edited under the supervision of M. E. J. Richardson, in collaboration with G. J. Jongeling-Vos and L. J. de Regt. 1994. Pp. cv, 365. (Brill, Leiden–New York-Köln. Price: fl 227.00/$129.75. ISBN 90 04 09696 5)

The first volume of the third edition of Koehler-Baumgartner (or HAL, as it became abbreviated) appeared in 1967, with the fifth and final volume soon to be printed (for reviews, see *B.L.* 1969, p. 65 [*Bible Bibliog.*, p. 191]; 1975, p. 114; 1984, p. 144; 1992, p. 136). More than a quarter of a century later, an English edition has now appeared. Considering the many potential users whose first language or main scholarly language is English, the project is well justified. Although an updating would have been desirable, time and resources have not allowed that, though the corrections in the later volumes of the German edition have been incorporated into the text. Also, an attempt has been made to bring consistency to the abbreviations and references. The various prefaces of the different volumes of the HAL, as well as those of the original Koehler-Baumgartner, have been included. Like HAL, the English edition is expected to be complete in five volumes; however, the publishing form is different: The volumes of HAL used a large-page format, with the idea that they could be finally issued (or rebound) into a single, if bulky, volume. The English edition has smaller pages and the volume is thicker; clearly, it is intended to form a five-volume set. One can argue for either alternative, though many will miss the convenience of a usable one-volume edition (which BDB and Gesenius-Buhl have provided all these years).

L. L. GRABBE

MEYER, RUDOLF: *Beiträge zur Geschichte von Text und Sprache des Alten Testaments. Gesammelte Aufsätze* (Beihefte zur Zeitschrift für die alttestamentliche Wissenschaft 209). Herausgegeben von Waltraut Bernhardt. 1993. Pp. viii, 259 + frontispiece. (de Gruyter, Berlin–New York. Price: DM 168.00. ISBN 3 11 013695 3; ISSN 0934 2575)

This very welcome volume contains reprints of 20 publications on text and language by the great Old Testament scholar and Semitist Rudolf Meyer

(1909–91). These are prefaced by a brief but fascinating biography written by Waltraut Bernhardt and supplemented with a bibliography of Meyer's works (19 books, 63 articles and 32 contributions to a reference works such as *TWNT* and *RGG*!). His *Hebräische Grammatik* may be regarded as a lasting memorial. Items reprinted here include several on one of M.'s themes, the Hebrew verbal system: 'Spuren eines westsemitischen Präsens-Futur . . .', 'Das hebräische Verbalsystem im Lichte . . .', 'Aspekt und Tempus im althebräischen Verbalsystem' and 'Zur Geschichte des hebräischen Verbums'. Several others are on aspects of the Masoretic text. As often with such collections, the inclusion of items which are otherwise difficult of access is particularly to be welcomed. Thus 'Gegensinn und Mehrdeutigkeit in der althebräischen Wort- und Begriffsbildung' from the *Sitzungsberichte der Sächsischen Akademie der Wissenschaften zu Leipzig.*   J. F. HEALEY

OREL, VLADIMIR E. and STOLBOVA, OLGA V.: *Hamito-Semitic Etymological Dictionary. Materials for a Reconstruction* (Handbuch der Orientalistik: Erste Abteilung, Der Nahe und Mittlere Osten: Band 18). 1995. Pp. xxxviii, 578. (Brill, Leiden–New York–Köln. Price: fl 350.00/$200.00. ISBN 90 04 10051 2; ISSN 0169 9423)

The 2,672 entries in this volume result from work initiated in 1986 in Moscow, comparing and analysing the lexical stocks of scores of languages and dialects. The introduction summarizes the authors' methods and assumptions (many of them treated at length in articles published in Russian), tabulates correspondences of consonants and vowels and explains types of metathesis and semantic shift accepted. Among those thanked for help I. M. Diakonoff's name should be noted. While the book is not immediately useful for elucidating meanings in biblical Hebrew or Aramaic, it emphasizes the enormous family that includes them, with a word such as **mawut* 'to die' common to Semitic, Berber, Egyptian, Chadic and Cushitic and, on the other hand, *nzl* 'to flow' appearing only in Hebrew and West Chadic. Some unexpected links are made, such a *bārā'* 'to create' with West Chadic *bār* 'build', then **būr* 'fortified place' (cf. Heb. *bīrā*). Many questions arise from the synchronic approach, for example, putting words of the Pyramid Texts beside terms current today, which the nature of the compilation cannot answer. The two-column index, set in small type on pp. 557–78, reveals that numerous words denote the same basic concept (e.g. 11 words for 'ant, insect', 54 for 'break'), contradicting the principle of linguistic economy. This immense work, which the editors describe as 'devoid of many simple human joys', will stimulate research and imagination in ways previously impossible in Semitic linguistics.   A. R. MILLARD

SCHOORS, A.: *The Preacher Sought to Find Pleasing Words. A Study of the Language of Qoheleth* (Orientalia Lovaniensia Analecta 41). 1992. Pp. xiv, 260. (Peeters/Departement Orientalistiek, Leuven. Price: BEF 1750. ISBN 90 6831 376 2)

This is a welcome addition to the continuing flood of books on Qohelet and, in particular, on the language of the book. S. explains the genesis of his book as the result of a 'partial dissatisfaction' with the work of C. F. Whitley which led him to organize his own research 'in the format of a grammar and a vocabulary' (p. 13). What we have here is Part One, the grammar and syntax; the vocabulary will be treated in a later volume. Hence, after a useful introductory survey of scholarly debate on the nature and date of the language, the main bulk of this work is laid out on the usual lines of a grammatical textbook: orthography and phonetics, morphology and syntax.

However, most of the material consists of a series of notes dealing with particular forms but written in dialogue with the works discussed in the introduction. Dahood (with his Ugaritic/Phoenician thesis) and, to a lesser extent, Fredericks (with his pre-exilic dating) are the main targets of criticism. S.'s preliminary conclusions support the general scholarly consensus that 'the language of Qoh is definitely late in the development of B[iblical] H[ebrew] and belongs to what scholars recently have called Late Biblical Hebrew' (p. 221).

A. P. HAYMAN

TAYLOR, BERNARD A.: *The Analytical Lexicon to the Septuagint. A Complete Parsing Guide.* 1994. Pp. xix, 460. (Zondervan, Grand Rapids MI. Price: $39.99. ISBN 0 310 53540 9)

This arises out of work on the Computer-Assisted Tools for Septuagint Study (CATSS) project. The lexicon is necessarily based on the Rahlfs text and excludes the data of the apparatus. All forms in that text are given a grammatical analysis or parsing and also the base form of the lexical entry; even the occasional error is cross-referenced to the correct form. The base form of verbs is that of the correct Hellenistic (*koine*) form even if that differs from classical Greek; one can understand this to be strictly correct, though inexperienced users who wish to look up the word in Liddel and Scott may not always find what they want. This is a new useful tool to be added to that growing number designed for the users of the Old Testament in its Greek versions.

L. L. GRABBE

WATSON, WILFRED G. E.: *Traditional Techniques in Classical Hebrew Verse* (Journal for the Study of the Old Testament Supplement 170). 1994. Pp. 534. (Sheffield Academic Press. Price: £55.00/$82.50. ISBN 1 85075 459 4; ISSN 0309 0787)

During and since the period in which W. was preparing his *Classical Hebrew Poetry* (*B.L.* 1986, pp. 81–82), he has published some forty articles on particular texts or stylistic features in Biblical Hebrew and other relevant ancient languages. Most happily, he has now been enabled to gather and arrange these scattered articles in such a way that, with the help of some new link pieces, they form a coherent whole, a sequel to his book presenting detailed examples of verse forms and techniques. The contents are arranged under the chapter-headings: Introduction, Conventions of Style, Half-line (Internal) Parallelism, Gender-matched Parallelism, Other Types of Parallelism, Word-Pairs, Chiasmus, Figurative Language, Preludes to Speech, and Patterns and Rhetorical Devices. The book is exhaustively indexed, and the editorial work is also to be highly praised. W.'s pair of volumes will surely long remain indispensable on their subject.

R. P. R. MURRAY

XELLA, P. (ed.): *Studi epigrafici e linguistici sul Vicino Oriente antico.* Vol. 11. 1994. Pp. 133. (Essedue edizioni, Verona. Price: Lire 45,000. ISBN 88 85697 41 0)

The articles of direct interest to OT scholars are a structural study of Psalm 106 (P. Auffret); an evaluation of the expression *byt dwd* ('house of David') in two ninth-century West Semitic inscriptions (A. Lemaire), and a lengthy survey of recent work on the 'Asherah of Yhwh' in the Kuntillet ʿAjrud inscriptions (P. Merlo). There is also a study of the cult of the dead during the ninth and eighth centuries at Samʾal (H. Niehr). Other contributions are on Ugaritic style (W. Watson), a reading in a Pylos tablet

(M. Negri), hieroglyphic Luwian (M. Poetto and N. Bolatti-Guzzo), an enigmatic Pharaoh (W. Huss), the Neo-Punic inscriptions from Mididi (F. Vattioni) and Sabaean culture during the first four centuries CE (A. Korotayev). There are also book reviews.

W. G. E. WATSON

ZADOK, RAN: *The Pre-Hellenistic Israelite Anthroponymy and Prosopography* (Orientalia Lovaniensia Analecta 28). 1988. Pp. xxv, 465. (Peeters/ Departement Orientalistiek, Leuven. Price: BEF 4950. ISBN 90 6831 120 4)

Z.'s well-known work on names in the ancient Near East continues with this useful volume. It is based mainly on the names in the Hebrew Bible but also includes those in epigraphic sources. The first part is devoted to a grammatical analysis of the names. The second part, on the prosopography, attempts to summarize in very abbreviated form the biblical data on various individuals. This is arranged in roughly chronological order. Z. admits some uncertainty and also recognizes that the biblical dating of some names is not necessarily reliable; however, he accepts conventional dating for the vast majority, a position which many will find problematic. Names in the epigraphic material are rightly treated separately from those in the Old Testament. Full indexes complete the usefulness of this industrious collection.

L. L. GRABBE

Books Received too Late for Notice in 1995

The books in the following list will be reviewed in the *Book List* for 1996.

ALDEN, ROBERT L.: *Job* (The New American Commentary). 1994. Pp. 432. (Broadman and Holman, Nashville TN. Price: $27.99. ISBN 0 8054 0111 3)

ASSAF, DAVID (ed.): *Proceedings of the Eleventh World Congress of Jewish Studies, Jerusalem, June 22–29, 1993. Division A: The Bible and Its World.* 1994. Pp. 246 (Eng.); 158 (Heb.). (World Union of Jewish Studies/Magnes Press, Jerusalem. Price: $20.00. ISSN 0333 9068)

ASSAF, DAVID (ed.): *Proceedings of the Eleventh World Congress of Jewish Studies, Jerusalem, June 22–29, 1993. Division B: The History of the Jewish People, Volume 1: From the Second Temple Period to Modern Times.* 1994. Pp. 194 (Eng.); 205 (Heb.). (World Union of Jewish Studies/Magnes Press, Jerusalem. Price: $20.00. ISSN 0333 9068)

AUBERT, JEAN-JACQUES: *Business Managers in Ancient Rome. A Social and Economic Study of the Institores 200 BC–AD 250* (Columbia Studies in the Classical Tradition 21). 1994. Pp. xv, 520. (Brill, Leiden–New York–Köln. Price: fl. 140.00/$80.00. ISBN 90 04 10038 5; ISSN 0166 1302)

AUS, ROGER DAVID: *Samuel, Saul and Jesus. Three Elderly Palestinian Jewish Christian Gospel Haggadoth* (South Florida Studies in the History of Judaism 105). 1994. Pp. xvi, 202. (Scholars Press, Atlanta. Price: $69.95. ISBN 1 55540 969 5)

BEATTIE, D. R. G. and McNAMARA, M. J. (eds): *The Aramaic Bible. Targums in their Historical Context* (Journal for the Study of the Old Testament Supplement 166). 1994. Pp. 470. (Sheffield Academic Press. Price: £40.00/$60.00. ISBN 1 1 85075 454 3; ISSN 0309 0787)

BEUKEN, W. A. M. (ed.): *The Book of Job* (Bibliotheca Ephemeridum Theologicarum Lovaniensium 114). 1994. Pp. x, 462. (Peeters/ University Press, Leuven Price: BEF 2400. ISBN (Peeters) 90 6831 652 4; (University) 90 6186 622 7)

BOYARIN, DANIEL: *Intertextuality and the Reading of Midrash* (Indiana Studies in Biblical Literature). 1994 (1990). Pp. xiii, 161. (Indiana University Press, Bloomington–Indianapolis; distributed in the U.K. by the Open University Press, Buckingham. Price: £27.50; paper £8.99. ISBN 0 253 31251 5; paper 0 253 20909 9)

BRAULIK, GEORG: *The Theology of Deuteronomy. Collected Essays of Georg Braulik, O.S.B.* (BIBAL Collected Essays 2). Translated by Ulrika Lindblad. 1994. Pp. ix, 302. (BIBAL Press, N. Richland Hills TX. Price: $18.95. ISBN 0 941037 30 4)

BRENNER, ATHALYA (ed.): *A Feminist Companion to Esther, Judith and Susanna* (The Feminist Companion to the Bible 7). 1995. Pp. 336. (Sheffield Academic Press. Price: $16.50/$24.50. ISBN 1 85075 527 2)

BRIEND, JACQUE and COTHENET, ÉDOUARD (eds): *Supplément au Dictionnaire de la Bible.* Vol. 12. Fasc. 69 (*Sermon sur la Montagne-Sexualité*). 1994. Cols 769–1024. (Letouzey & Ané, Paris. Price: Fr 316. ISBN (series) 2 7063 0161 9; (vol. 12) 2 7063 0188 0)

BUTLER, TRENT C. (general ed.): *Holman Bible Dictionary.* 1991. Pp. xxx, 1450 + 8 maps. (Broadman and Holman, Nashville TN. Price: $34.99. ISBN 1 55819 053 8)

CATE, ROBERT L.: *An Introduction to the Historical Books of the Old Testament.* 1994. Pp. xii, 175. (Broadman and Holman, Nashville TN. Price: $16.99. ISBN 0 8054 1044 9)

COOGAN, MICHAEL D.; EXUM, J. CHERYL; and STAGER, LAWRENCE E. (eds): *Scripture and Other Artifacts. Essays on the Bible and Archaeology in Honor of Philip J. King.* 1994. Pp. xxvii, 452. (Westminster/John Knox, Louisville KY. Price: $25.00. ISBN 0 664 22036 3)

COOPER, LAMAR EUGENE, SR: *Ezekiel* (The New American Commentary). 1994. Pp. 440. (Broadman and Holman, Nashville TN. Price: $27.99. ISBN 0 8054 0117 2)

CORNELIUS, IZAK: *The Iconography of the Canaanite Gods Reshef and Ba'al. Late Bronze and Iron Age Periods (c. 1500–1000 BCE)* (Orbis Biblicus et Orientalis 140). 1994. Pp. 298 + 54 plates and 53 figures. (Universitätsverlag, Freiburg (Schweiz); Vandenhoeck & Ruprecht, Göttingen. Price: SwF 120.00/DM 140.00/AS 1092. ISBN (Universitätsverlag) 3 7278 0983 3; (Vandenhoeck & Ruprecht) 3 525 53775 1)

CULLEY, ROBERT C. and ROBINSON, ROBERT B. (eds): *Textual Determinacy. Part One* (Semeia 52). 1993. Pp. xiii, 171. (Scholars Press, Atlanta. Price: $19.95; member price $14.95. ISSN 0095 571X)

DERRETT, J. DUNCAN M.: *Studies in the New Testament. Volume Six: Jesus among Biblical Exegetes.* 1995. Pp. x, 251. (Brill, Leiden–New York–Köln. Price: fl. 125.00/$71.50. ISBN 90 04 10228 0)

DOCKERY, DAVID S. (general ed.): *Holman Bible Handbook.* 1992. Pp. 896. (Broadman and Holman, Nashville TN. Price: £29.99. ISBN 1 55819 332 4)

DOCKERY, DAVID S.; MATHEWS, KENNETH A.; and SLOAN, ROBERT B. (eds): *Foundations for Biblical interpretation. A Complete Library of Tools and Resources.* 1994. Pp. xviii, 614. (Broadman and Holman, Nashville TN. Price: $29.99. ISBN 0 8054 1039 2)

DRESNER, SAMUEL H.: *Rachel.* 1994. Pp. xvi, 256. (Fortress, Minneapolis. Price: $15.00. ISBN 0 8006 2777 6)

FERNÁNDEZ MARCOS, NATALIO: *Scribes and Translators. Septuagint and Old Latin in the Books of Kings* (Supplements to Vetus Testamentum 54). 1994. Pp. x, 98 + 3 figures. (Brill, Leiden–New York–Köln. Price: fl. 100.00/$57.25. ISBN 90 04 10043 1; ISSN 0083 5889)

FERNÁNDEZ TEJERO, EMILIA: *El cantar más bello. El Cantar de los cantares de Salomón.* 1994. Pp. 111. (Editorial Trotta, Madrid. ISBN 84 8164 018 2)

FISCHER, GEORG S. J. and OESCH, JOSEF M. (eds): *Zeitschrift für Katholische Theologie. Für Univ.–Prof. Dr. Arnold Gamper SJ zum 70. Geburtstag.* Vol. 116. 1994. Pp. 387–493. (Theologische Fakultät, Innsbruck. Price: DM 20.00/AS 120. ISSN 0044 2895)

GOLDINGAY, JOHN: *Models for Scripture.* 1994. Pp. xi, 420. (Eerdmans. Grand Rapids MI; Paternoster, Carlisle. Price: $19.99/£13.99. ISBN 0 8028 0146 3)

GOODMAN-THAU, EVELINE: *Zeitbruch. Zur messianischen Grunderfahrung in der jüdischen Tradition.* 1995. Pp. 216. (Akademie Verlag, Berlin. Price: DM 78.00. ISBN 3 05 002511 5)

GUNKEL, HERMANN: *The Stories of Genesis.* Translated by John J. Scullion; edited by William R. Scott. 1994. Pp. xix, 155. (BIBAL Press, N. Richland Hills TX. Price: $15.95. ISBN 0 941037 21 5)

HENTSCHEL, G.: *2 Samuel.* (Die Neue Echter Bibel: Kommentar zum Alten Testament mit der Einheitsübersetzung 34). 1994. Pp. 112. (Echter Verlag, Würzburg. Price: DM 28.00/SwF 29.00/AS 219. ISBN 3 429 01634 7)

HOUSE, PAUL R.: *Old Testament Survey.* 1994. Pp. 270. (Broadman and Holman, Nashville TN. Price: $16.99. ISBN 0 8054 1015 5)

JACOBS, IRVING: *The Midrashic Process. Tradition and Interpretation in Rabbinic Judaism.* 1995. Pp. xiii, 218. (Cambridge University Press. Price: £35.00. ISBN 0 521 46174 X)

JASPER, DAVID and LEADBETTER, MARK (eds): *In Good Company. Essays in Honor of Robert Detweiler* (American Academy of Religion Studies in Religion 71). 1994. Pp. xviii, 455. (Scholars Press, Atlanta. Price: $44.95. ISBN 0 7885 0039 2)

JENNI, ERNST: *Die hebräischen Präpositionen. Band 2: Die Präposition Kaph.* 1994. Pp. 195. (Kohlhammer, Stuttgart. Price: DM 98.00/SwF 98.00/AS 765. ISBN 3 17 012688 1)

184

184 BOOKS RECEIVED

Justin, Epitome of the Philippic History of Pompeius Trogus (Classical Resources Series 3). Translated by J. C. Yardley, with introduction and explanatory notes by R. Devlin. 1994. (Scholars Press, Atlanta. Price: $44.95; paper $29.95. ISBN 1 55540 950 4; paper 1 55540 951 2)

KELLENBACH, KATHARINA VON: *Anti-Judaism in Feminist Religious Writings* (American Academy of Religion). 1994. Pp. x, 173. (Scholars Press, Atlanta. Price: $29.95; paper $17.95. ISBN 0 7885 0043 0; paper 0 7885 0044 9)

LASSERRE, GUY: *Synopse des lois du Pentateque* (Supplements to Vetus Testamentum 59). 1994. Pp. xxx, 242. (Brill, Leiden–New York–Köln. Price: fl. 150/$85.75. ISBN 90 04 10202 7; ISSN 0083 5889)

LINDENBERGER, JAMES M.: *Ancient Aramaic and Hebrew Letters* (Society of Biblical Literature Writings from the Ancient World Series 4). Edited by K. H. Richards. 1994. Pp. xv, 155. (Scholars Press, Atlanta. Price: $44.95; paper $29.95. ISBN 1 55540 839 7; paper 1 55540 840 0)

MALBON, ELIZABETH STRUTHERS and BERLIN, ADELE (eds): *Characterization in Biblical Literature*. (Semeia 63). 1993. Pp. viii, 227. (Scholars Press, Atlanta. Price: $19.95; member price $14.95. ISSN 0095 571X)

MALKIN, I. and RUBINSOHN, Z. M. (eds): *Leaders and Masses in the Roman World. Studies in Honor of Zvi Yavetz* (Mnemosyne Supplement 139). 1995. Pp. xvii, 243. (Brill, Leiden–New York–Köln. Price: fl. 110.00/ $63.00. ISBN 90 04 09917 4; ISSN 0169 8958)

MARX, ALFRED: *Les offrandes végétales dans l'Ancien Testament. Du tribut d'hommage au repas eschatologique* (Supplements to Vetus Testamentum 57). 1994. Pp. xiii, 186. (Brill, Leiden–New York–Köln. ISBN 90 04 10136 5; ISSN 0083 5889)

MCCONVILLE, J. G. and MILLAR, J. G.: *Time and Place in Deuteronomy* (Journal for the Study of the Old Testament Supplement 179). 1994. Pp. 155. (Sheffield Academic Press. Price: £25.00/$37.50. ISBN 1 85075 494 2; ISSN 0309 0787)

MILLER, JOHN W.: *The Origins of the Bible. Rethinking Canon History*. 1994. Pp. vii, 250. (Paulist Press, New York–Mahwah NJ. Price: $18.95. ISBN 0 8091 3522 1)

MUELLER, JAMES R.: *The Five Fragments of the* Apocryphon of Ezekiel. *A Critical Study* (Journal for the Study of the Pseudepigrapha Supplement 5). 1994. Pp. 196. (Sheffield Academic Press. Price: £27.50/$41.00. ISBN 1 85075 195 1; ISSN 0951 8215)

NEUSNER, JACOB (ed.): *Judaism in Late Antiquity. Part 1: The Literary and Archaeological Sources* (Handbuch der Orientalistik: Erste Abteilung, Der Nahe und Mittlere Osten: Band 17/1). 1995. Pp. xiv, 276. (Brill, Leiden–New York–Köln. Price: fl. 140.00/$80.00. ISBN 90 04 10129 2; ISSN 0169 9423)

NEUSNER, JACOB (ed.): *Judaism in Late Antiquity. Part 2: Historical Syntheses* (Handbuch der Orientalistik: Erste Abteilung, Der Nahe und Mittlere Osten: Band 17/2). 1995. Pp. xiv, 318. (Brill, Leiden–New York–Köln. Price: fl. 200.00/$114.50. ISBN 90 04 10130 6; ISSN 0169 9423).

NEUSNER, JACOB: *What is Midrash?* and *A Midrash Reader* (South Florida Studies in the History of Judaism 106). 1994. (2nd printing). Pp. x, 276. (Scholars Press, Atlanta. Price: $74.95. ISBN 1 55540 982 2; originally 0 8006 2433 5; 0 8006 0472 5)

NEYTON, ANDRÉ: *Lumières sur le paganisme antique*. 1995. Pp. 125. (Letouzey et Ané, Paris. Price: Fr 88.00. ISBN 2 7063 0196 1)

O'CONNELL, ROBERT H.: *Concentricity and Continuity. The Literary Structure of Isaiah* (Journal for the Study of the Old Testament Supplement 188). 1994. Pp. 272. (Sheffield Academic Press. Price: £32.59/$58.50. ISBN 1 85075 521 3; ISSN 0309 0787)

PASSAMANECK, S. M. and FINLEY, M. (eds): *Jewish Law Association Studies VII: The Paris Conference Volume* (Jewish Law Association Papers and

Proceedings). 1994. Pp. viii, 245. (Scholars Press, Atlanta. Price: $59.95. ISBN 1 55540 899 0)

PEELS. H. G. L.: *The Vengeance of God. The Meaning of the Root NQM and the Function of the NQM-Texts in the Context of Divine Revelation in the Old Testament* (Oudtestamentische Studiën 31). 1995. Pp. xiv, 326. (Brill, Leiden–New York–Köln. Price: fl. 135.00/$77.25. ISBN 90 04 10164 0; ISSN 0169 7226)

PERDUE, LEO G.: *The Collapse of History. Reconstructing Old Testament Theology* (Overtures to Biblical Theology). 1994. Pp. xvi, 317. (Fortress, Minneapolis. Price: $14.00. ISBN 0 8006 1563 8)

POINSETT, BRENDA: *Old Testament Survey. A Student's Guide*. 1994. Pp. v, 119. (Broadman and Holman, Nashville TN. Price: $7.99. ISBN 0 8054 1086 4)

POMYKALA, KENNETH E.: *The Davidic Dynasty Tradition in Early Judaism. Its History and Significance for Messianism* (Society of Biblical Literature Early Judaism and Its Literature 7). 1995. Pp. xv, 308. (Scholars Press, Atlanta. Price: $39.95; paper $24.95. ISBN 0 7885 0068 6; paper 0 7885 0069 4)

POTTER, DAVID: *Prophets and Emperors. Human and Divine Authority from Augustus to Theodosius* (Revealing Antiquity 7). 1994. Pp. viii, 281. (Harvard University Press, Cambridge MA and London. Price: $53.95/ £35.95. ISBN 0 674 71565 9)

QUACK, JOACHIM FRIEDRICH: *Die Lehren des Ani. Ein neuägyptischer Weisheitstext in seinem kulturellen Umfeld* (Orbis Biblicus et Orientalis 141). 1994. Pp. x, 338 + 2 plates. (Universitätsverlag, Freiburg (Schweiz); Vandenhoeck & Ruprecht, Göttingen. Price: SwF 98.00/DM 118.00/ AS 921. ISBN (Universitätsverlag) 3 7278 0984 1; (Vandenhoeck & Ruprecht) 3 525 53776 X)

REEVES, JOHN C. and KAMPEN, JOHN (eds): *Pursuing the Text. Studies in Honor of Ben Zion Wacholder on the Occasion of his Seventieth Birthday* (Journal for the Study of the Old Testament Supplement 184). 1994. Pp. 434. (Sheffield Academic Press. Price: £47.50/$71.00. ISBN 1 85075 501 9; ISSN 0309 0787)

RUNIA, DAVID T. (ed.): *The Studia Philonica Annual. Studies in Hellenistic Judaism* (Brown Judaic Studies 287). Vol. 5. 1993. Pp. viii, 256. (Scholars Press, Atlanta. Price: $44.95. ISBN 1 55540 917 2)

RUNIA, DAVID T. (ed.): *The Studia Philonica Annual. Studies in Hellenistic Judaism* (Brown Judaic Studies 299). Vol. 6. 1994. Pp. 229. (Scholars Press, Atlanta. Price: $44.95. ISBN 0 7885 0030 9)

SCHRAMM, BROOKS: *The Opponents of Third Isaiah. Reconstructing the Cultic History of the Restoration* (Journal for the Study of the Old Testament Supplement 193). 1995. Pp. 216. (Sheffield Academic Press. Price: £30.00/$45.00. ISBN 1 85075 538 8; ISSN 0309 0787)

SCHREINER, JOSEF: *Theologie des Alten Testaments* (Die Neue Echter Bible: Ergänzungsband zum Alten Testament 1). 1995. Pp. 349. (Echter Verlag, Würzburg. Price: DM 54.00/SwF 54.00/AS 421. ISBN 3 429 01669 X)

SMITH, GARY V.: *The Prophets as Preachers. An Introduction to the Hebrew Prophets*. 1994. Pp. xi, 372. (Broadman and Holman, Nashville TN. Price: $27.99. ISBN 0 8054 1610 2)

STIPP, HERMAN-JOSEF: *Das masoretische und alexandrinische Sondergut des Jeremiabuches. Textgeschichtlicher Rang, Eigenarten. Triebkräfte* (Orbis Biblicus et Orientalis 36). 1994. Pp. vii, 186. (Universitätsverlag, Freiburg (Schweiz); Vandenhoeck & Ruprecht, Göttingen. Price: SwF 58.00/ DM 57.00/AS 523. ISBN (Universitätsverlag) 3 7278 0956 6; (Vandenhoeck & Ruprecht) 3 525 53771 9)

TOV, EMANUEL (ed.), with the collaboration of Stephen J. Pfann: *Companion Volume to the Dead Sea Scrolls Microfiche Edition*. 1995 (2nd revised edn). Pp. 187. (Brill, Leiden–New York–Köln. Price: fl. 140.00/$80.00. ISBN 90 04 10288 4)

186 BOOKS RECEIVED

ULRICH, EUGENE and CROSS, FRANK MOORE (eds): *Discoveries in the Judaean Desert. Volume 12: Qumran Cave 4: VII Genesis to Numbers.* With J. R. Davila, N. Jastram, J. E. Sanderson, E. Tov, J. Strugnell. 1994. Pp. xv, 272 + 49 plates. (Clarendon Press, Oxford. Price: £70.00. ISBN 0 19 826365 1)

USSISHKIN, DAVID: *The Village of Silwan. The Necropolis from the Period of the Judean Kingdom.* 1993. Pp. xi, 364. (Israel Exploration Society, Jerusalem. ISBN 965 221 018 8)

VARGON, SHMUEL: *spr mykh. 'ywnym wpyrwšym (The Book of Micah. A Study and Commentary).* 1994. Pp. 280 (Heb.). (Bar-Ilan University Press, Ramat-Gan. ISBN 965 226 128 9)

VERMES, GEZA: *The Dead Sea Scrolls in English.* 1994. (4th edn, revised and extended). Pp. lvii, 392. (Penguin, London. Price: £8.99. ISBN 0 14 023730 5)

Vetus Latina. Die Reste der altlateinischen Bibel nach Petrus Sabatier neu gesammelt und herausgegeben von der Erzabtei Beuron. 12 (Pars II): *Esaias.* Herausgegeben von Roger Gryson. Fascicule 3: Is 41, 21–44, 4. 1994. Pp. 961–1040. (Herder, Freiburg. ISBN 3 451 00123 3; ISSN 0571 9070)

WUNSCH, CORNELIA: *XXV. Deutscher Orientalistentag vom 8. bis 13.4.1991 in München. Vorträge* (Zeitschrift der Deutschen Morgenländischen Gesellschaft Supplement 10). 1994. Pp. ix, 540. (Franz Steiner, Stuttgart. Price: DM 128.00/SwF 128.00/AS 999)

Index of Authors

(N.B. — Names occurring more than once in the same review or on the same page are listed on their first occurrence only)

Index of Periodicals and Series

The Society for Old Testament Study is a British Society for Old Testament scholars. Candidates for membership, which is not confined to British subjects, must be nominated by two members of the Society. Residents of the British Isles are normally admitted to ordinary membership and non-residents to associate membership. All correspondence concerning domestic affairs of the Society should be sent to:

Dr K. J. Dell
Ripon College
Cuddesdon
Oxford
OX44 9EX